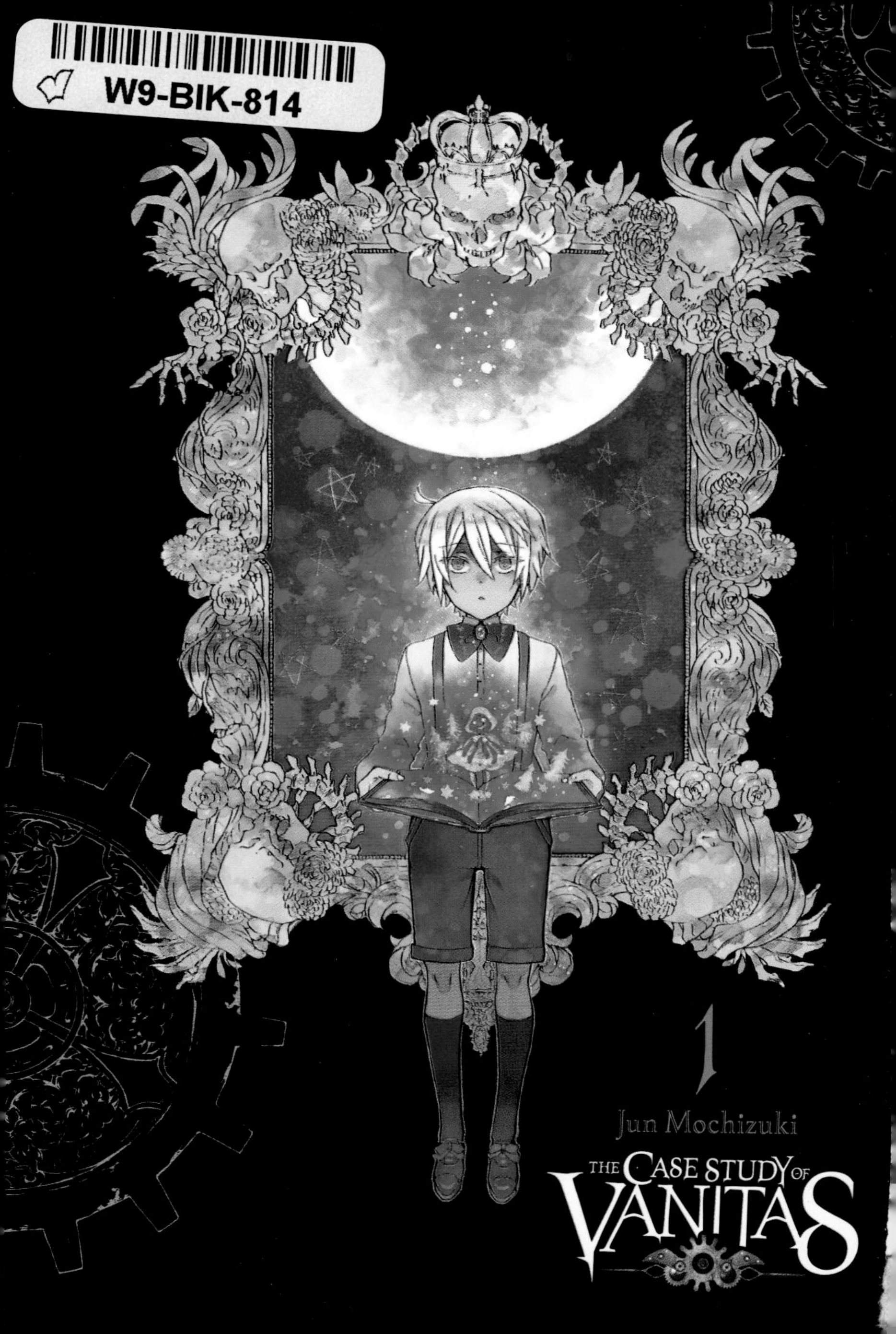

1

Jun Mochizuki

THE CASE STUDY OF VANITAS

The Case Study of Vanitas

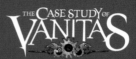

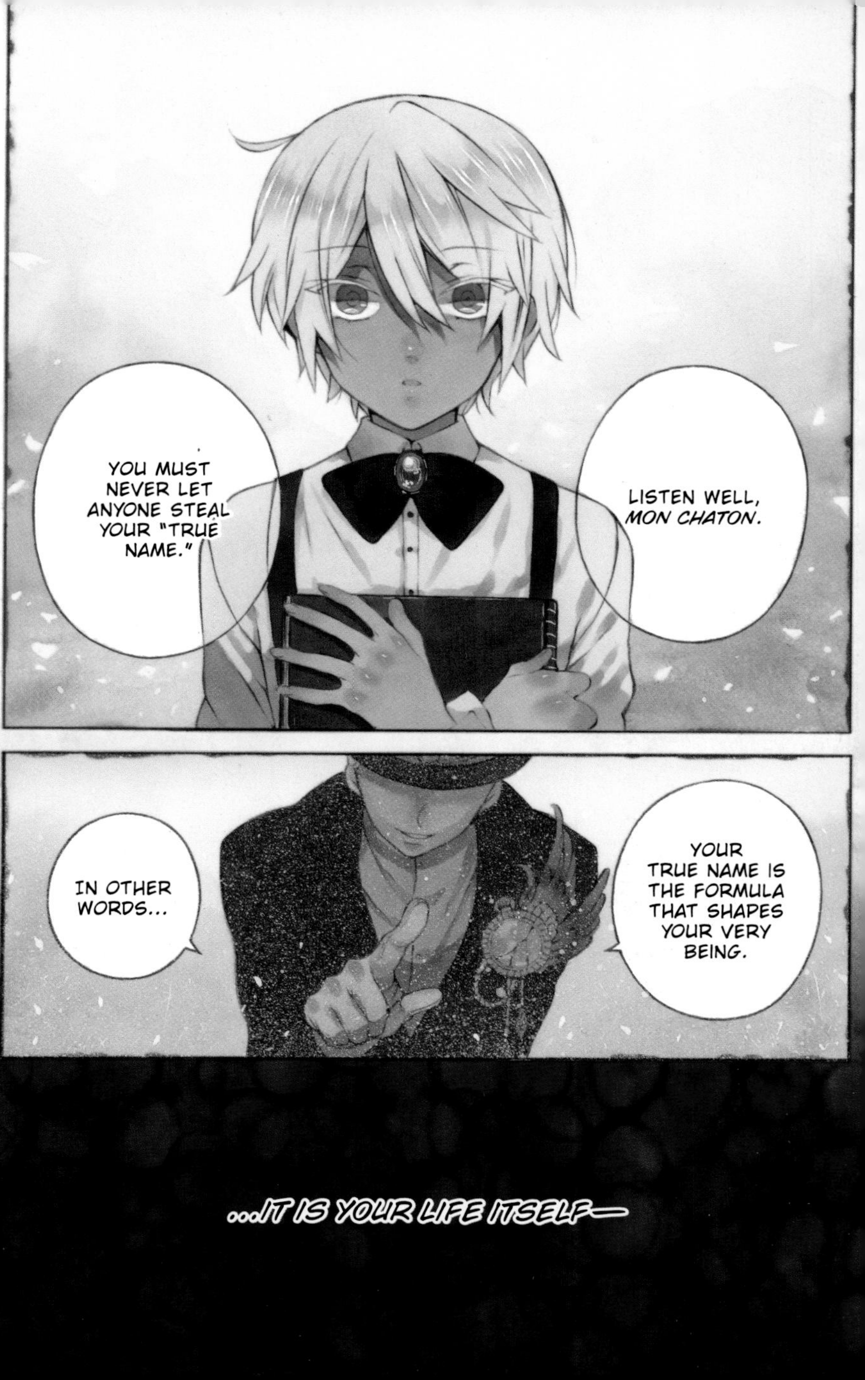
LISTEN WELL, *MON CHATON*.
YOU MUST NEVER LET ANYONE STEAL YOUR "TRUE NAME."
YOUR TRUE NAME IS THE FORMULA THAT SHAPES YOUR VERY BEING.
IN OTHER WORDS...
...IT IS YOUR LIFE ITSELF—

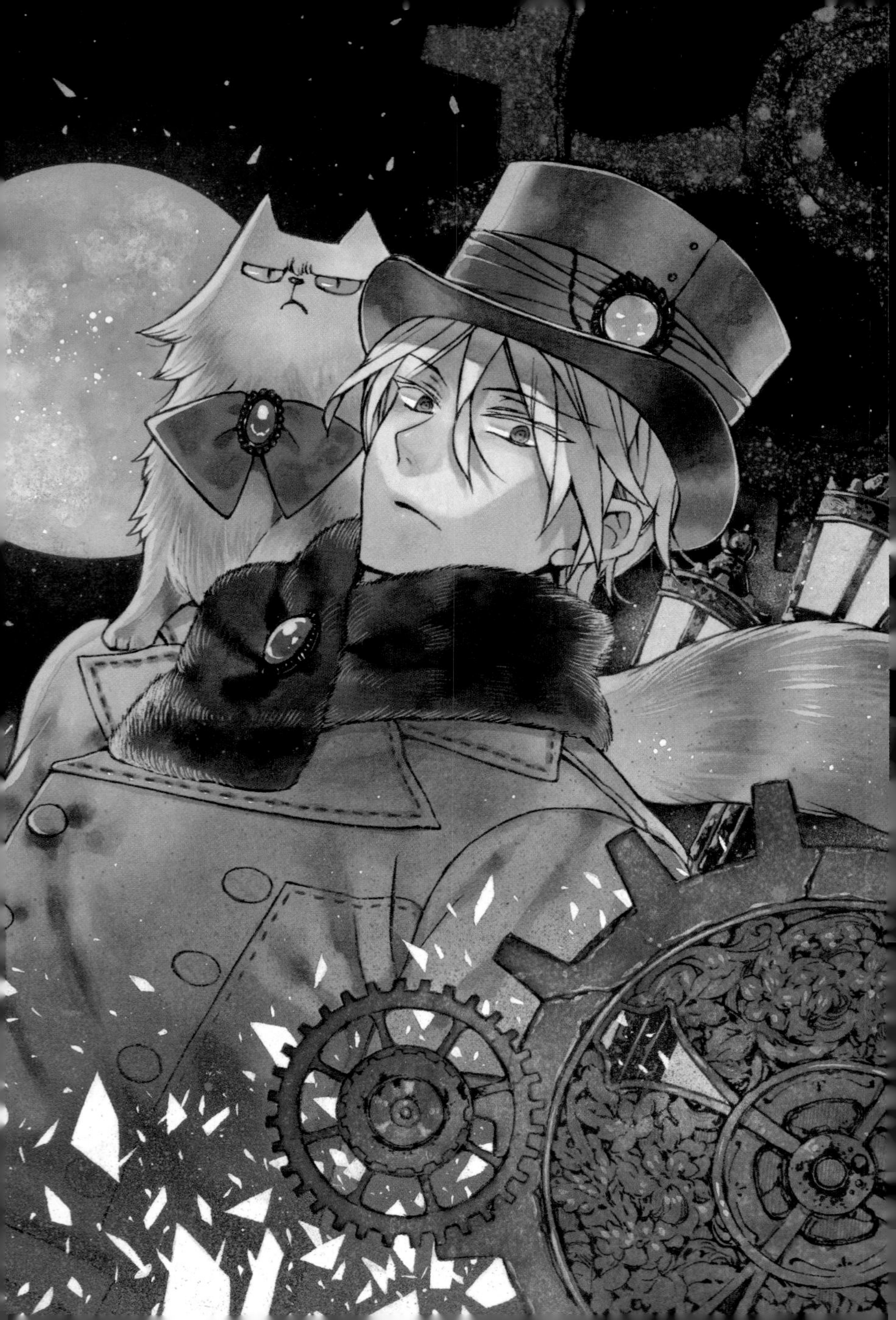

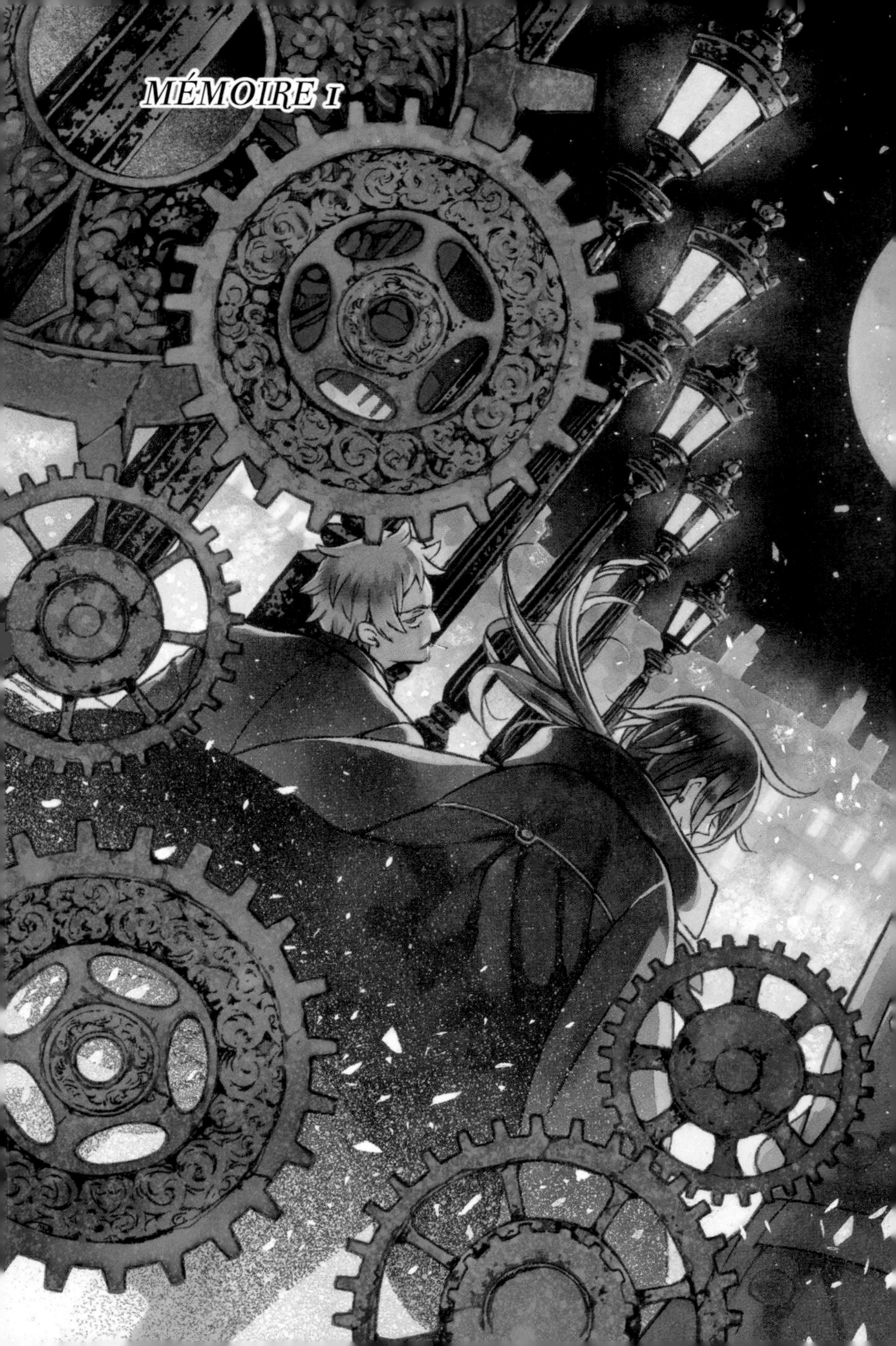
MÉMOIRE 1

Les Mémoires de Vanitas

THE CASE STUDY OF VANITAS

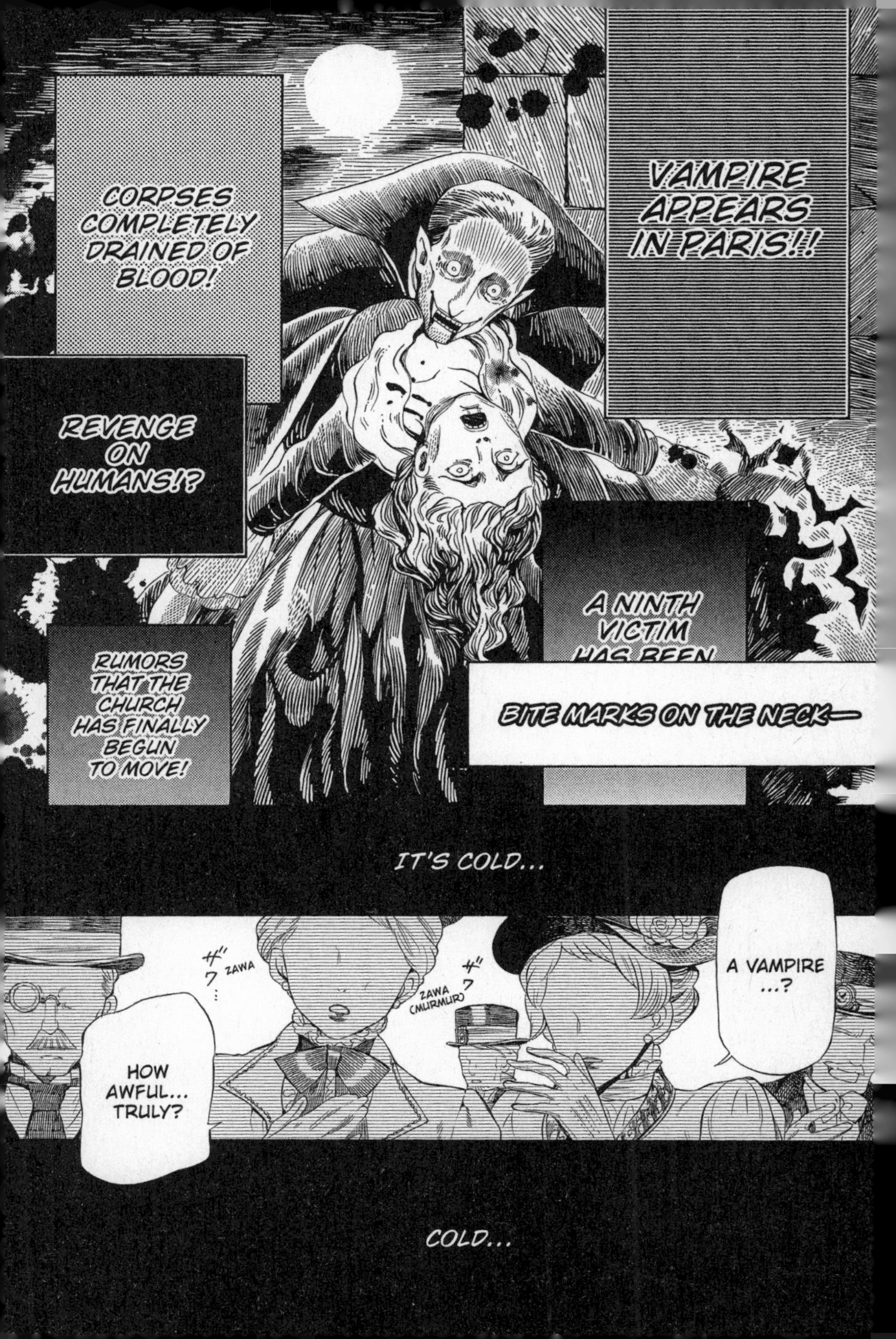
VAMPIRE APPEARS IN PARIS!!
CORPSES COMPLETELY DRAINED OF BLOOD!
REVENGE ON HUMANS!?
A NINTH VICTIM HAS BEEN
BITE MARKS ON THE NECK—
RUMORS THAT THE CHURCH HAS FINALLY BEGUN TO MOVE!
IT'S COLD...
A VAMPIRE ...?
ザワ ZAWA (MURMUR)
ザワ... ZAWA
HOW AWFUL... TRULY?
COLD...

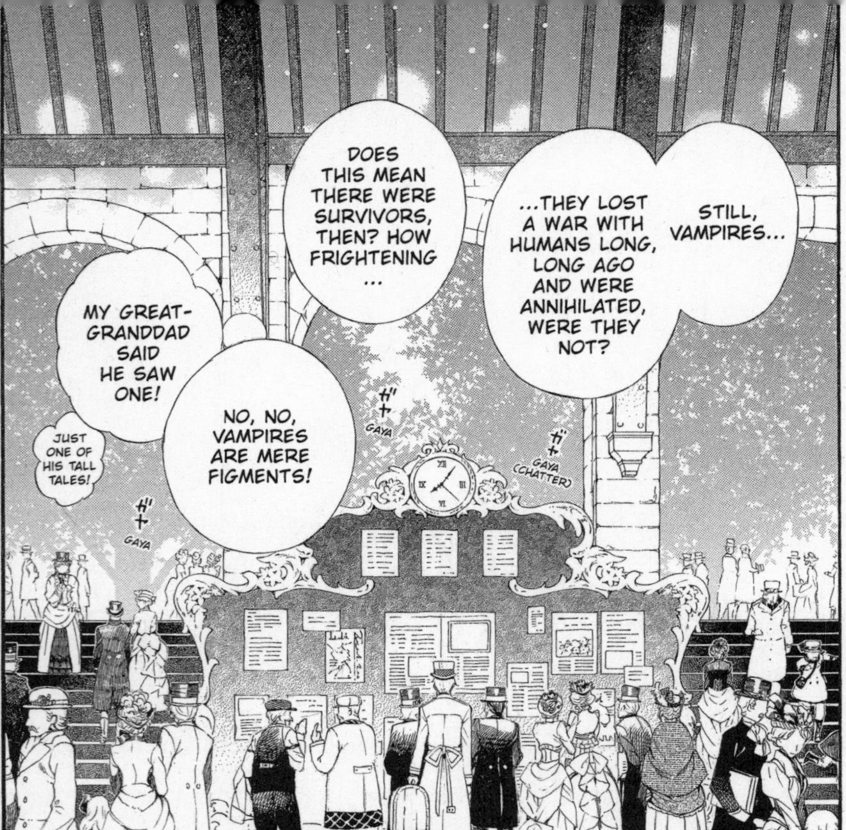
STILL, VAMPIRES...
...THEY LOST A WAR WITH HUMANS LONG, LONG AGO AND WERE ANNIHILATED, WERE THEY NOT?
DOES THIS MEAN THERE WERE SURVIVORS, THEN? HOW FRIGHTENING...
ガヤ GAYA (CHATTER)
ガヤ GAYA
NO, NO, VAMPIRES ARE MERE FIGMENTS!
MY GREAT-GRANDDAD SAID HE SAW ONE!
JUST ONE OF HIS TALL TALES!
ガヤ GAYA

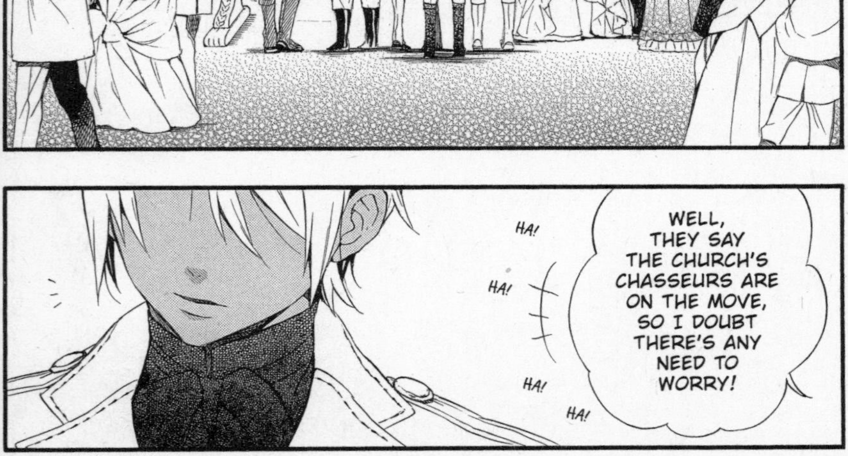
WELL, THEY SAY THE CHURCH'S CHASSEURS ARE ON THE MOVE, SO I DOUBT THERE'S ANY NEED TO WORRY!
HA! HA! HA! HA!

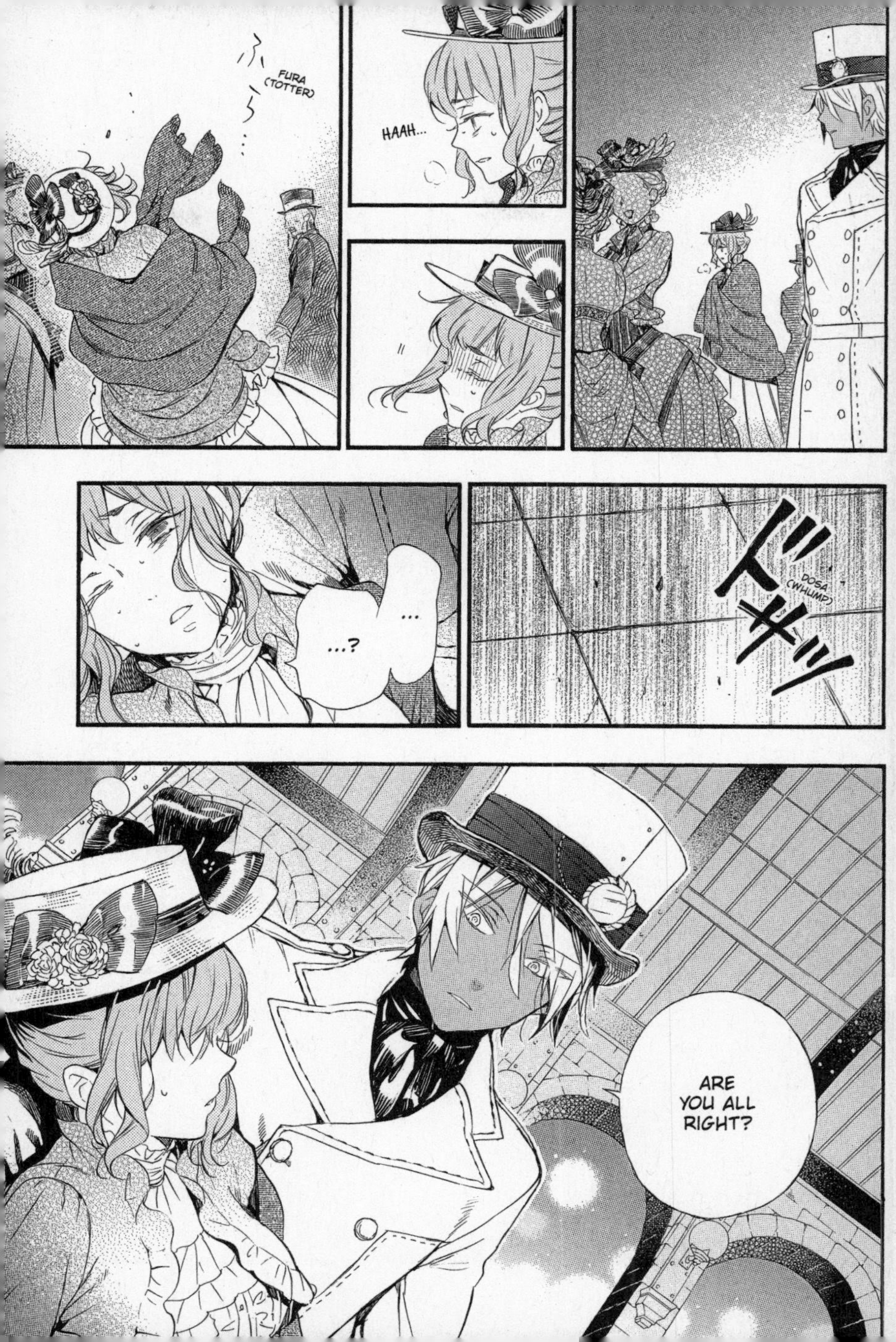
HAAH...
ふら…
FURA (TOTTER)
ドサッ
DOSA (WHUMP)
...
...?
ARE YOU ALL RIGHT?

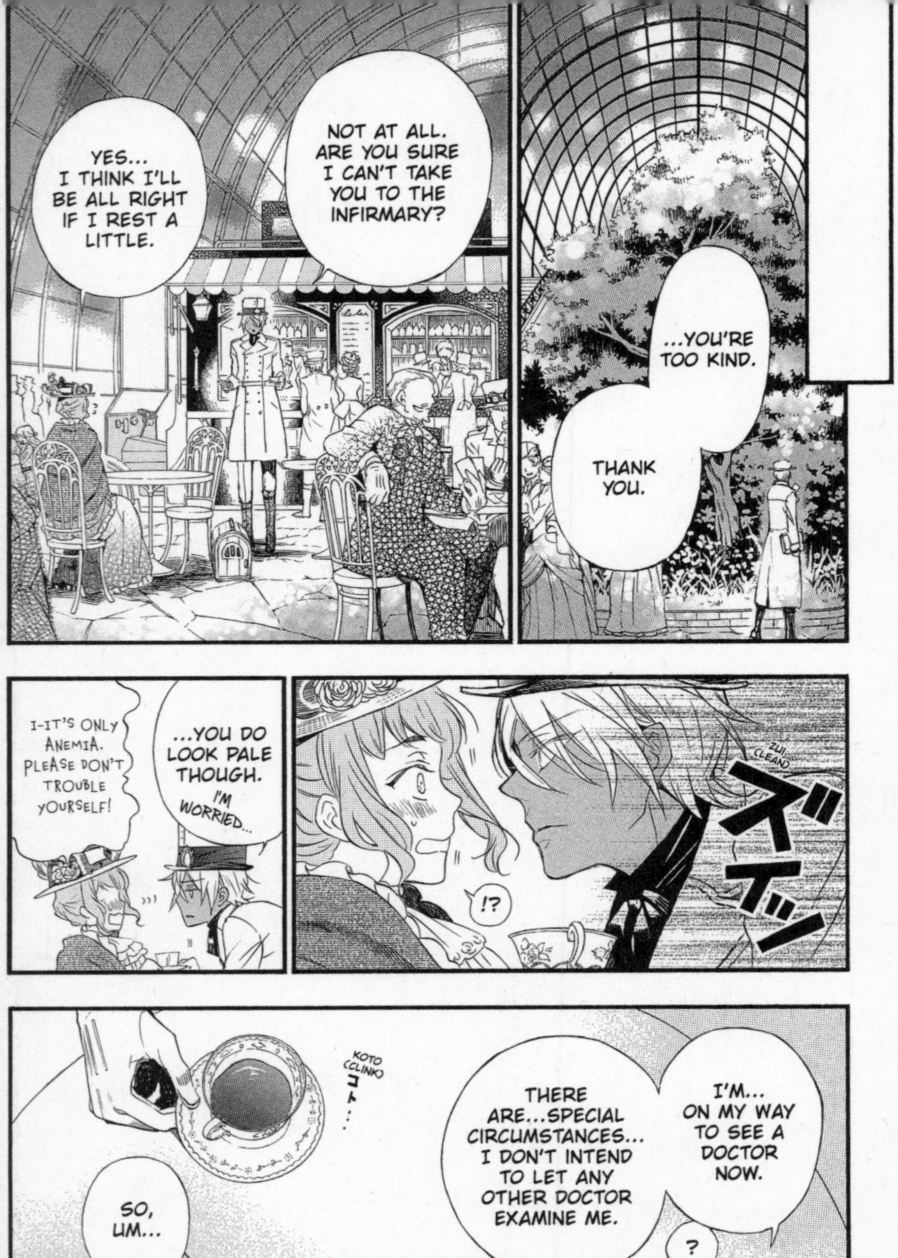
...YOU'RE TOO KIND.
THANK YOU.
NOT AT ALL. ARE YOU SURE I CAN'T TAKE YOU TO THE INFIRMARY?
YES... I THINK I'LL BE ALL RIGHT IF I REST A LITTLE.
ZUI (LEAN)
ズイ
!?
...YOU DO LOOK PALE THOUGH.
I'M WORRIED...
I-IT'S ONLY ANEMIA. PLEASE DON'T TROUBLE YOURSELF!
I'M... ON MY WAY TO SEE A DOCTOR NOW.
?
THERE ARE...SPECIAL CIRCUMSTANCES... I DON'T INTEND TO LET ANY OTHER DOCTOR EXAMINE ME.
KOTO (CLINK)
コト…
SO, UM...

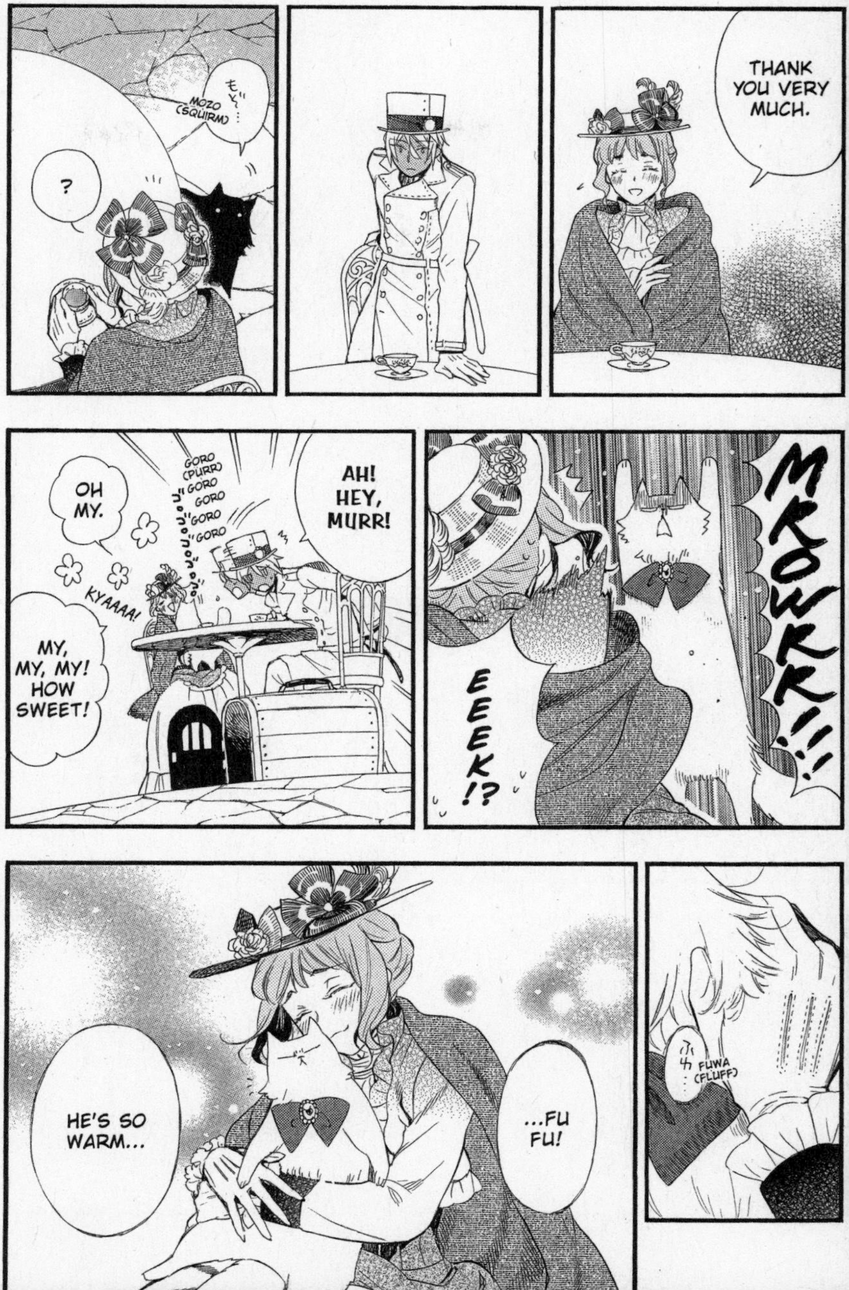
THANK YOU VERY MUCH.
もぞ…
MOZO (SQUIRM)
?
MROWRR!!!
EEEK!?
AH! HEY, MURR!
GORO (PURR) GORO GORO GORO GORO
OH MY.
KYAAAA!
MY, MY, MY! HOW SWEET!
ふわ…
FUWA (FLUFF)
...FU FU!
HE'S SO WARM...

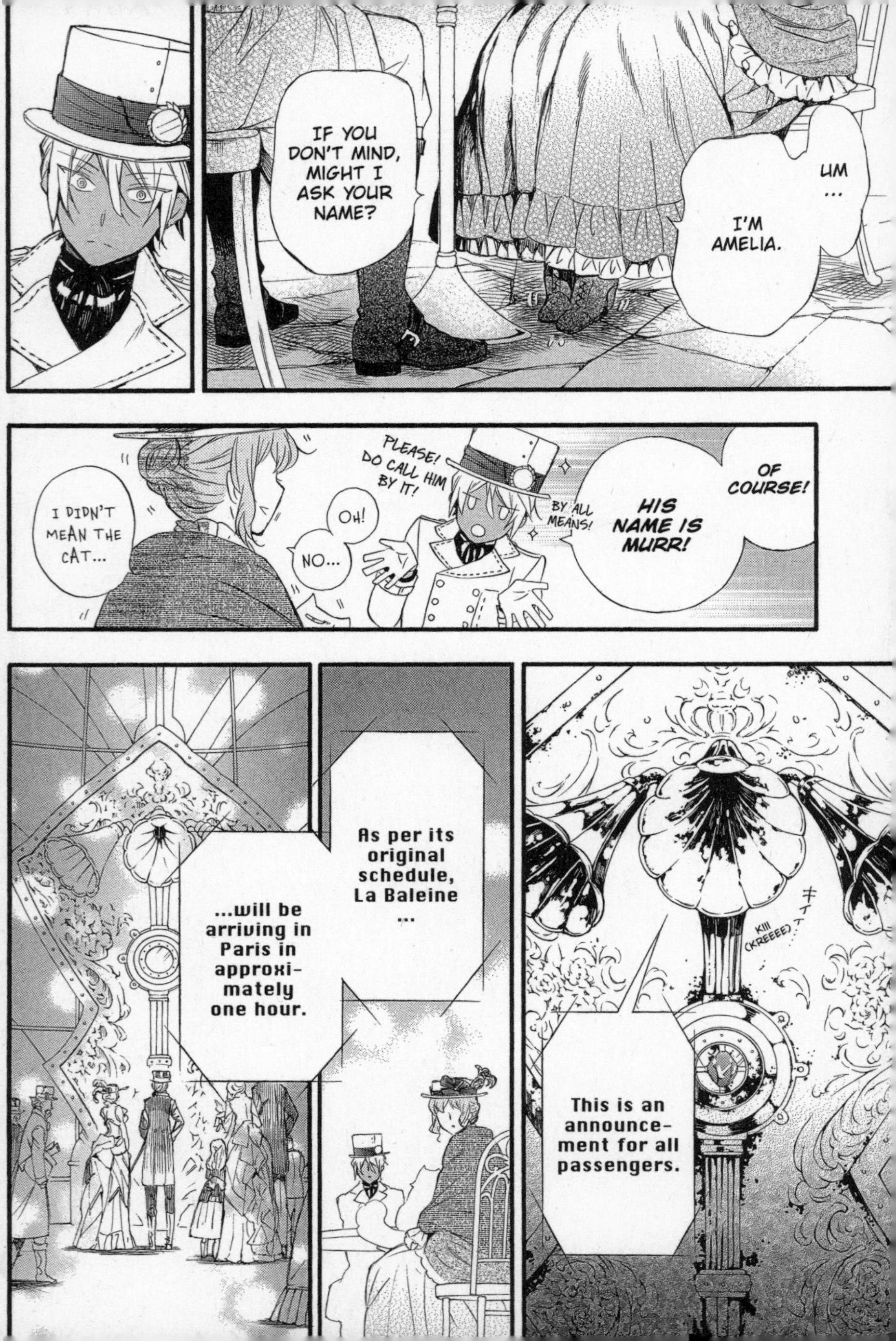
IF YOU DON'T MIND, MIGHT I ASK YOUR NAME?
UM ... I'M AMELIA.
OF COURSE! HIS NAME IS MURR!
BY ALL MEANS!
PLEASE! DO CALL HIM BY IT!
OH! NO...
I DIDN'T MEAN THE CAT...
This is an announcement for all passengers.
KIII (KREEEE)
As per its original schedule, La Baleine ...
...will be arriving in Paris in approximately one hour.

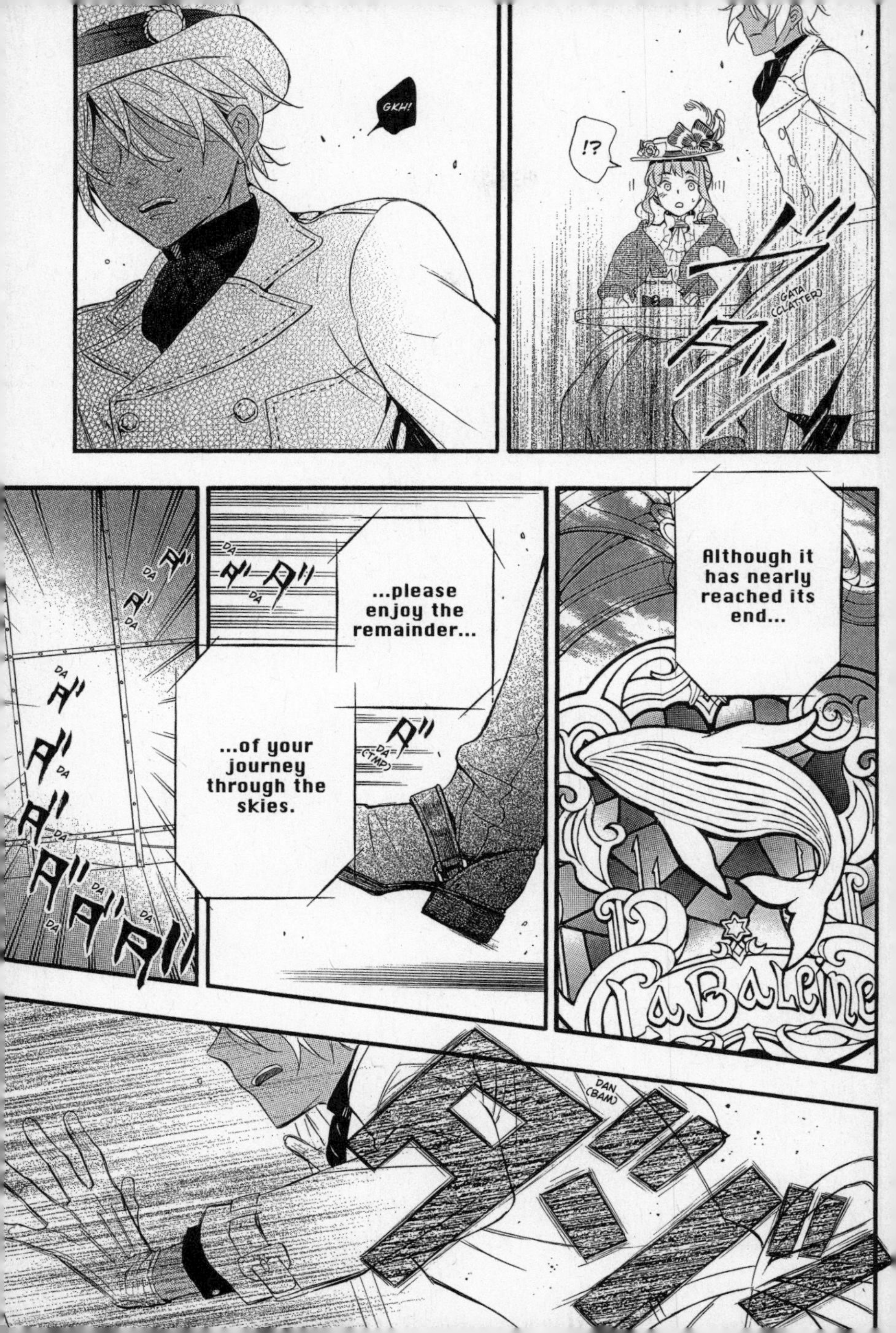
!?
GATA (CLATTER)
GKH!
Although it has nearly reached its end...
La Baleine
DA DA
...please enjoy the remainder...
DA (TMP)
...of your journey through the skies.
DA DA DA DA DA DA DA DA
DAN (BAM)

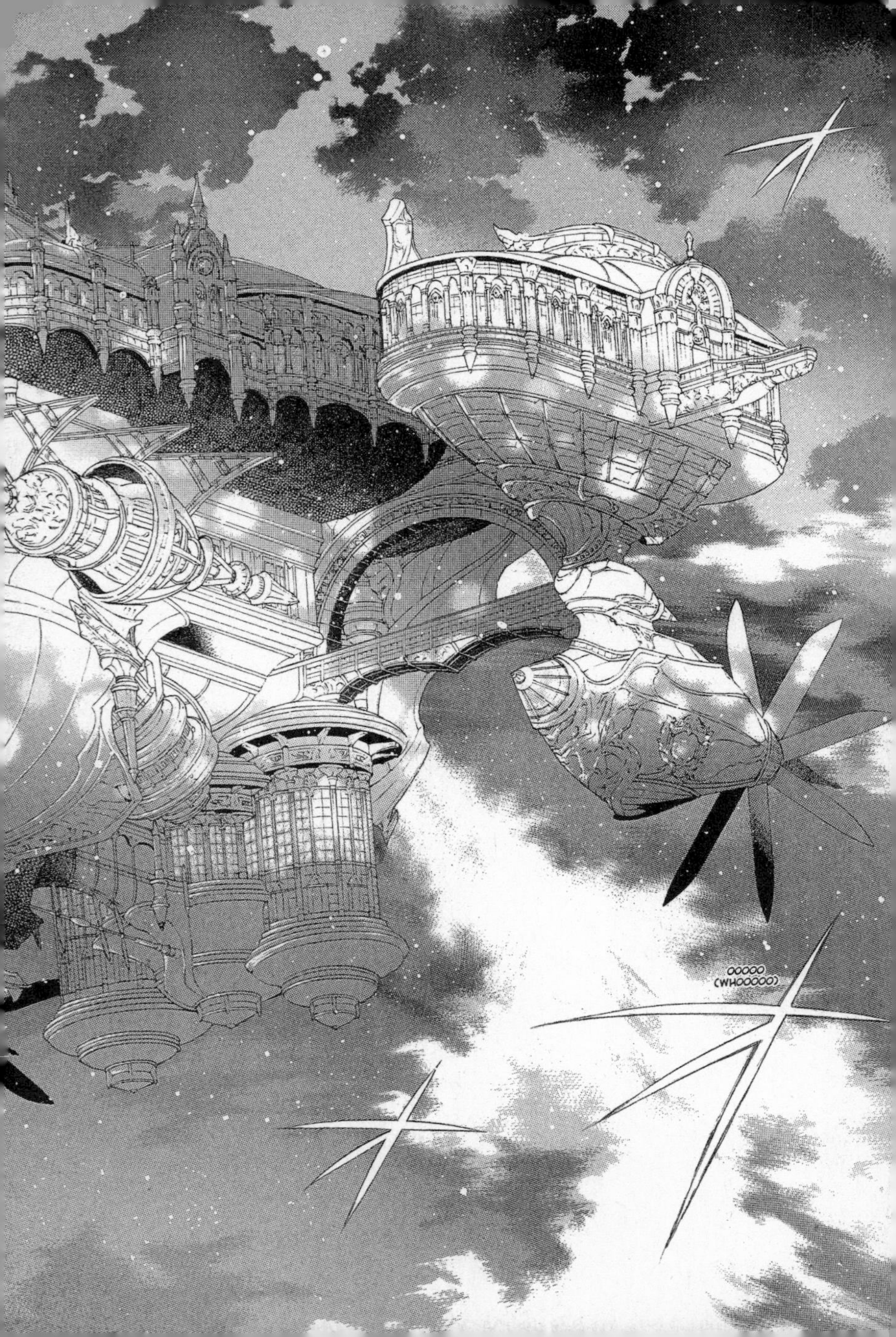
OOOOO
(WHOOOOO)

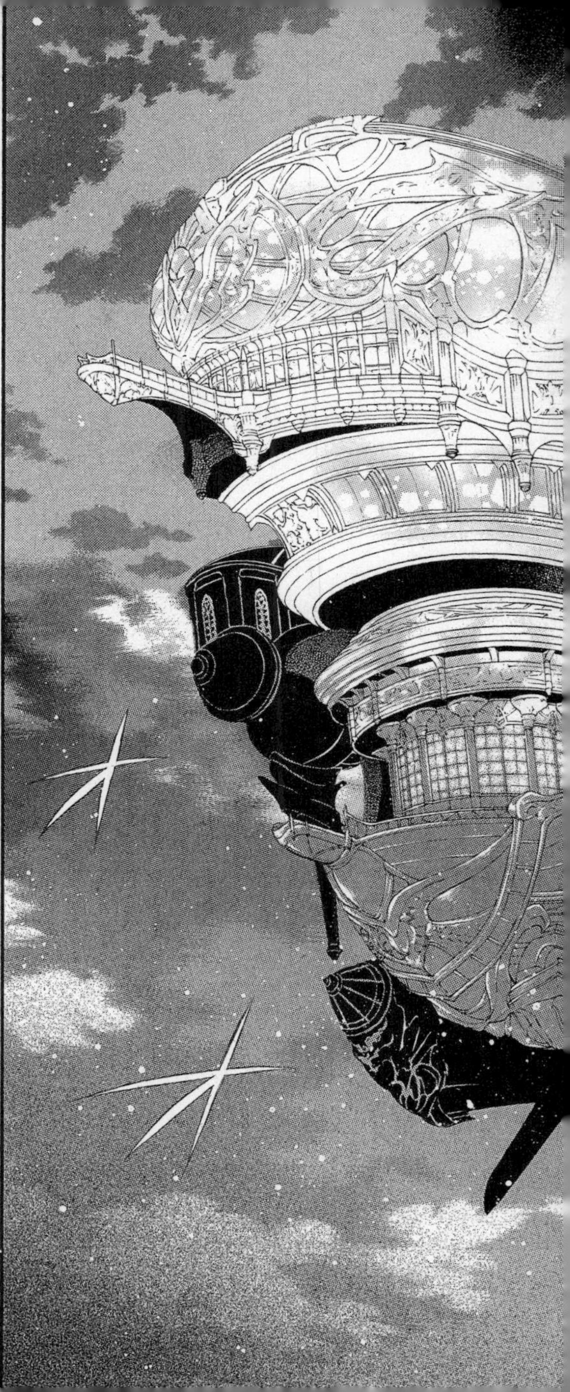
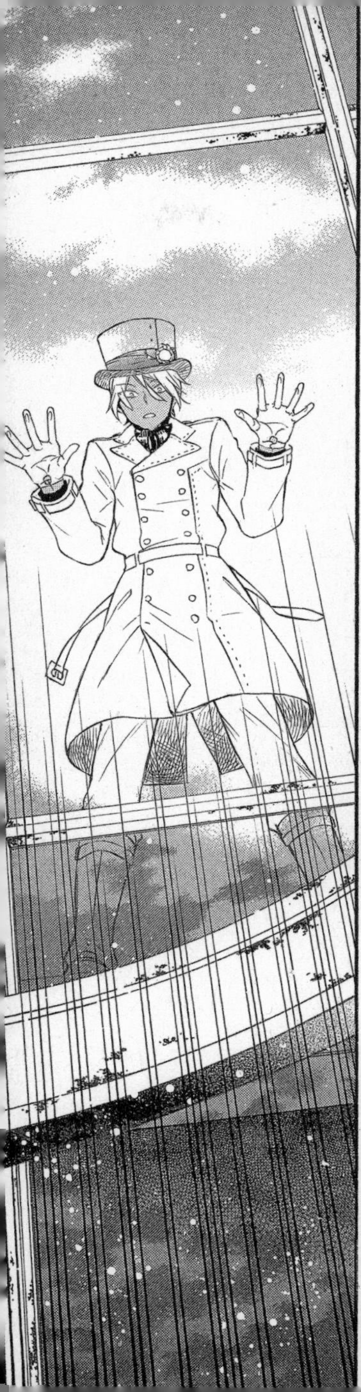

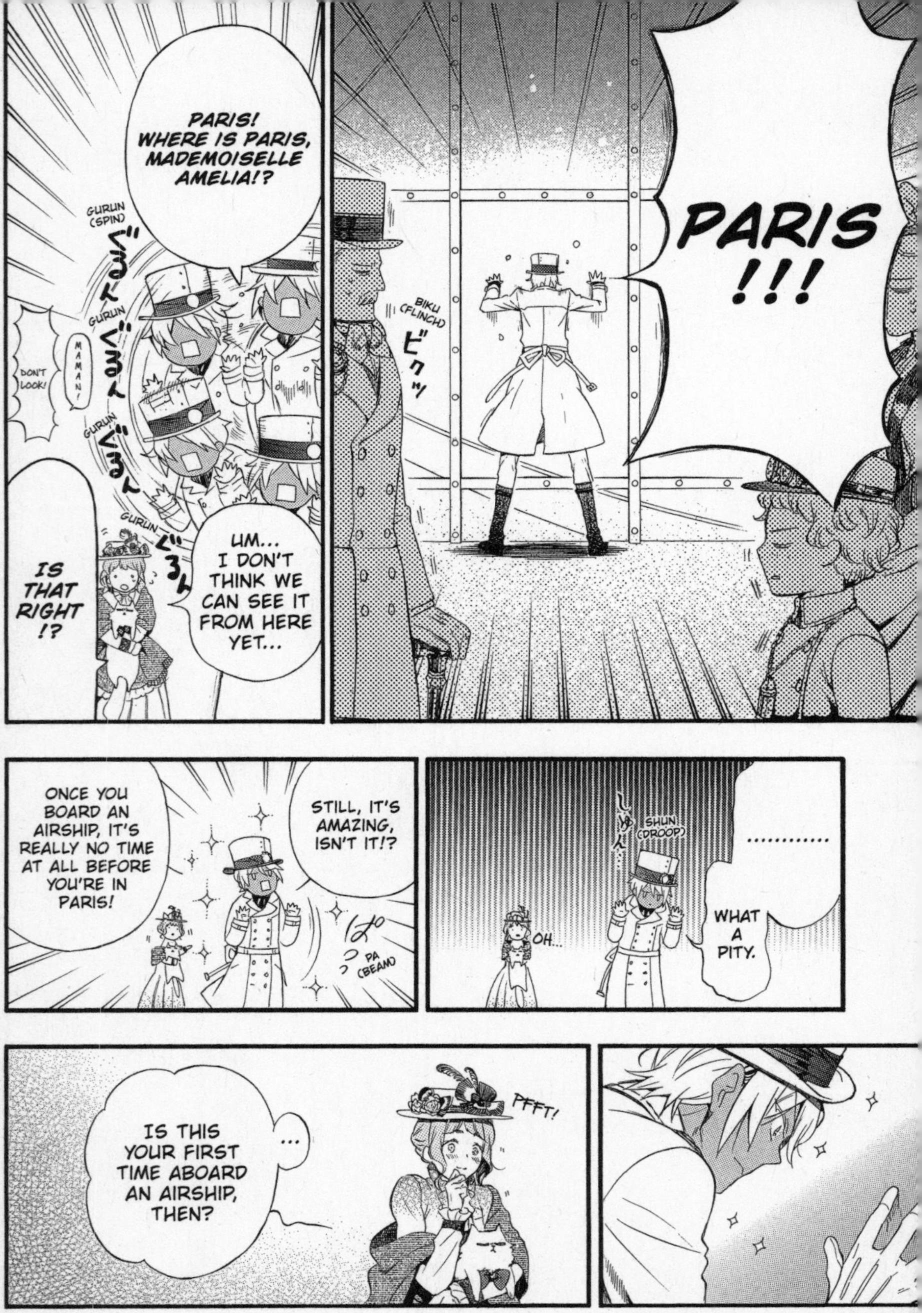
PARIS !!!
BIKU (FLINCH)
ビクッ
PARIS! WHERE IS PARIS, MADEMOISELLE AMELIA!?
GURUN (SPIN)
ぐるん
GURUN
ぐるん
GURUN
ぐるん
GURUN
ぐるん
MAMAN!
DON'T LOOK!
UM... I DON'T THINK WE CAN SEE IT FROM HERE YET...
IS THAT RIGHT!?
SHUN (DROOP)
....
WHAT A PITY.
OH...
STILL, IT'S AMAZING, ISN'T IT!?
ONCE YOU BOARD AN AIRSHIP, IT'S REALLY NO TIME AT ALL BEFORE YOU'RE IN PARIS!
PA (BEAM)
PFFT!
...
IS THIS YOUR FIRST TIME ABOARD AN AIRSHIP, THEN?

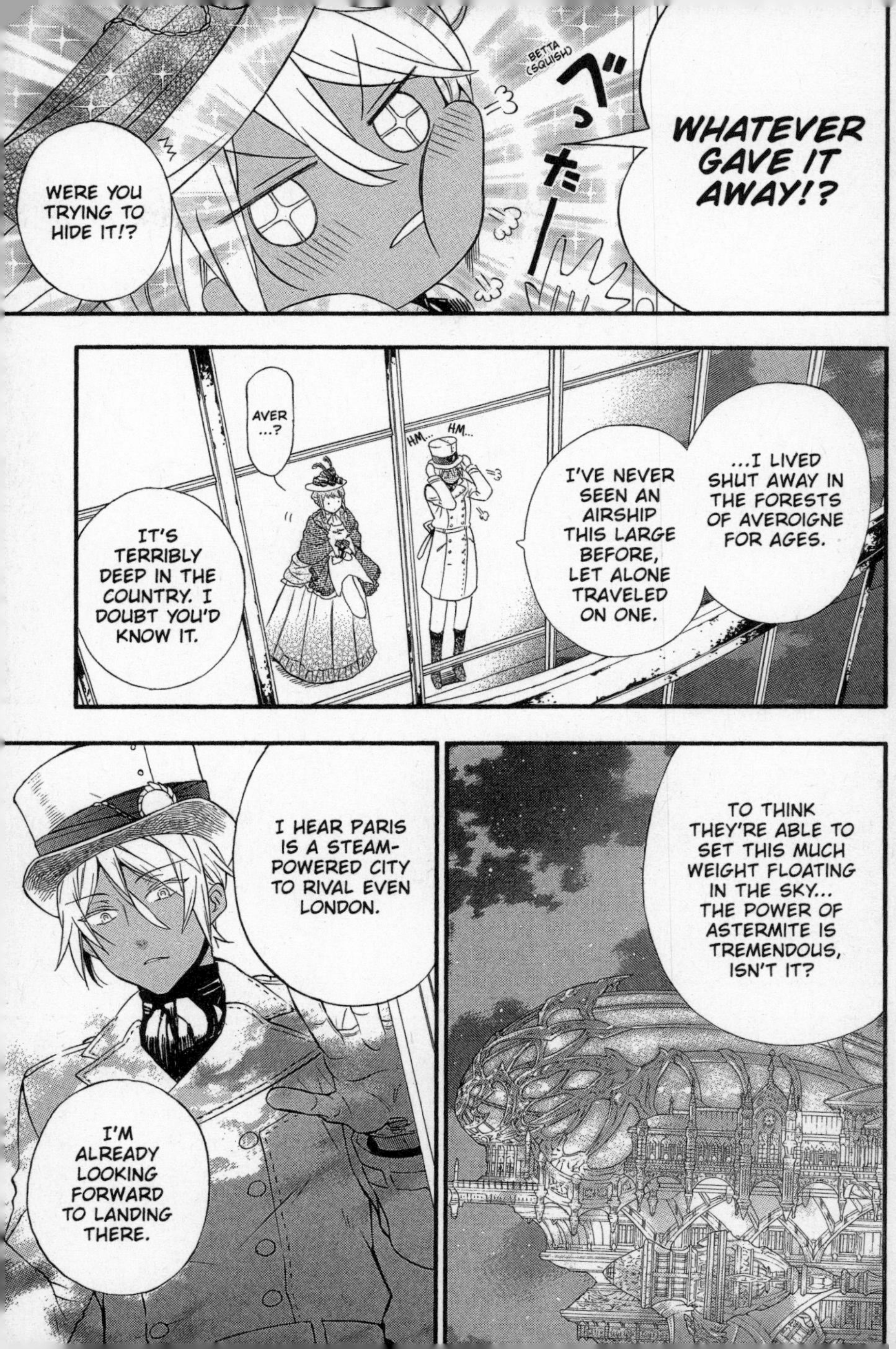
WHATEVER GAVE IT AWAY!?
BETTA (SQUISH)
ベったー
WERE YOU TRYING TO HIDE IT!?
...I LIVED SHUT AWAY IN THE FORESTS OF AVEROIGNE FOR AGES.
I'VE NEVER SEEN AN AIRSHIP THIS LARGE BEFORE, LET ALONE TRAVELED ON ONE.
HM... HM...
AVER ...?
IT'S TERRIBLY DEEP IN THE COUNTRY. I DOUBT YOU'D KNOW IT.
TO THINK THEY'RE ABLE TO SET THIS MUCH WEIGHT FLOATING IN THE SKY... THE POWER OF ASTERMITE IS TREMENDOUS, ISN'T IT?
I HEAR PARIS IS A STEAM-POWERED CITY TO RIVAL EVEN LONDON.
I'M ALREADY LOOKING FORWARD TO LANDING THERE.

...ARE YOU VISITING PARIS FOR SIGHT-SEEING?

...

"SOME-THING"...?

NO. I'M LOOKING FOR SOME-THING.

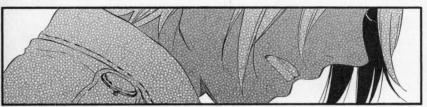

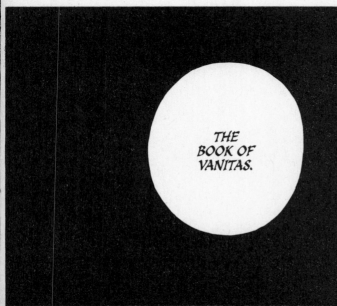

THE BOOK OF VANITAS.

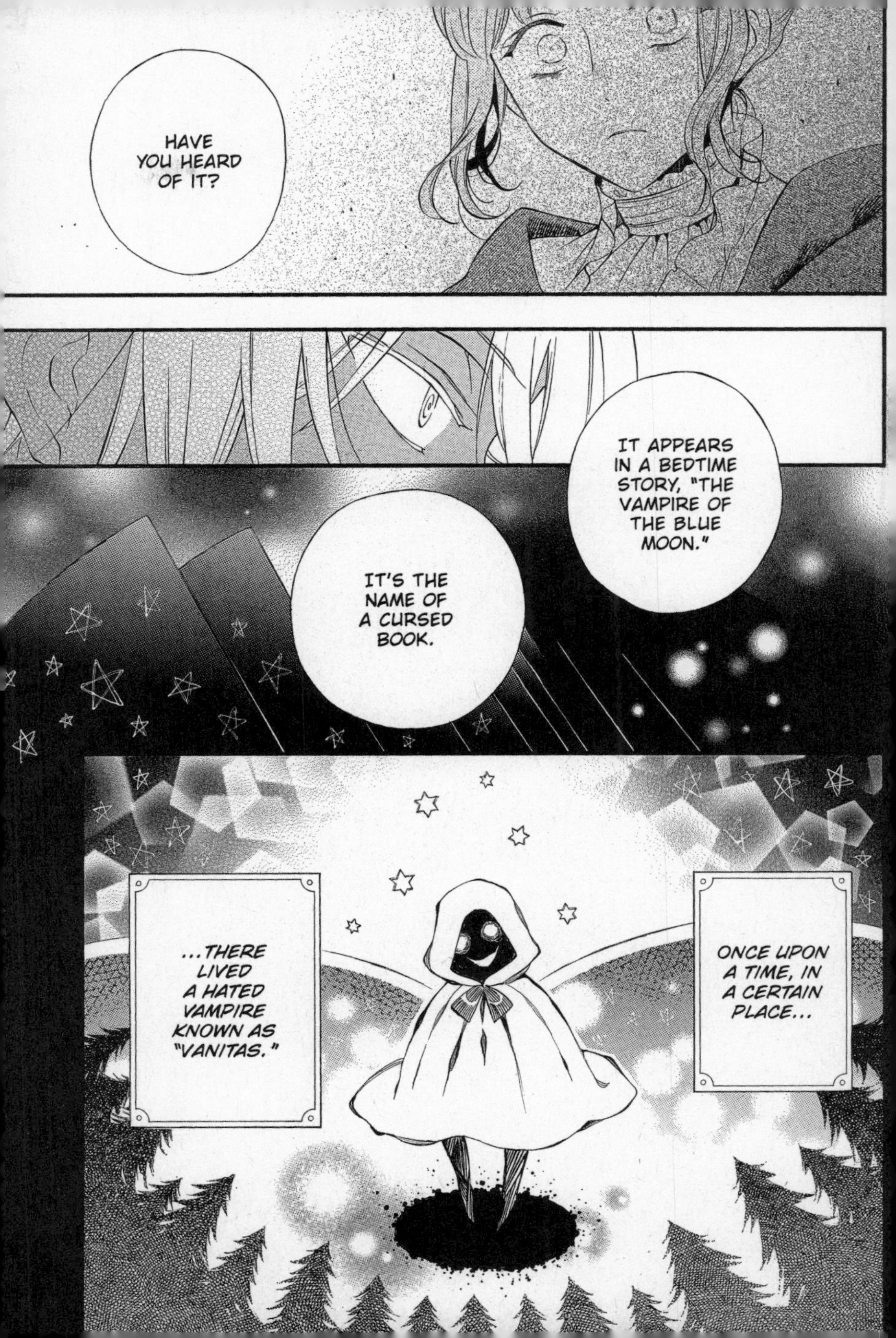
HAVE YOU HEARD OF IT?
IT APPEARS IN A BEDTIME STORY, "THE VAMPIRE OF THE BLUE MOON."
IT'S THE NAME OF A CURSED BOOK.
ONCE UPON A TIME, IN A CERTAIN PLACE...
...THERE LIVED A HATED VAMPIRE KNOWN AS "VANITAS."

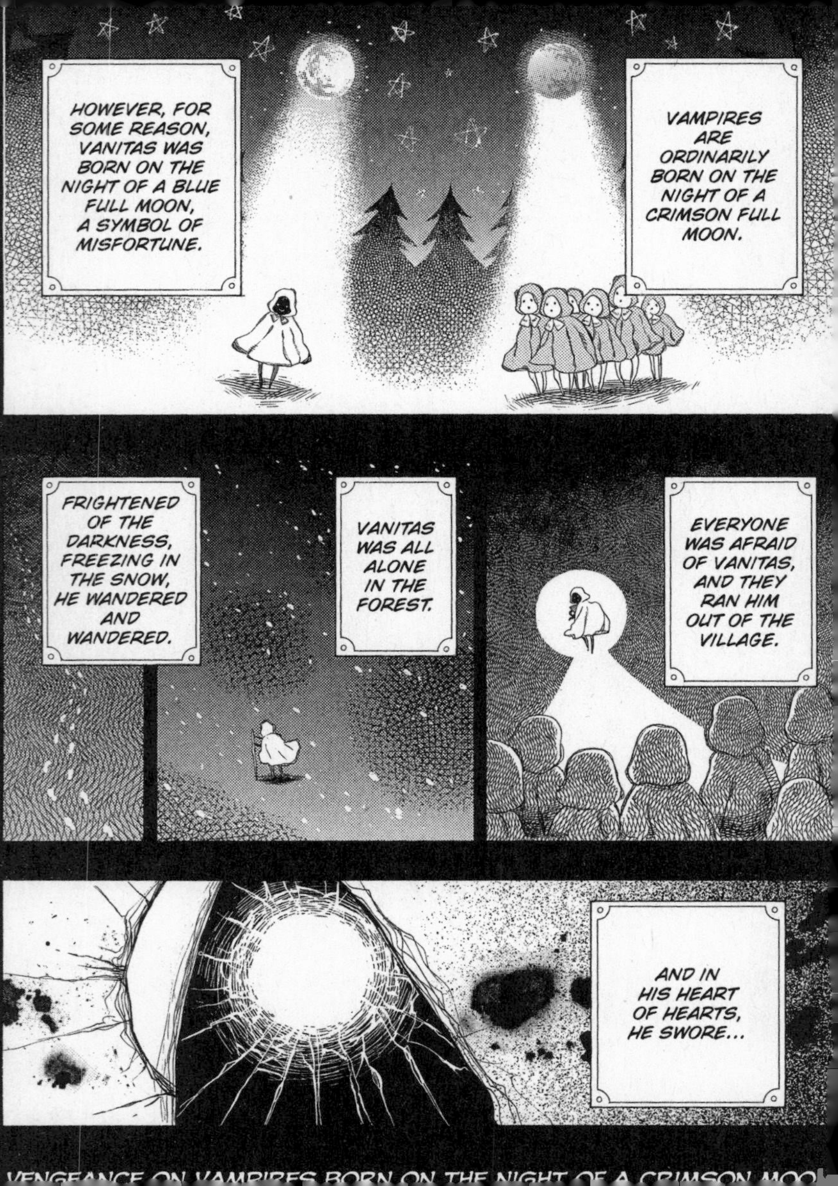

VAMPIRES ARE ORDINARILY BORN ON THE NIGHT OF A CRIMSON FULL MOON.
HOWEVER, FOR SOME REASON, VANITAS WAS BORN ON THE NIGHT OF A BLUE FULL MOON, A SYMBOL OF MISFORTUNE.
EVERYONE WAS AFRAID OF VANITAS, AND THEY RAN HIM OUT OF THE VILLAGE.
VANITAS WAS ALL ALONE IN THE FOREST.
FRIGHTENED OF THE DARKNESS, FREEZING IN THE SNOW, HE WANDERED AND WANDERED.
AND IN HIS HEART OF HEARTS, HE SWORE...
VENGEANCE ON VAMPIRES BORN ON THE NIGHT OF A CRIMSON MOO

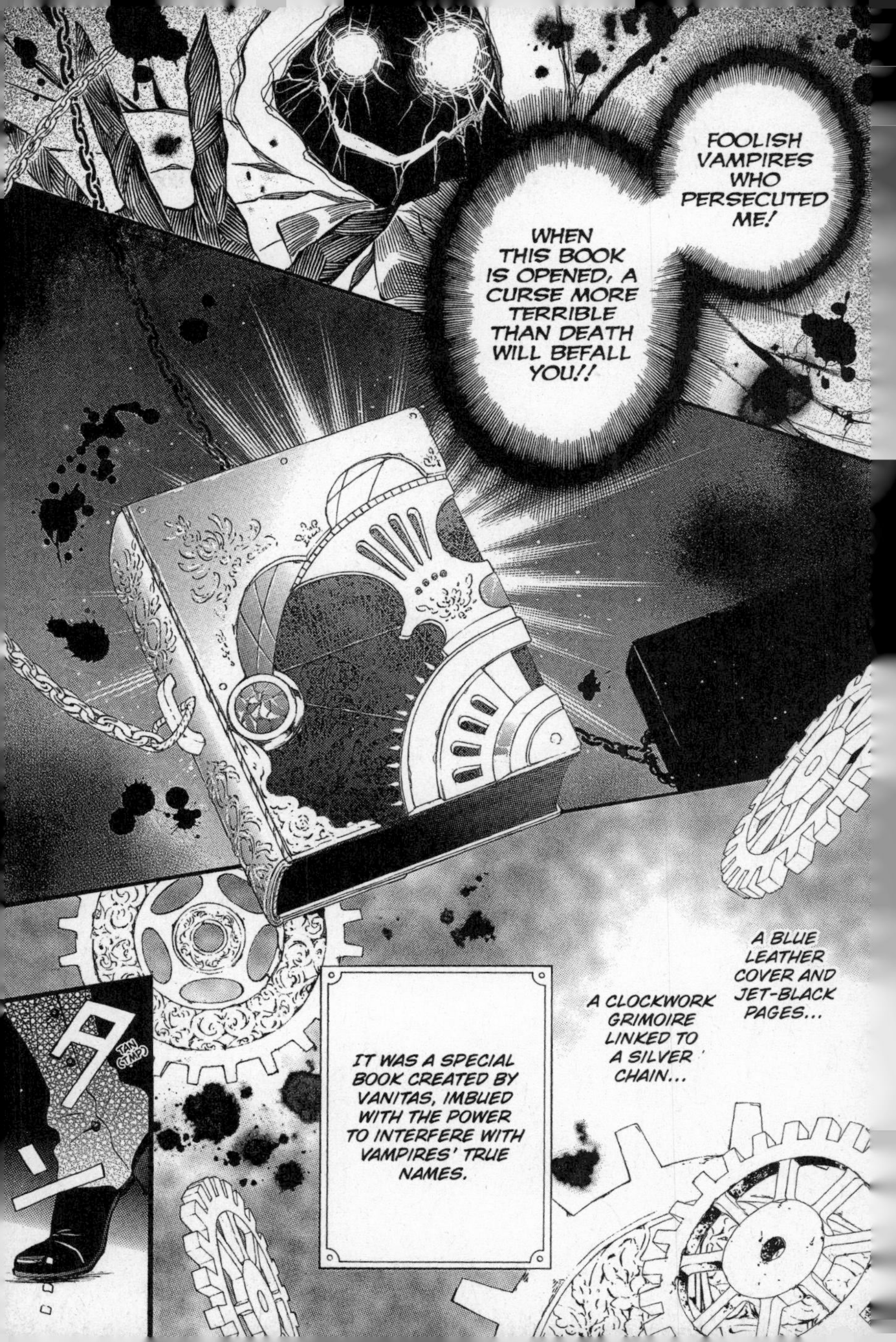
FOOLISH VAMPIRES WHO PERSECUTED ME!
WHEN THIS BOOK IS OPENED, A CURSE MORE TERRIBLE THAN DEATH WILL BEFALL YOU!!
A BLUE LEATHER COVER AND JET-BLACK PAGES...
A CLOCKWORK GRIMOIRE LINKED TO A SILVER CHAIN...
IT WAS A SPECIAL BOOK CREATED BY VANITAS, IMBUED WITH THE POWER TO INTERFERE WITH VAMPIRES' TRUE NAMES.
TAN (TMP)

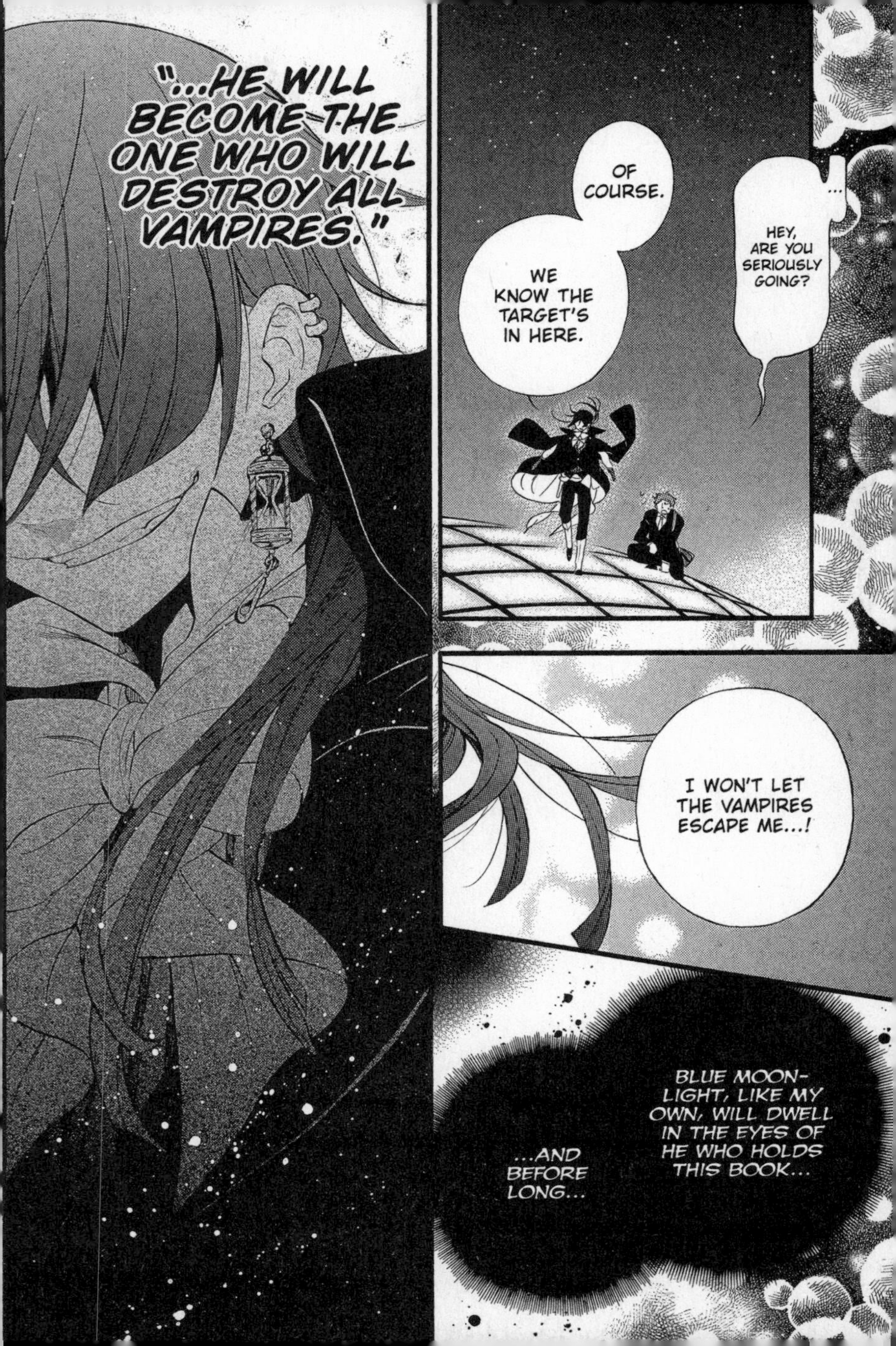
...
HEY, ARE YOU SERIOUSLY GOING?
OF COURSE.
WE KNOW THE TARGET'S IN HERE.
I WON'T LET THE VAMPIRES ESCAPE ME...!
BLUE MOON-LIGHT, LIKE MY OWN, WILL DWELL IN THE EYES OF HE WHO HOLDS THIS BOOK...
...AND BEFORE LONG...
"...HE WILL BECOME THE ONE WHO WILL DESTROY ALL VAMPIRES."

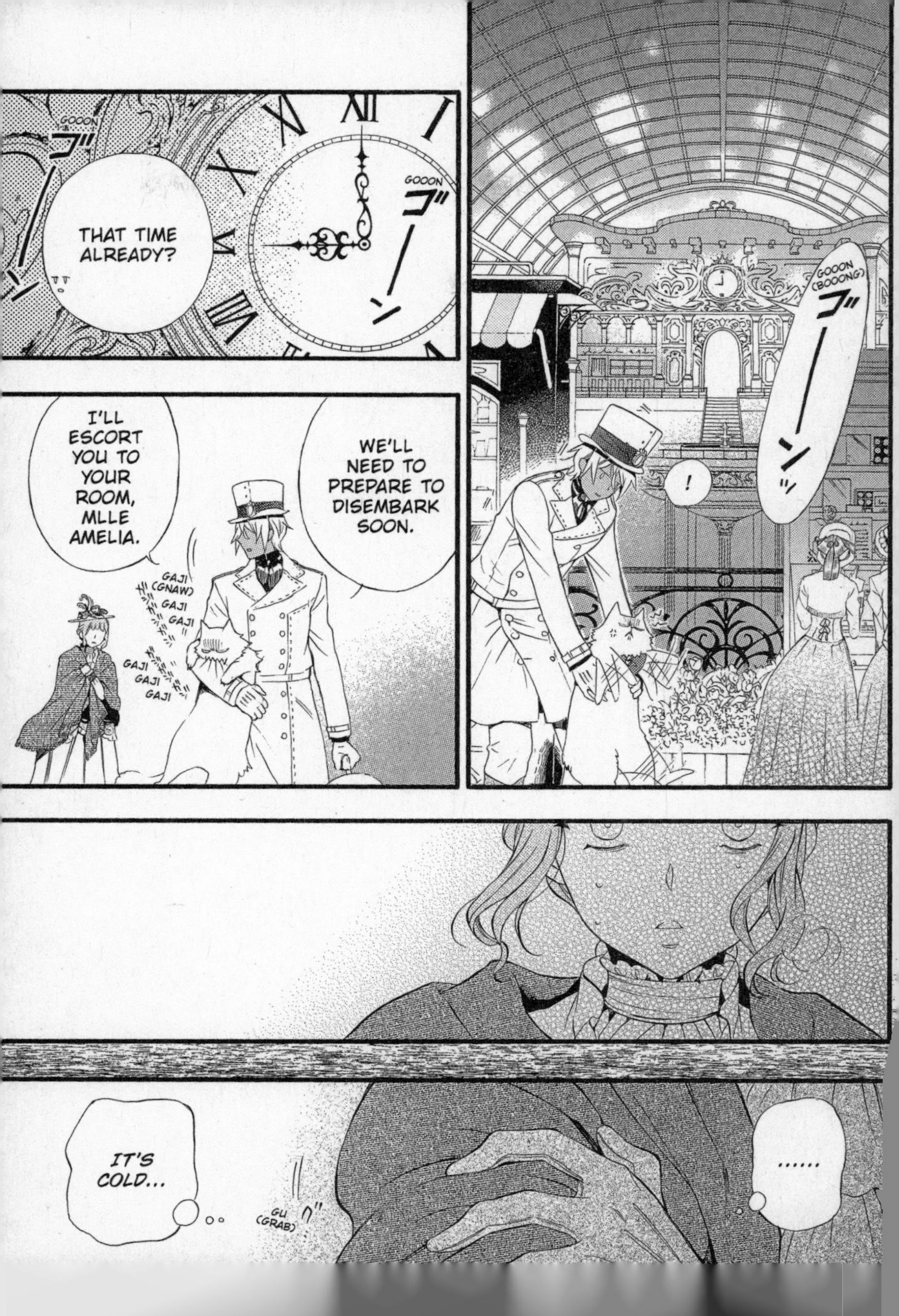
GOOON (BOOONG)
ゴーンッ
!
GOOON
ゴーン
GOOON
ゴ
THAT TIME ALREADY?
WE'LL NEED TO PREPARE TO DISEMBARK SOON.
I'LL ESCORT YOU TO YOUR ROOM, MLLE AMELIA.
GAJI (GNAW) GAJI GAJI
GAJI GAJI GAJI
......
GU (GRAB)
IT'S COLD...

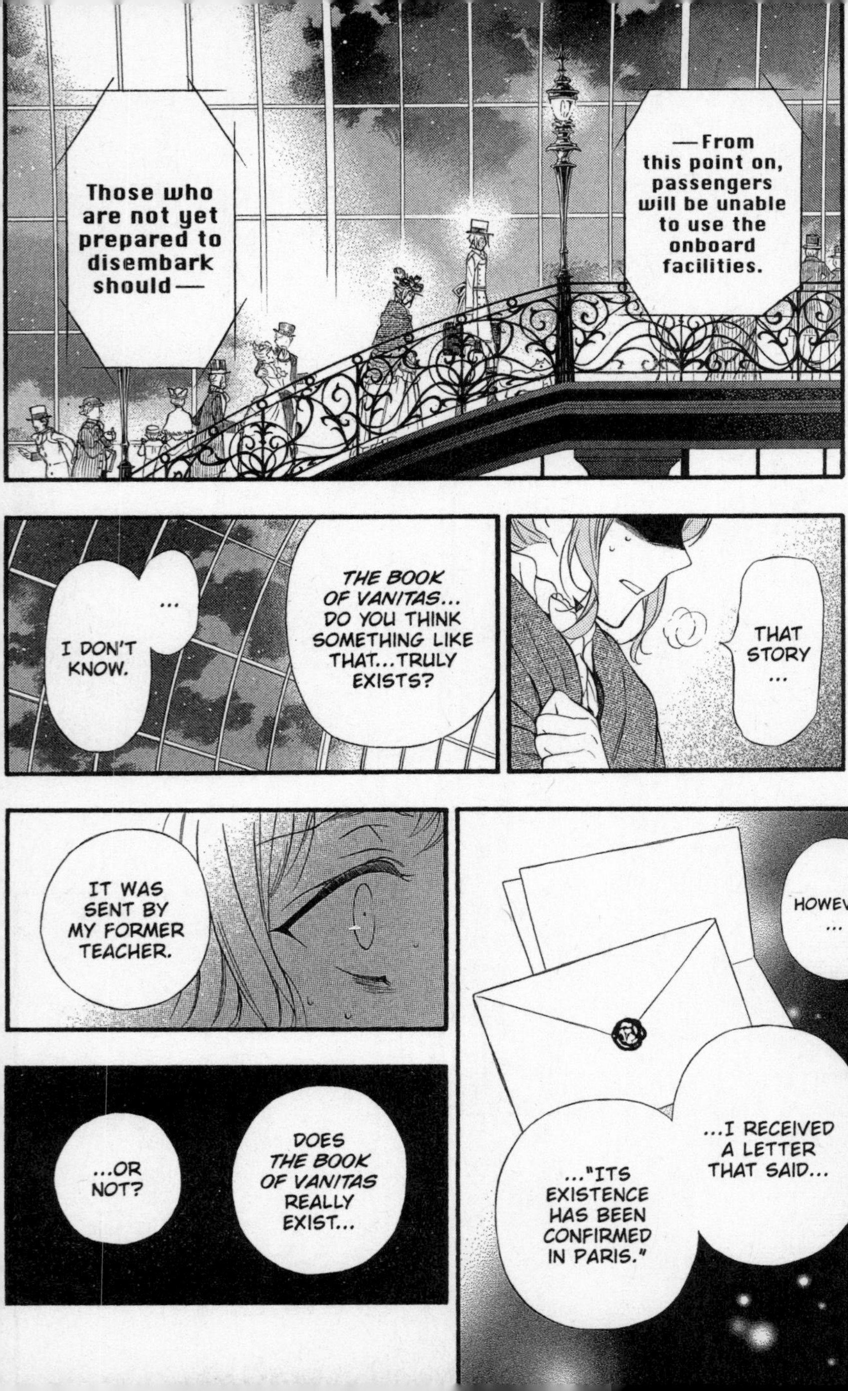
—From this point on, passengers will be unable to use the onboard facilities.
Those who are not yet prepared to disembark should—
THAT STORY ...
THE BOOK OF VANITAS... DO YOU THINK SOMETHING LIKE THAT...TRULY EXISTS?
...
I DON'T KNOW.
HOWEVER ...
...I RECEIVED A LETTER THAT SAID...
..."ITS EXISTENCE HAS BEEN CONFIRMED IN PARIS."
IT WAS SENT BY MY FORMER TEACHER.
DOES THE BOOK OF VANITAS REALLY EXIST...
...OR NOT?

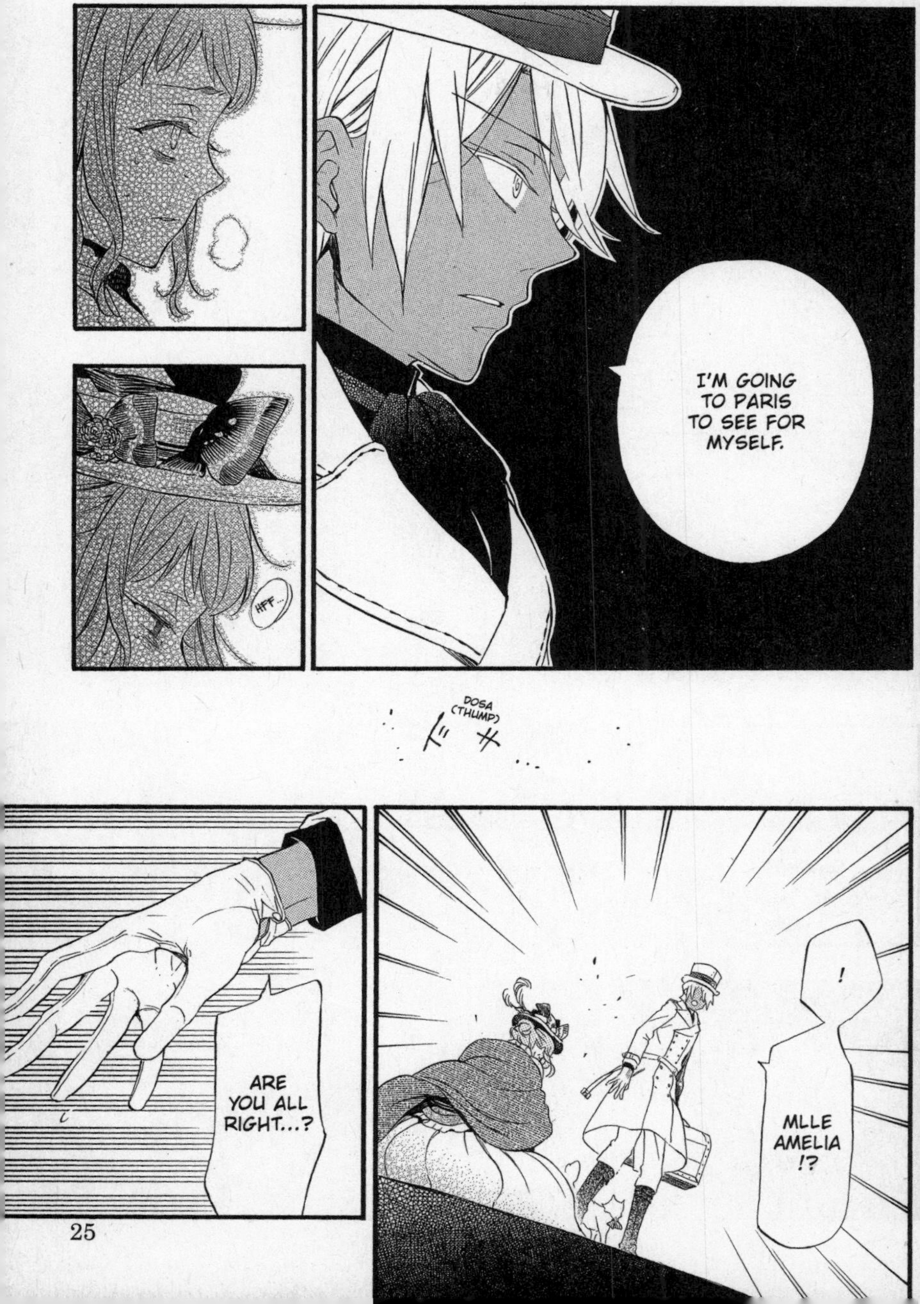
I'M GOING TO PARIS TO SEE FOR MYSELF.
HFF...
DOSA (THUMP)
!
MLLE AMELIA !?
ARE YOU ALL RIGHT...?

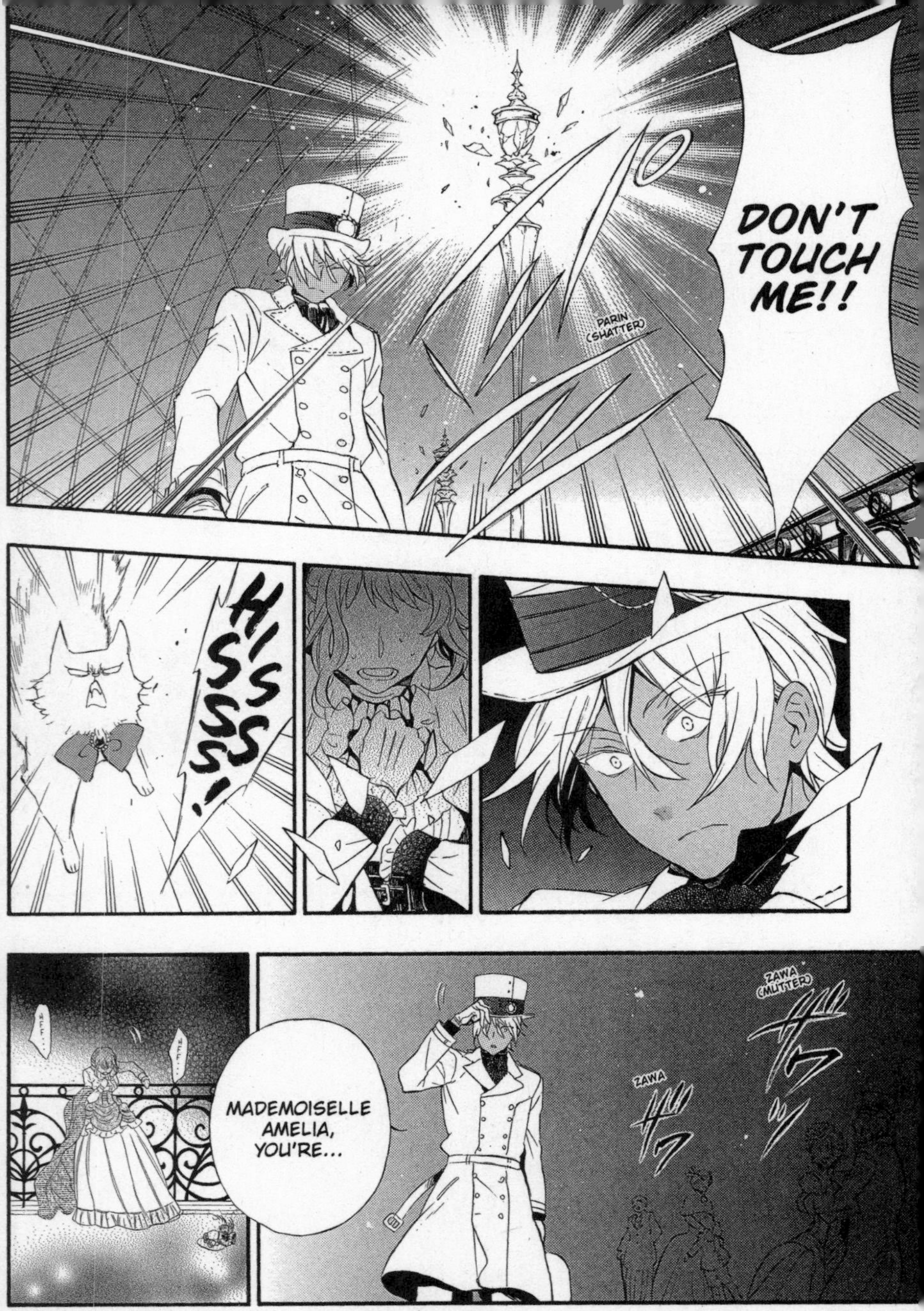
DON'T TOUCH ME!!
PARIN (SHATTER)
HISSSSS!
ZAWA (MUTTER)
ザワッ
ZAWA
ザワ
MADEMOISELLE AMELIA, YOU'RE...
HFF...
HFF...

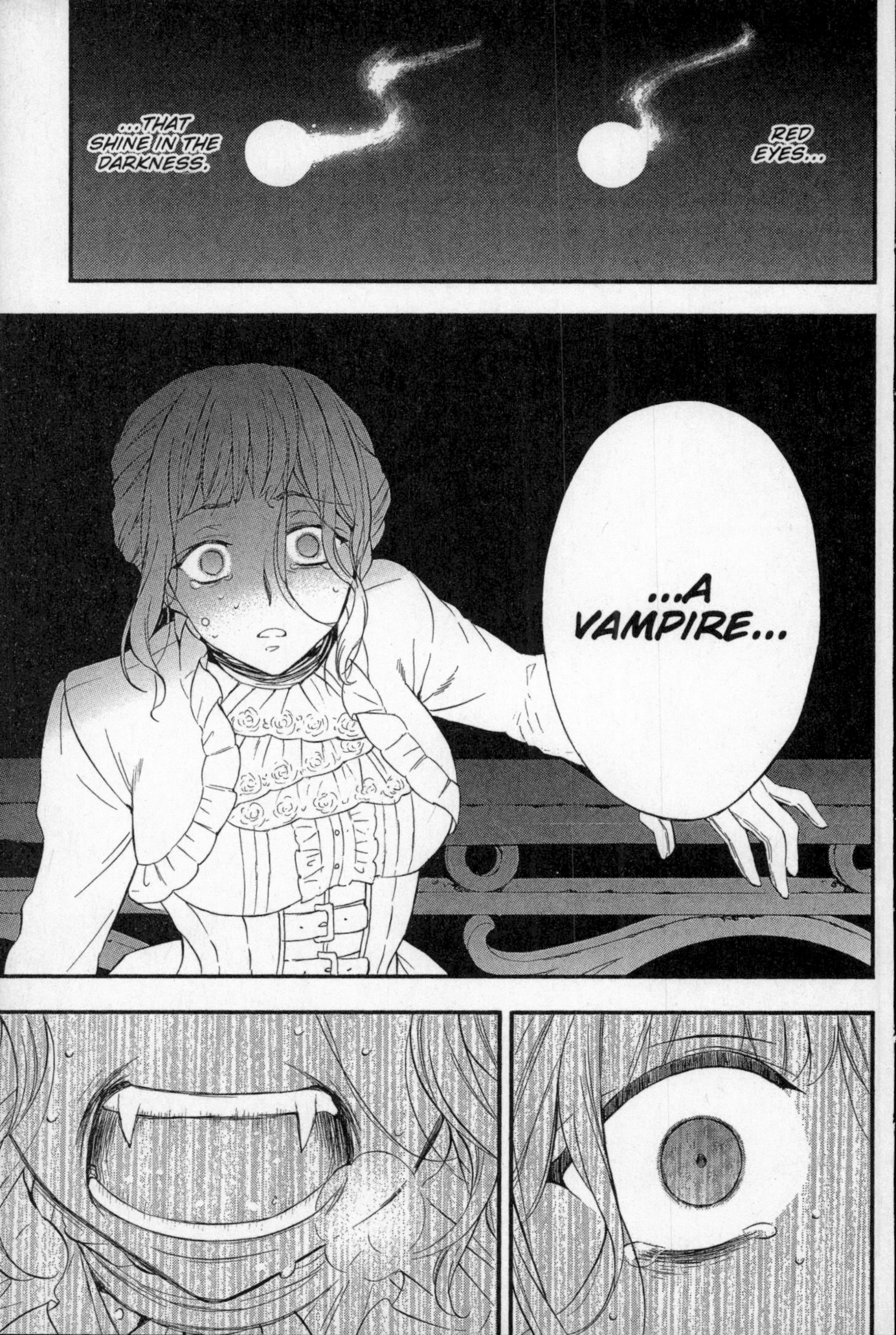
RED EYES...
...THAT SHINE IN THE DARKNESS.
...A VAMPIRE...

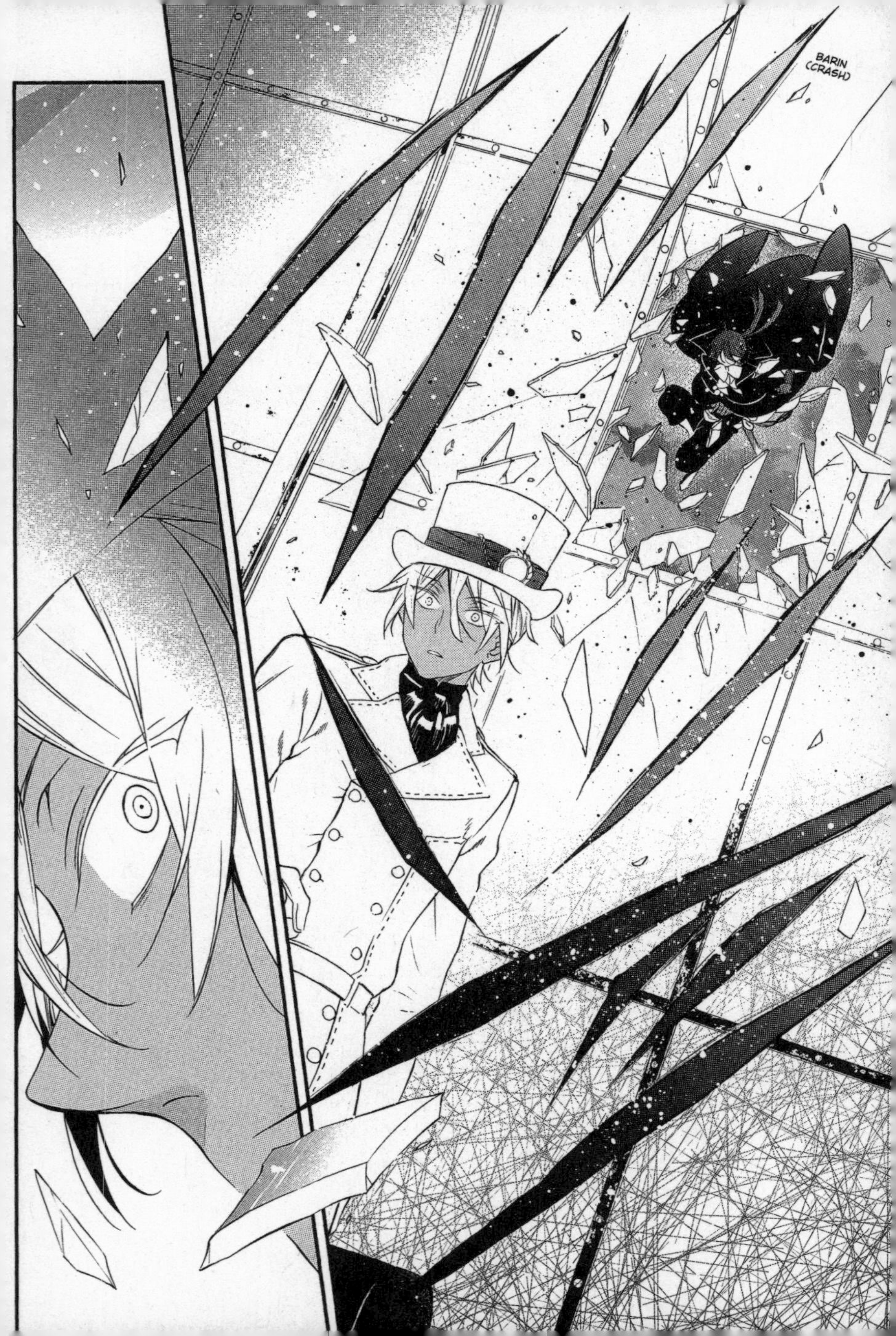
BARIN
(CRASH)

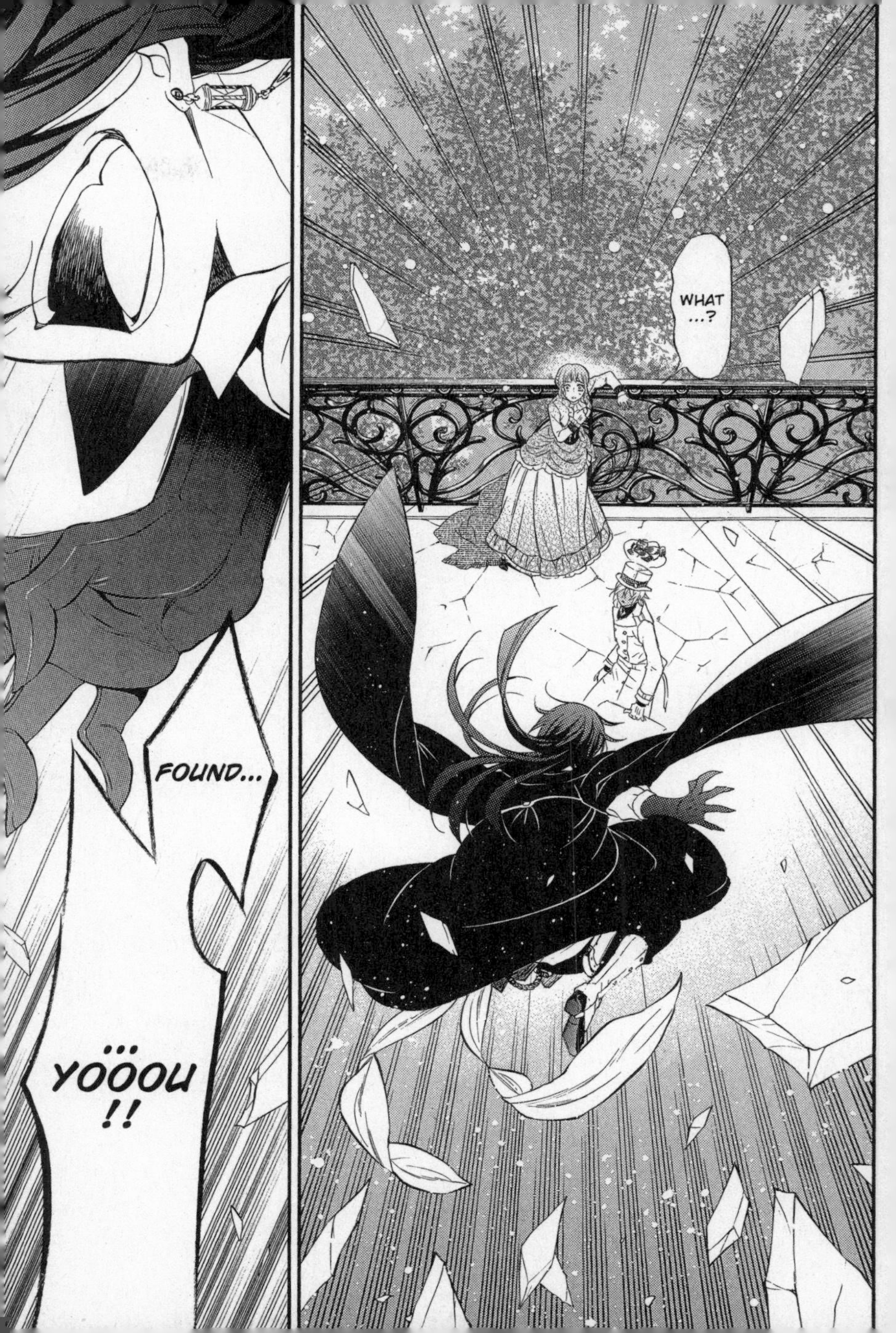
WHAT ...?
FOUND...
... YOÖOU !!

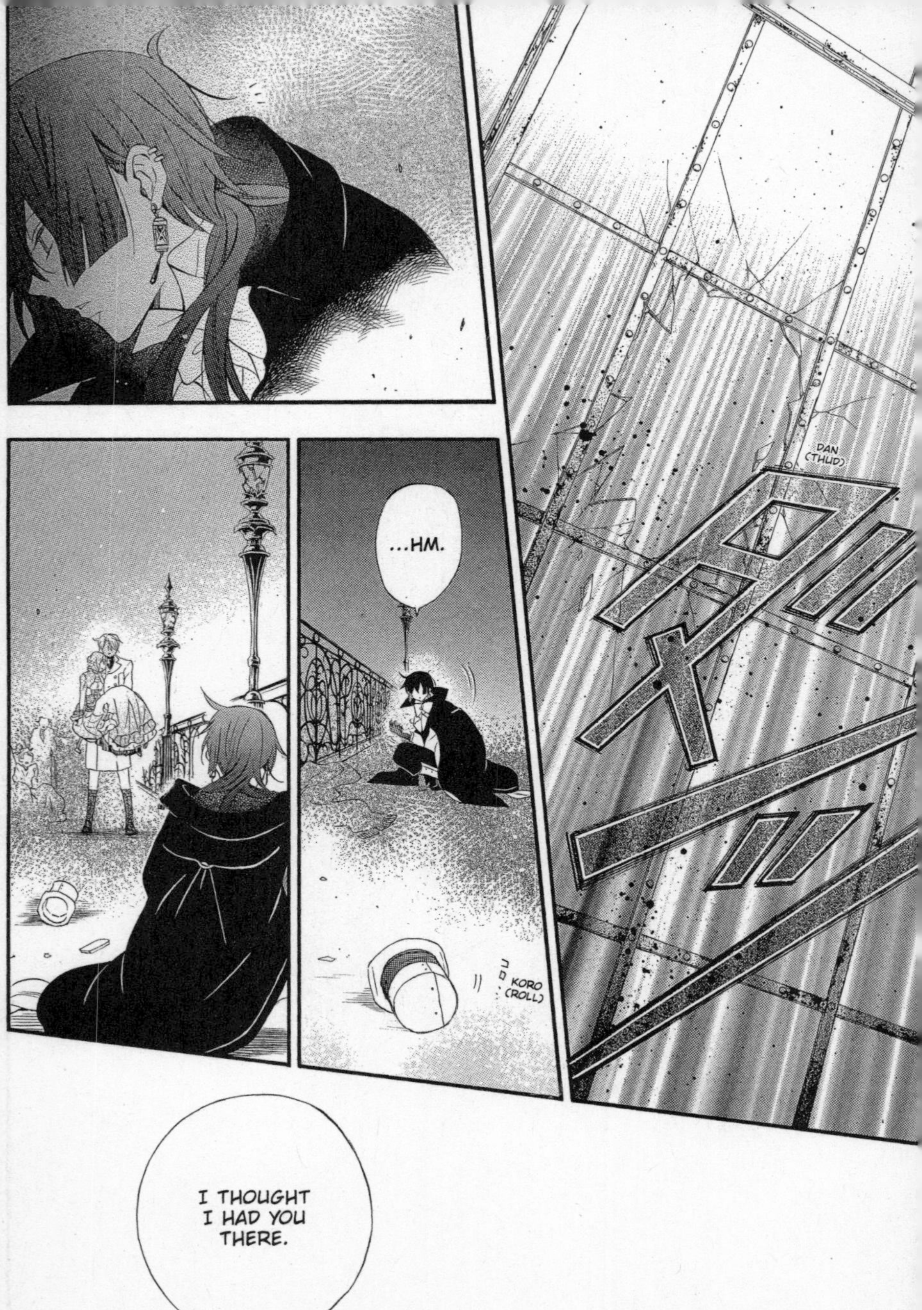
DAN (THUD)
...HM.
KORO (ROLL)
I THOUGHT I HAD YOU THERE.

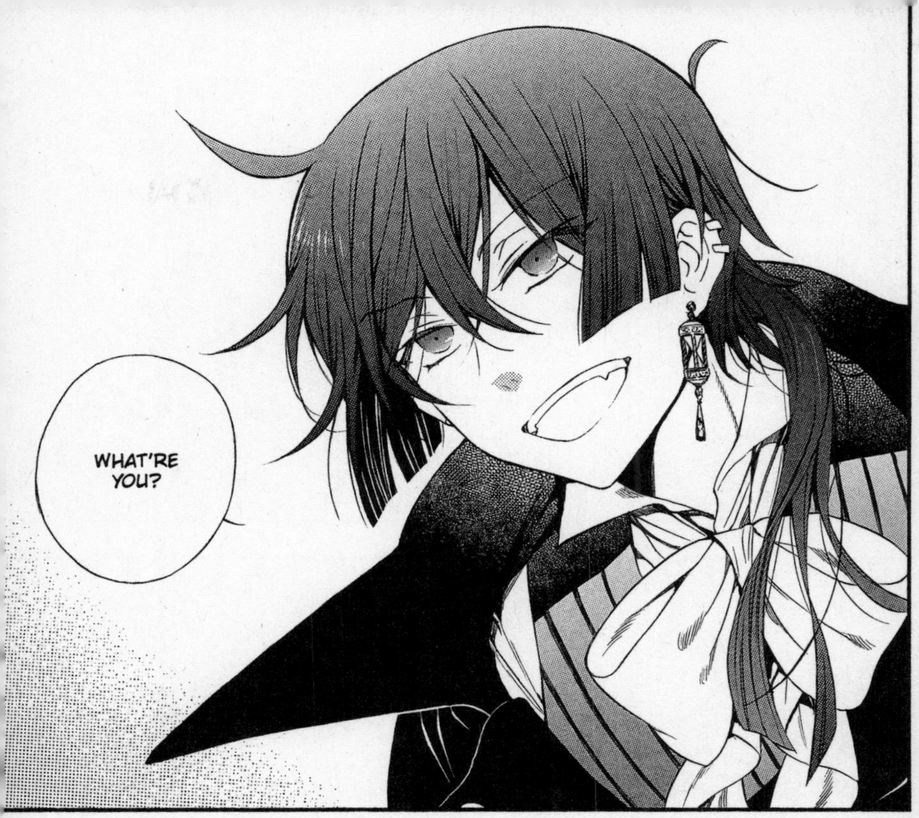
WHAT'RE YOU?

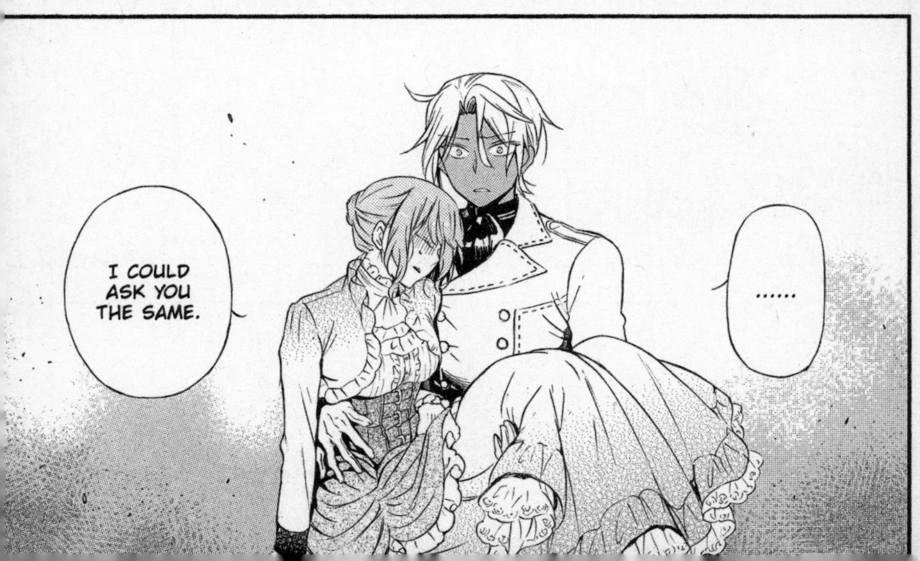
......
I COULD ASK YOU THE SAME.

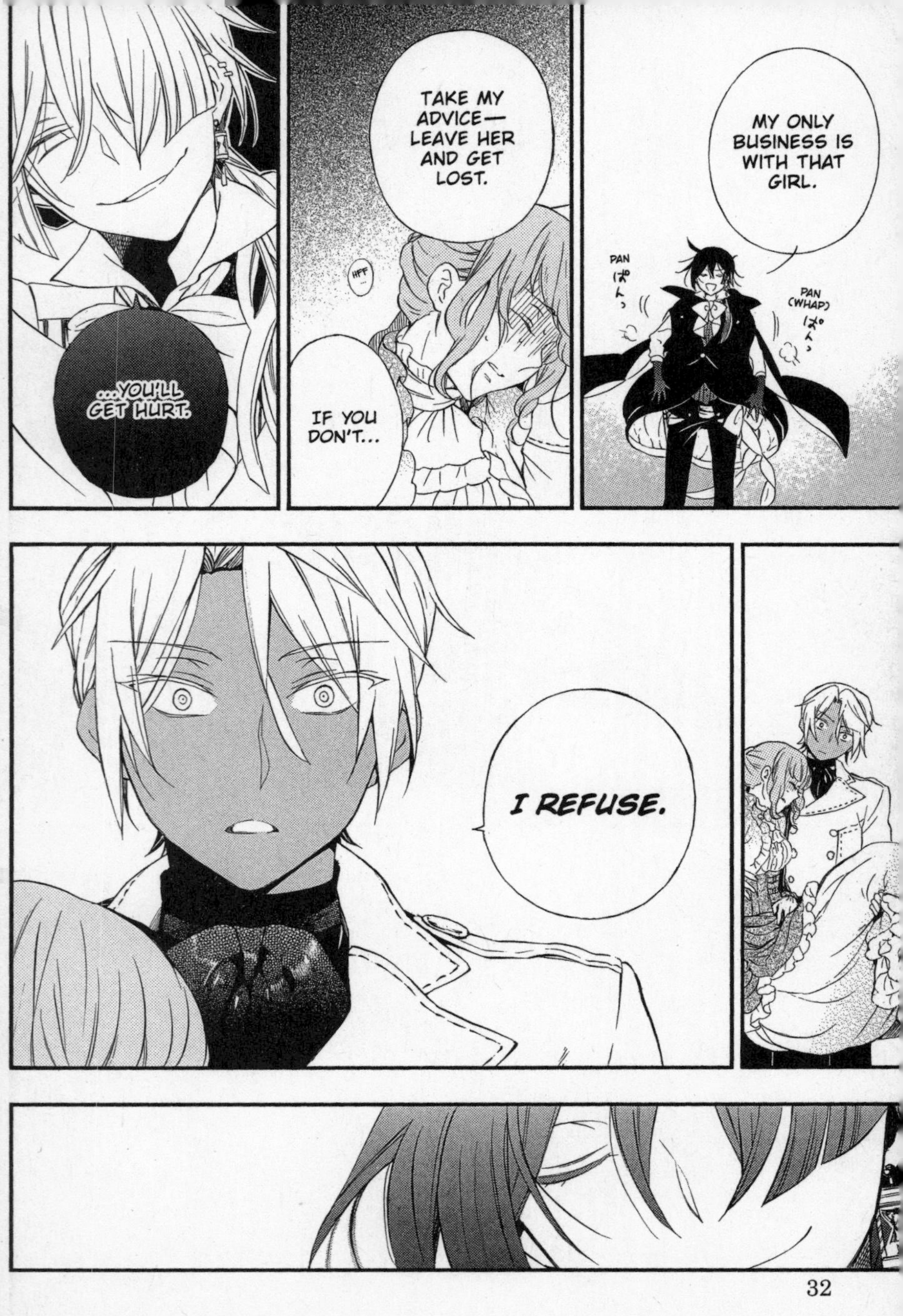

MY ONLY BUSINESS IS WITH THAT GIRL.
PAN (WHAP) ぱんっ
PAN ぱんっ
TAKE MY ADVICE—LEAVE HER AND GET LOST.
HFF...
IF YOU DON'T...
...YOU'LL GET HURT.
I REFUSE.

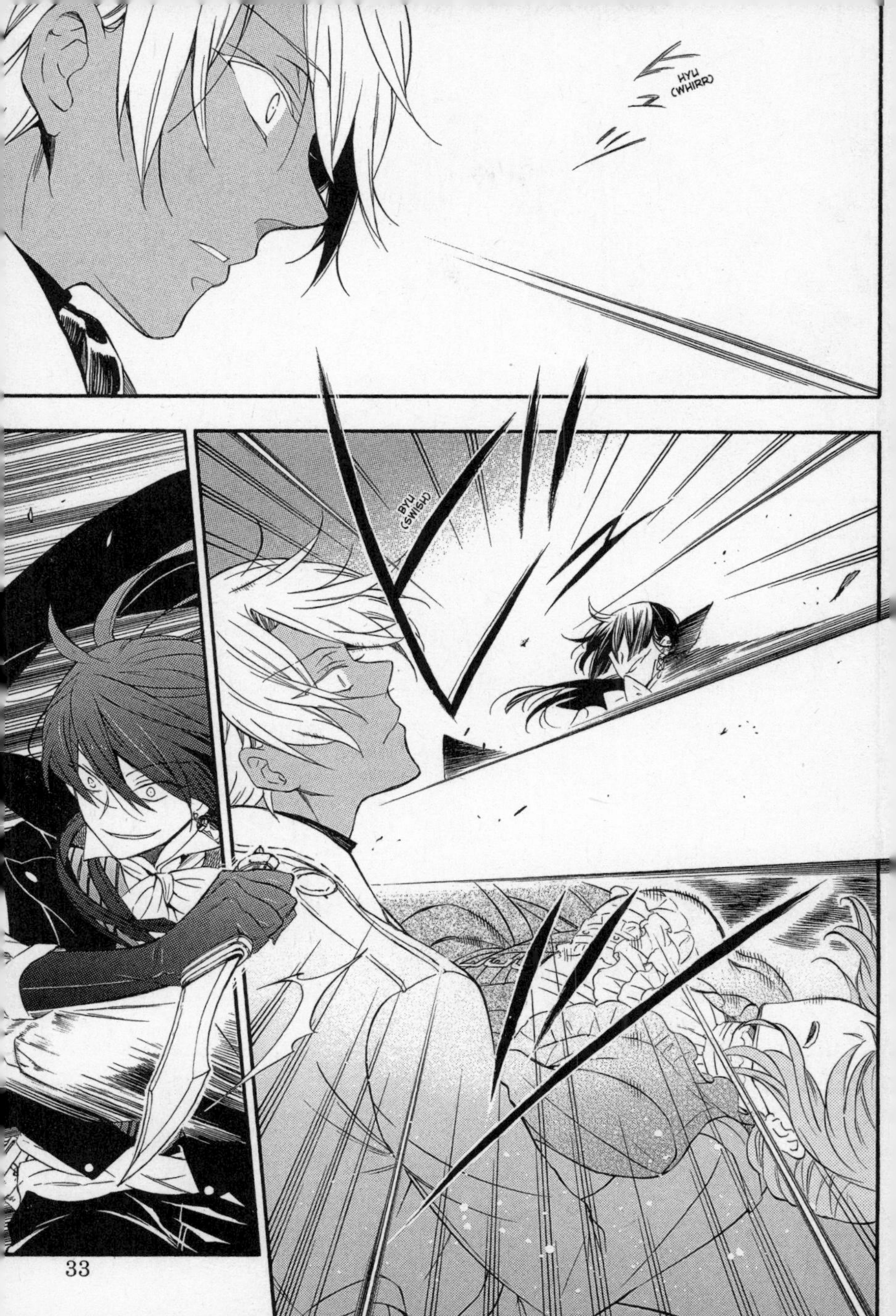
HYU (WHIRR)
BYU (SWISH)

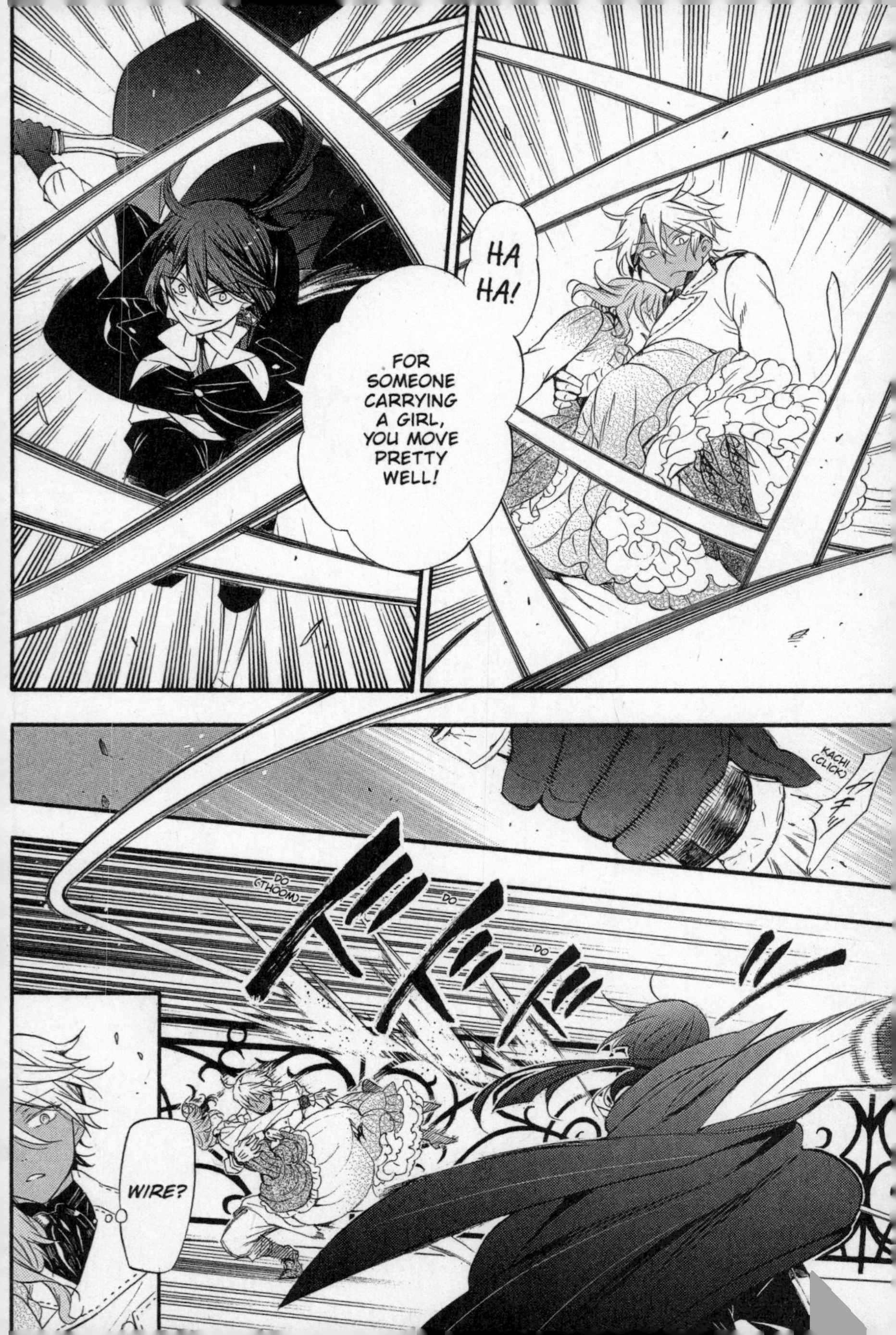
HA HA!
FOR SOMEONE CARRYING A GIRL, YOU MOVE PRETTY WELL!
KACHI (CLICK)
DO (THOOM)
DO
DO
WIRE?

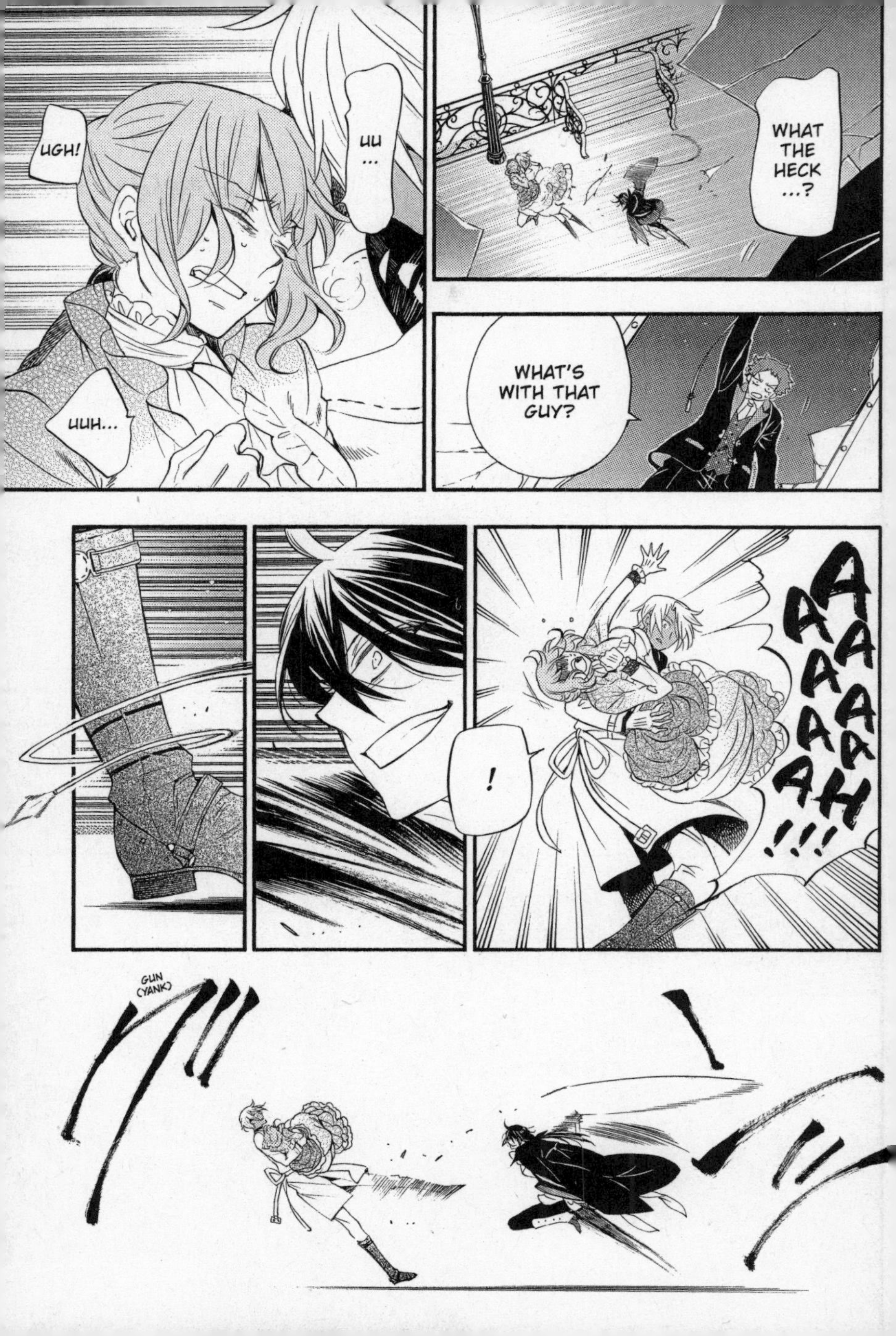
WHAT THE HECK ...?
WHAT'S WITH THAT GUY?
UU ...
UGH!
UUH...
AAAAAAAAH!!!
!
GUN (YANK)

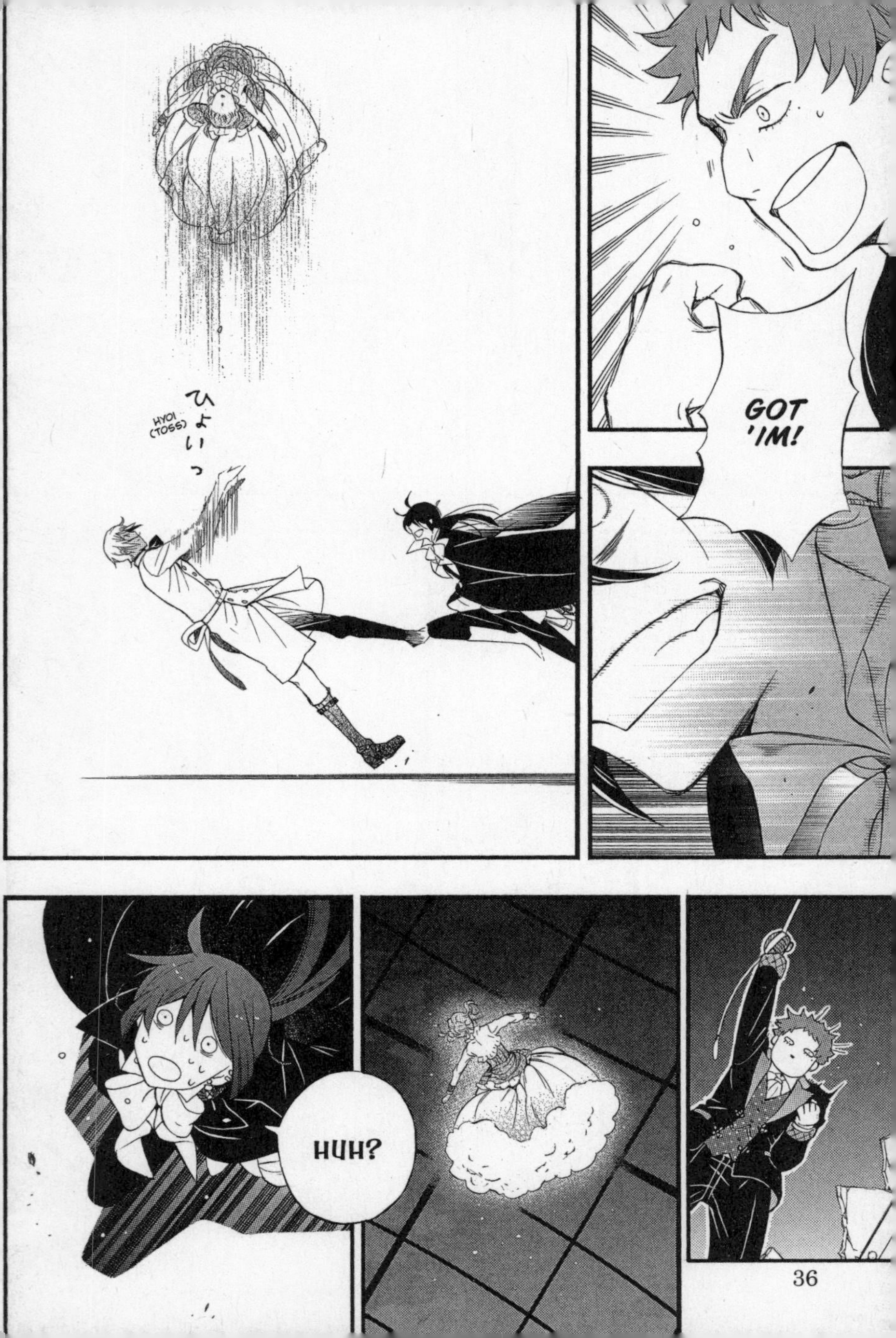
GOT 'IM!
ひょいっ
HYOI (TOSS)
HUH?

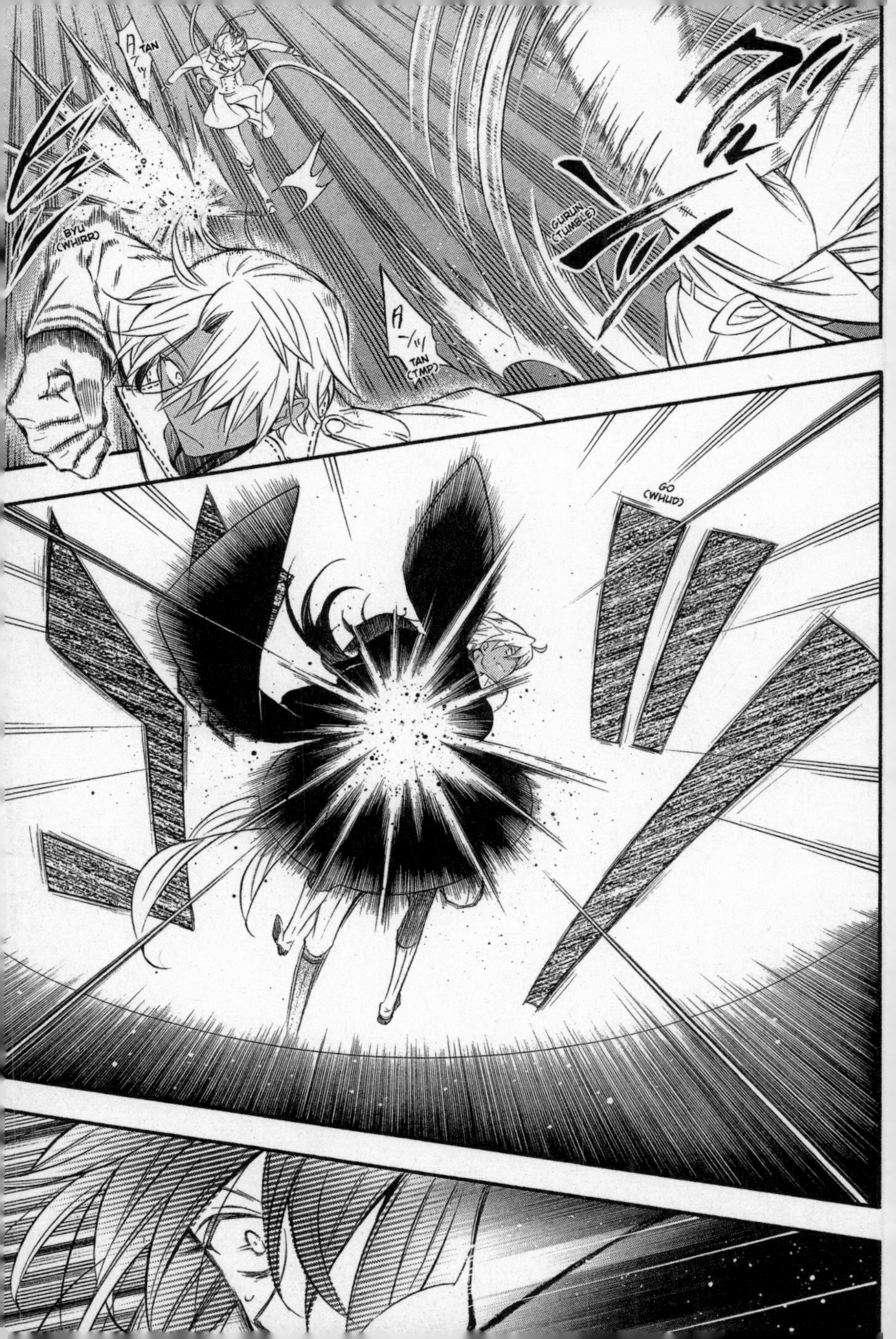
GURUN (TUMBLE)
TAN
TAN (TMP)
BYU (WHIRR)
GO (WHUD)

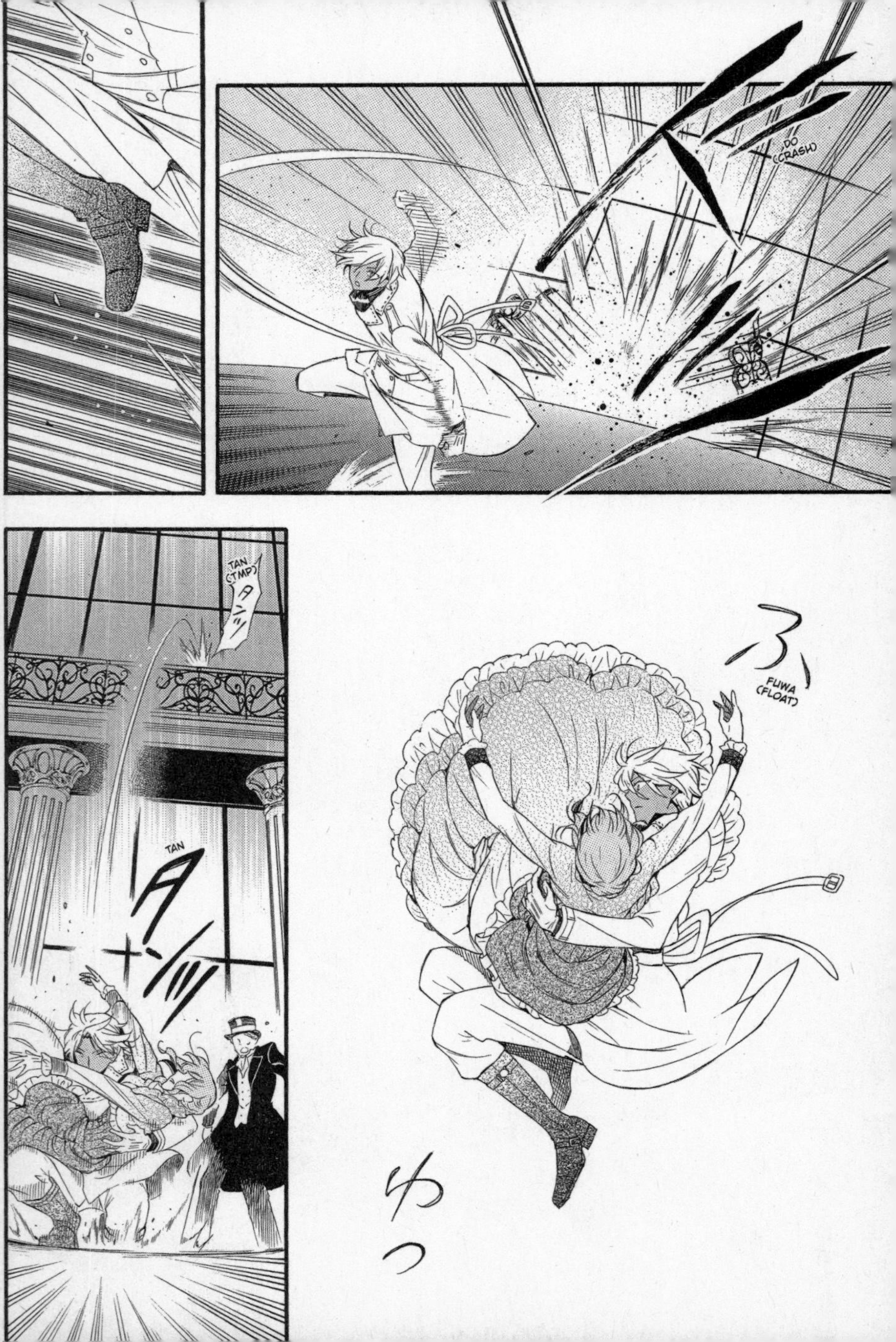

DO (CRASH)
FUWA (FLOAT)
TAN (TMP)
TAN

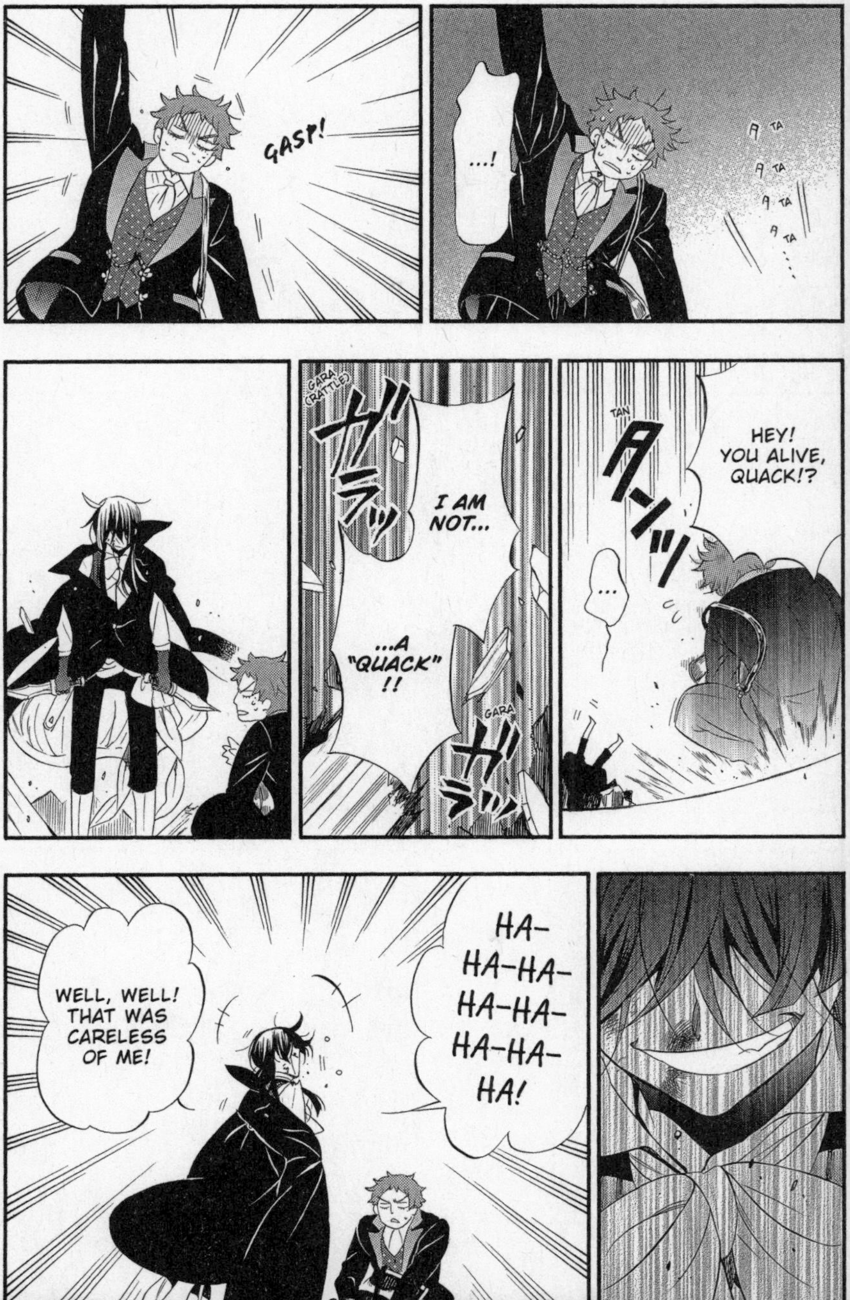
...!
TA
TA
TA
TA
GASP!
TAN
HEY! YOU ALIVE, QUACK!?
...
GARA (RATTLE)
I AM NOT...
...A "QUACK" !!
GARA
HA-HA-HA-HA-HA-HA-HA-HA-HA!
WELL, WELL! THAT WAS CARELESS OF ME!

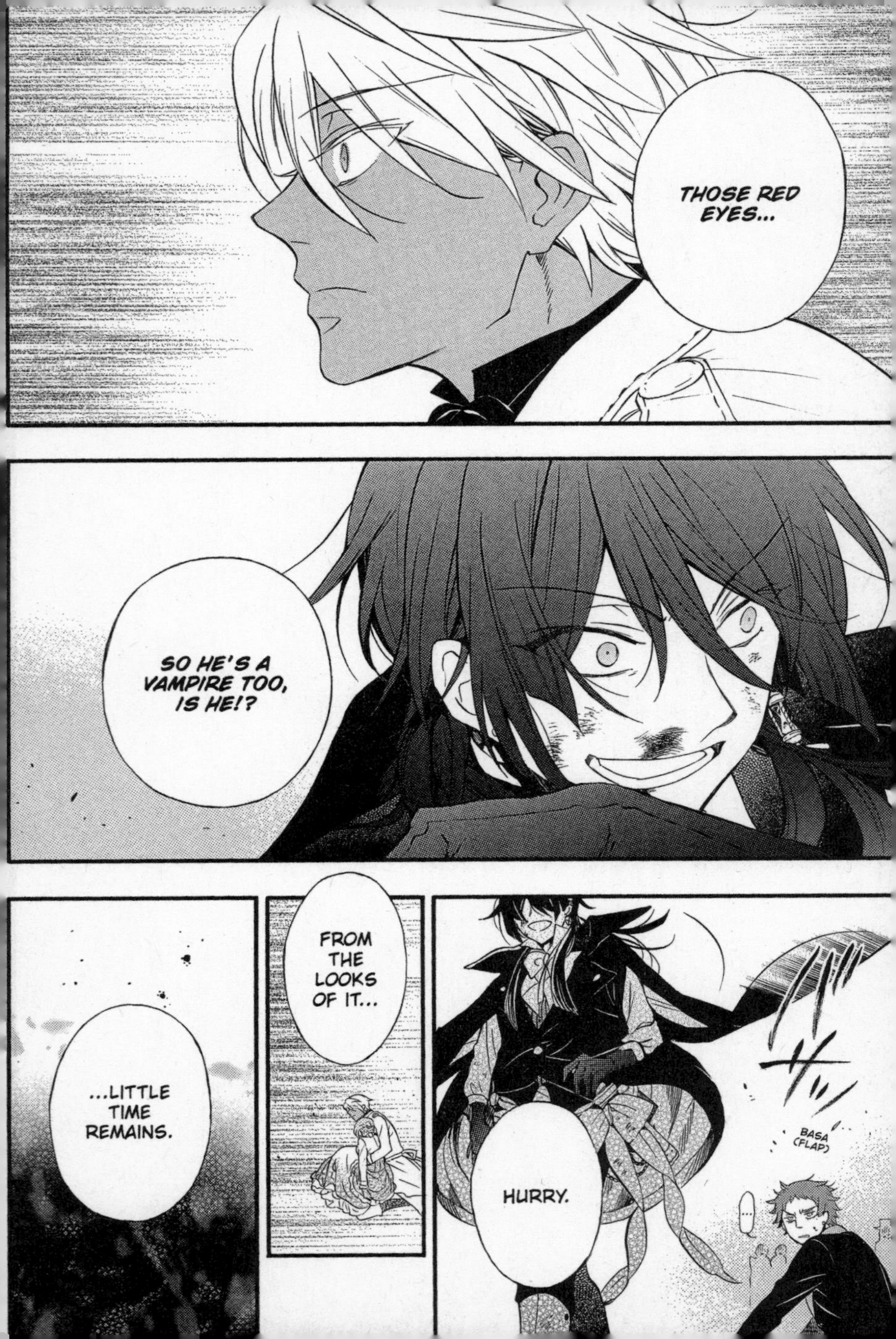
THOSE RED EYES...
SO HE'S A VAMPIRE TOO, IS HE!?
HURRY.
BASA (FLAP)
...
FROM THE LOOKS OF IT...
...LITTLE TIME REMAINS.

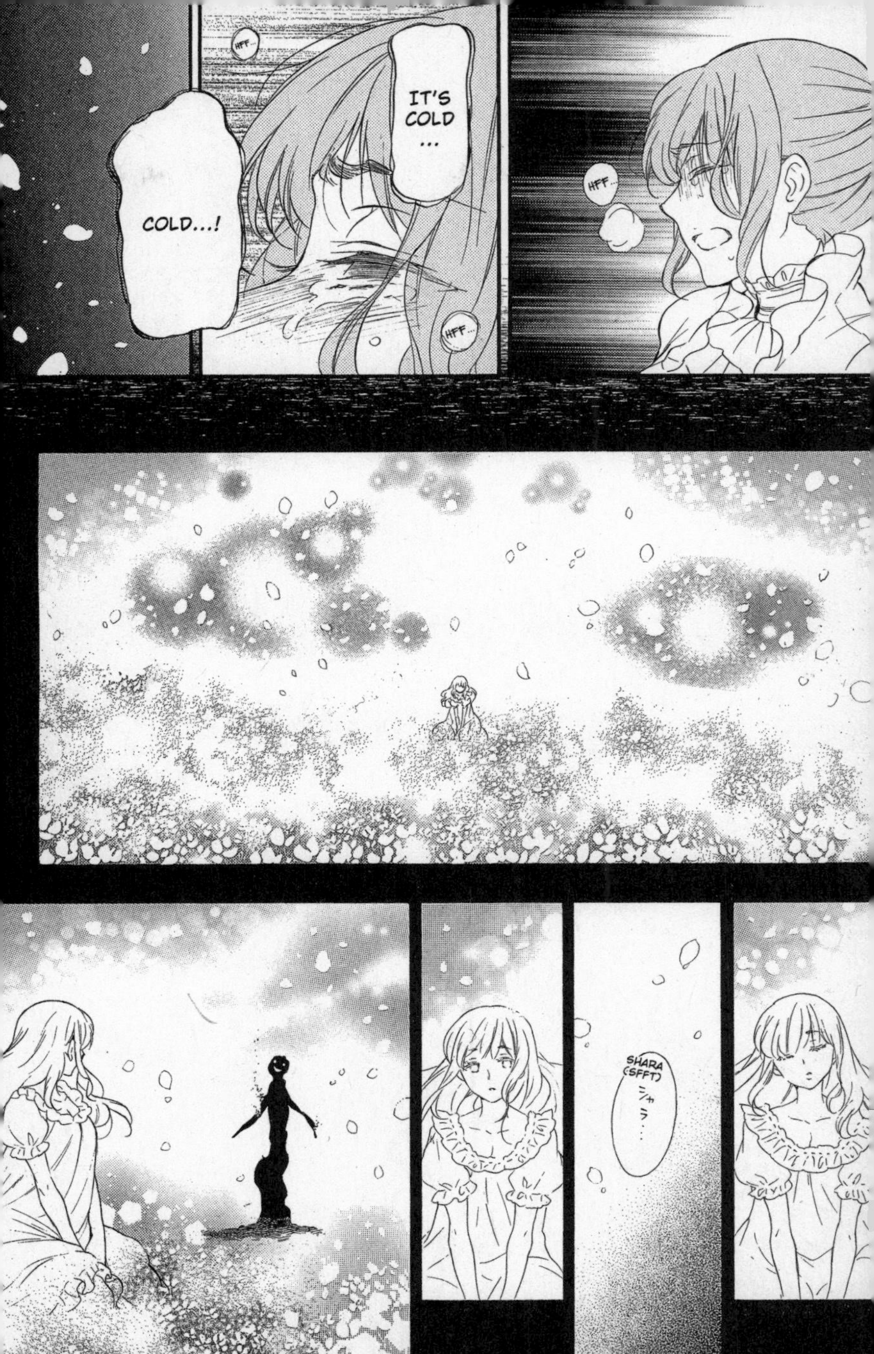
HFF...
HFF...
IT'S COLD ...
HFF...
COLD...!
SHARA (SFFT)
シャラ...

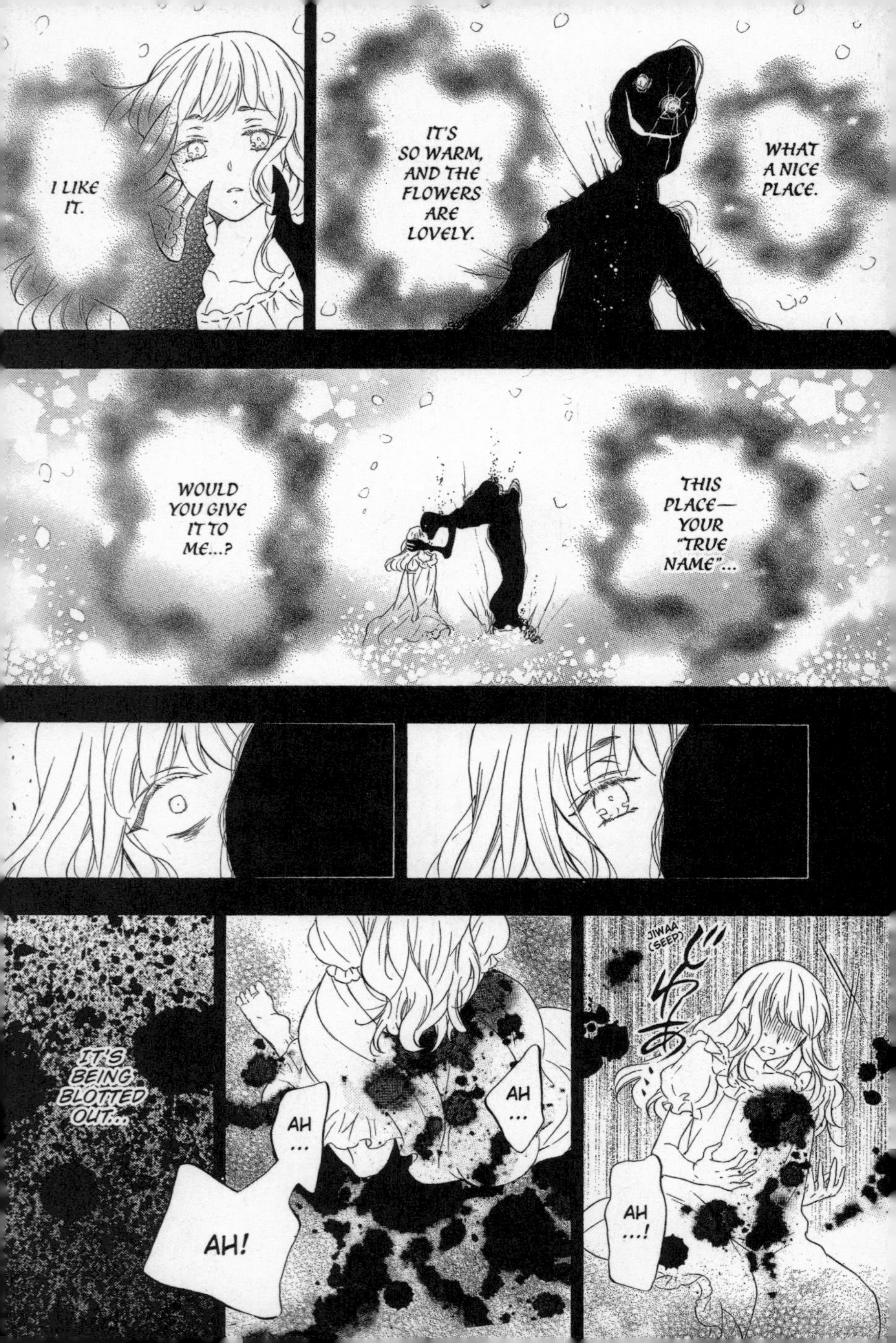
WHAT A NICE PLACE.
IT'S SO WARM, AND THE FLOWERS ARE LOVELY.
I LIKE IT.
THIS PLACE— YOUR "TRUE NAME"...
WOULD YOU GIVE IT TO ME...?
JIWAA (SEEP)
AH ...!
AH ...
AH ...
AH!
IT'S BEING BLOTTED OUT...

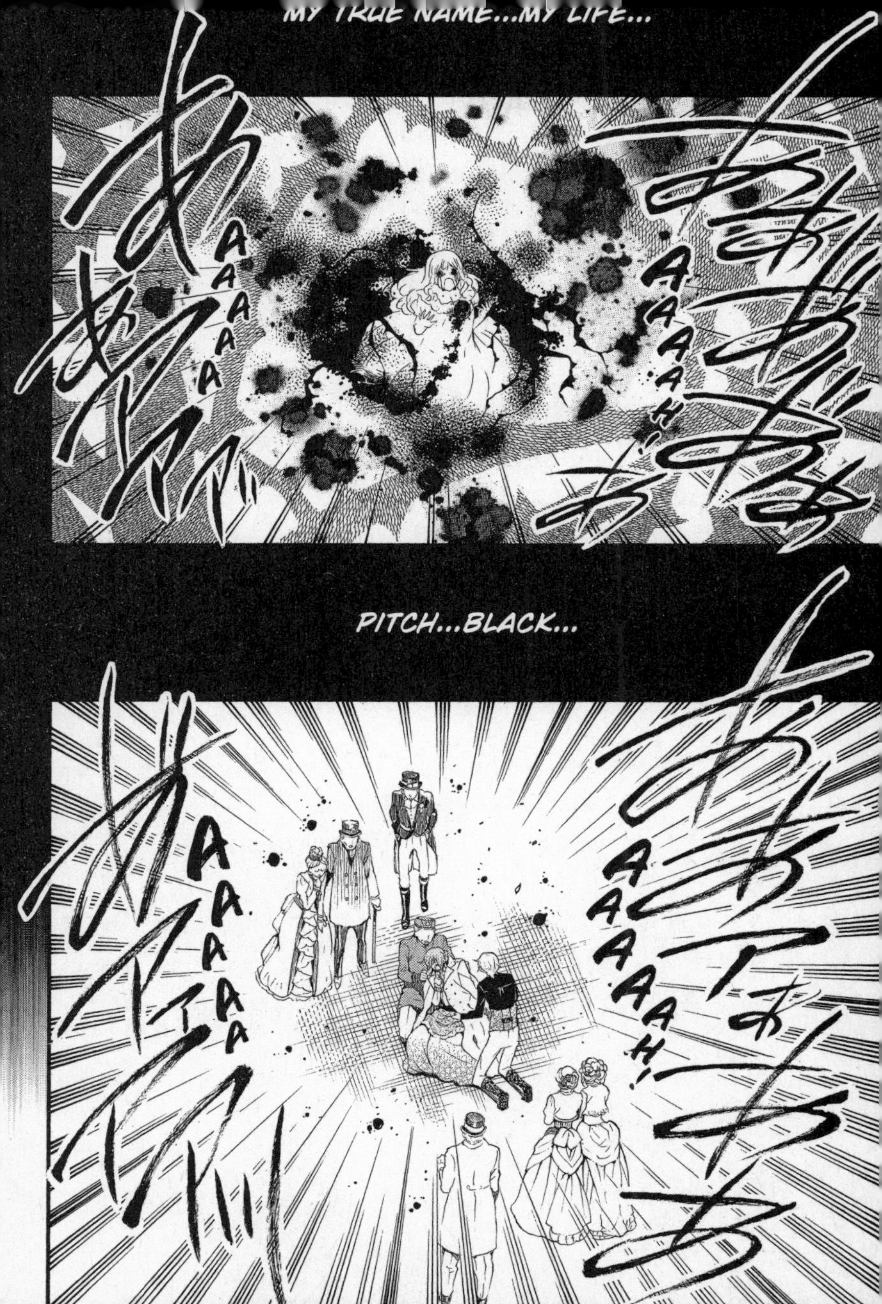
MY TRUE NAME...MY LIFE...
AAAAAH!
AAAAAA
PITCH...BLACK...
AAAAAAAAH!
AAAAAAAA

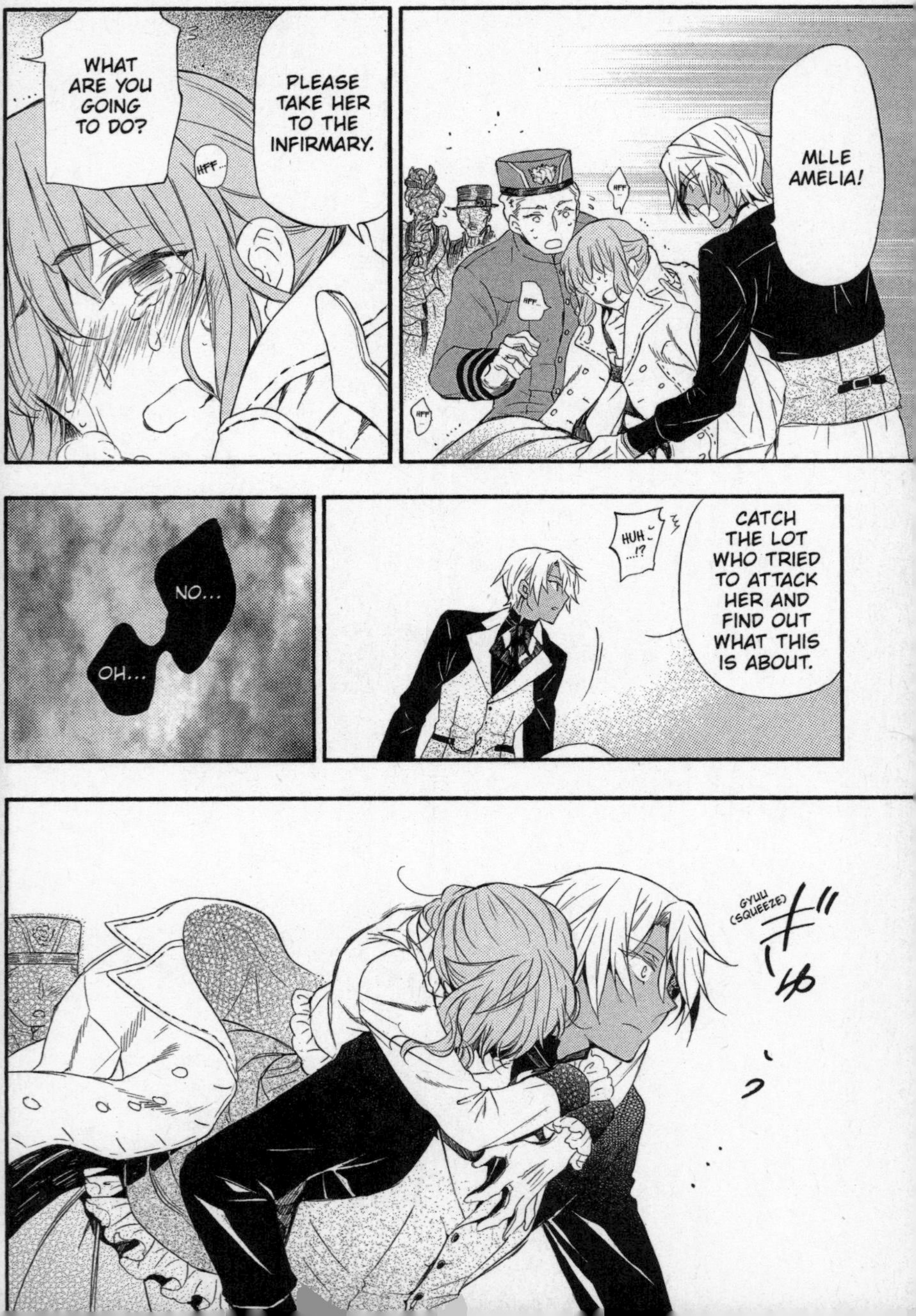
MLLE AMELIA!
HFF...
HFF...
HFF...
PLEASE TAKE HER TO THE INFIRMARY.
WHAT ARE YOU GOING TO DO?
HFF...
CATCH THE LOT WHO TRIED TO ATTACK HER AND FIND OUT WHAT THIS IS ABOUT.
HUH...!?
NO...
OH...
GYUU (SQUEEZE)

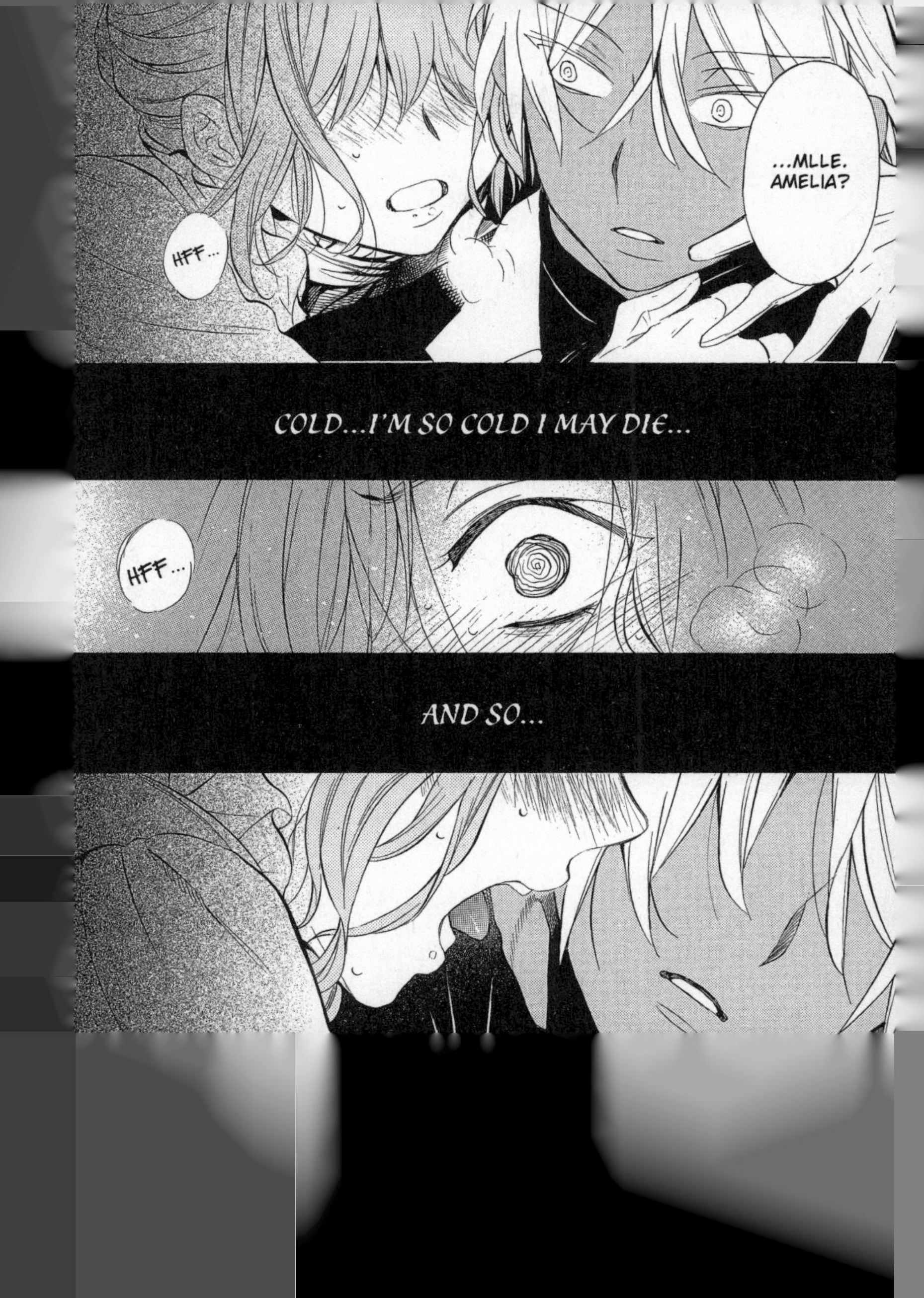
...MLLE. AMELIA?
HFF...
COLD...I'M SO COLD I MAY DIE...
HFF...
AND SO...

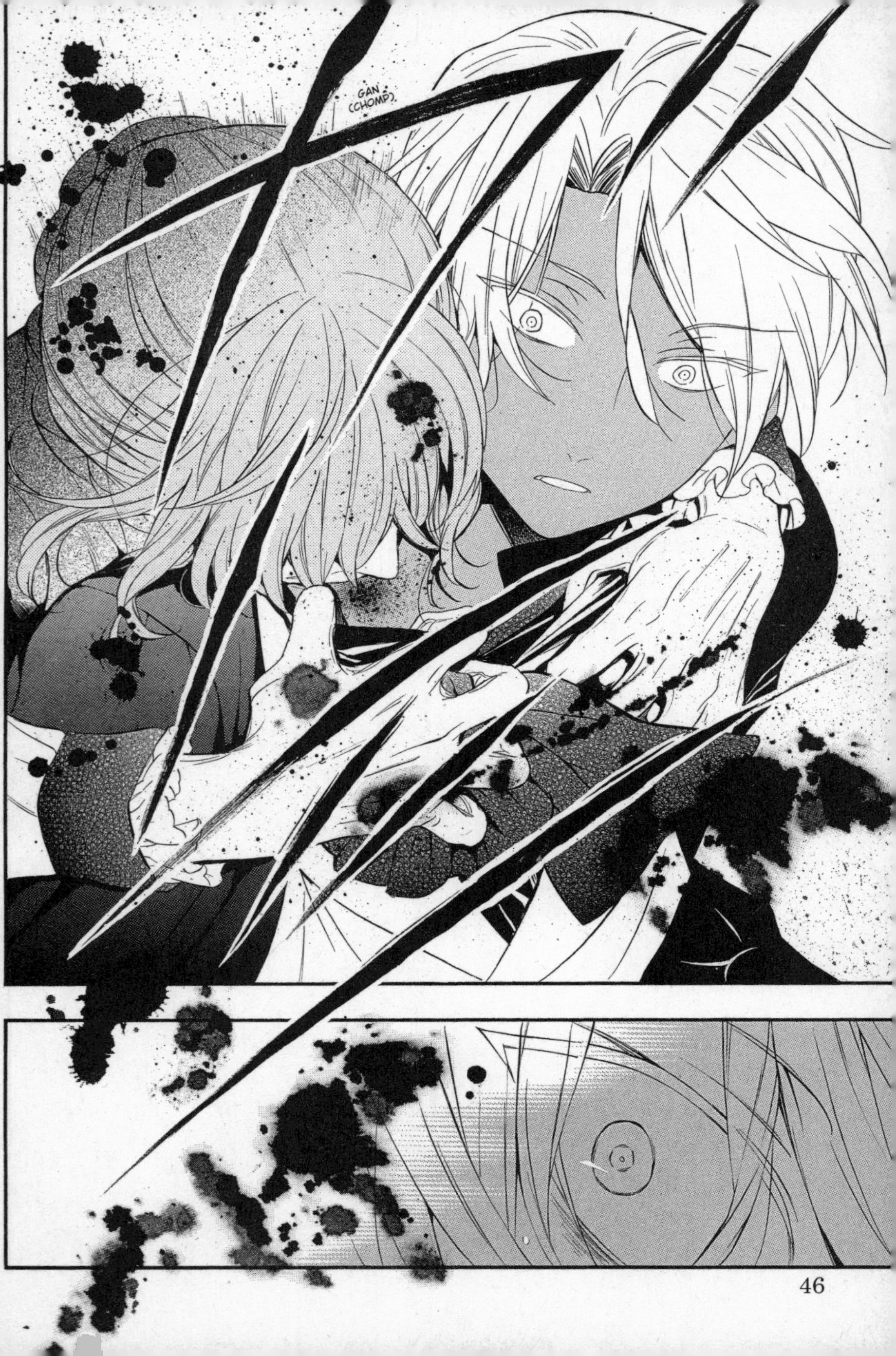
GAN
(CHOMP)

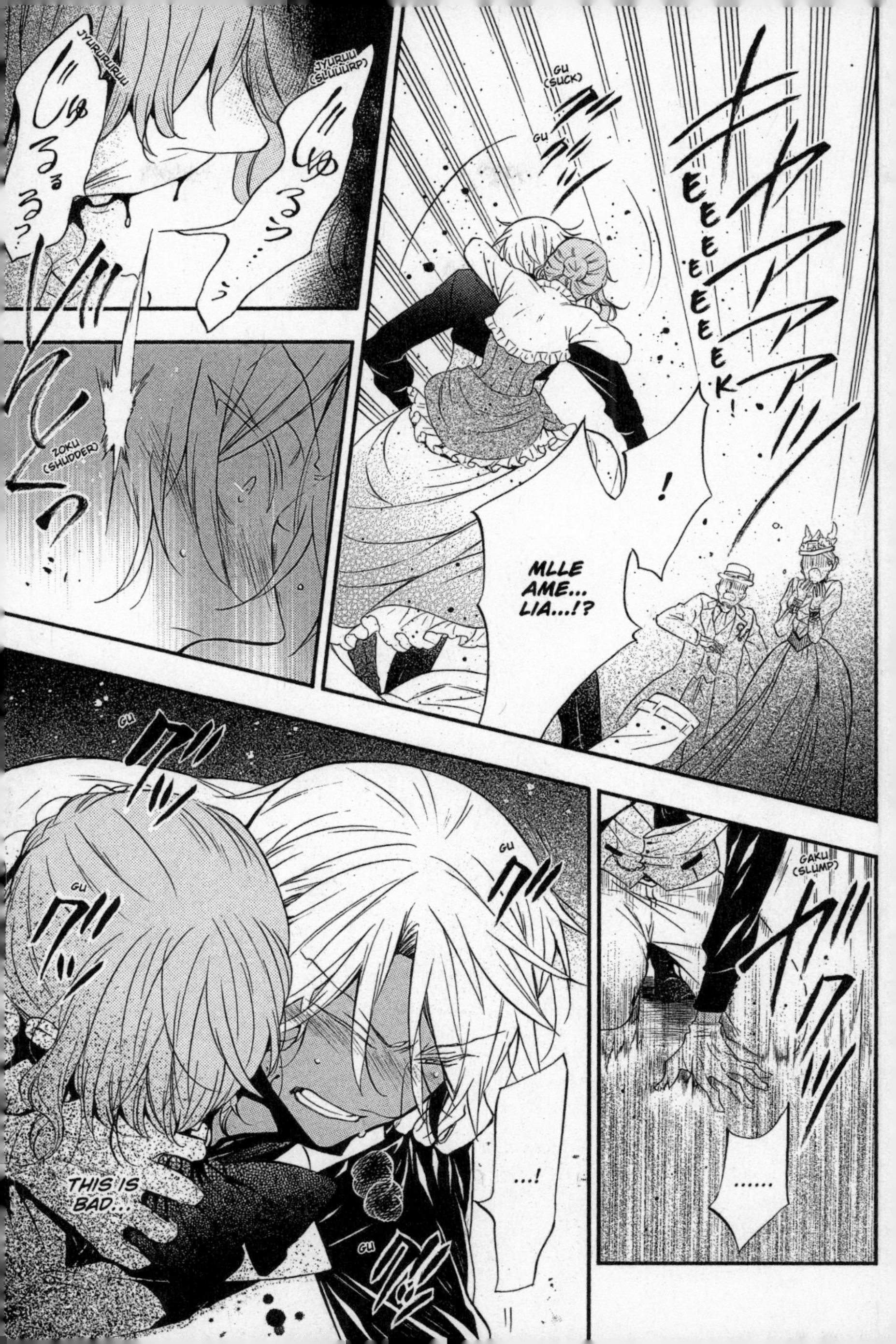

GU (SUCK)
GU
EEEEEEEEK!
!
MLLE AME... LIA...!?
JYURURURU
JYURURU (SLUUURP)
ZOKU (SHUDDER)
GAKU (SLUMP)
......
GU
GU
GU
...!
THIS IS BAD...
GU

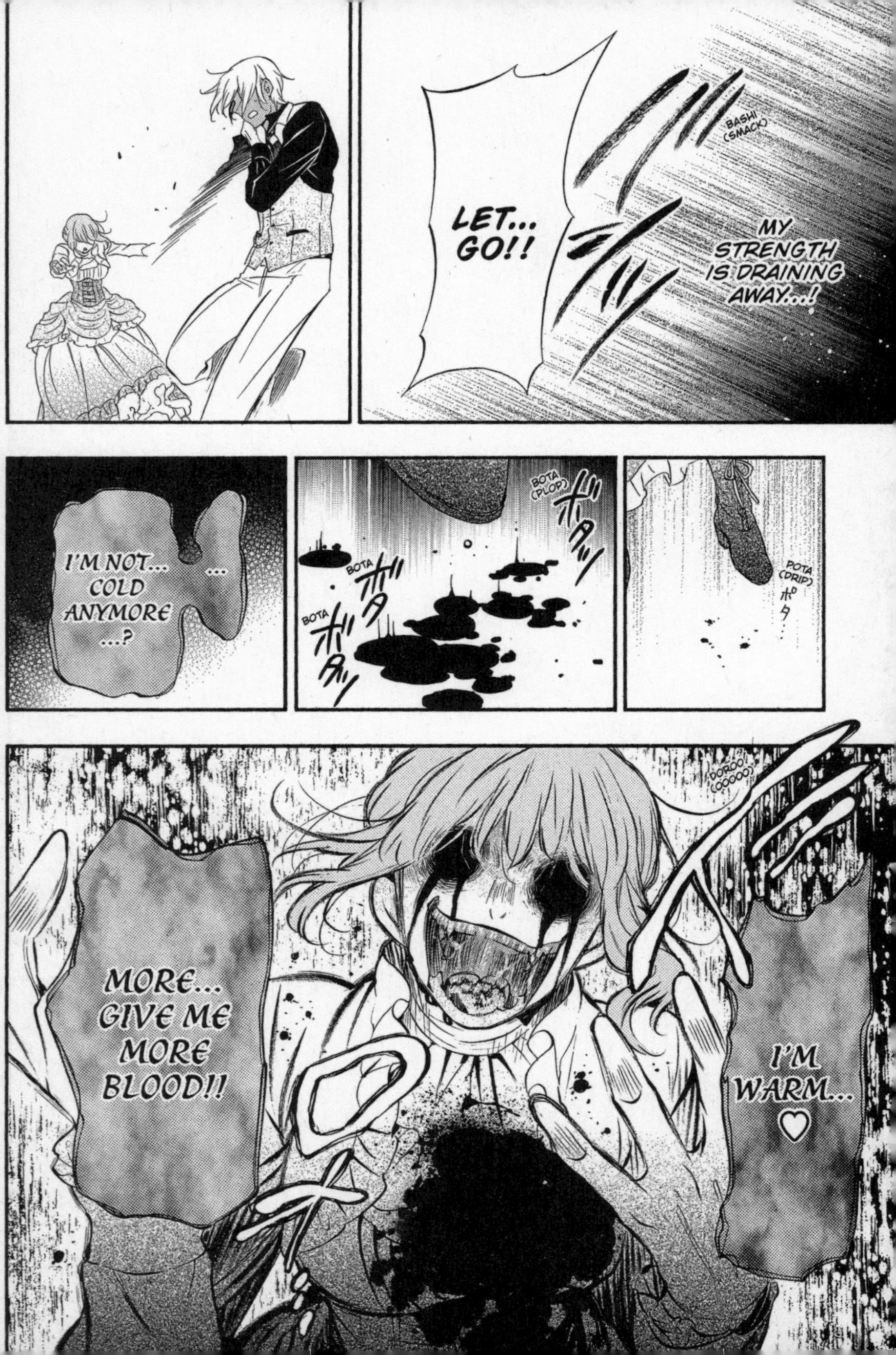
BASHI (SMACK)
MY STRENGTH IS DRAINING AWAY...!
LET... GO!!
POTA (DRIP)
ポタ
BOTA (PLOP)
ボタッ
BOTA
ボタ
BOTA
ボタッ
...
I'M NOT... COLD ANYMORE ...?
DOROO (OOOOO)
I'M WARM... ♡
MORE... GIVE ME MORE BLOOD!!

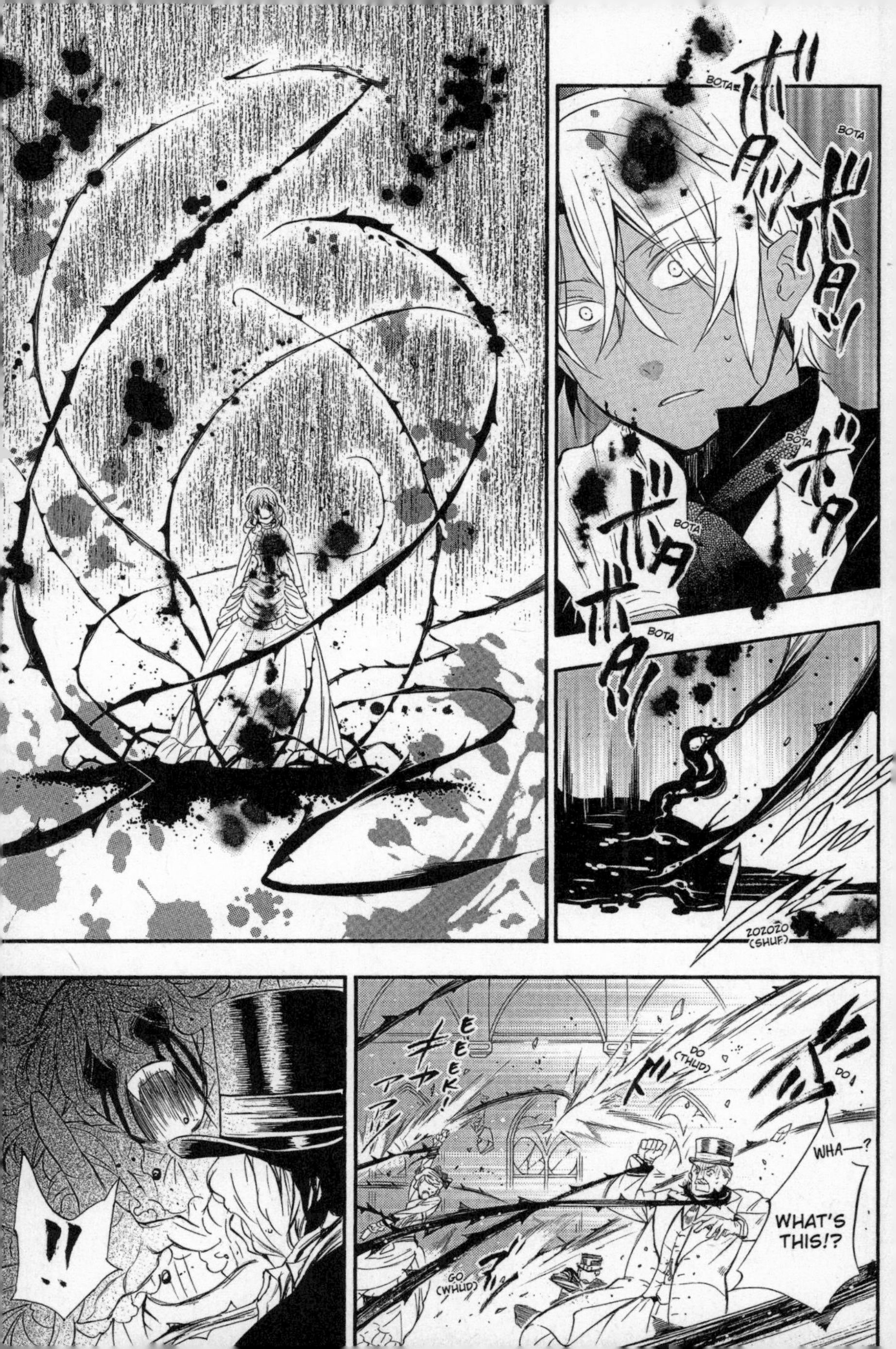
BOTA
BOTA
BOTA
BOTA
BOTA
ZOZOZO (SHUF)
DO
DO (THUD)
WHA—?
EEEEK!
WHAT'S THIS!?
GO (WHUD)
!!

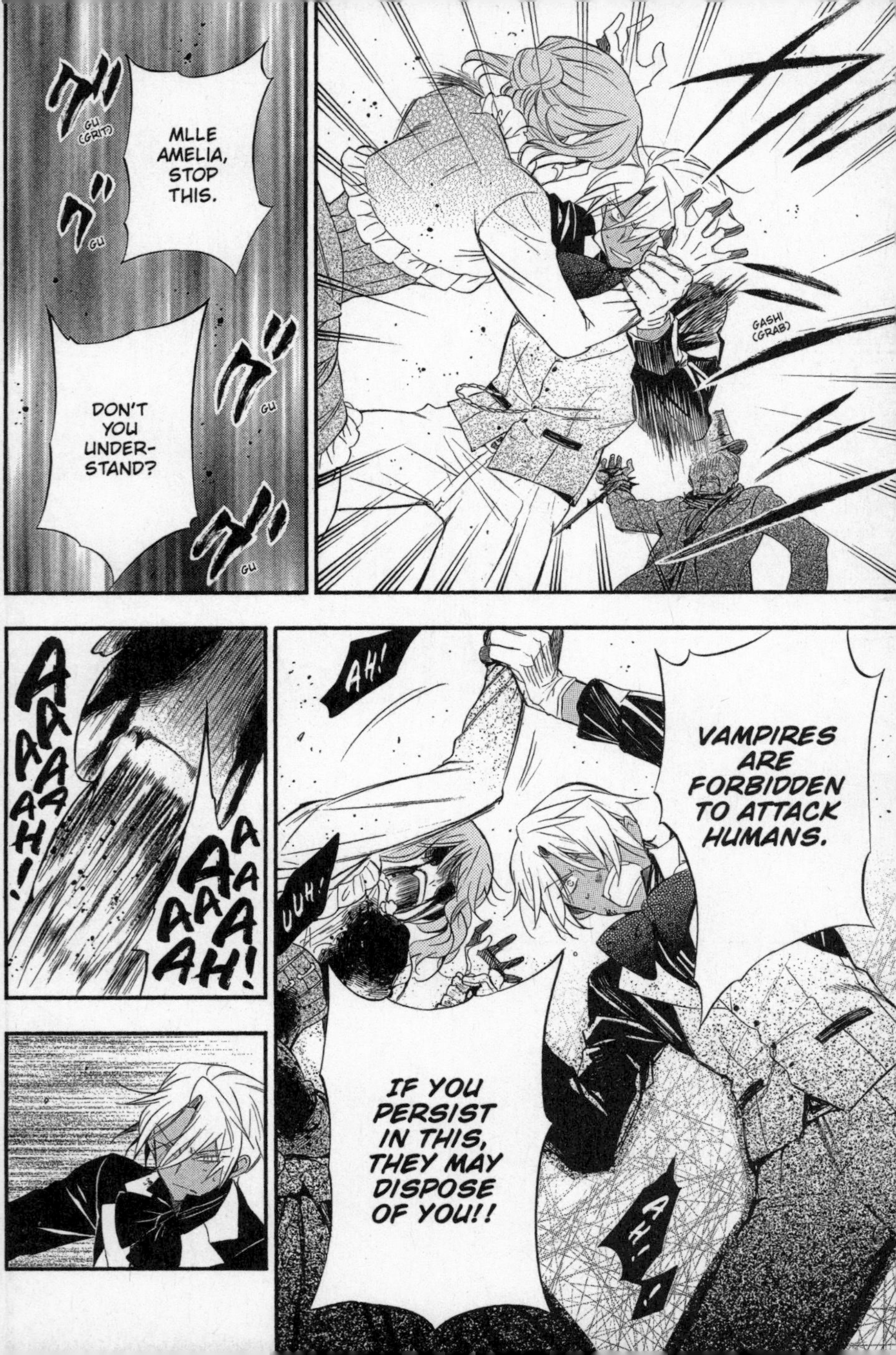
GASHI (GRAB)
MLLE AMELIA, STOP THIS.
GU (GRIT)
GU
DON'T YOU UNDER-STAND?
GU
GU
AH!
VAMPIRES ARE FORBIDDEN TO ATTACK HUMANS.
UUH!
IF YOU PERSIST IN THIS, THEY MAY DISPOSE OF YOU!!
AH!
AAAAAAAAAH!
AAAAAAH!

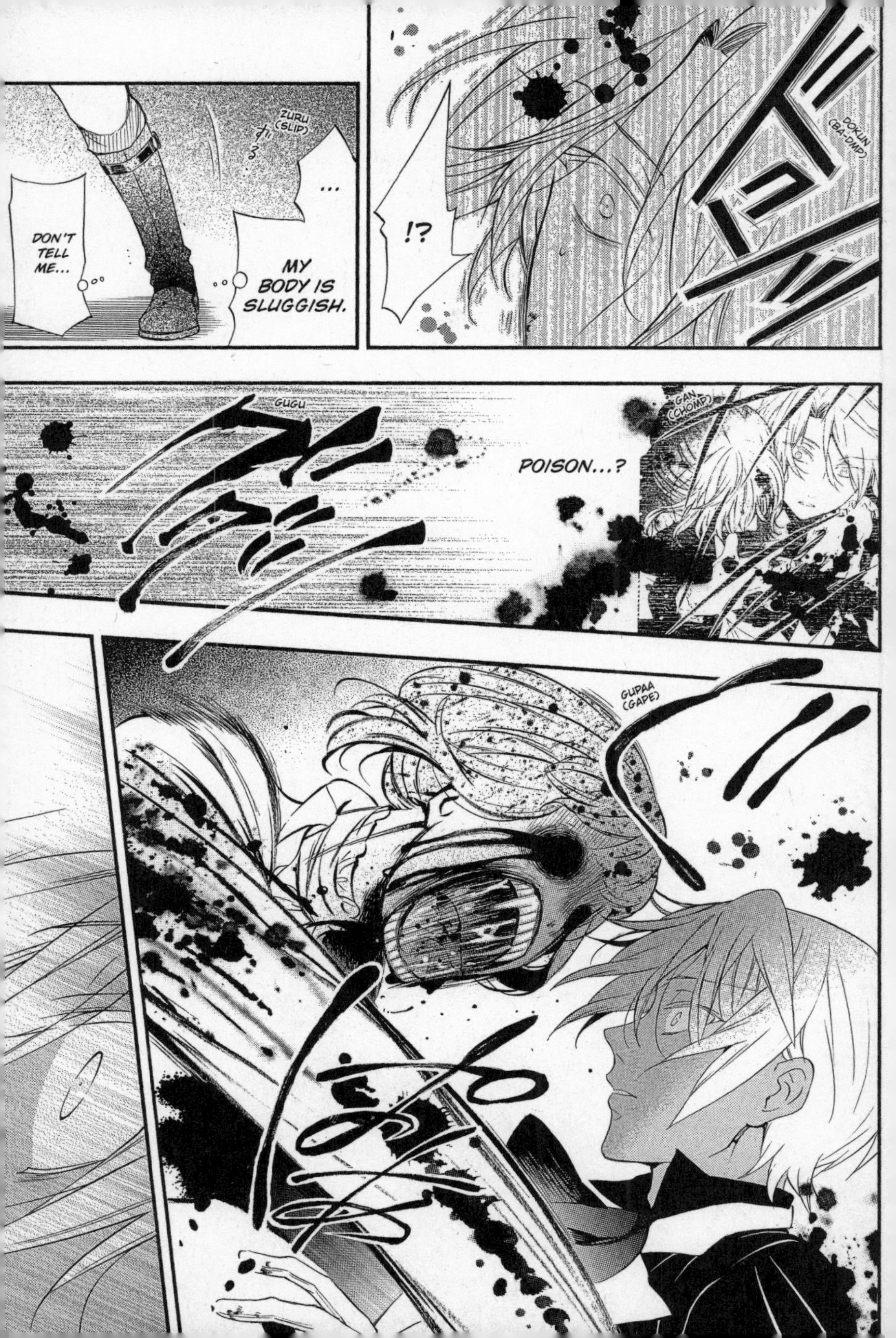
DOKUN (BA-DMP)
!?
ZURU (SLIP)
ずる
...
MY BODY IS SLUGGISH.
DON'T TELL ME...
GAN (CHOMP)
POISON...?
GUGU
GUPAA (GAPE)

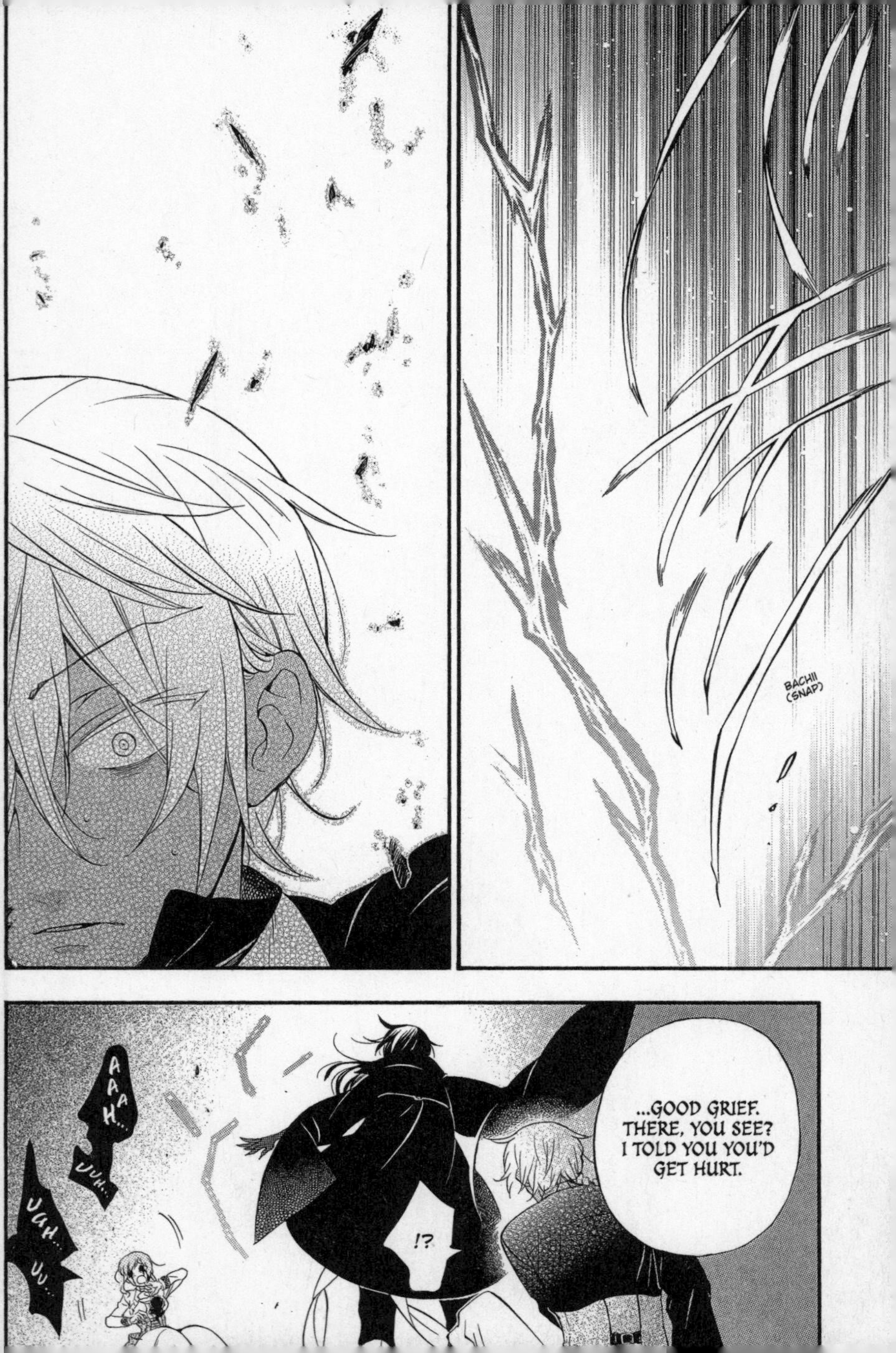
BACHII (SNAP)
...GOOD GRIEF. THERE, YOU SEE? I TOLD YOU YOU'D GET HURT.
!?
AAAH... UUH...
UGH... UU...

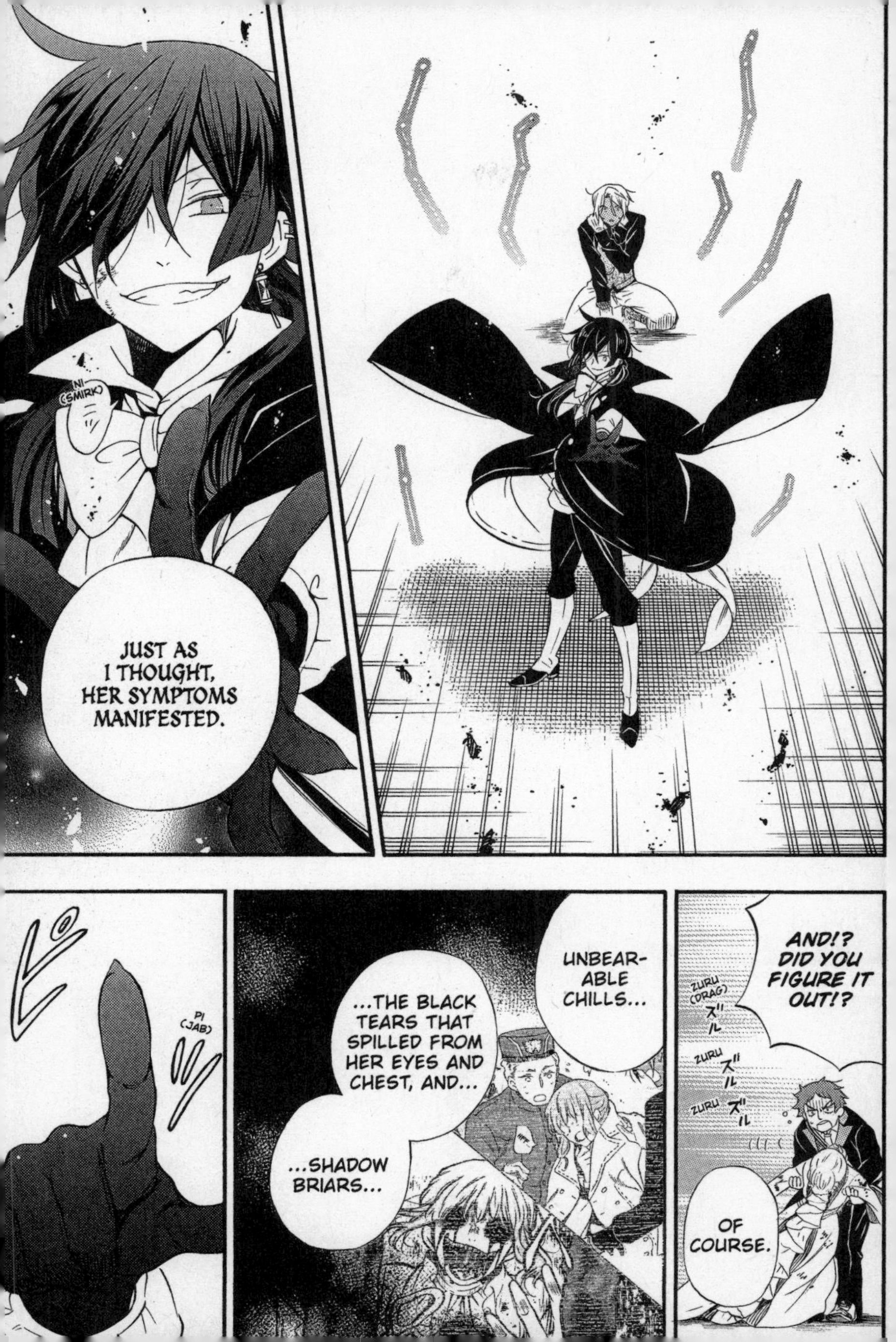
NI (SMIRK)
JUST AS I THOUGHT, HER SYMPTOMS MANIFESTED.
AND!? DID YOU FIGURE IT OUT!?
ZURU (DRAG) ズル
ZURU ズル
ZURU ズル
OF COURSE.
UNBEAR-ABLE CHILLS...
...THE BLACK TEARS THAT SPILLED FROM HER EYES AND CHEST, AND...
...SHADOW BRIARS...
PI (JAB)

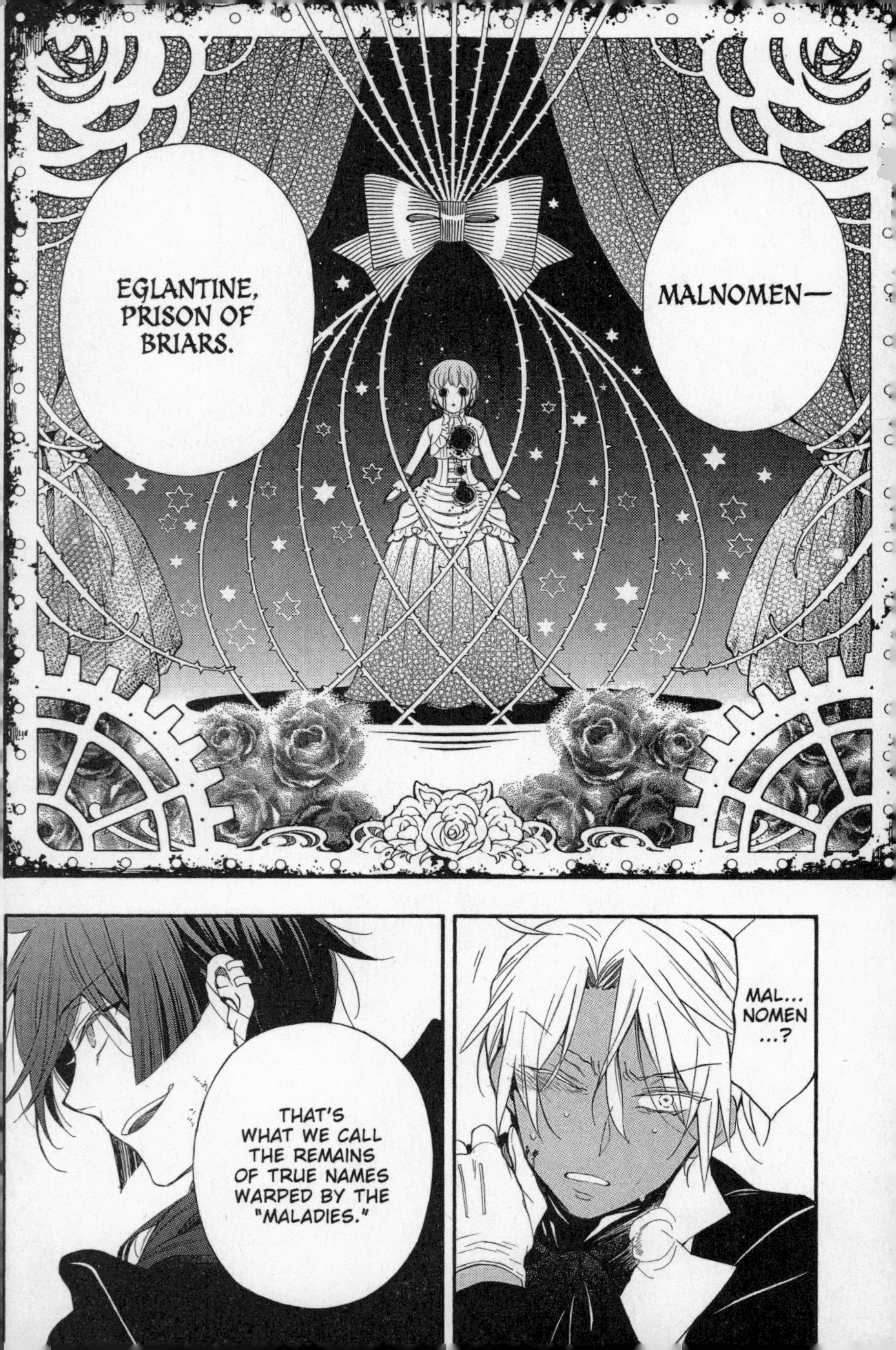
MALNOMEN—
EGLANTINE, PRISON OF BRIARS.
MAL... NOMEN ...?
THAT'S WHAT WE CALL THE REMAINS OF TRUE NAMES WARPED BY THE "MALADIES."

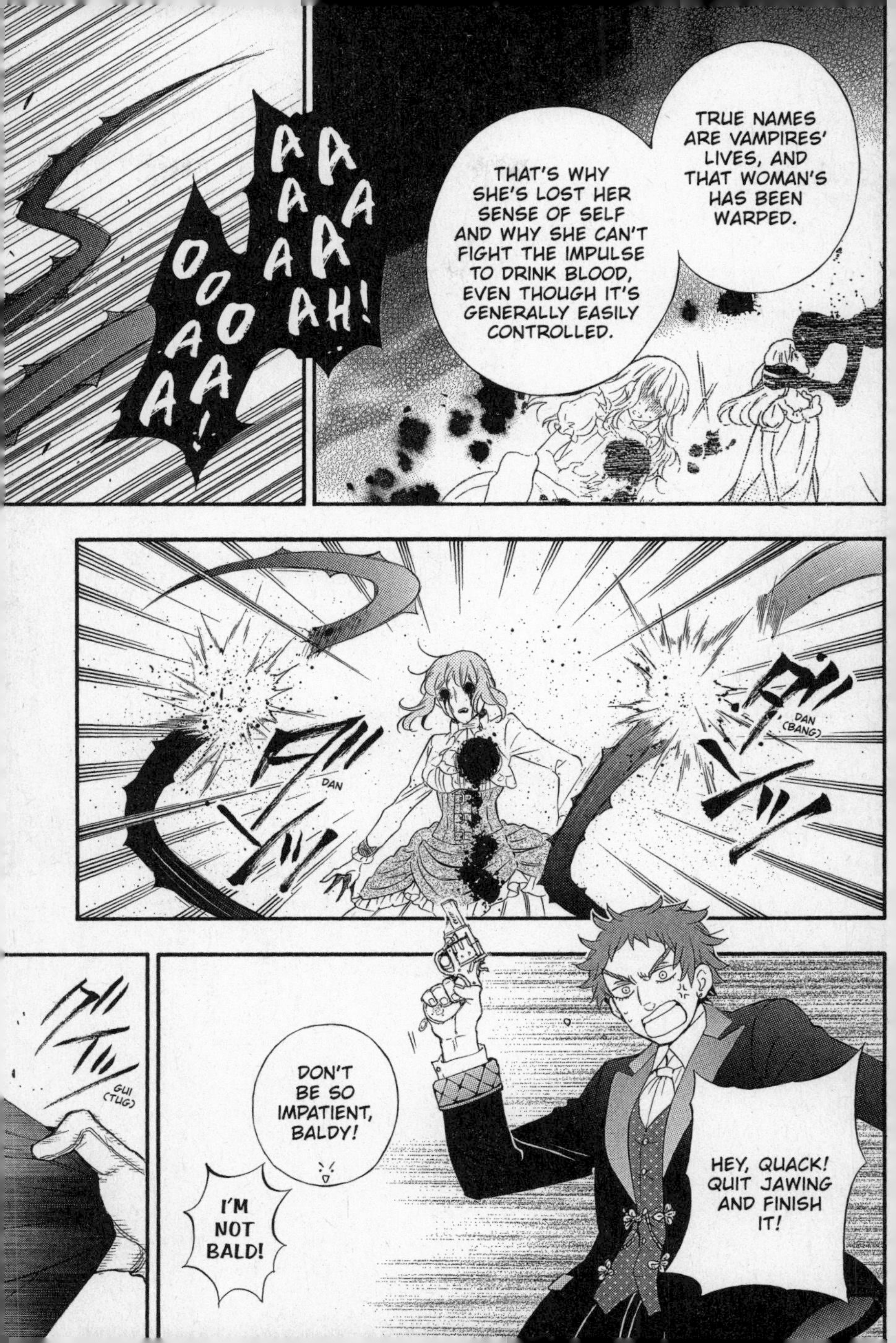
TRUE NAMES ARE VAMPIRES' LIVES, AND THAT WOMAN'S HAS BEEN WARPED.
THAT'S WHY SHE'S LOST HER SENSE OF SELF AND WHY SHE CAN'T FIGHT THE IMPULSE TO DRINK BLOOD, EVEN THOUGH IT'S GENERALLY EASILY CONTROLLED.
AAAAAAAH!
OOOAAAA!
DAN (BANG)
DAN
HEY, QUACK! QUIT JAWING AND FINISH IT!
DON'T BE SO IMPATIENT, BALDY!
I'M NOT BALD!
GUI (TUG)

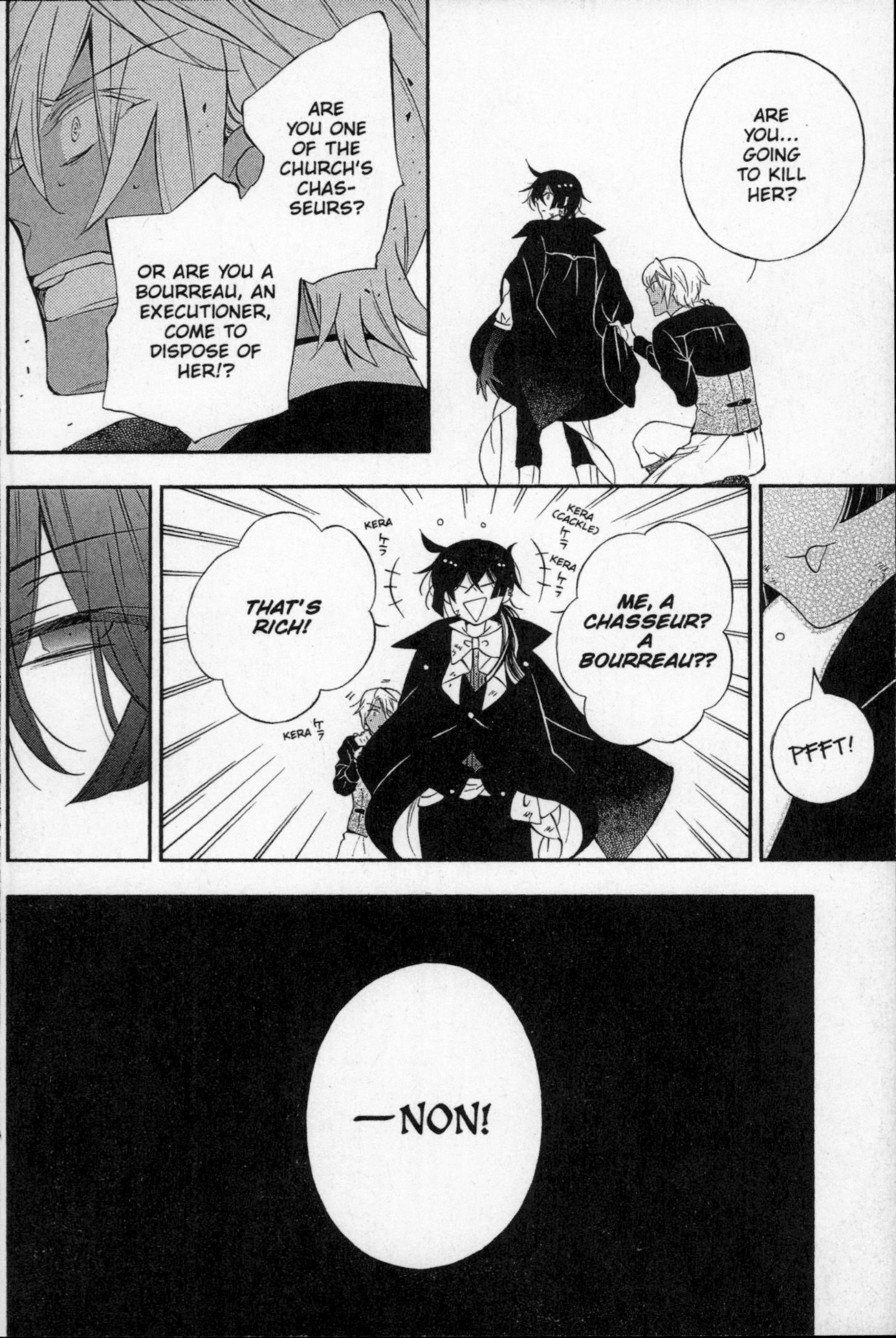
ARE YOU... GOING TO KILL HER?
ARE YOU ONE OF THE CHURCH'S CHAS-SEURS?
OR ARE YOU A BOURREAU, AN EXECUTIONER, COME TO DISPOSE OF HER!?
PFFT!
KERA (CACKLE) ケラ
KERA ケラ
ME, A CHASSEUR? A BOURREAU??
KERA ケラ
THAT'S RICH!
KERA ケラ
—NON!

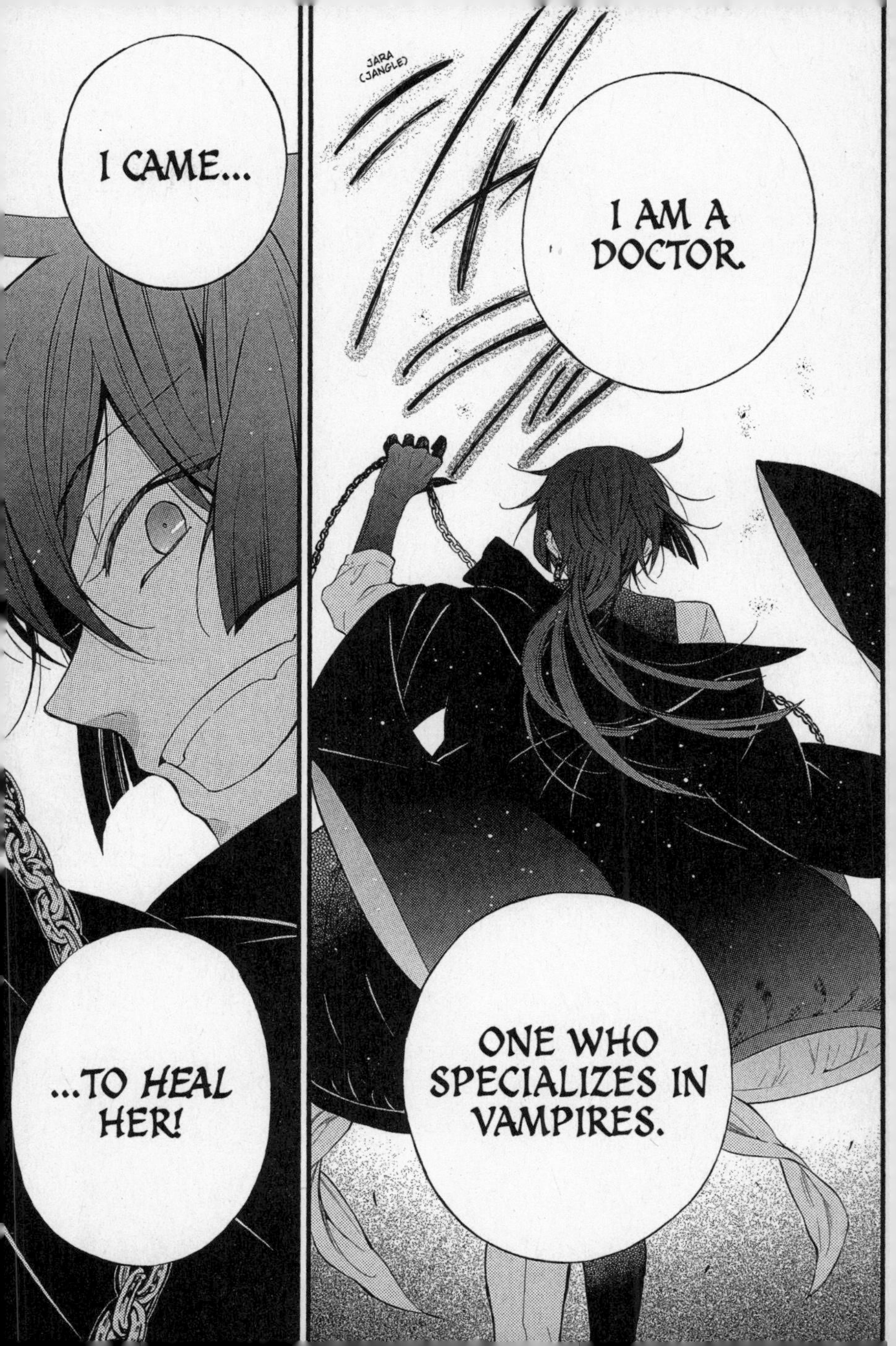
JARA (JANGLE)
I AM A DOCTOR.
ONE WHO SPECIALIZES IN VAMPIRES.
I CAME...
...TO *HEAL* HER!

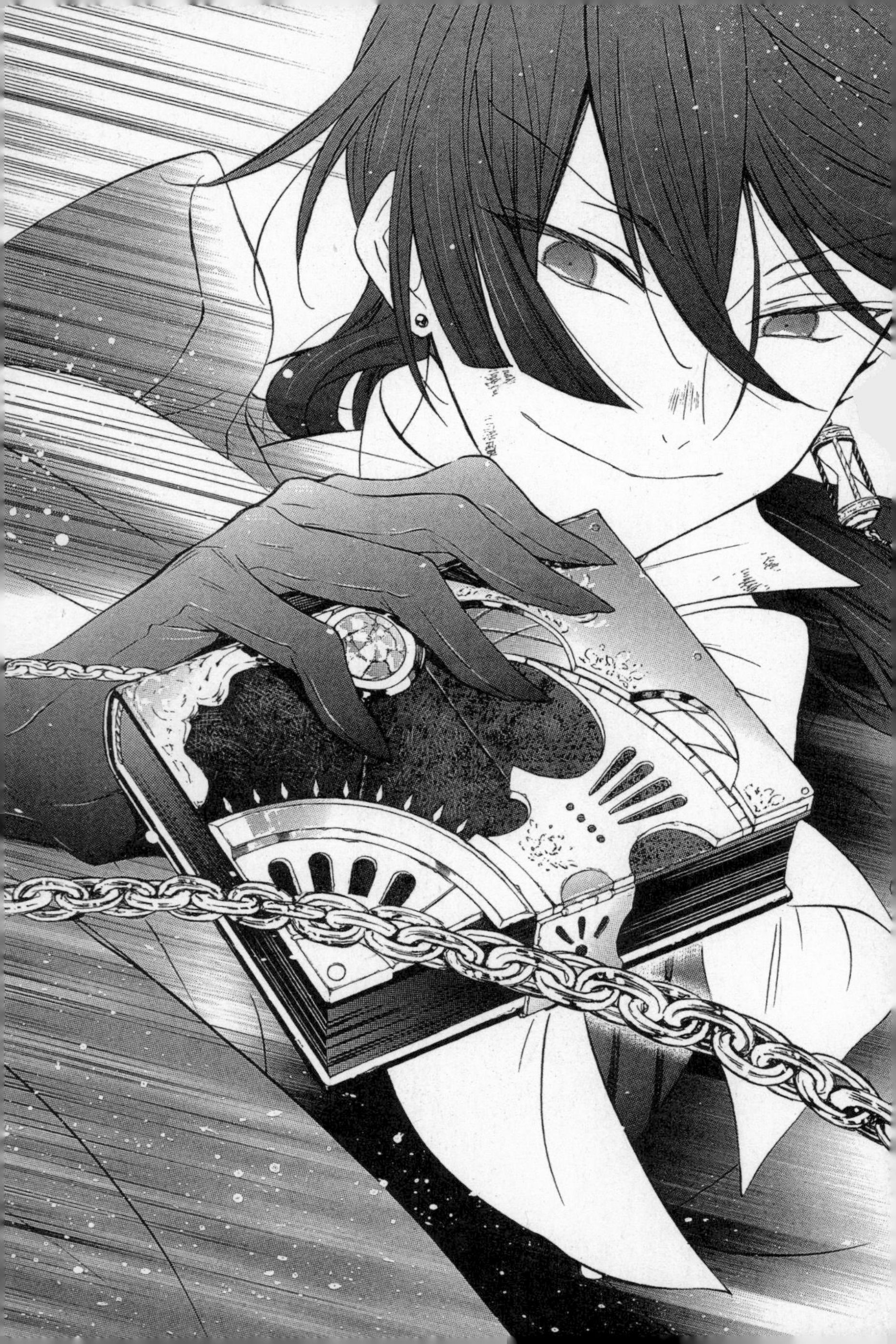

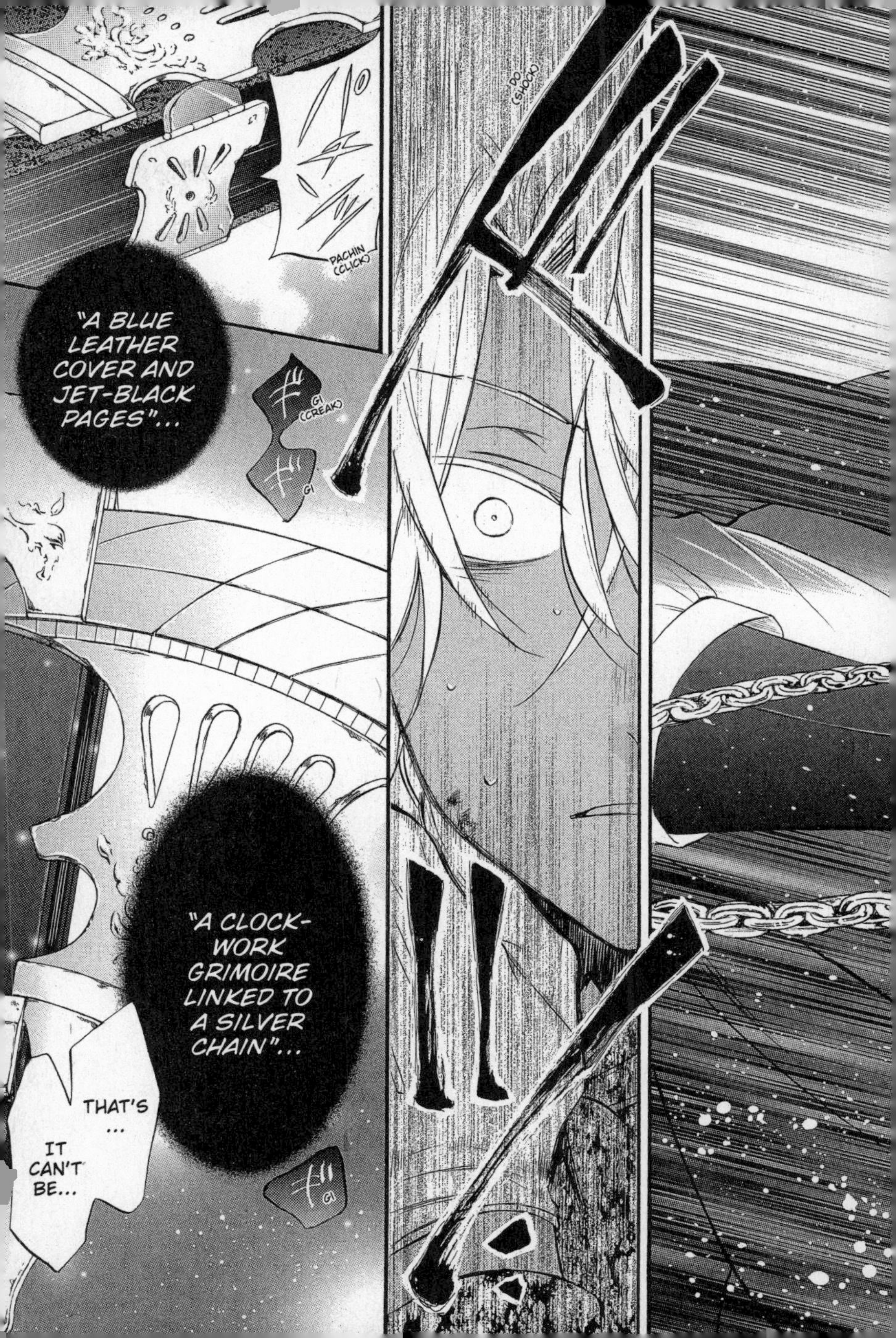
DO (SHOCK)
PACHIN (CLICK)
GI (CREAK)
GI
"A BLUE LEATHER COVER AND JET-BLACK PAGES"...
"A CLOCK-WORK GRIMOIRE LINKED TO A SILVER CHAIN"...
GI
THAT'S ...
IT CAN'T BE...

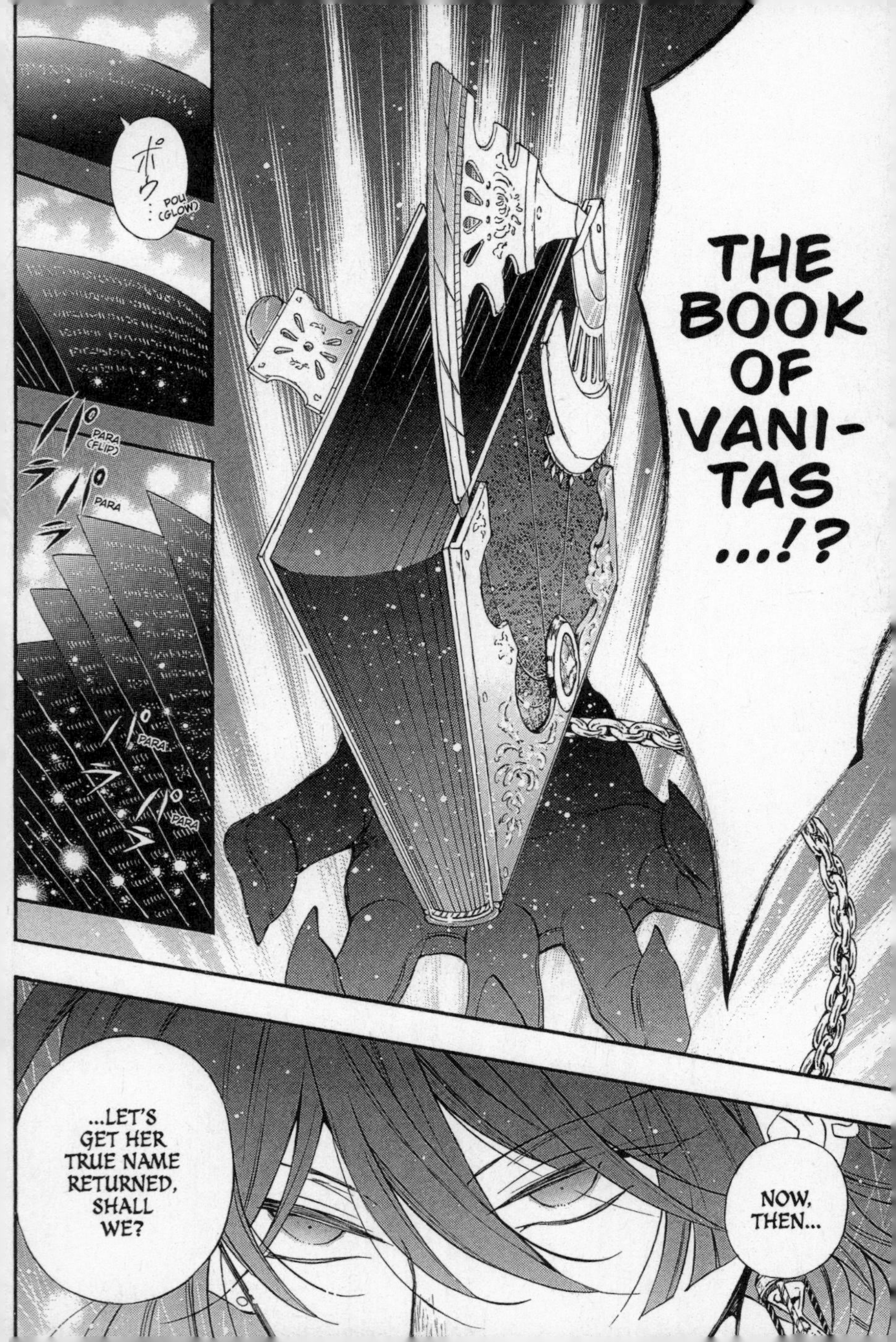
THE BOOK OF VANI-TAS ...!?
ポゥ…
POU (GLOW)
パラ
PARA (FLIP)
パラ
PARA
パラ
PARA
パラ
PARA
NOW, THEN...
...LET'S GET HER TRUE NAME RETURNED, SHALL WE?

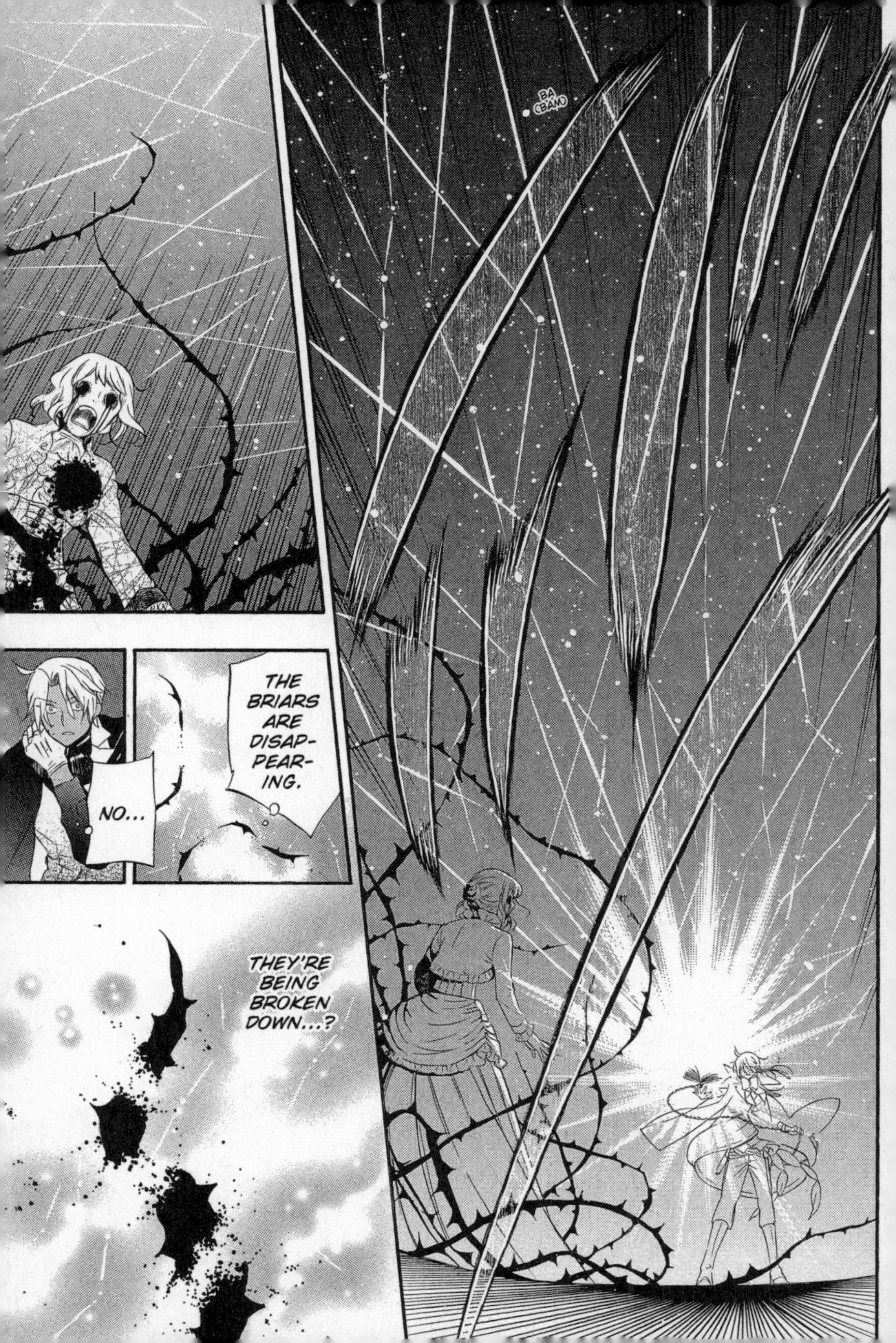
BA (BAM)
THE BRIARS ARE DISAP-PEAR-ING.
NO...
THEY'RE BEING BROKEN DOWN...?

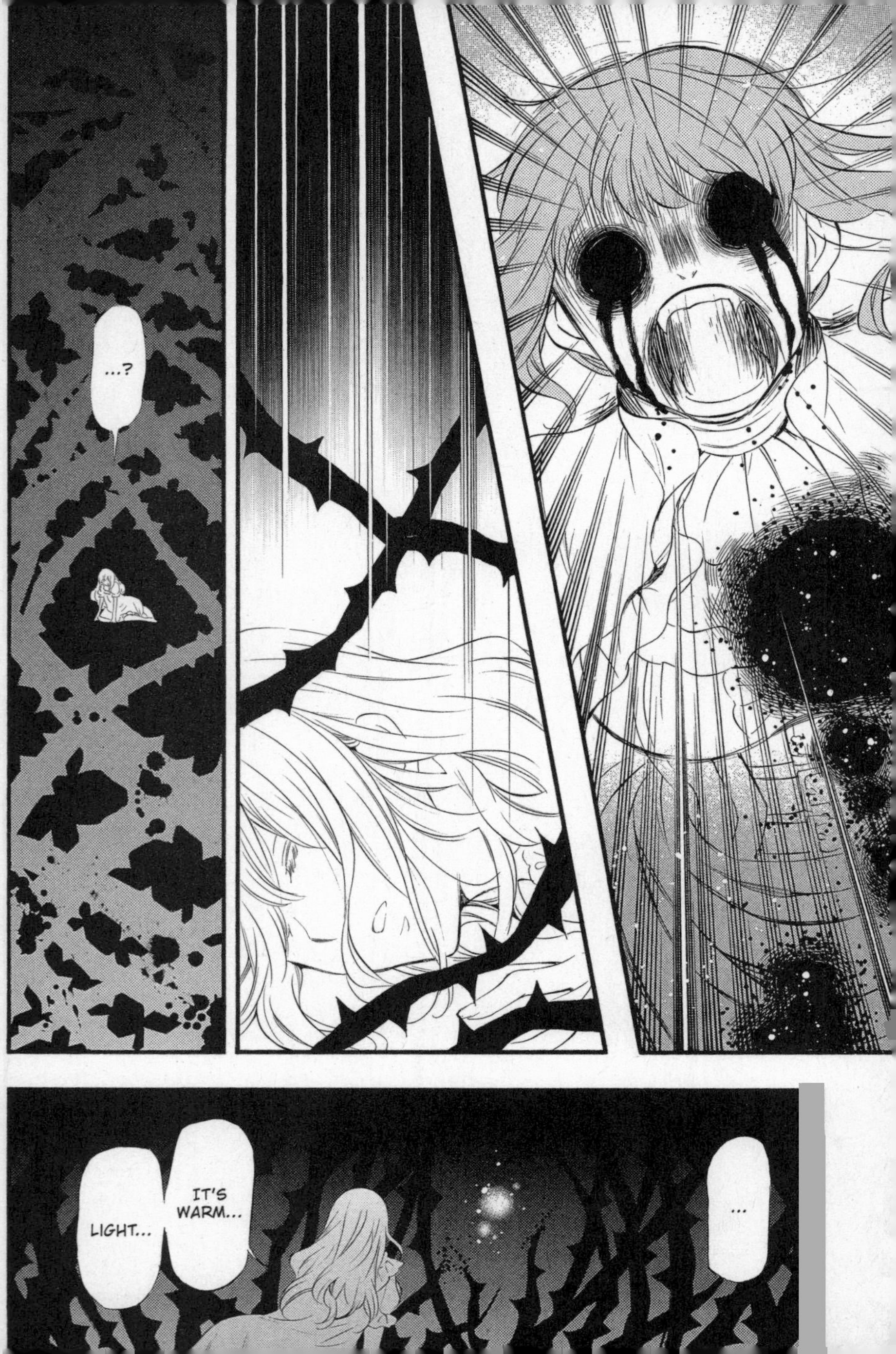
...?
...
IT'S WARM...
LIGHT...

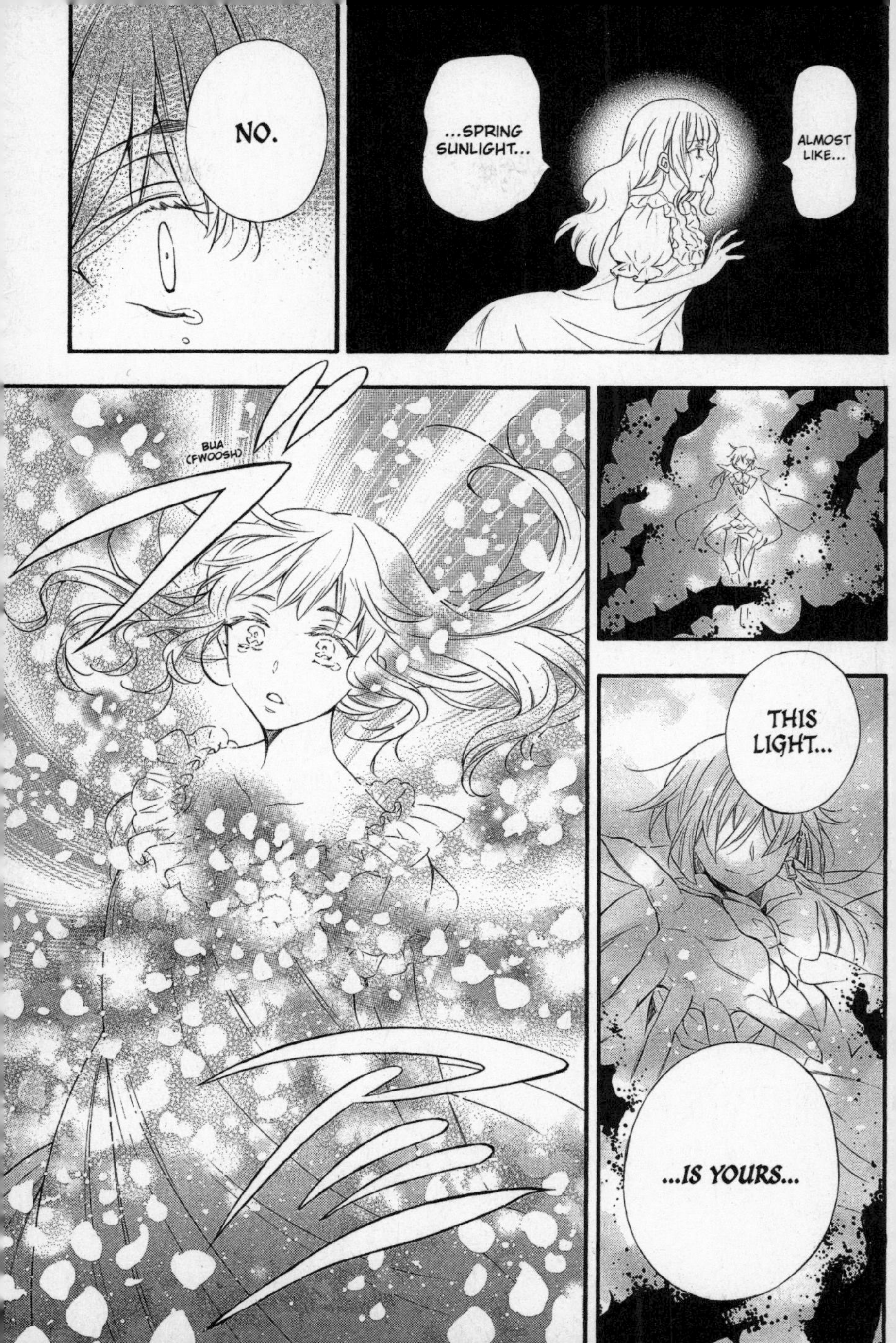
ALMOST LIKE...
...SPRING SUNLIGHT...
NO.
THIS LIGHT...
...IS YOURS...
BUA (FWOOSH)

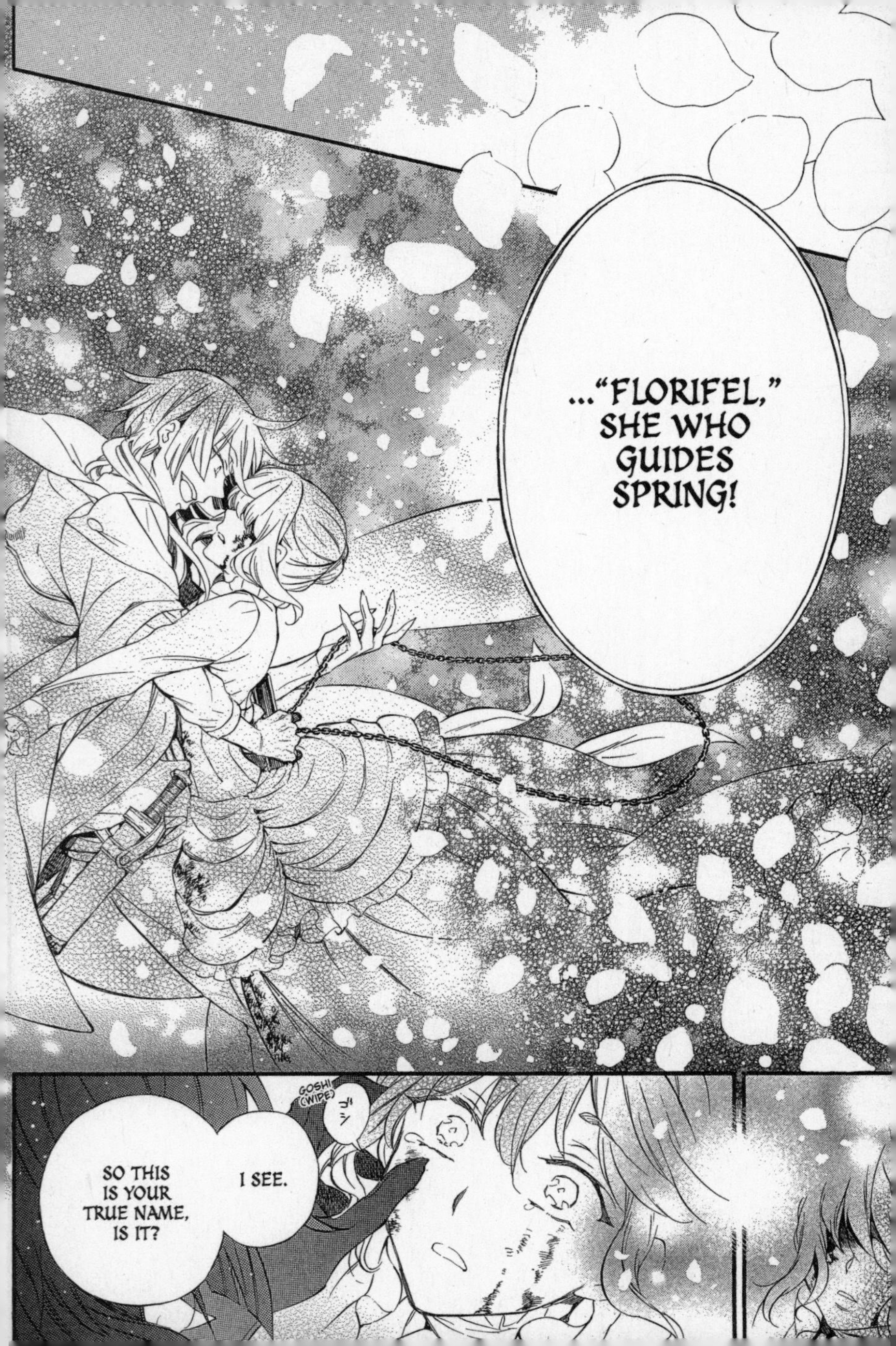
..."FLORIFEL," SHE WHO GUIDES SPRING!
GOSHI (WIPE)
I SEE.
SO THIS IS YOUR TRUE NAME, IS IT?

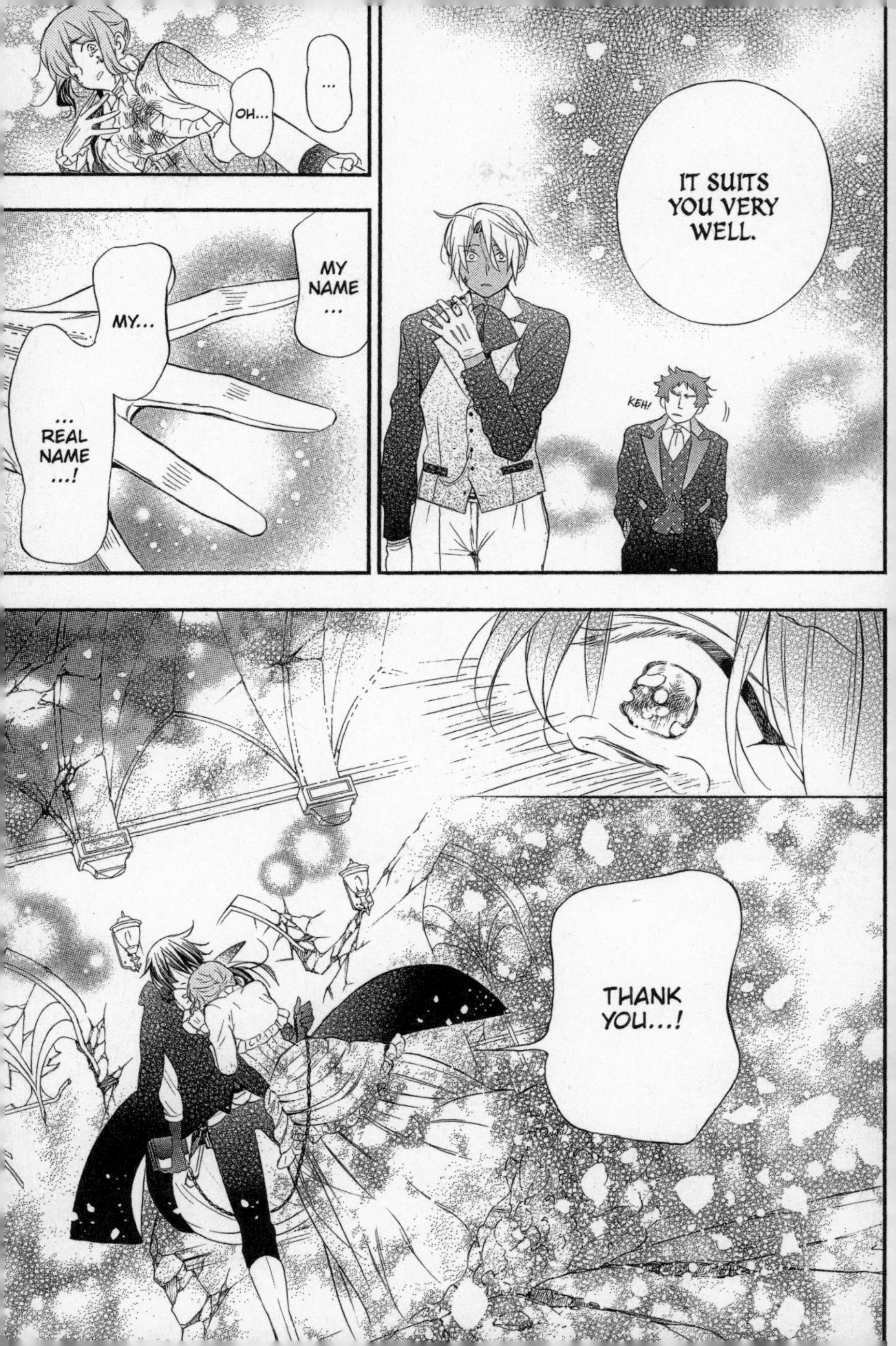
IT SUITS YOU VERY WELL.
KEH!
...
OH...
MY NAME ...
MY...
... REAL NAME ...!
THANK YOU...!

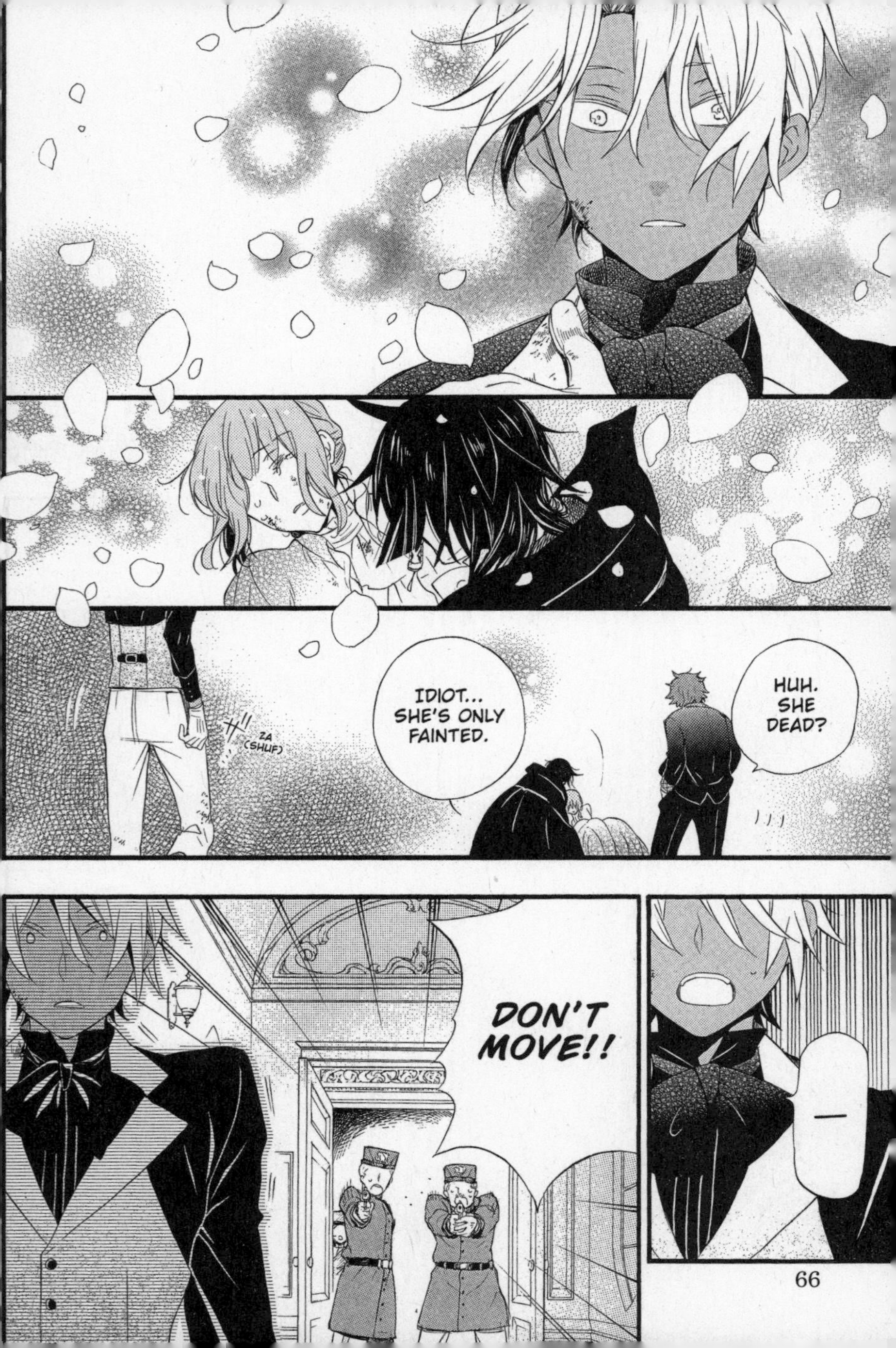
HUH. SHE DEAD?
IDIOT... SHE'S ONLY FAINTED.
ZA (SHUF)
—
DON'T MOVE!!

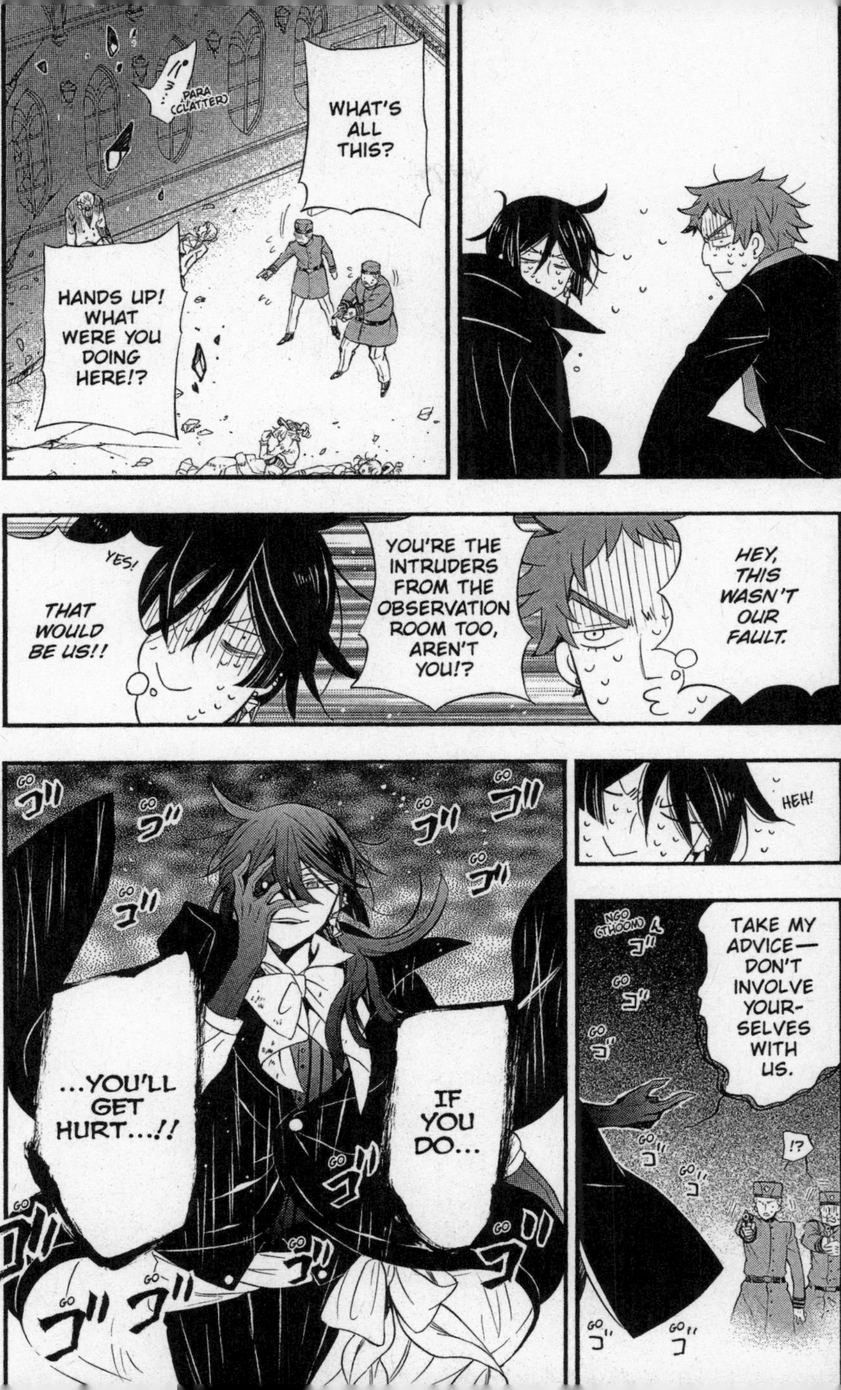
WHAT'S ALL THIS?
PARA (CLATTER)
HANDS UP! WHAT WERE YOU DOING HERE!?
HEY, THIS WASN'T OUR FAULT.
YOU'RE THE INTRUDERS FROM THE OBSERVATION ROOM TOO, AREN'T YOU!?
YES!
THAT WOULD BE US!!
HEH!
TAKE MY ADVICE—DON'T INVOLVE YOURSELVES WITH US.
NGO (THOOM)
GO
!?
IF YOU DO...
...YOU'LL GET HURT...!!
GO

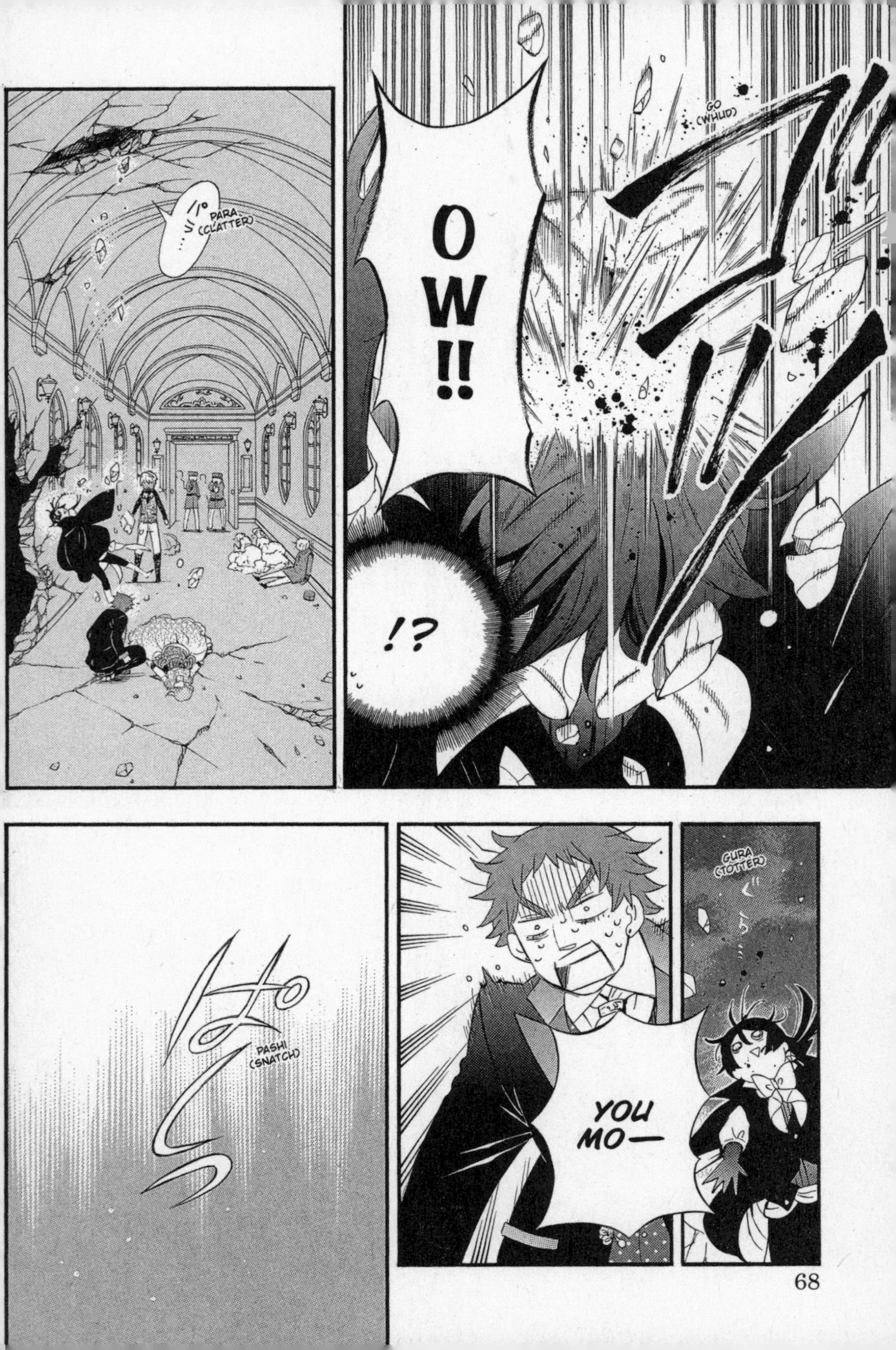
GO (WHUD)
OW!!
!?
PARA (CLATTER)
GURA (TOTTER)
YOU MO—
PASHI (SNATCH)

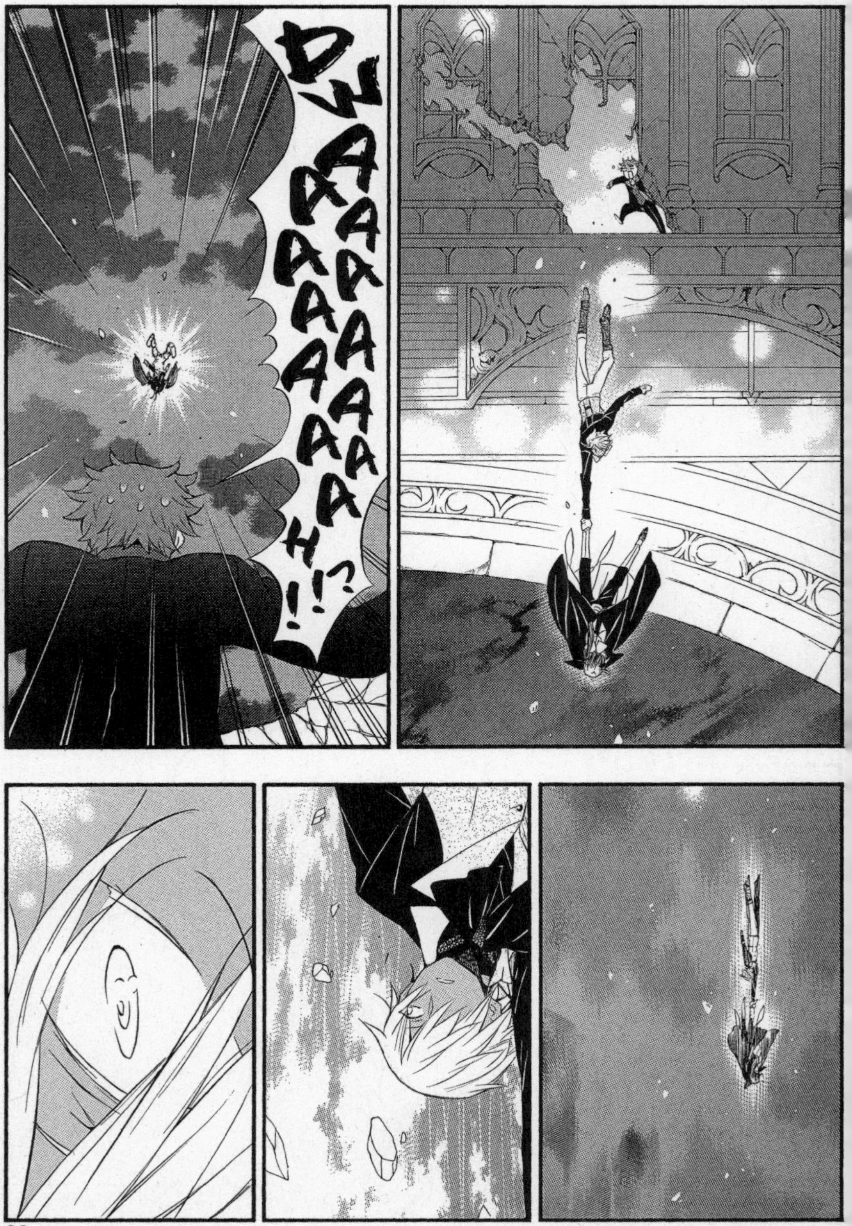
DWAAAAAAAAAAAAH!!?

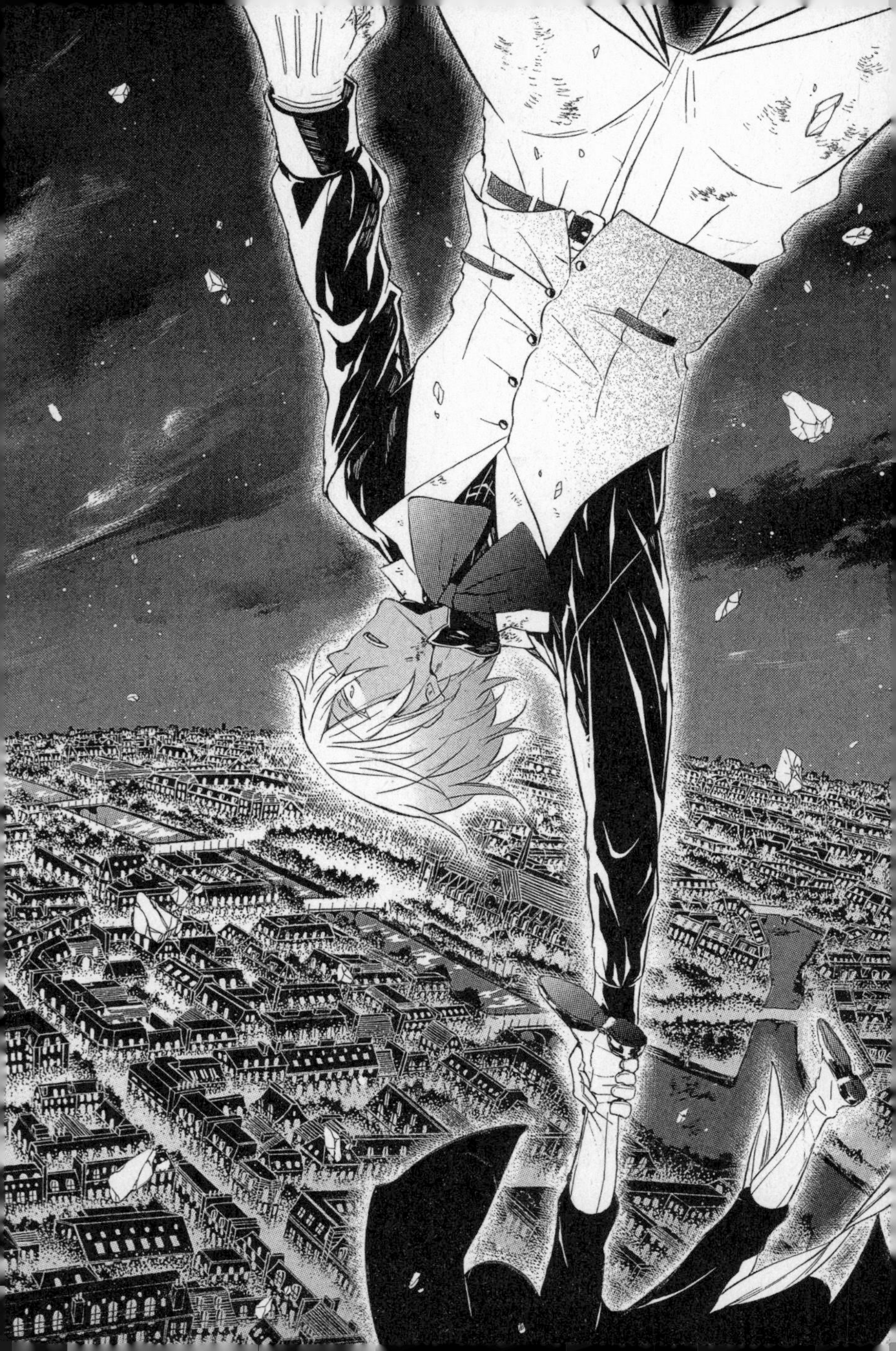

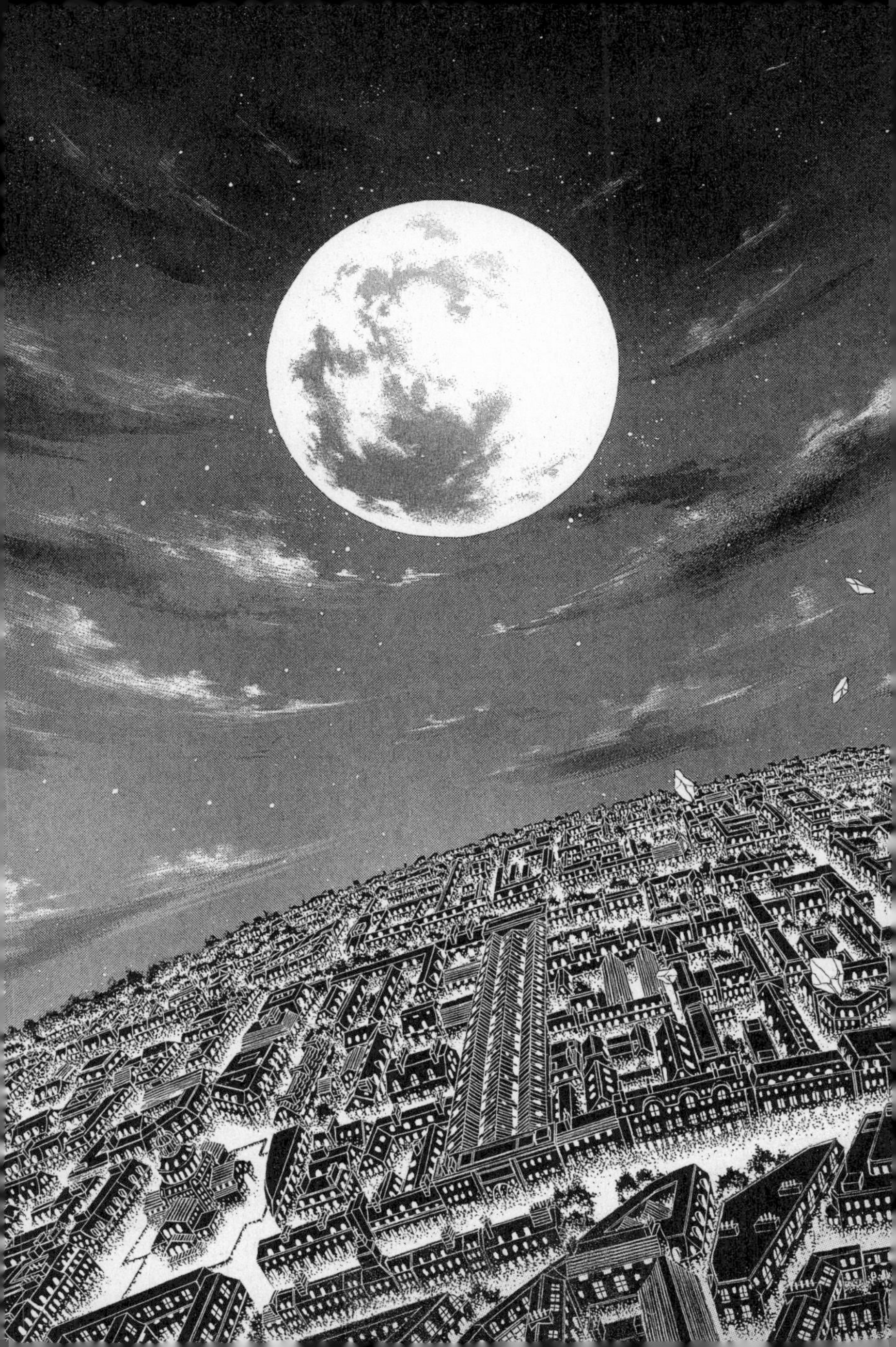

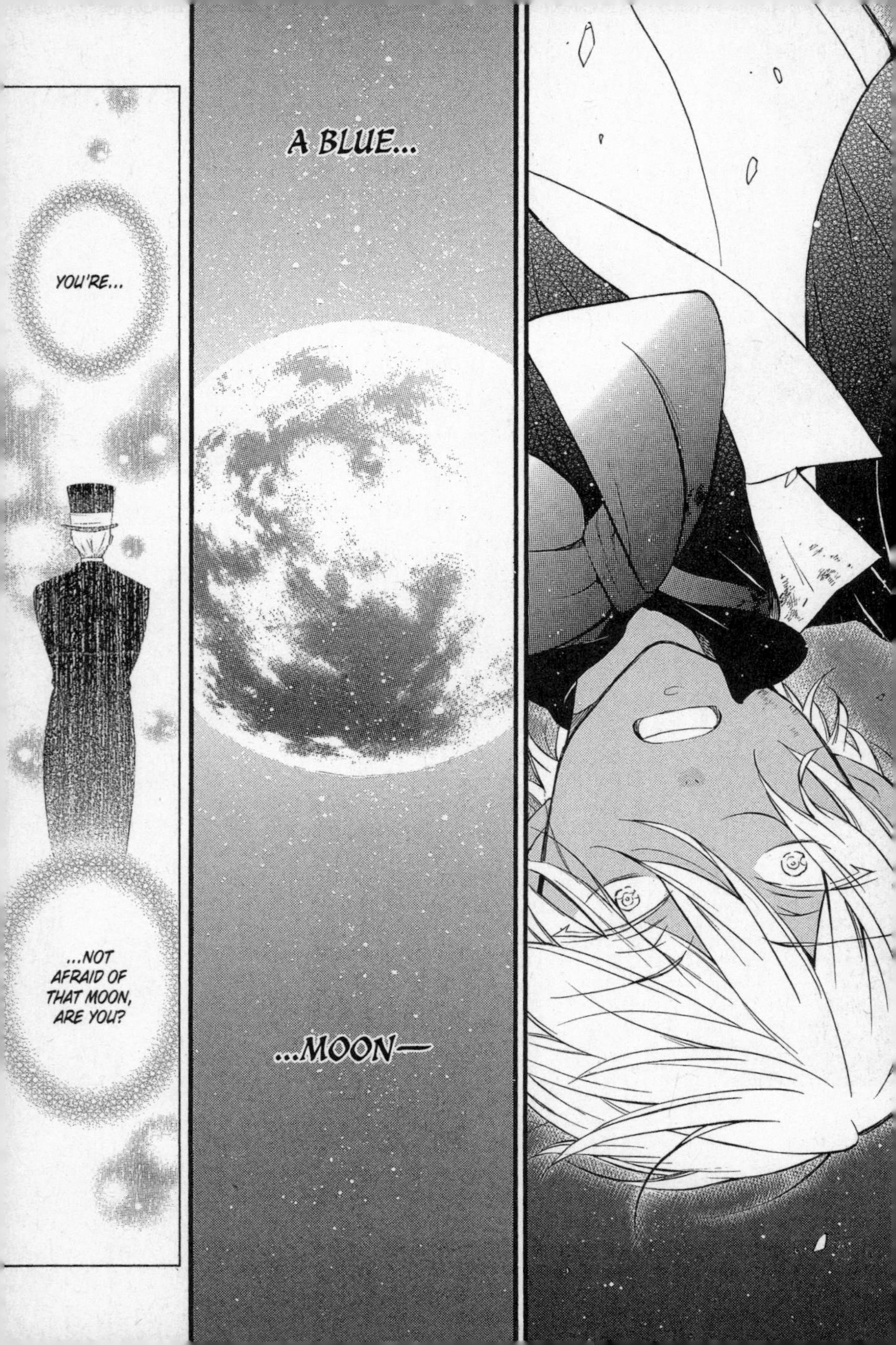
A BLUE...
...MOON—
YOU'RE...
...NOT AFRAID OF THAT MOON, ARE YOU?

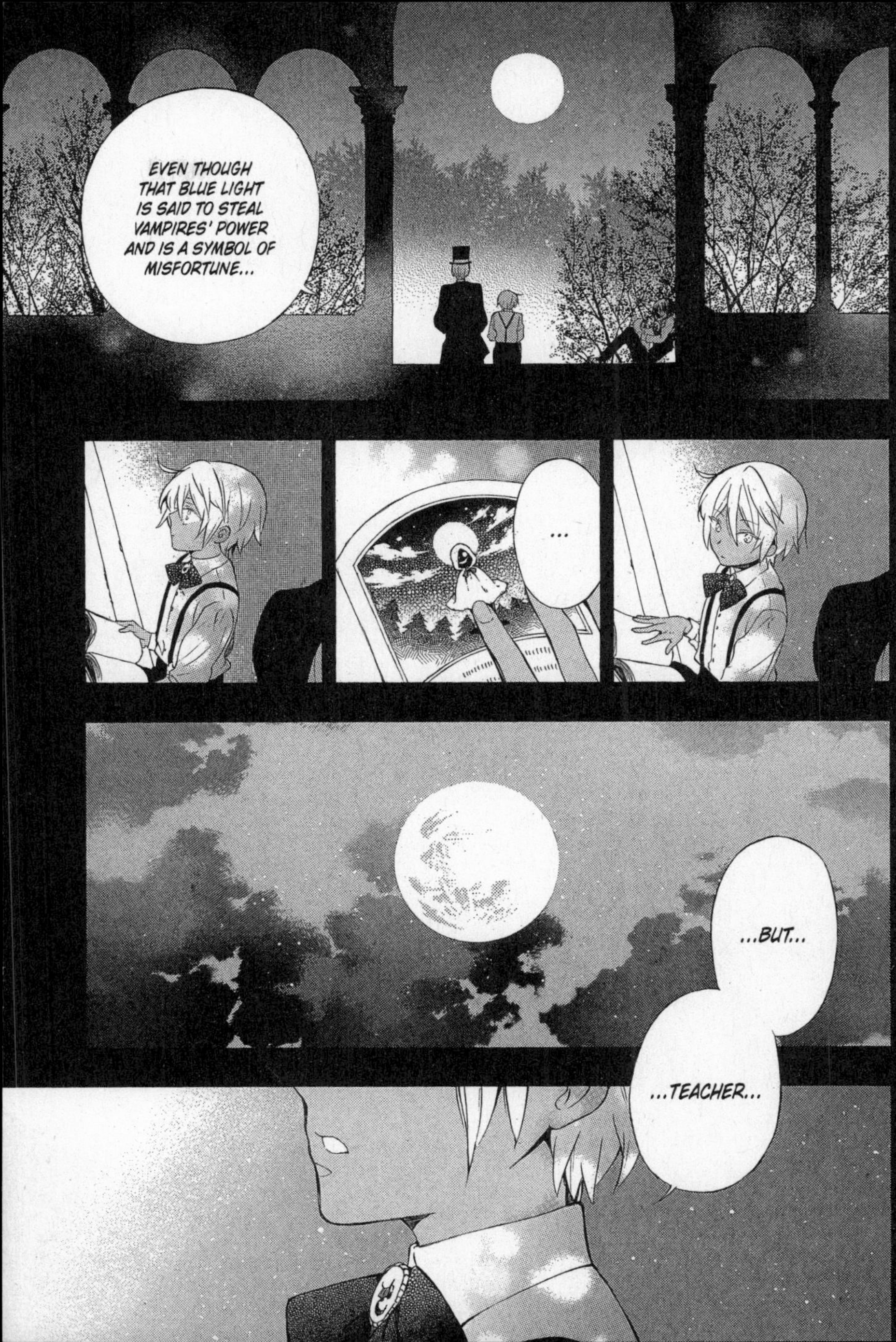
EVEN THOUGH THAT BLUE LIGHT IS SAID TO STEAL VAMPIRES' POWER AND IS A SYMBOL OF MISFORTUNE...
...
...BUT...
...TEACHER...

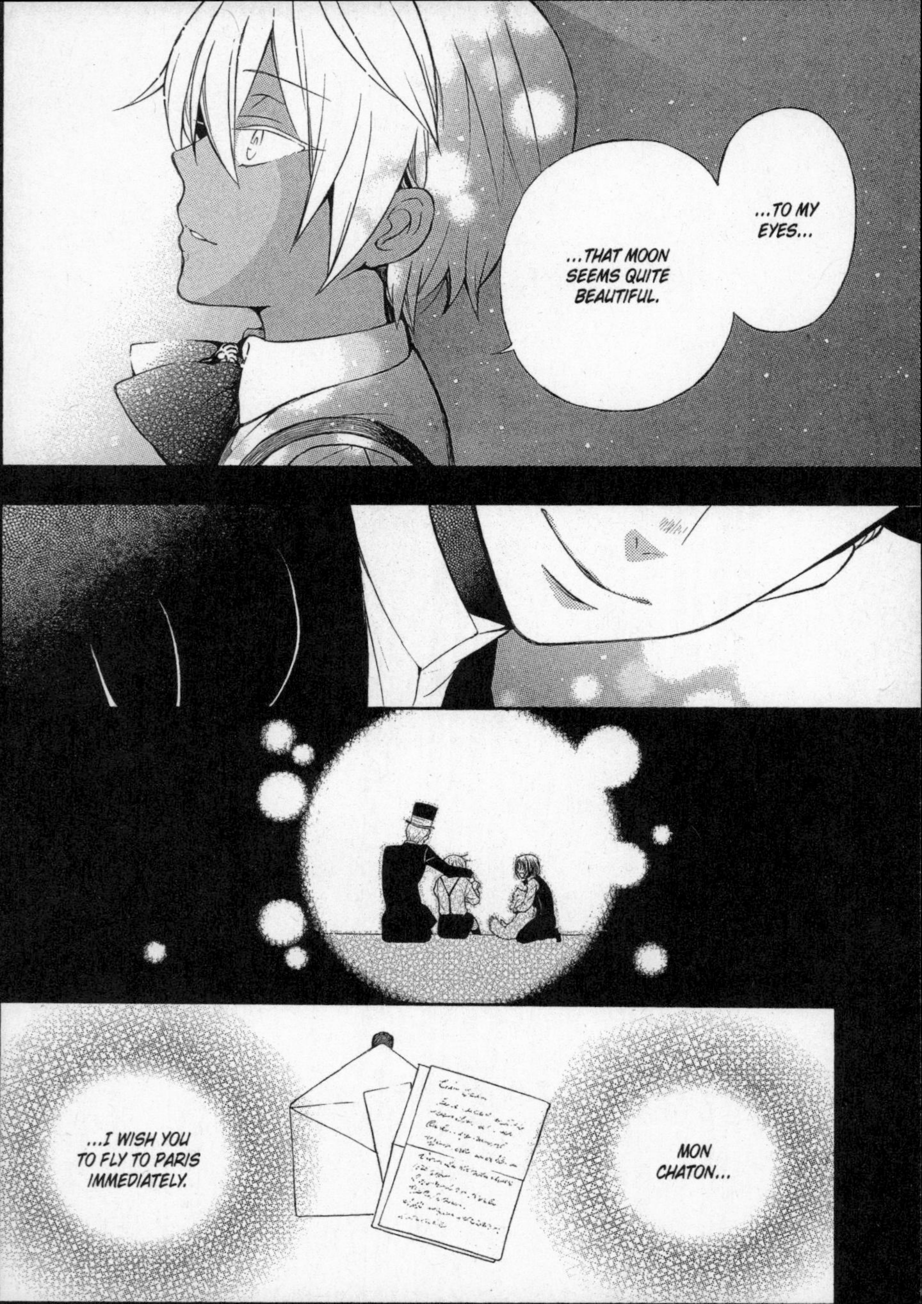
...TO MY EYES...
...THAT MOON SEEMS QUITE BEAUTIFUL.
MON CHATON...
...I WISH YOU TO FLY TO PARIS IMMEDIATELY.

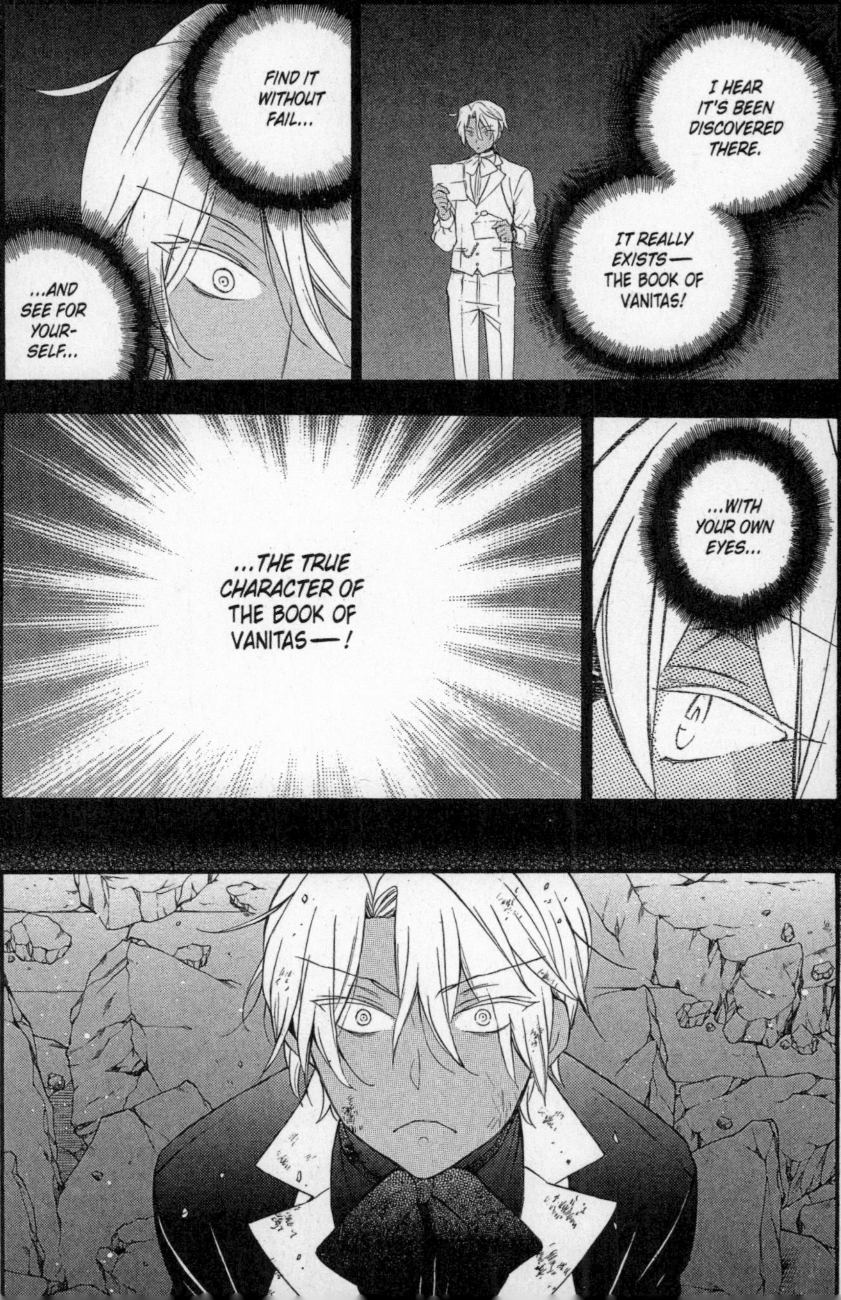
I HEAR IT'S BEEN DISCOVERED THERE.
IT REALLY EXISTS— THE BOOK OF VANITAS!
FIND IT WITHOUT FAIL...
...AND SEE FOR YOUR-SELF...
...WITH YOUR OWN EYES...
...THE TRUE CHARACTER OF THE BOOK OF VANITAS—!

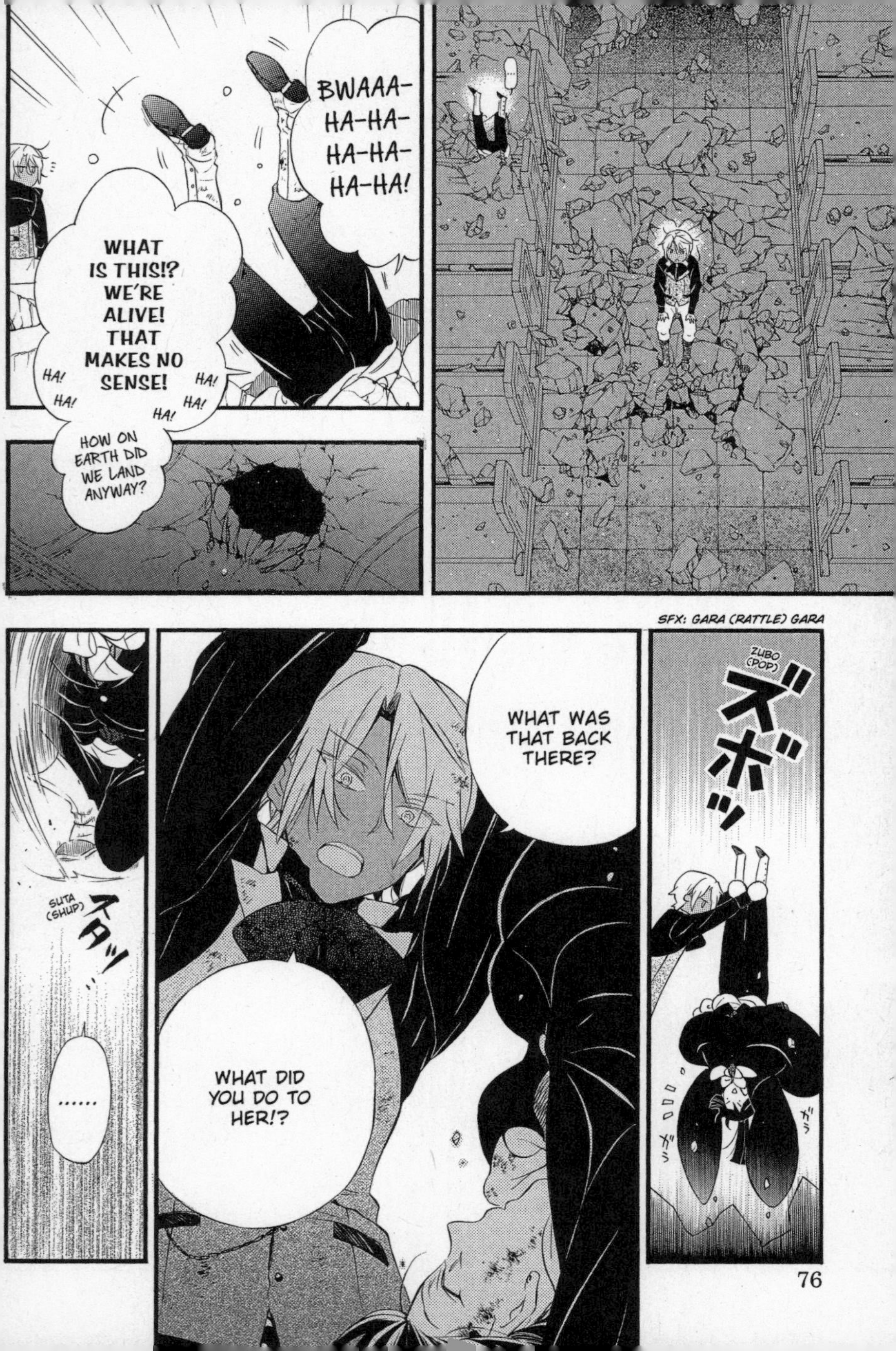
...
BWAAA-HA-HA-HA-HA-HA-HA!
WHAT IS THIS!? WE'RE ALIVE! THAT MAKES NO SENSE!
HA! HA! HA! HA! HA!
HOW ON EARTH DID WE LAND ANYWAY?
SFX: GARA (RATTLE) GARA
ZUBO (POP)
ズボッ
ガラ
ガラ
WHAT WAS THAT BACK THERE?
WHAT DID YOU DO TO HER!?
SUTA (SHUP)
スタッ
......

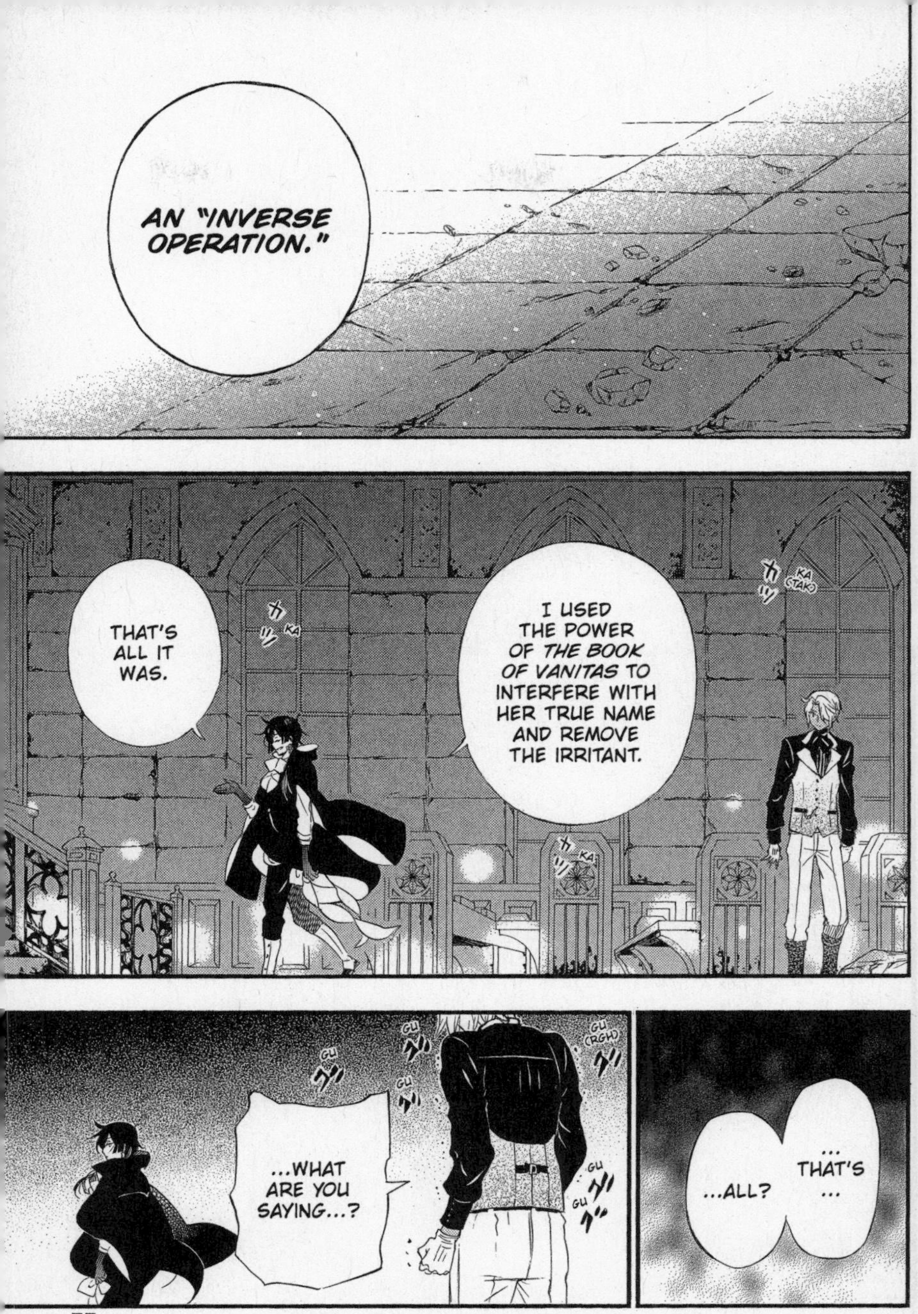
AN "INVERSE OPERATION."
KA (TAK)
I USED THE POWER OF THE BOOK OF VANITAS TO INTERFERE WITH HER TRUE NAME AND REMOVE THE IRRITANT.
KA
THAT'S ALL IT WAS.
KA
... THAT'S ...
...ALL?
GU (RGH)
GU
GU
GU
GU
GU
...WHAT ARE YOU SAYING...?

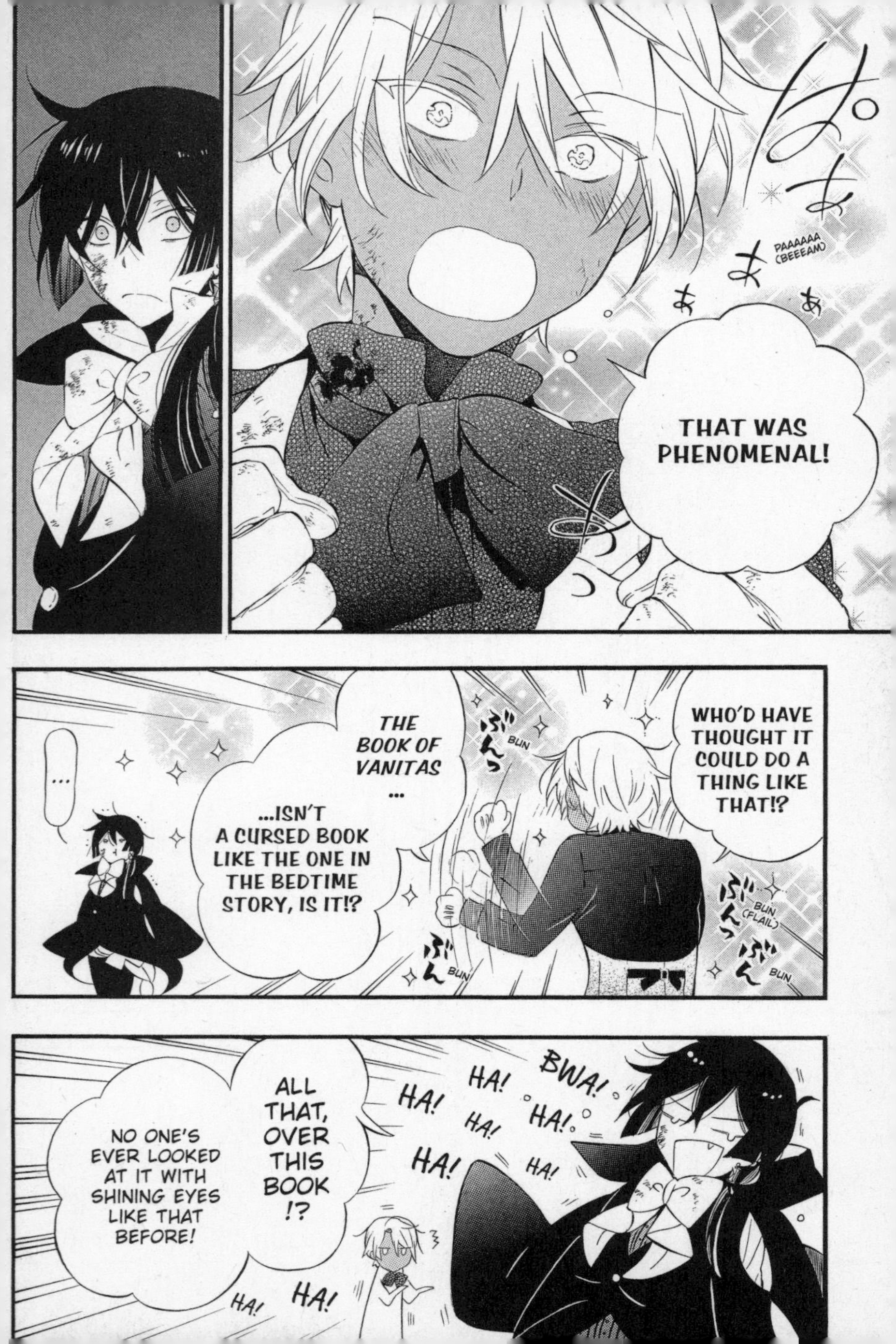
PAAAAAA (BEEEAM)
THAT WAS PHENOMENAL!
WHO'D HAVE THOUGHT IT COULD DO A THING LIKE THAT!?
BUN
THE BOOK OF VANITAS ...
...ISN'T A CURSED BOOK LIKE THE ONE IN THE BEDTIME STORY, IS IT!?
BUN (FLAIL)
BUN
BUN
...
BWA! HA! HA! HA! HA! HA! HA!
ALL THAT, OVER THIS BOOK !?
NO ONE'S EVER LOOKED AT IT WITH SHINING EYES LIKE THAT BEFORE!
HA! HA!

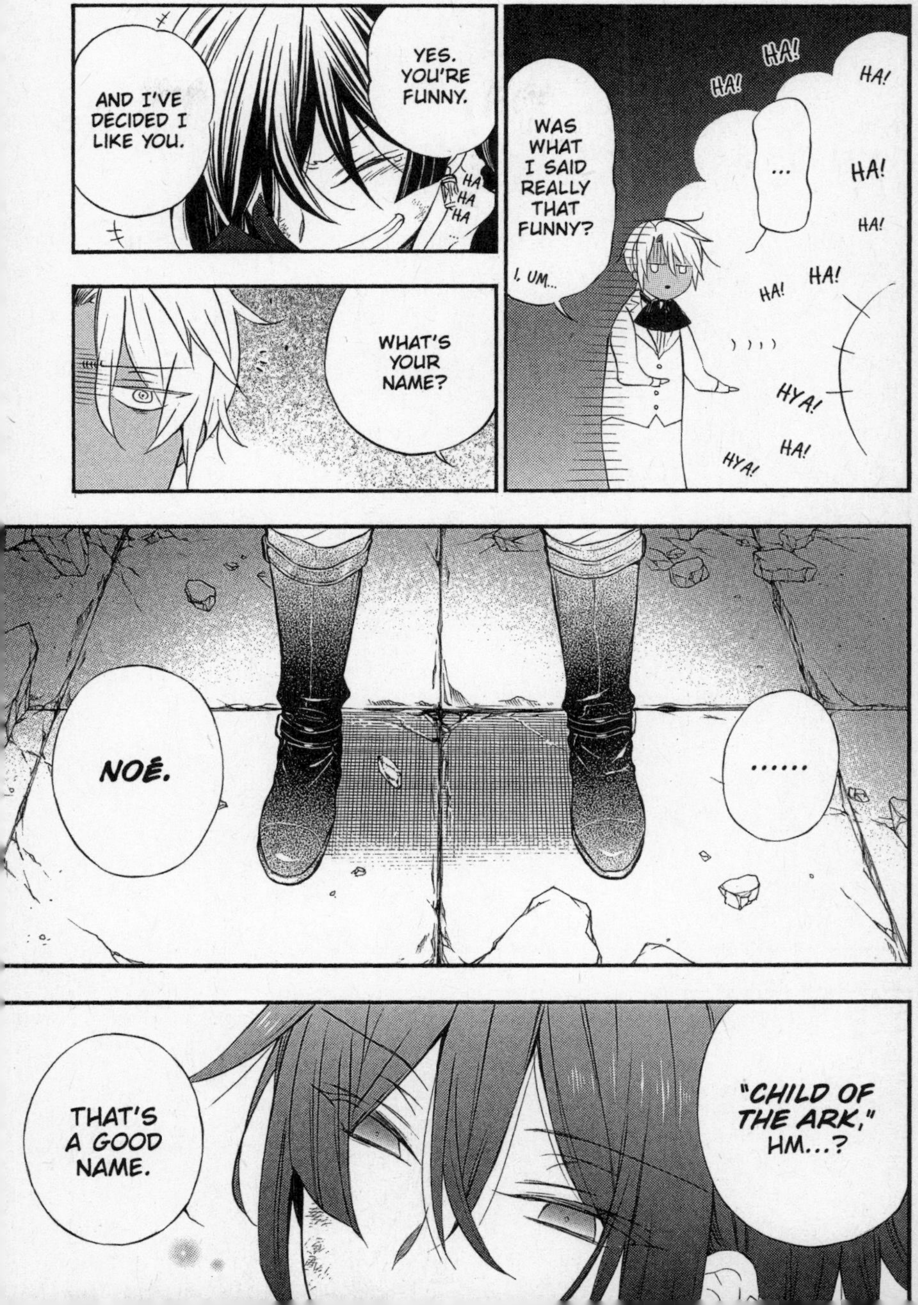
WAS WHAT I SAID REALLY THAT FUNNY?
I, UM...
HA!
HA!
HA!
...
HA!
HA!
HA!
HA!
HYA!
HA!
HYA!
YES. YOU'RE FUNNY.
AND I'VE DECIDED I LIKE YOU.
HA HA HA HA ...
WHAT'S YOUR NAME?
......
NOÉ.
"CHILD OF THE ARK," HM...?
THAT'S A GOOD NAME.

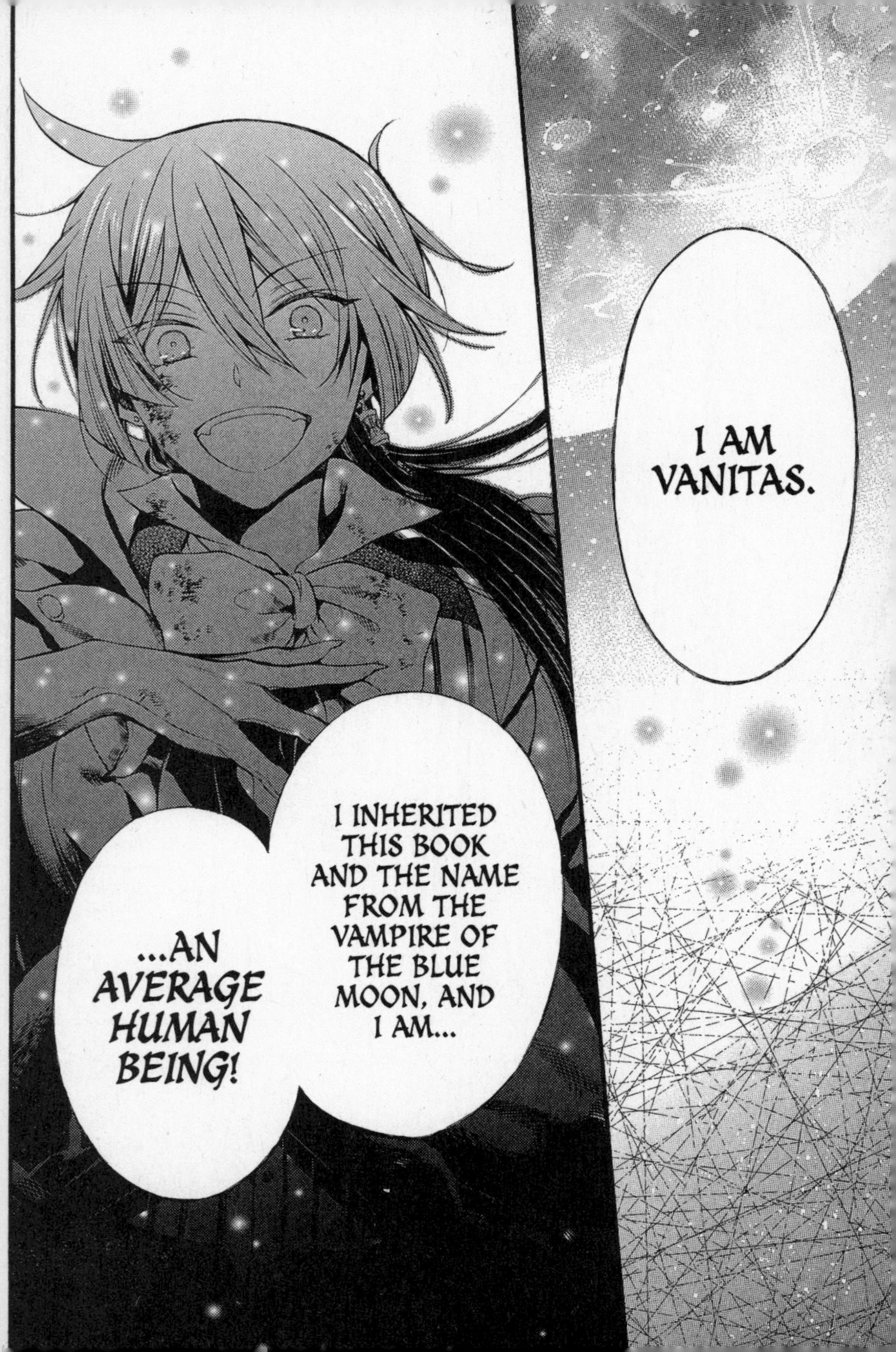
I AM VANITAS.
I INHERITED THIS BOOK AND THE NAME FROM THE VAMPIRE OF THE BLUE MOON, AND I AM...
...AN AVERAGE HUMAN BEING!

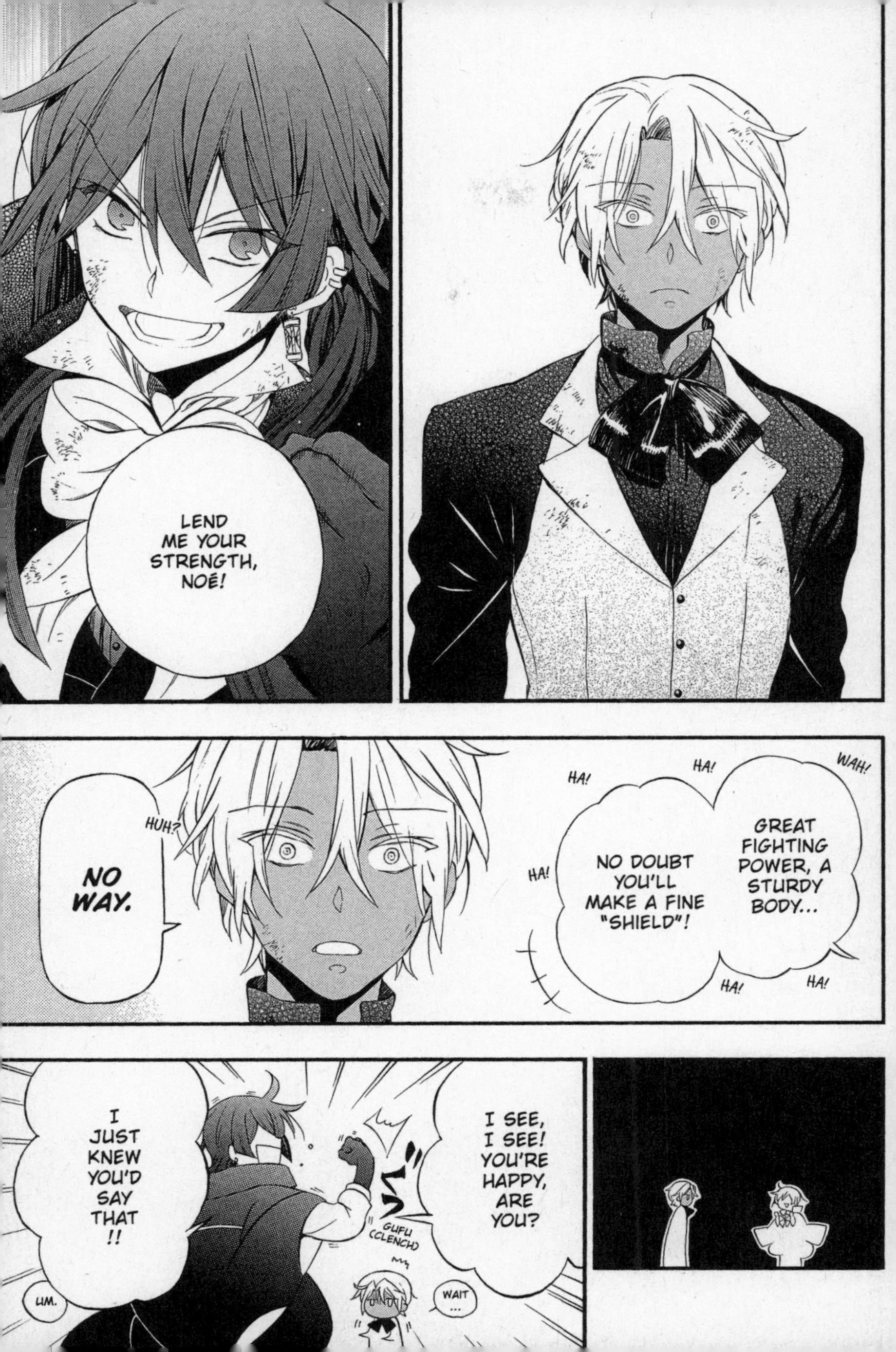
LEND ME YOUR STRENGTH, NOÉ!
WAH!
HA!
GREAT FIGHTING POWER, A STURDY BODY...
HA!
NO DOUBT YOU'LL MAKE A FINE "SHIELD"!
HA!
HA!
HA!
HUH?
NO WAY.
I SEE, I SEE! YOU'RE HAPPY, ARE YOU?
GUFU (CLENCH)
WAIT ...
I JUST KNEW YOU'D SAY THAT !!
UM.

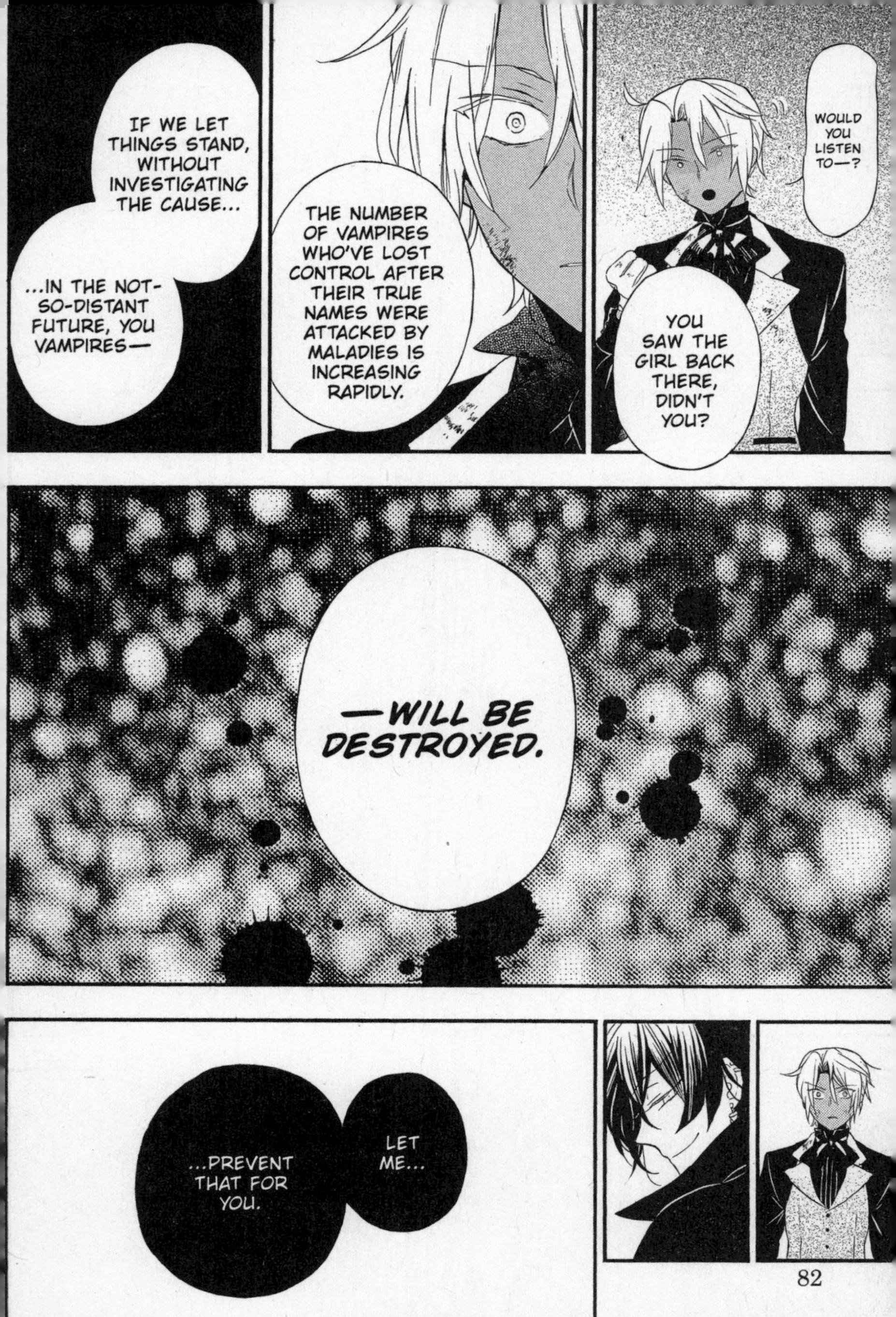
WOULD YOU LISTEN TO—?
YOU SAW THE GIRL BACK THERE, DIDN'T YOU?
THE NUMBER OF VAMPIRES WHO'VE LOST CONTROL AFTER THEIR TRUE NAMES WERE ATTACKED BY MALADIES IS INCREASING RAPIDLY.
IF WE LET THINGS STAND, WITHOUT INVESTIGATING THE CAUSE...
...IN THE NOT-SO-DISTANT FUTURE, YOU VAMPIRES—
—WILL BE DESTROYED.
LET ME...
...PREVENT THAT FOR YOU.

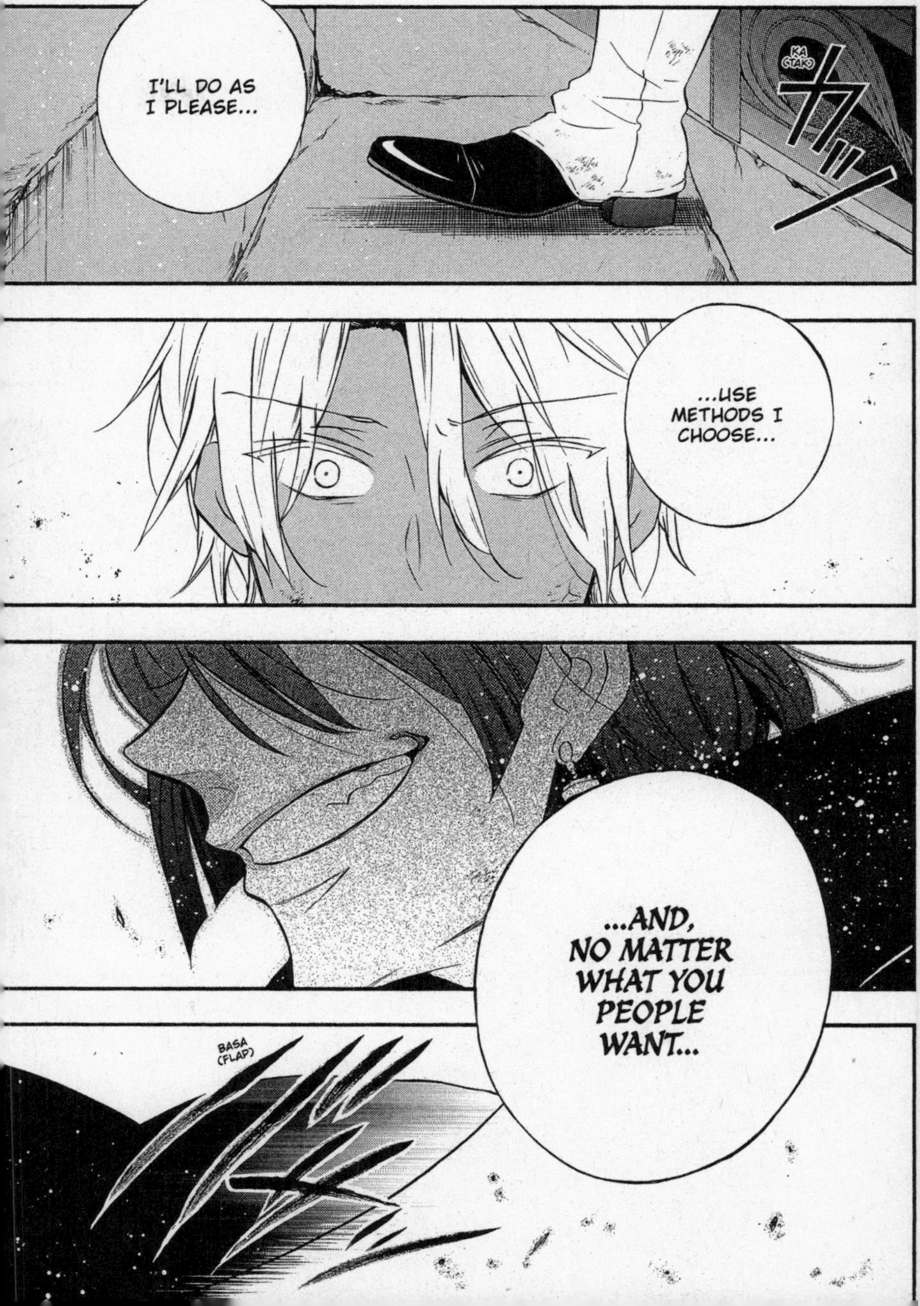
KA (TAK)
I'LL DO AS I PLEASE...
...USE METHODS I CHOOSE...
...AND, NO MATTER WHAT YOU PEOPLE WANT...
BASA (FLAP)

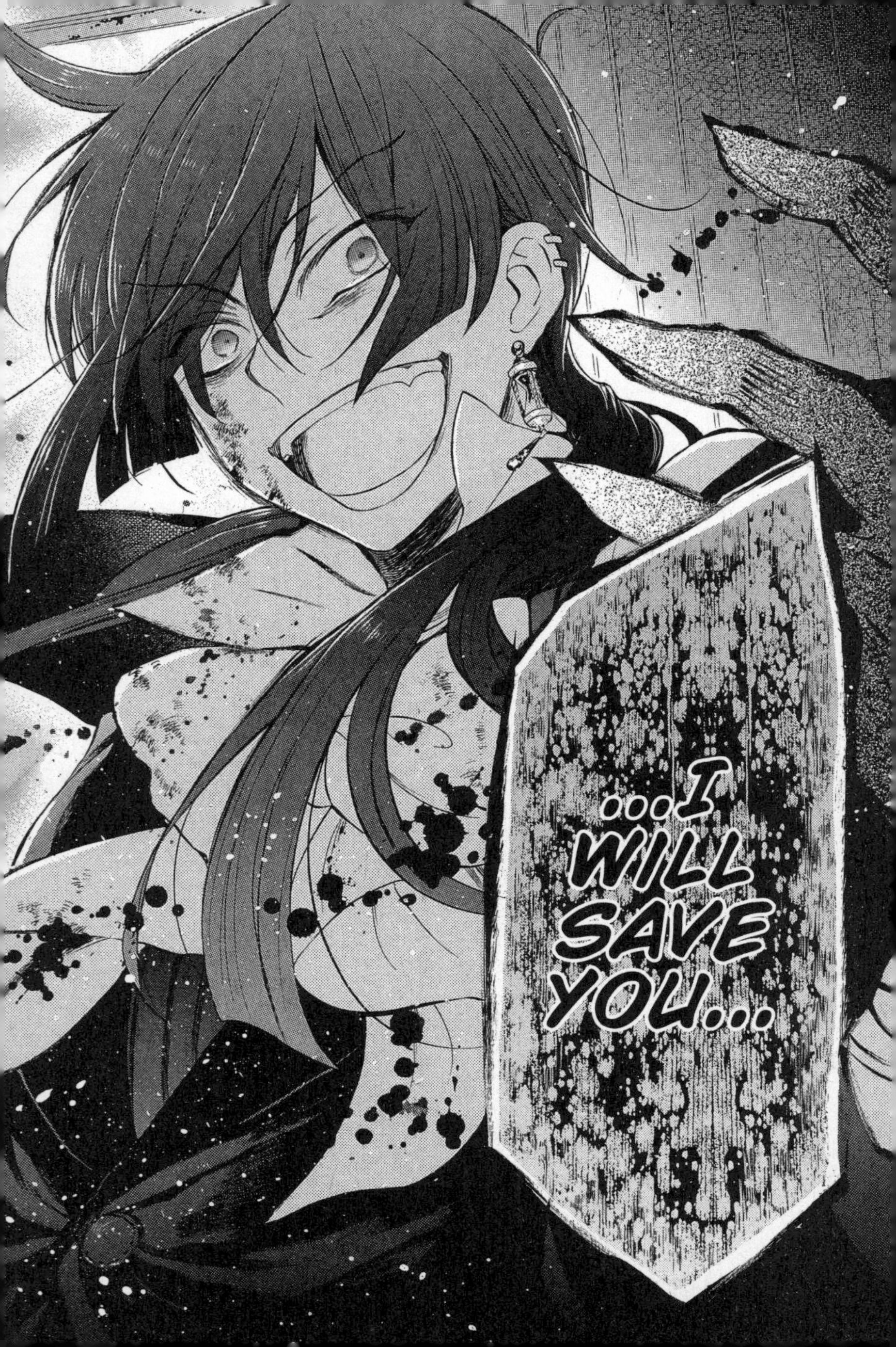
...I WILL SAVE YOU...

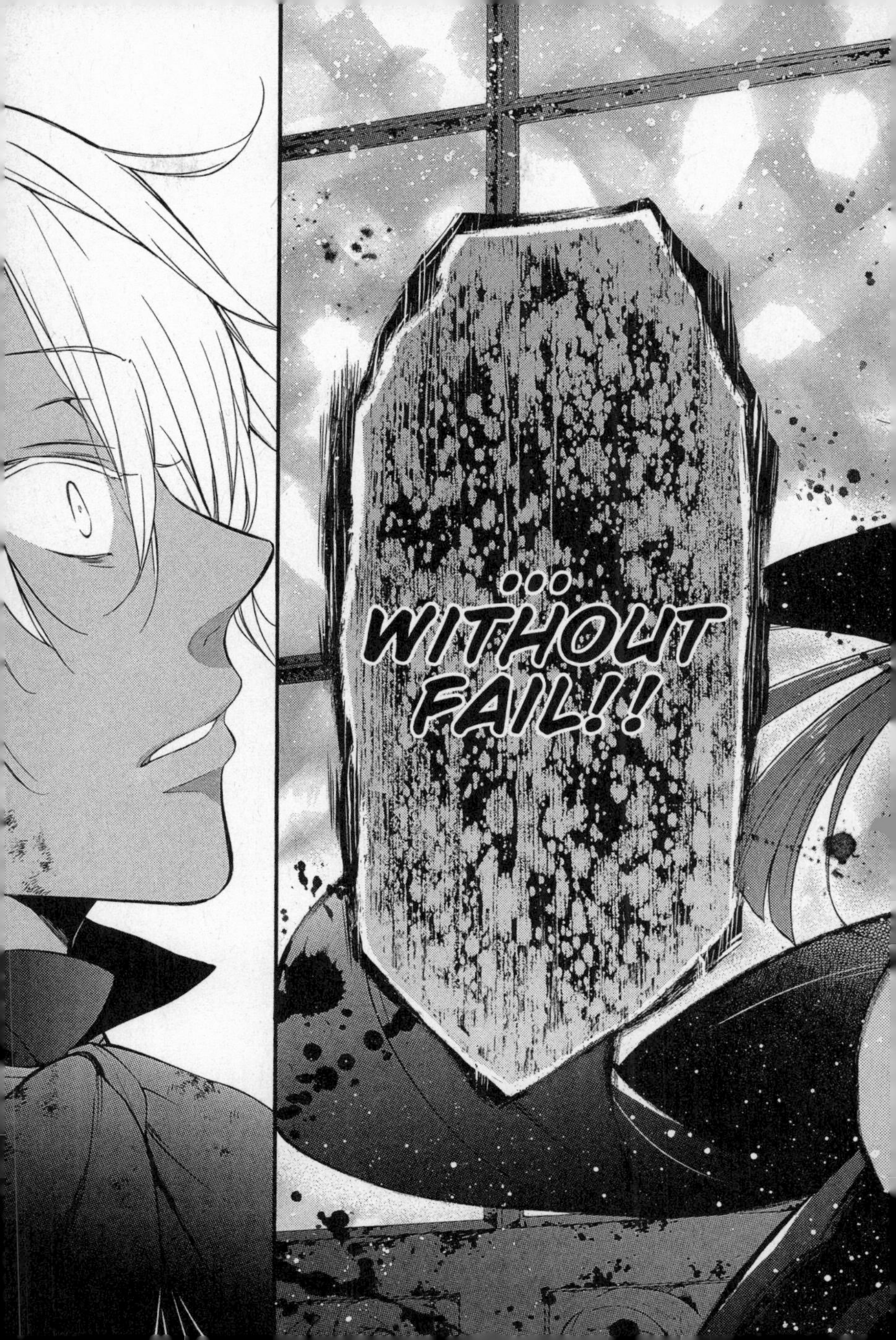
...WITHOUT FAIL!!

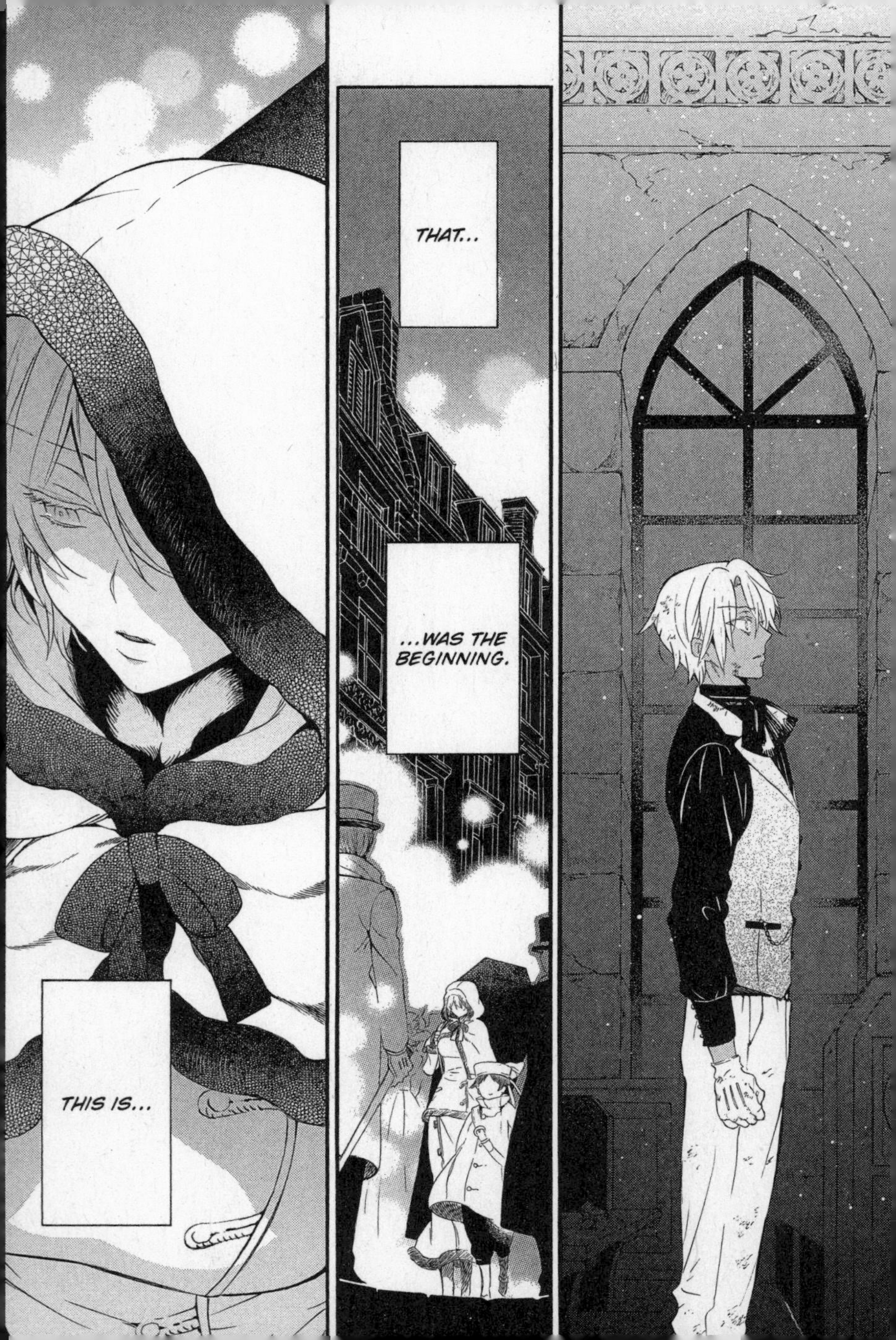
THAT...
...WAS THE BEGINNING.
THIS IS...

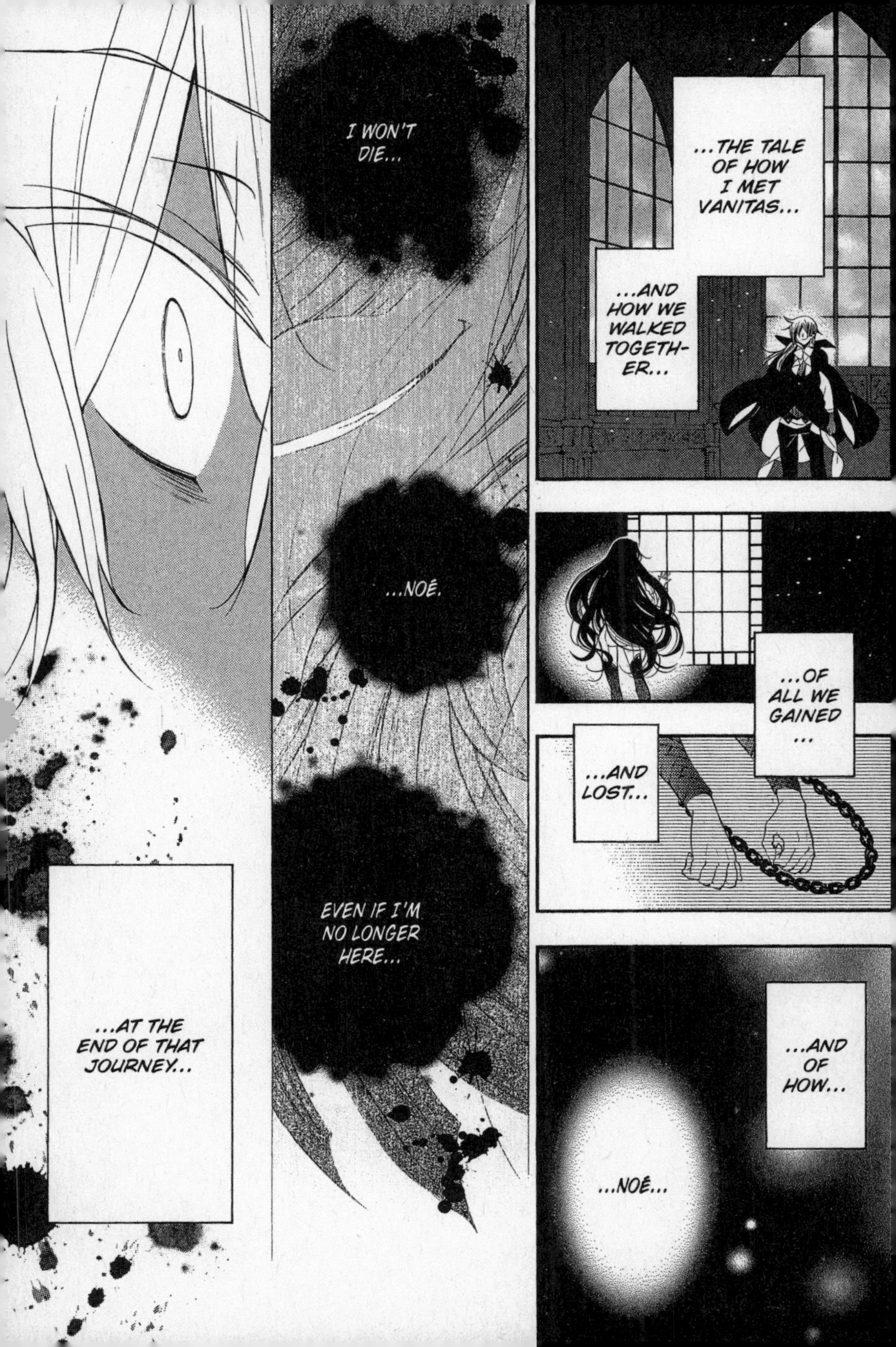
...THE TALE OF HOW I MET VANITAS...
...AND HOW WE WALKED TOGETHER...
...OF ALL WE GAINED...
...AND LOST...
...AND OF HOW...
...NOÉ...
I WON'T DIE...
...NOÉ.
EVEN IF I'M NO LONGER HERE...
...AT THE END OF THAT JOURNEY...

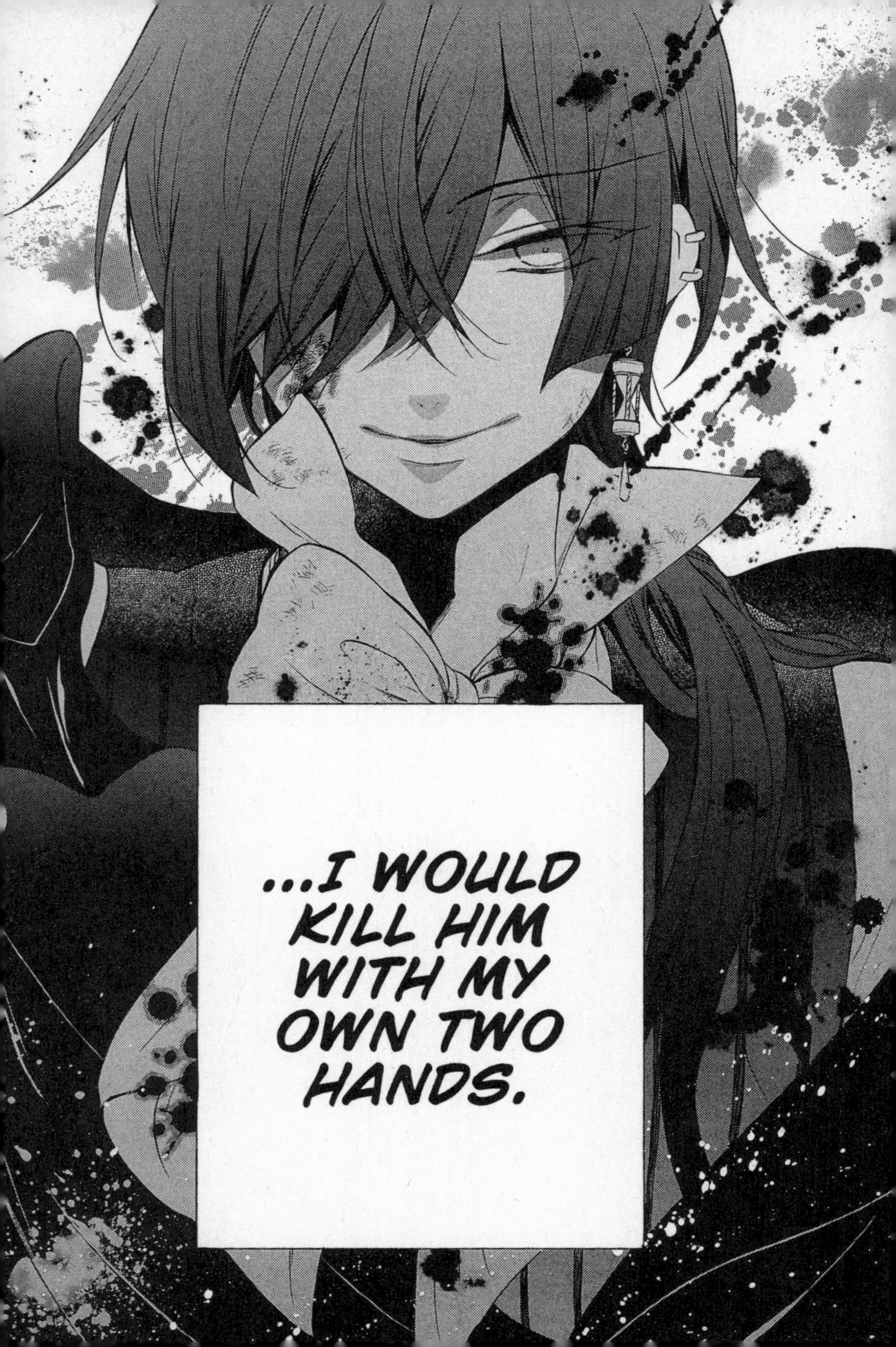
...I WOULD KILL HIM WITH MY OWN TWO HANDS.

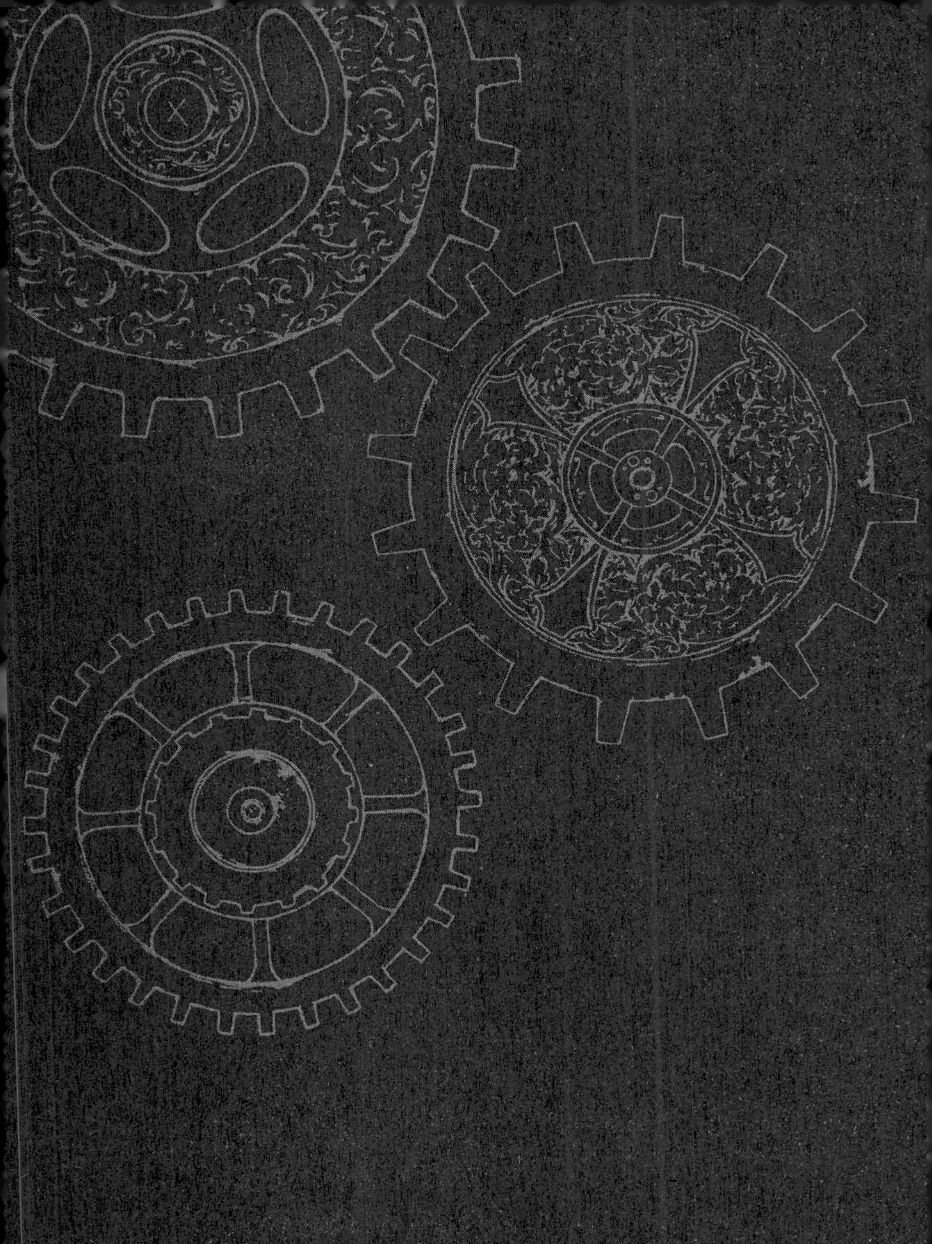

Mémoire 1 Vanitas IN THE EVENT OF RUSTY HOPES

Les Mémoires de Vanitas

THE CASE STUDY OF VANITAS

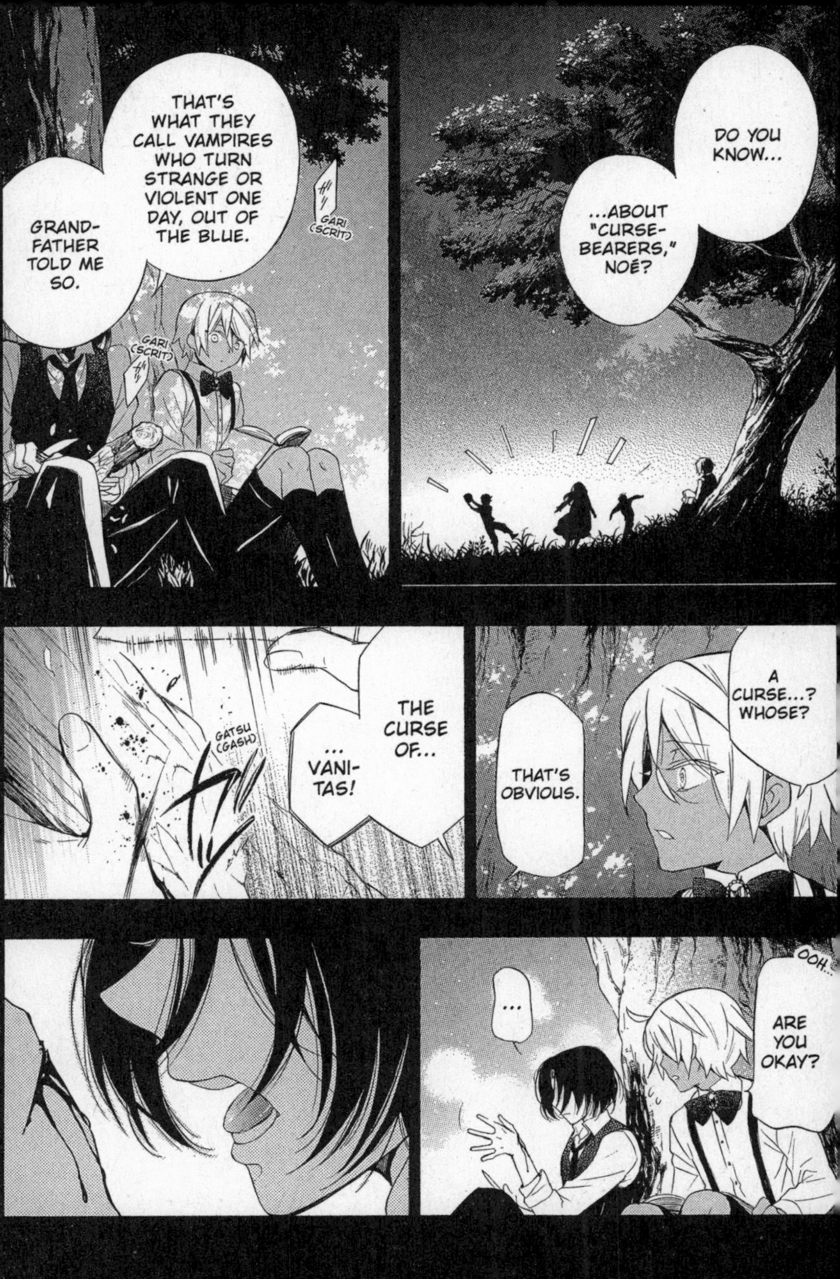
DO YOU KNOW...
...ABOUT "CURSE-BEARERS," NOÉ?
THAT'S WHAT THEY CALL VAMPIRES WHO TURN STRANGE OR VIOLENT ONE DAY, OUT OF THE BLUE.
GARI (SCRIT)
GRAND-FATHER TOLD ME SO.
GARI (SCRIT)
A CURSE...? WHOSE?
THAT'S OBVIOUS.
THE CURSE OF...
...VANI-TAS!
GATSU (GASH)
OOH...
ARE YOU OKAY?
...

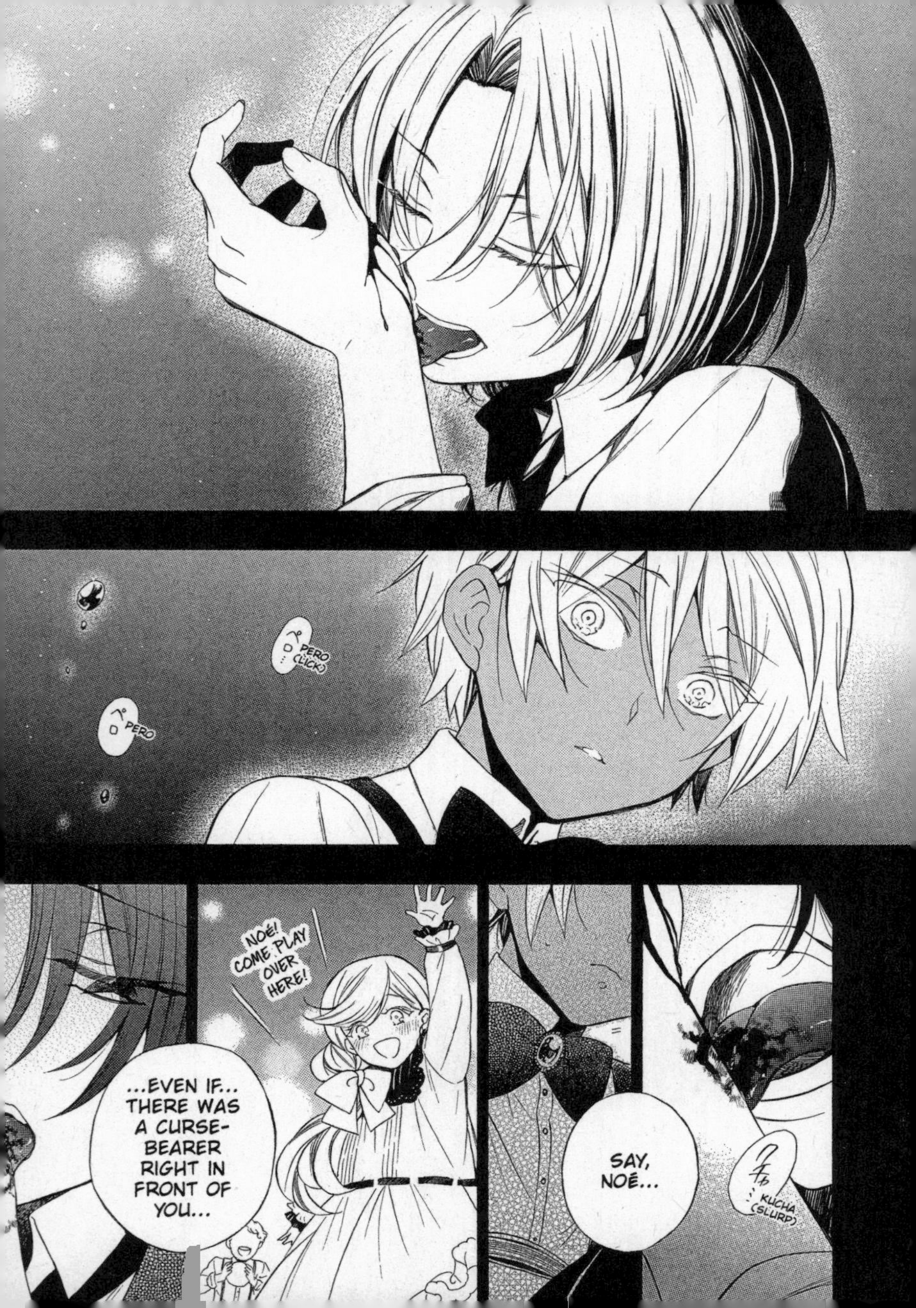
ぺロ… PERO (LICK)
ぺロ PERO
クチャ… KUCHA (SLURP)
SAY, NOÉ...
NOÉ! COME PLAY OVER HERE!
...EVEN IF... THERE WAS A CURSE-BEARER RIGHT IN FRONT OF YOU...

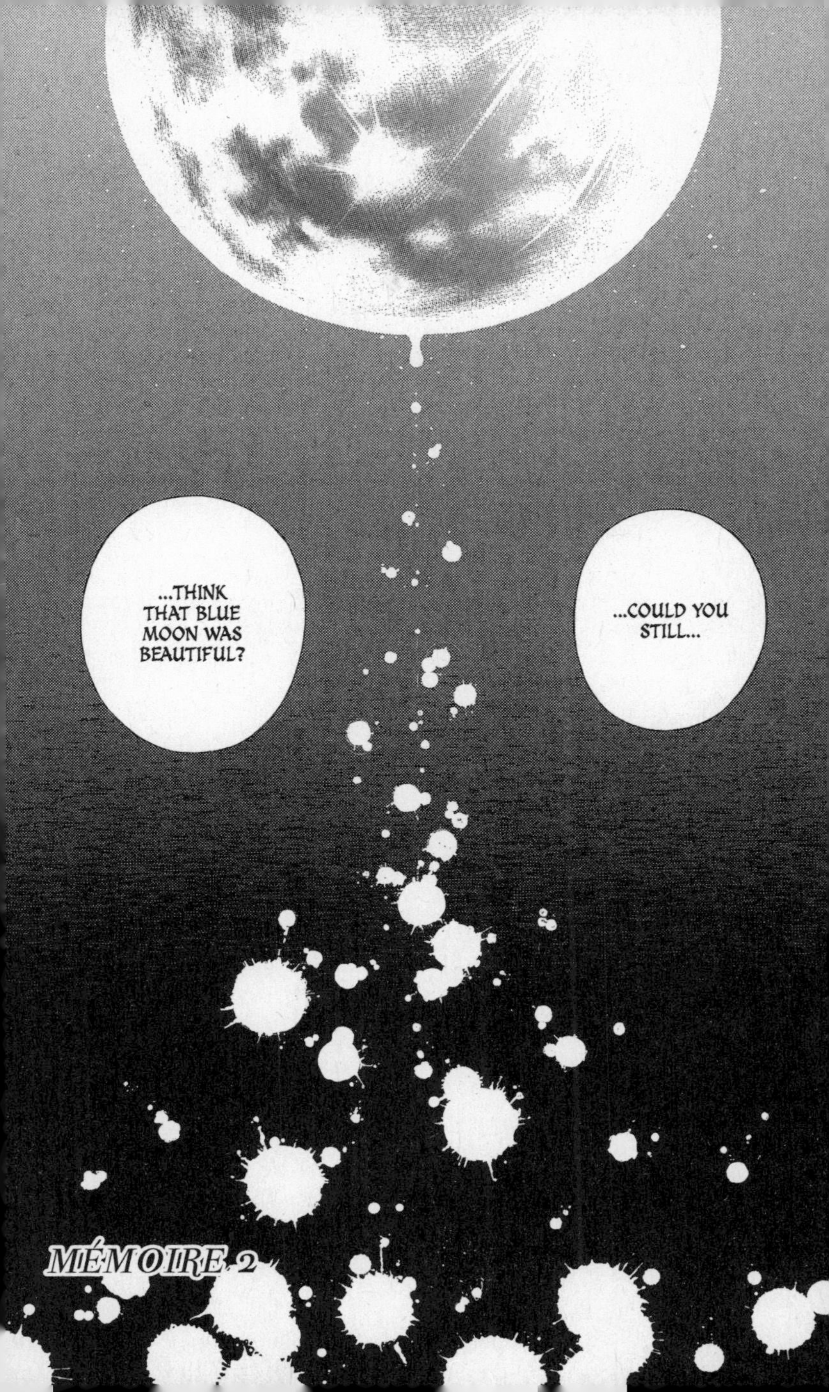

MÉMOIRE 2

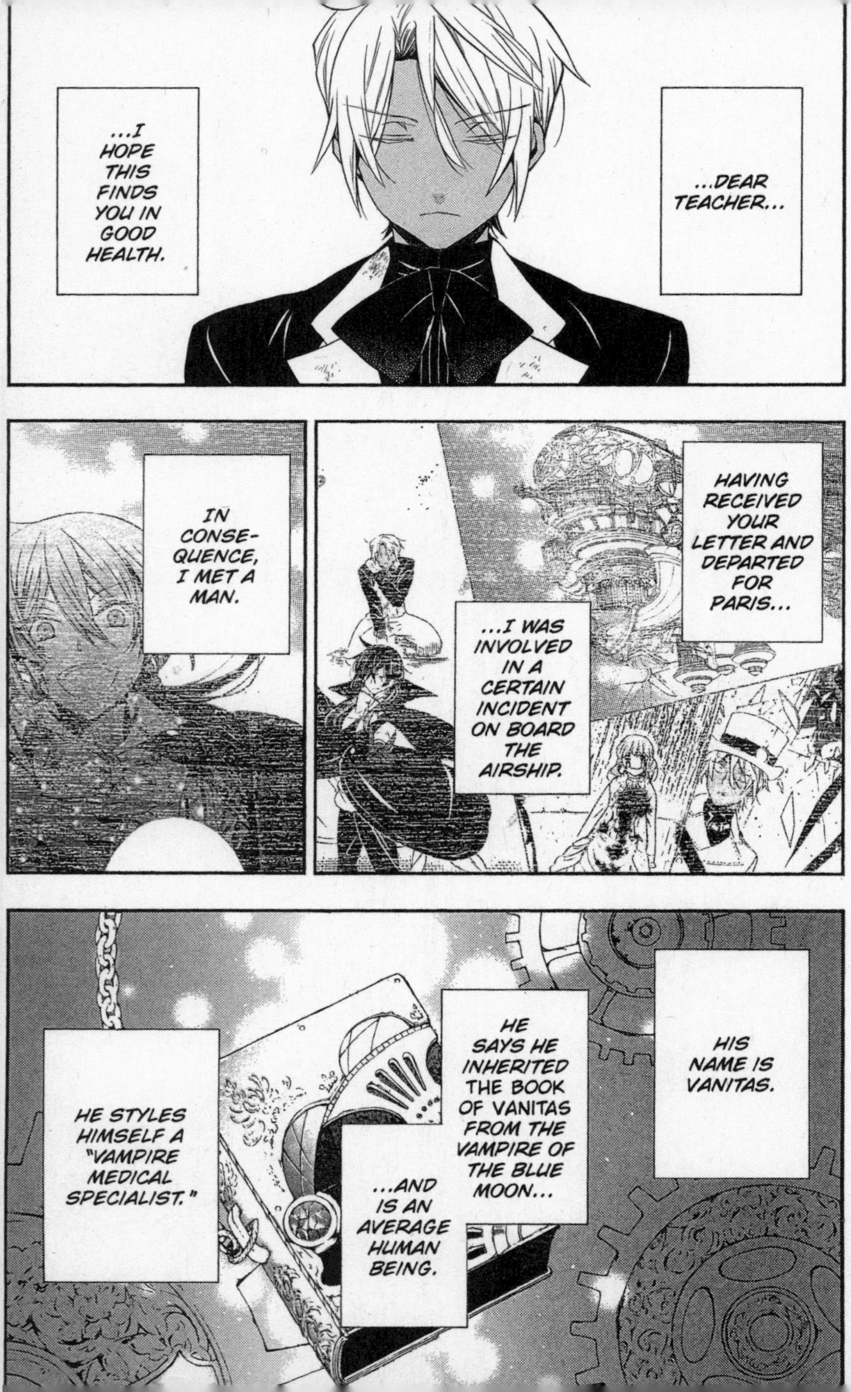
...DEAR TEACHER...
...I HOPE THIS FINDS YOU IN GOOD HEALTH.
HAVING RECEIVED YOUR LETTER AND DEPARTED FOR PARIS...
...I WAS INVOLVED IN A CERTAIN INCIDENT ON BOARD THE AIRSHIP.
IN CONSEQUENCE, I MET A MAN.
HIS NAME IS VANITAS.
HE SAYS HE INHERITED THE BOOK OF VANITAS FROM THE VAMPIRE OF THE BLUE MOON...
...AND IS AN AVERAGE HUMAN BEING.
HE STYLES HIMSELF A "VAMPIRE MEDICAL SPECIALIST."

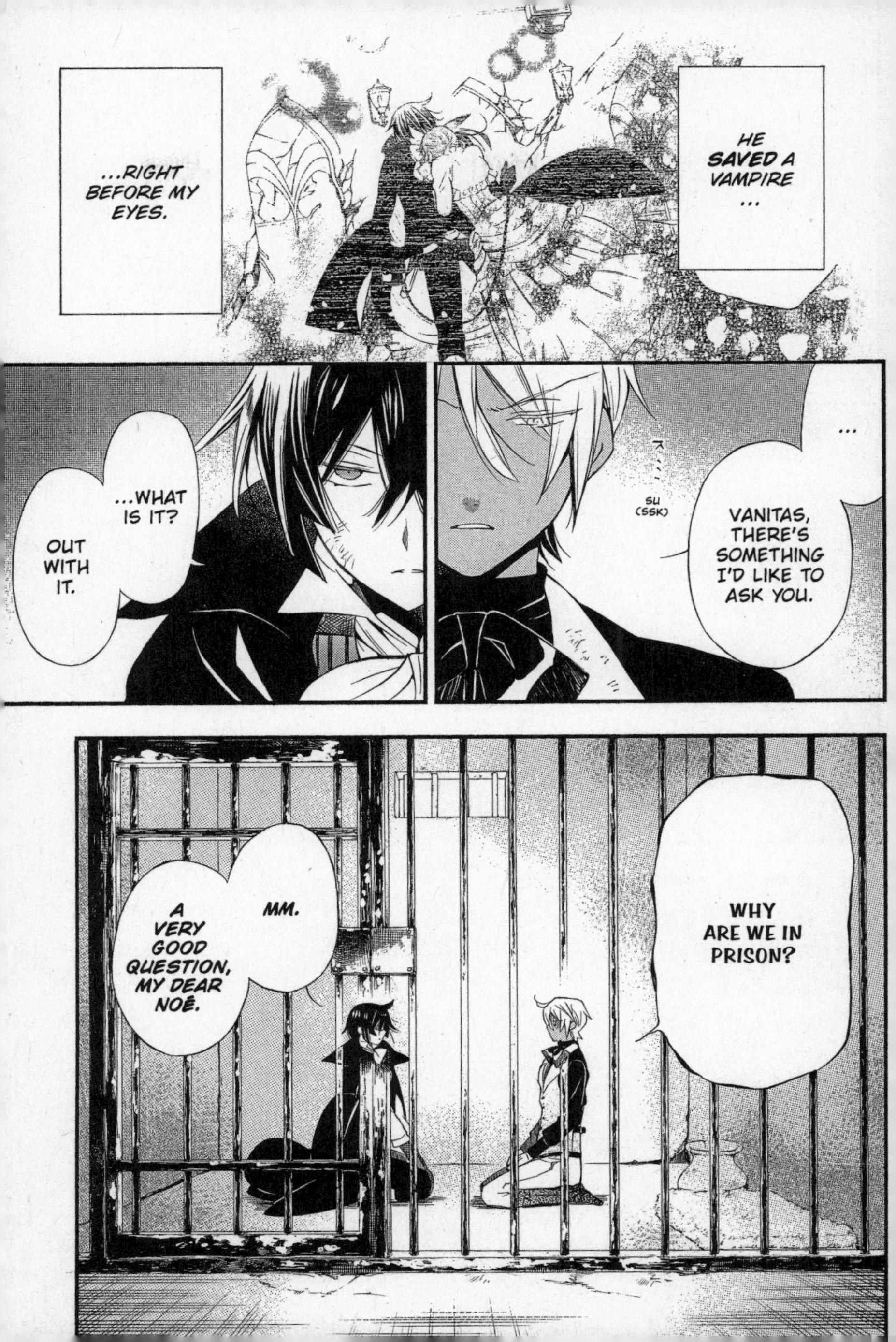
HE SAVED A VAMPIRE ...
...RIGHT BEFORE MY EYES.
...
SU (SSK)
VANITAS, THERE'S SOMETHING I'D LIKE TO ASK YOU.
...WHAT IS IT?
OUT WITH IT.
WHY ARE WE IN PRISON?
MM.
A VERY GOOD QUESTION, MY DEAR NOÉ.

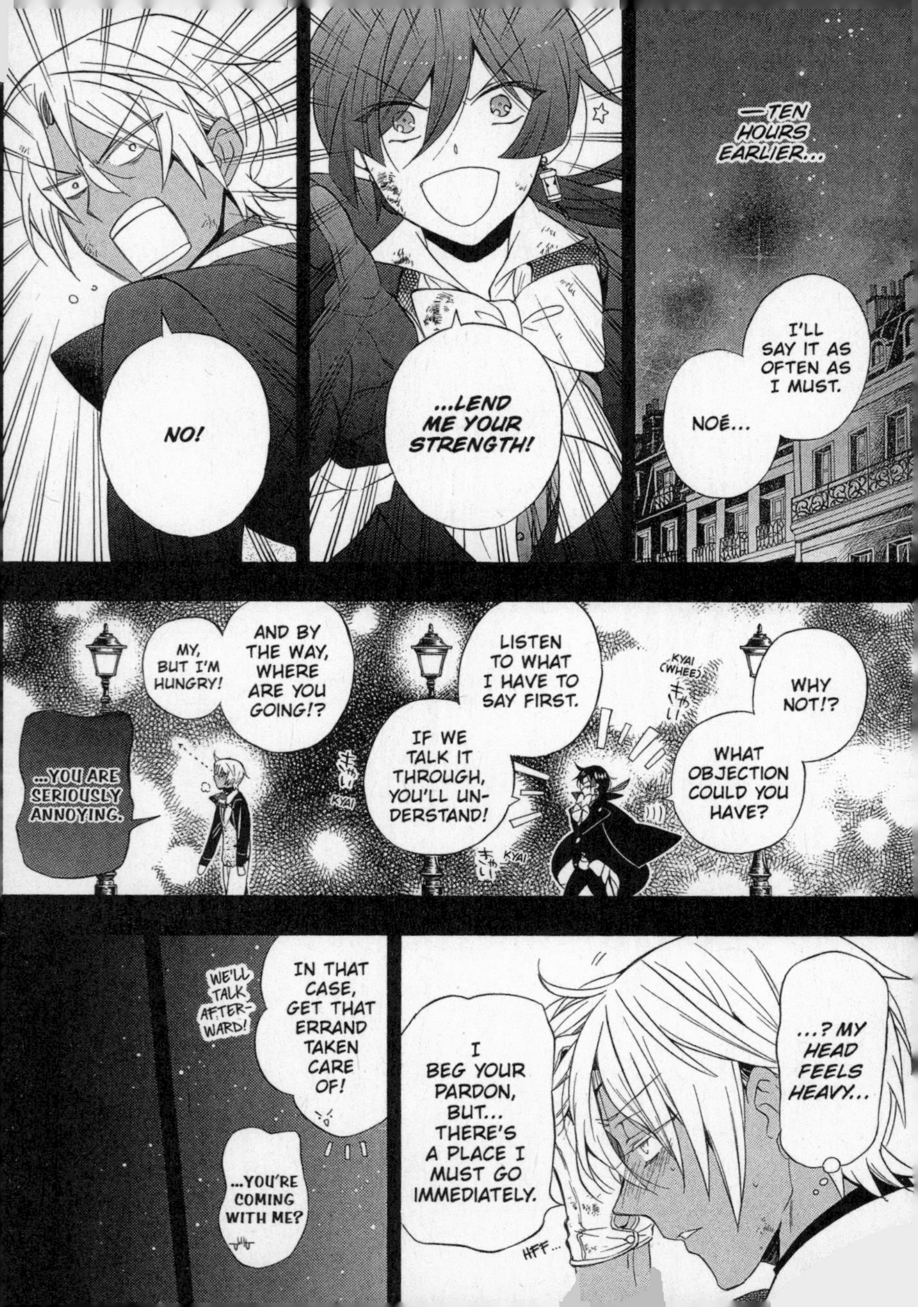
—TEN HOURS EARLIER...
I'LL SAY IT AS OFTEN AS I MUST.
NOÉ...
...LEND ME YOUR STRENGTH!
NO!
WHY NOT!?
WHAT OBJECTION COULD YOU HAVE?
KYAI (WHEE)
LISTEN TO WHAT I HAVE TO SAY FIRST.
IF WE TALK IT THROUGH, YOU'LL UN-DERSTAND!
KYAI
KYAI
AND BY THE WAY, WHERE ARE YOU GOING!?
MY, BUT I'M HUNGRY!
...YOU ARE SERIOUSLY ANNOYING.
...? MY HEAD FEELS HEAVY...
I BEG YOUR PARDON, BUT... THERE'S A PLACE I MUST GO IMMEDIATELY.
HFF...
IN THAT CASE, GET THAT ERRAND TAKEN CARE OF!
WE'LL TALK AFTER-WARD!
...YOU'RE COMING WITH ME?

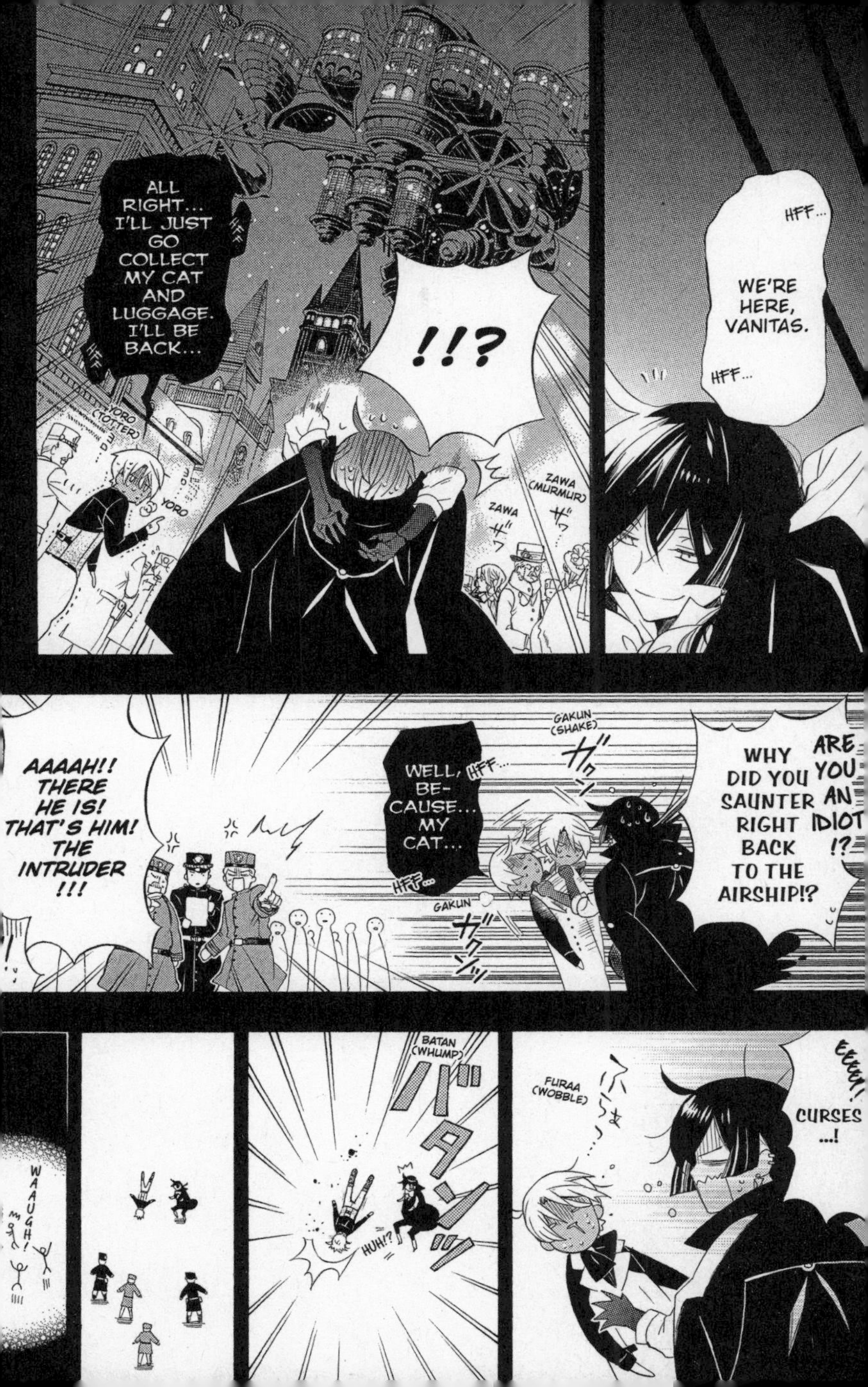
HFF...
WE'RE HERE, VANITAS.
HFF...
!!?
ALL RIGHT... I'LL JUST GO COLLECT MY CAT AND LUGGAGE. I'LL BE BACK...
ZAWA (MURMUR)
ZAWA
YORO (TOTTER)
YORO
ARE YOU AN IDIOT!?
WHY DID YOU SAUNTER RIGHT BACK TO THE AIRSHIP!?
GAKUN (SHAKE)
WELL, BE-CAUSE... MY CAT...
HFF...
HFF...
GAKUN
AAAAH!! THERE HE IS! THAT'S HIM! THE INTRUDER!!!
CURSES...!
FURAA (WOBBLE)
BATAN (WHUMP)
HUH!?
WAAAUGH!

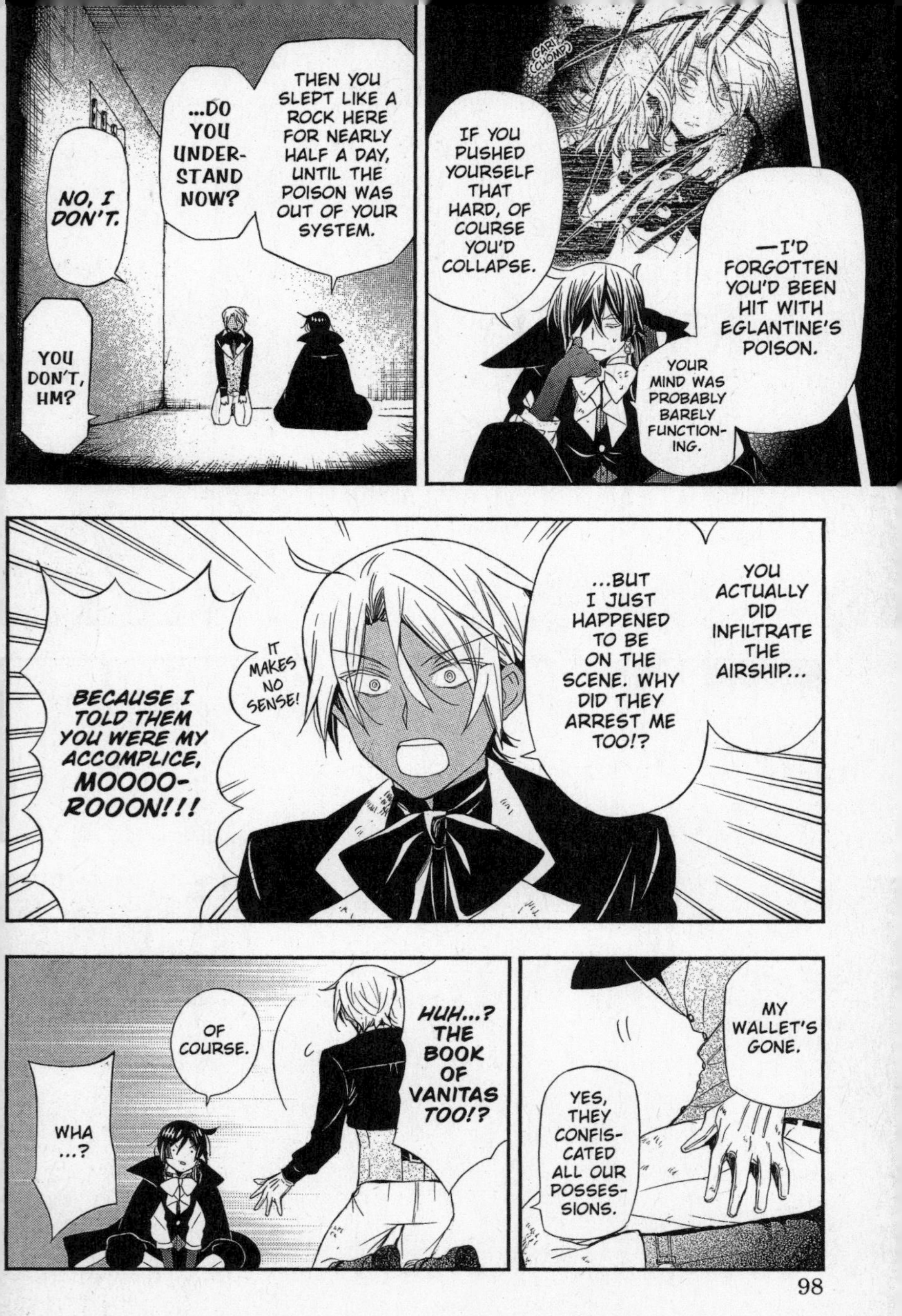
GARI (CHOMP)
—I'D FORGOTTEN YOU'D BEEN HIT WITH EGLANTINE'S POISON.
YOUR MIND WAS PROBABLY BARELY FUNCTIONING.
IF YOU PUSHED YOURSELF THAT HARD, OF COURSE YOU'D COLLAPSE.
THEN YOU SLEPT LIKE A ROCK HERE FOR NEARLY HALF A DAY, UNTIL THE POISON WAS OUT OF YOUR SYSTEM.
...DO YOU UNDERSTAND NOW?
NO, I DON'T.
YOU DON'T, HM?
YOU ACTUALLY DID INFILTRATE THE AIRSHIP...
...BUT I JUST HAPPENED TO BE ON THE SCENE. WHY DID THEY ARREST ME TOO!?
IT MAKES NO SENSE!
BECAUSE I TOLD THEM YOU WERE MY ACCOMPLICE, MOOOO-ROOON!!!
MY WALLET'S GONE.
YES, THEY CONFISCATED ALL OUR POSSESSIONS.
HUH...? THE BOOK OF VANITAS TOO!?
OF COURSE.
WHA ...?

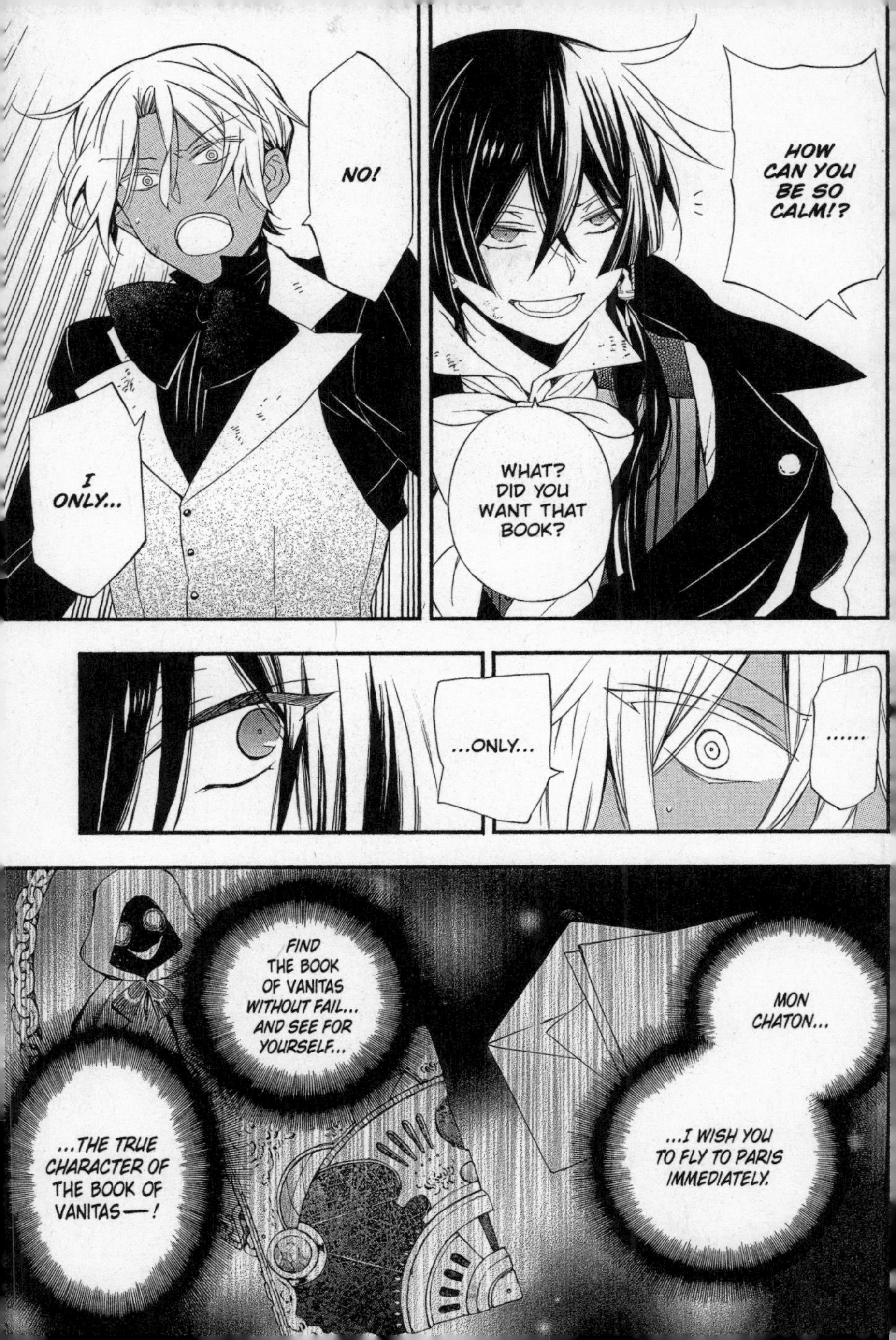
HOW CAN YOU BE SO CALM!?
WHAT? DID YOU WANT THAT BOOK?
NO!
I ONLY...
......
...ONLY...
MON CHATON...
...I WISH YOU TO FLY TO PARIS IMMEDIATELY.
FIND THE BOOK OF VANITAS WITHOUT FAIL... AND SEE FOR YOURSELF...
...THE TRUE CHARACTER OF THE BOOK OF VANITAS—!

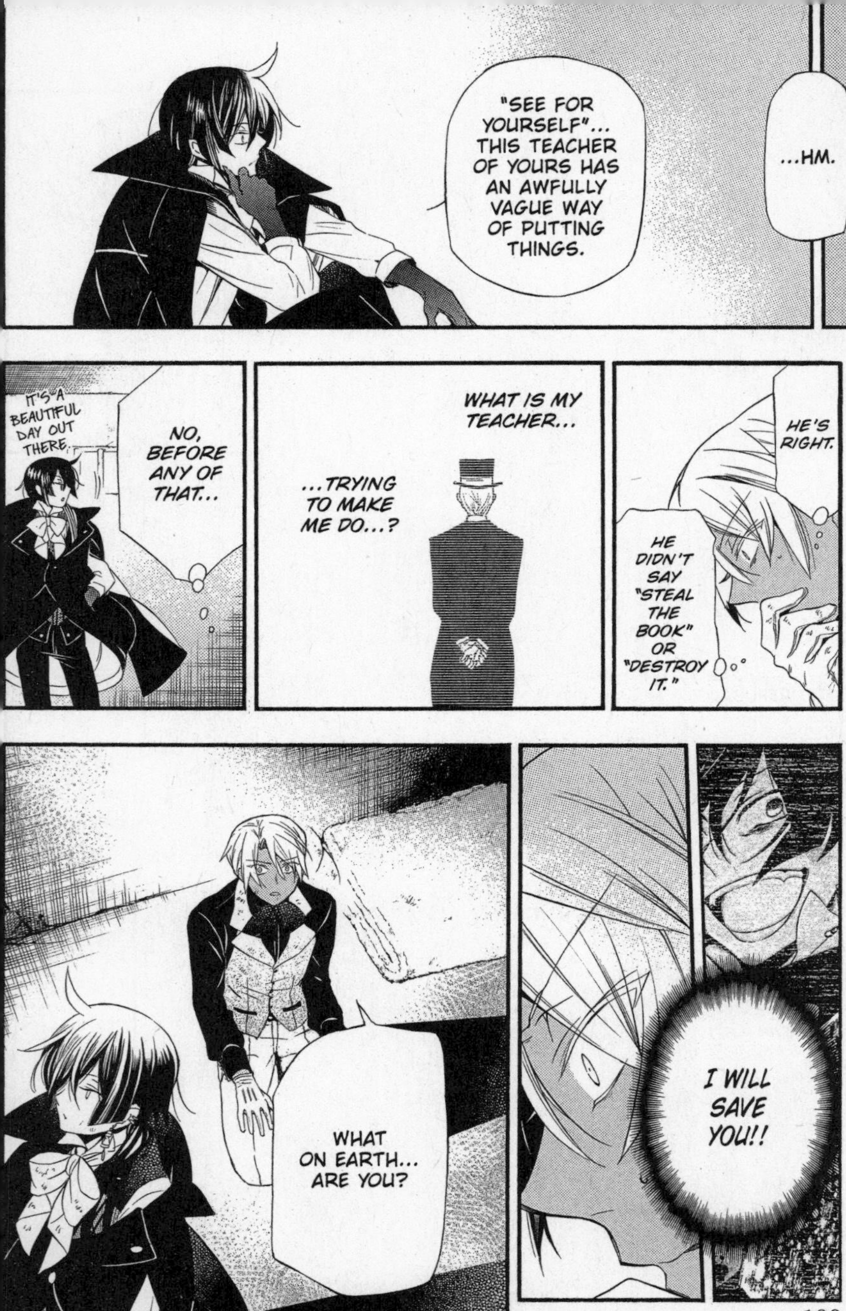
...HM.
"SEE FOR YOURSELF"... THIS TEACHER OF YOURS HAS AN AWFULLY VAGUE WAY OF PUTTING THINGS.
HE'S RIGHT.
HE DIDN'T SAY "STEAL THE BOOK" OR "DESTROY IT."
WHAT IS MY TEACHER...
...TRYING TO MAKE ME DO...?
NO, BEFORE ANY OF THAT...
IT'S A BEAUTIFUL DAY OUT THERE.
I WILL SAVE YOU!!
WHAT ON EARTH... ARE YOU?

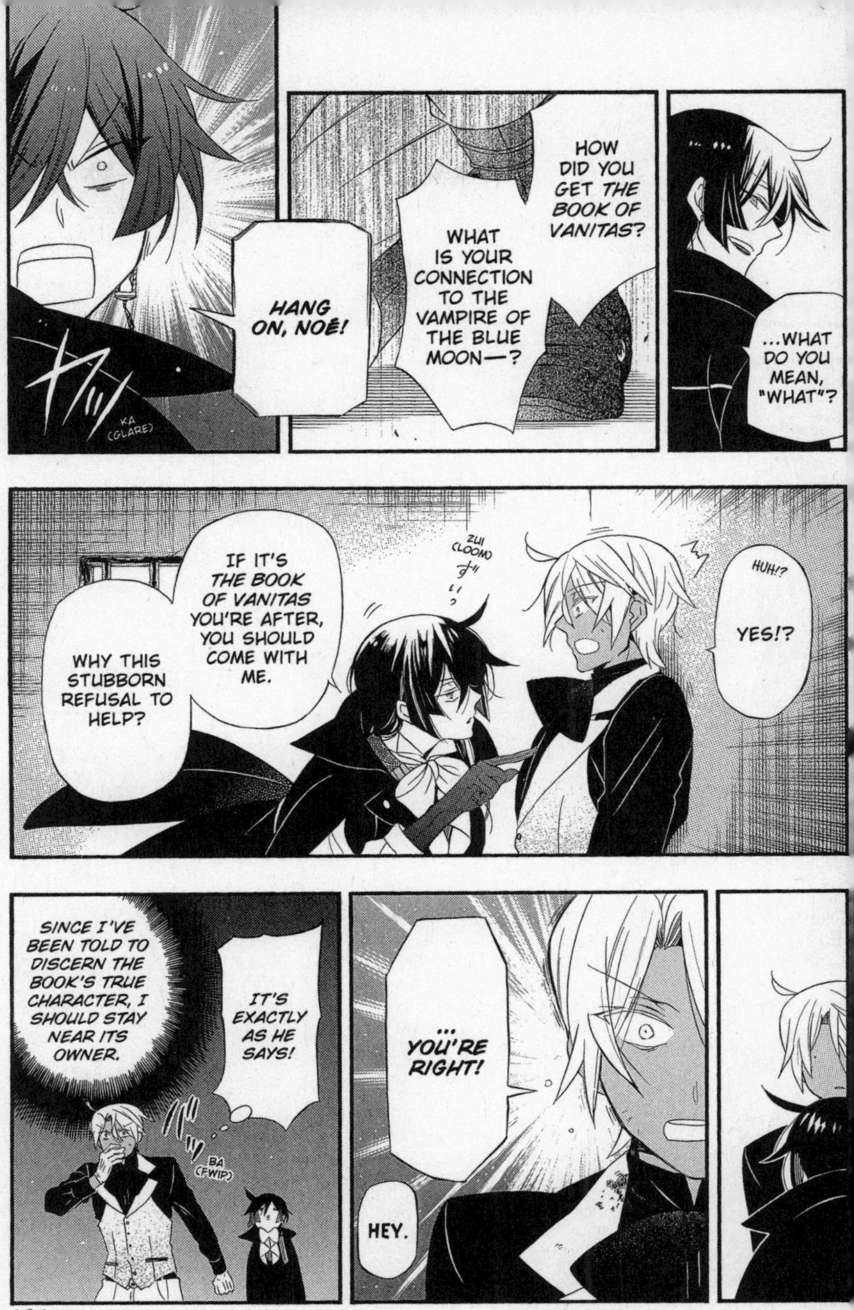
...WHAT DO YOU MEAN, "WHAT"?
HOW DID YOU GET *THE BOOK OF VANITAS*?
WHAT IS YOUR CONNECTION TO THE VAMPIRE OF THE BLUE MOON—?
HANG ON, NOÉ!
KA (GLARE)
HUH!?
YES!?
ZUI (LOOM)
IF IT'S *THE BOOK OF VANITAS* YOU'RE AFTER, YOU SHOULD COME WITH ME.
WHY THIS STUBBORN REFUSAL TO HELP?
...YOU'RE RIGHT!
HEY.
IT'S EXACTLY AS HE SAYS!
SINCE I'VE BEEN TOLD TO DISCERN THE BOOK'S TRUE CHARACTER, I SHOULD STAY NEAR ITS OWNER.
BA (FWIP)

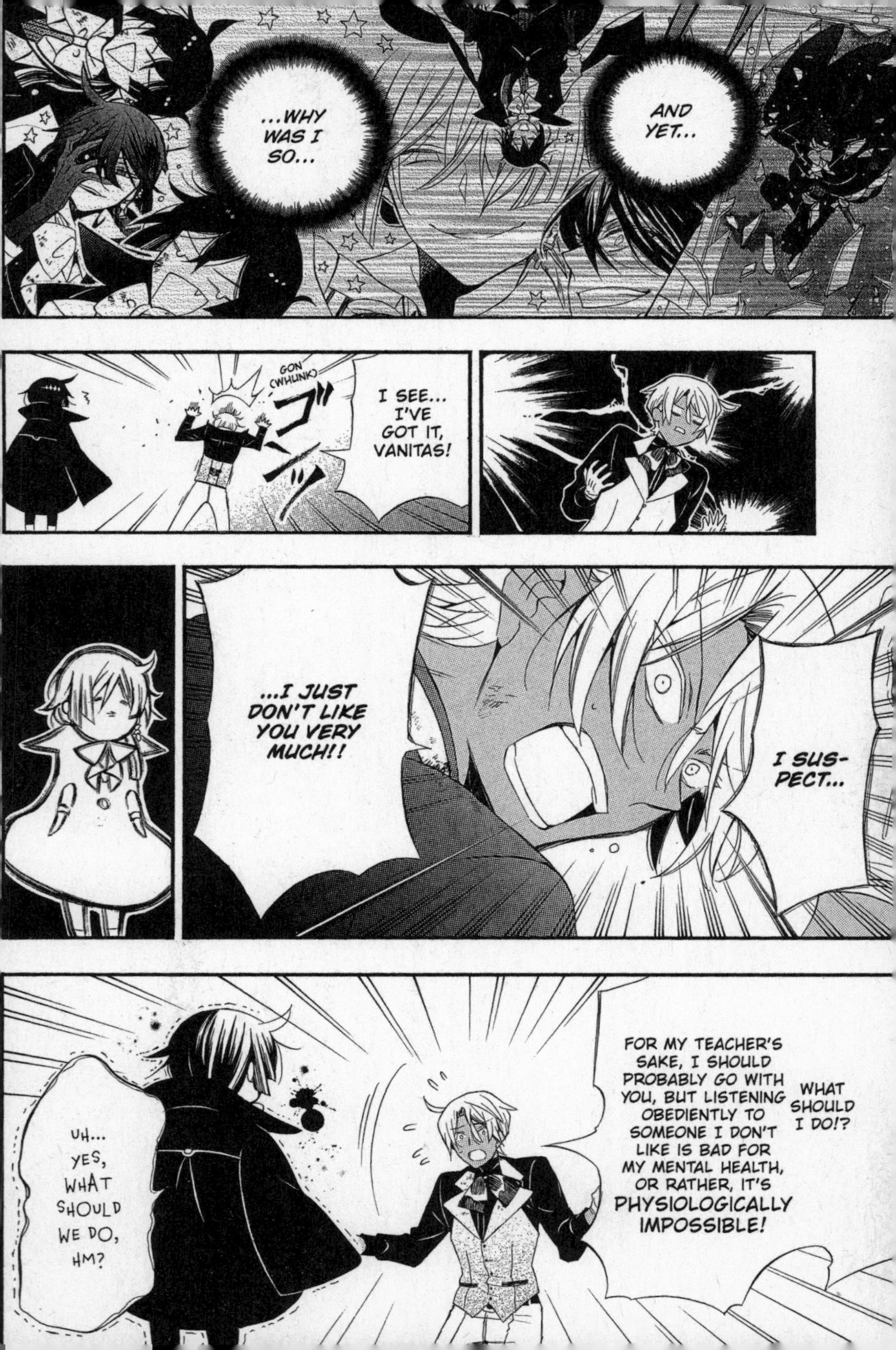
AND YET...
...WHY WAS I SO...
...
GON (WHUNK)
ゴン
I SEE... I'VE GOT IT, VANITAS!
I SUS-PECT...
...I JUST DON'T LIKE YOU VERY MUCH!!
WHAT SHOULD I DO!?
FOR MY TEACHER'S SAKE, I SHOULD PROBABLY GO WITH YOU, BUT LISTENING OBEDIENTLY TO SOMEONE I DON'T LIKE IS BAD FOR MY MENTAL HEALTH, OR RATHER, IT'S PHYSIOLOGICALLY IMPOSSIBLE!
UH... YES, WHAT SHOULD WE DO, HM?

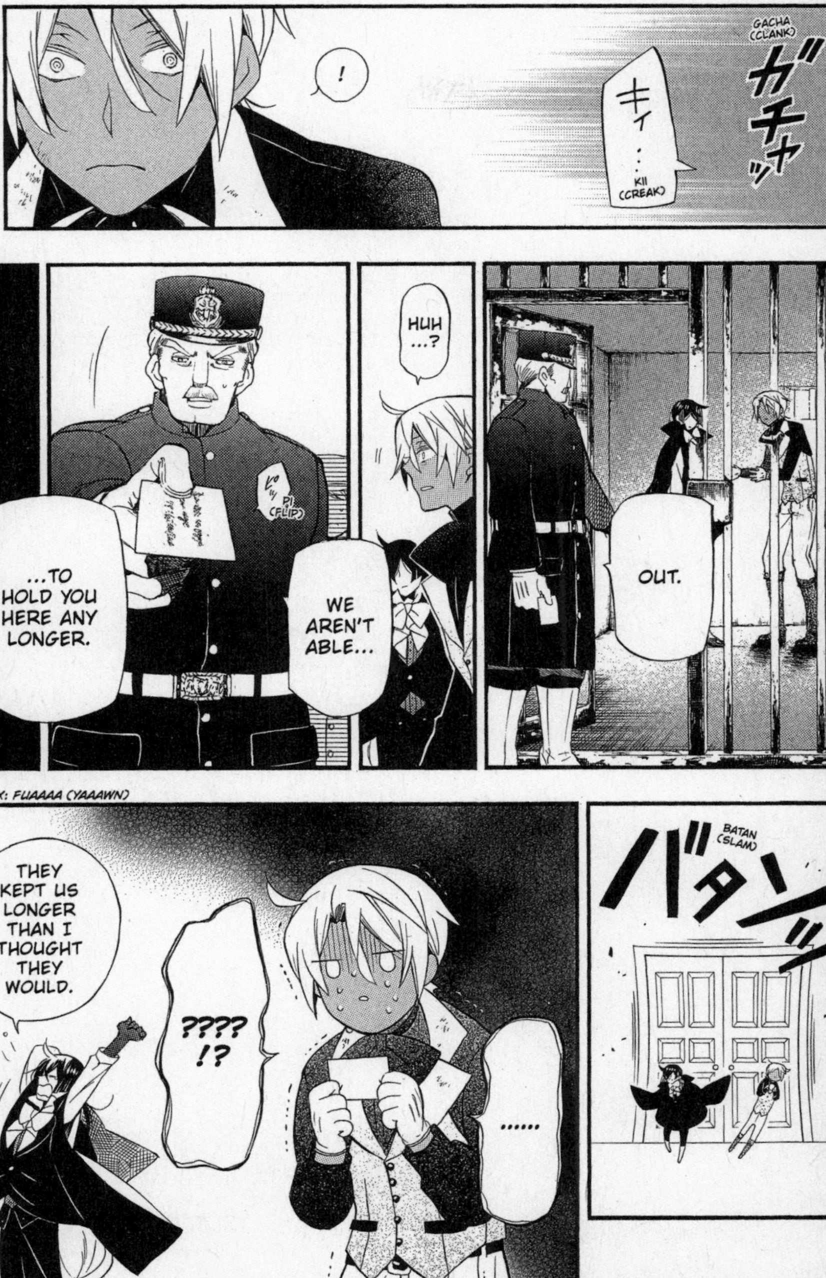
GACHA (CLANK)
ガチャッ
キィ…
KII (CREAK)
!
OUT.
HUH …?
WE AREN'T ABLE…
…TO HOLD YOU HERE ANY LONGER.
PI (FLIP)
SFX: FUAAAA (YAAAWN)
BATAN (SLAM)
バタンッ
……
????!?
THEY KEPT US LONGER THAN I THOUGHT THEY WOULD.

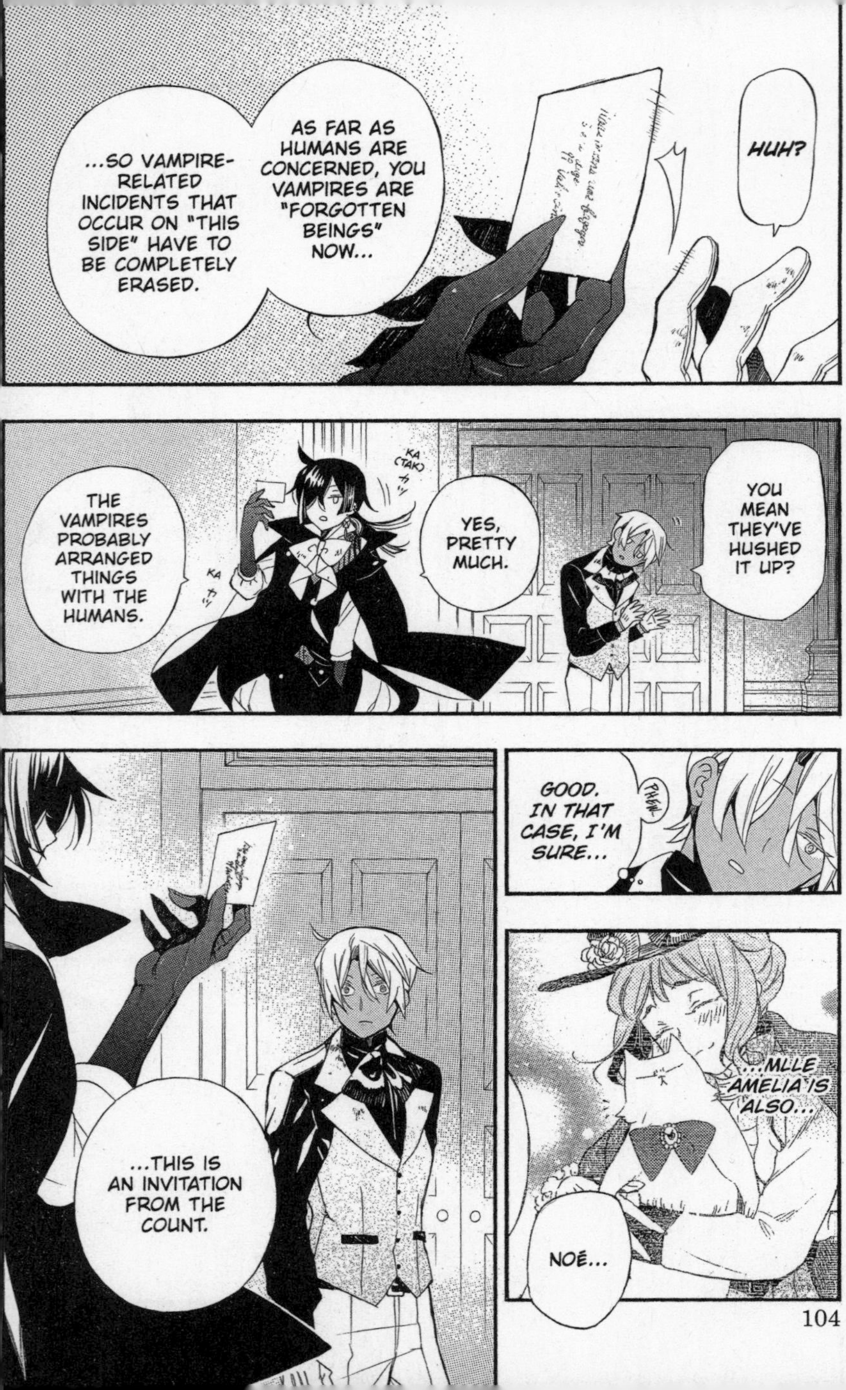
HUH?
AS FAR AS HUMANS ARE CONCERNED, YOU VAMPIRES ARE "FORGOTTEN BEINGS" NOW...
...SO VAMPIRE-RELATED INCIDENTS THAT OCCUR ON "THIS SIDE" HAVE TO BE COMPLETELY ERASED.
YOU MEAN THEY'VE HUSHED IT UP?
YES, PRETTY MUCH.
KA (TAK)
KA
THE VAMPIRES PROBABLY ARRANGED THINGS WITH THE HUMANS.
PHEW
GOOD. IN THAT CASE, I'M SURE...
...MLLE AMELIA IS ALSO...
NOÉ...
...THIS IS AN INVITATION FROM THE COUNT.

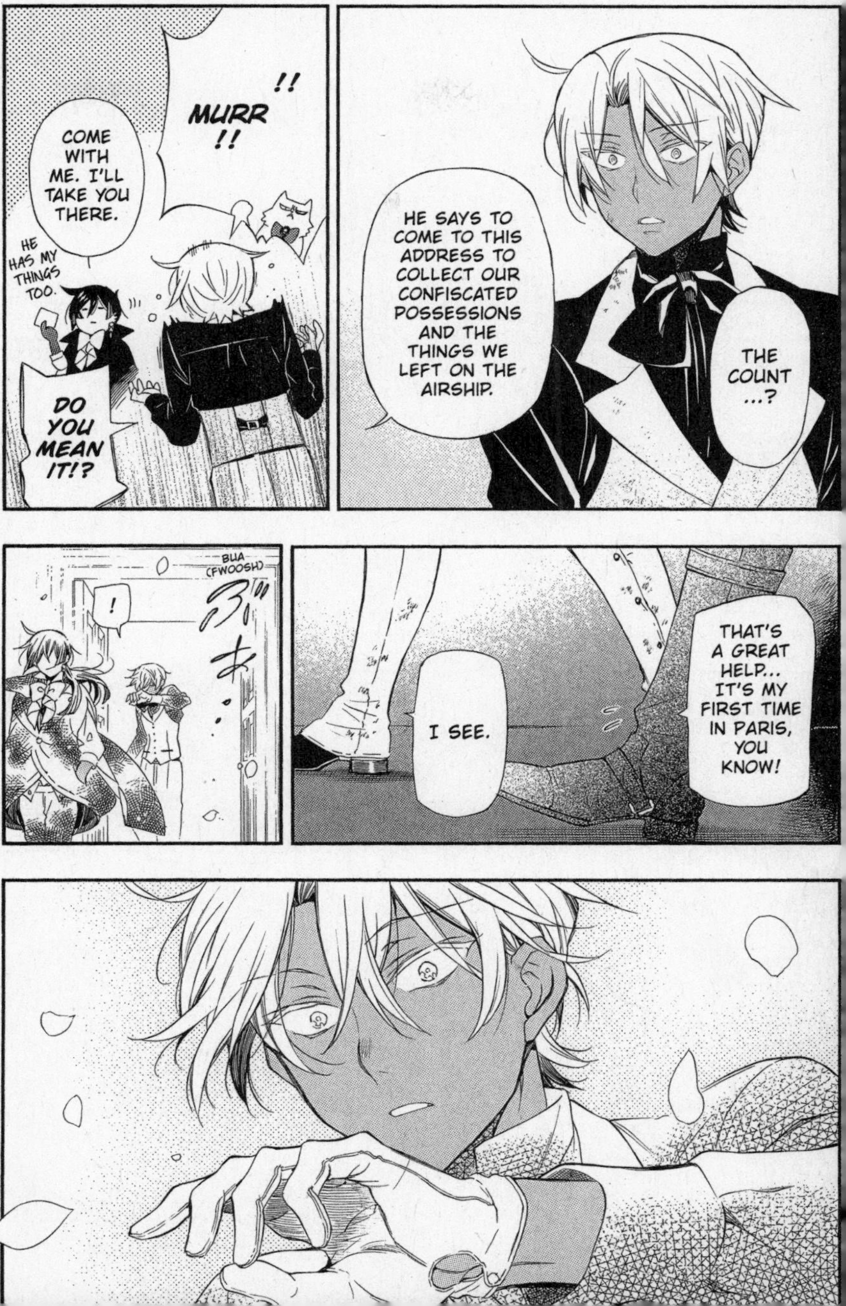
THE COUNT ...?
HE SAYS TO COME TO THIS ADDRESS TO COLLECT OUR CONFISCATED POSSESSIONS AND THE THINGS WE LEFT ON THE AIRSHIP.
!!
MURR !!
COME WITH ME. I'LL TAKE YOU THERE.
HE HAS MY THINGS TOO.
DO YOU MEAN IT!?
THAT'S A GREAT HELP... IT'S MY FIRST TIME IN PARIS, YOU KNOW!
I SEE.
BUA (FWOOSH)
!

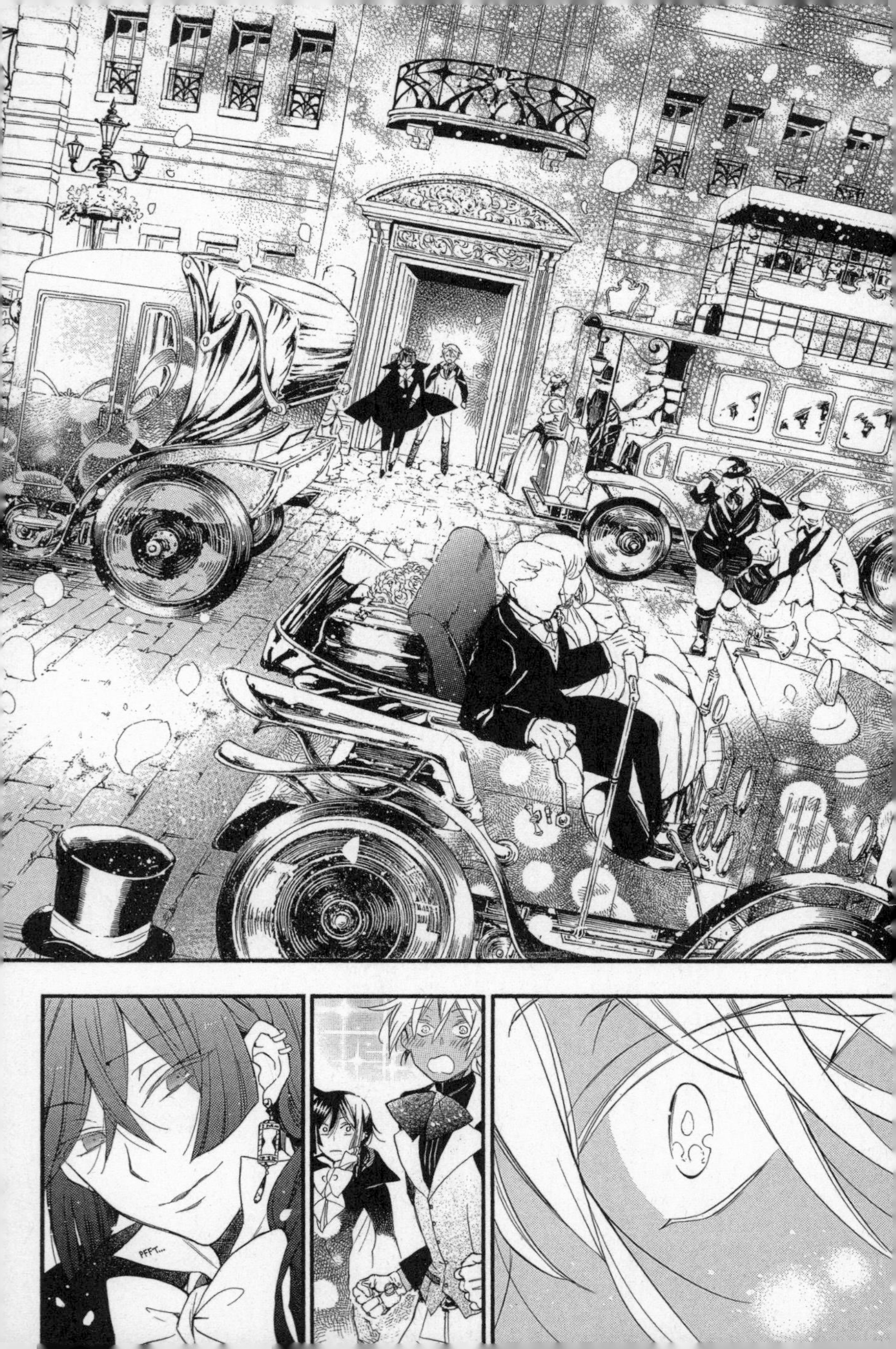
PFFT...

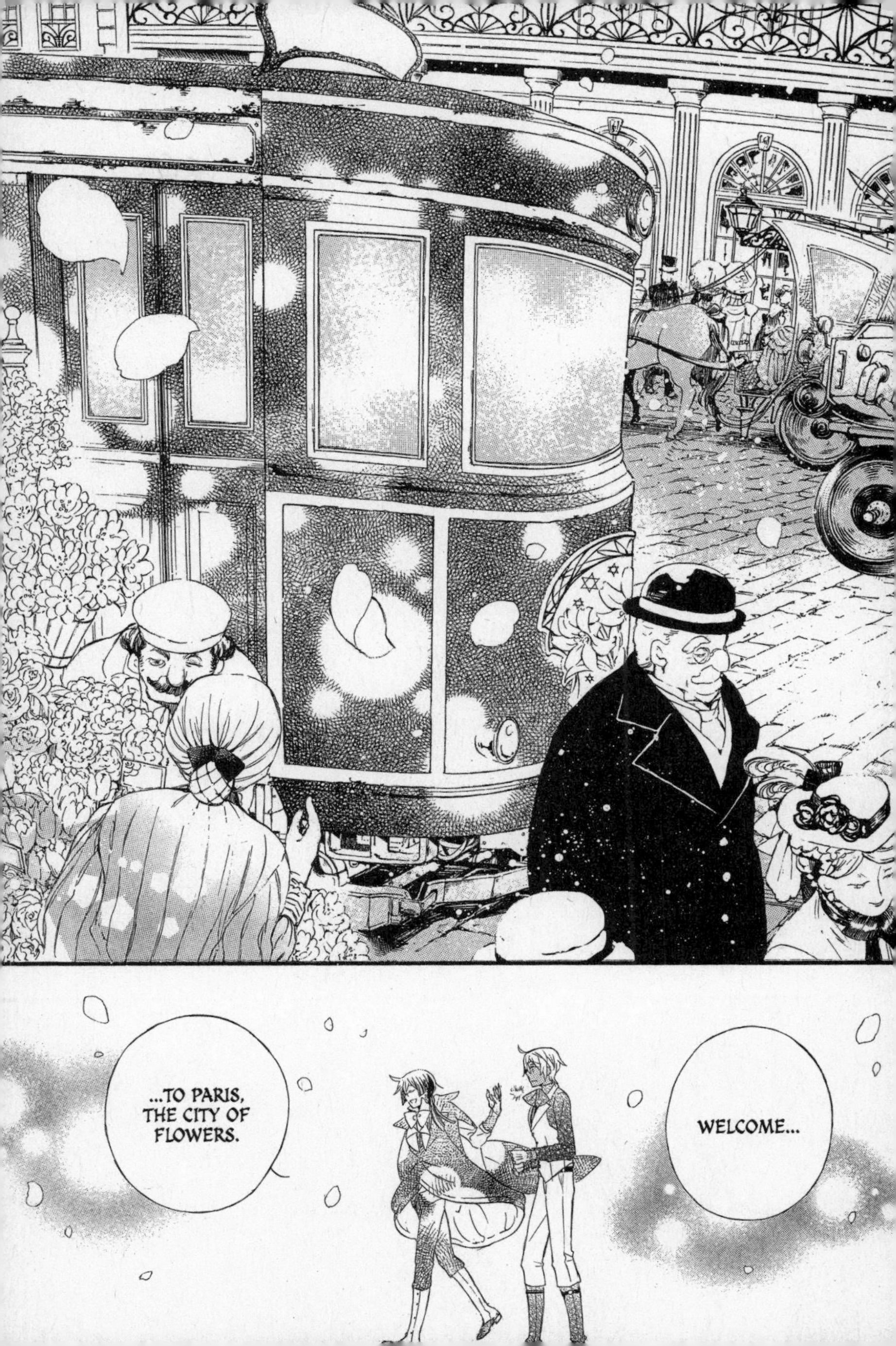
WELCOME...
...TO PARIS, THE CITY OF FLOWERS.

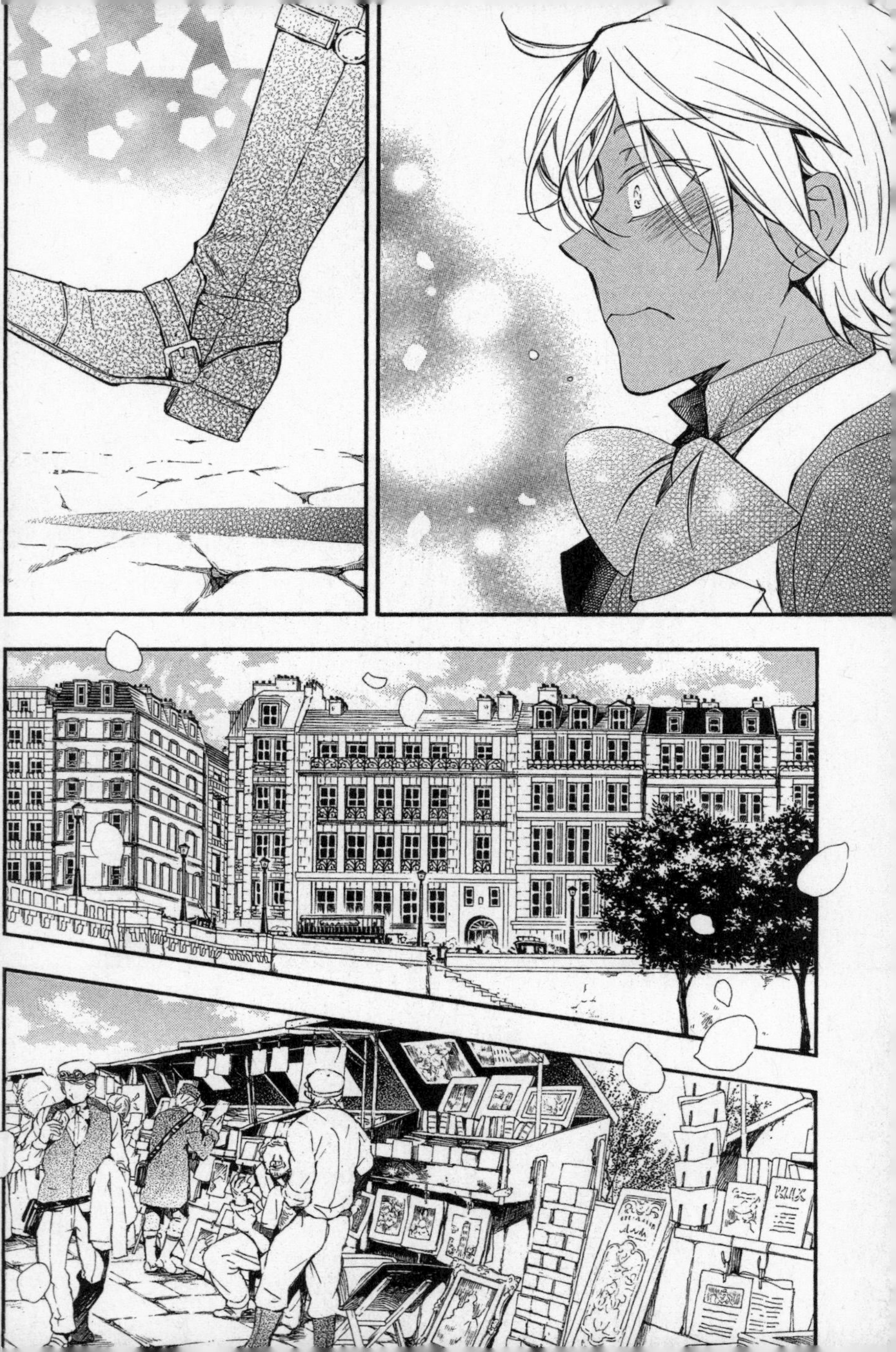

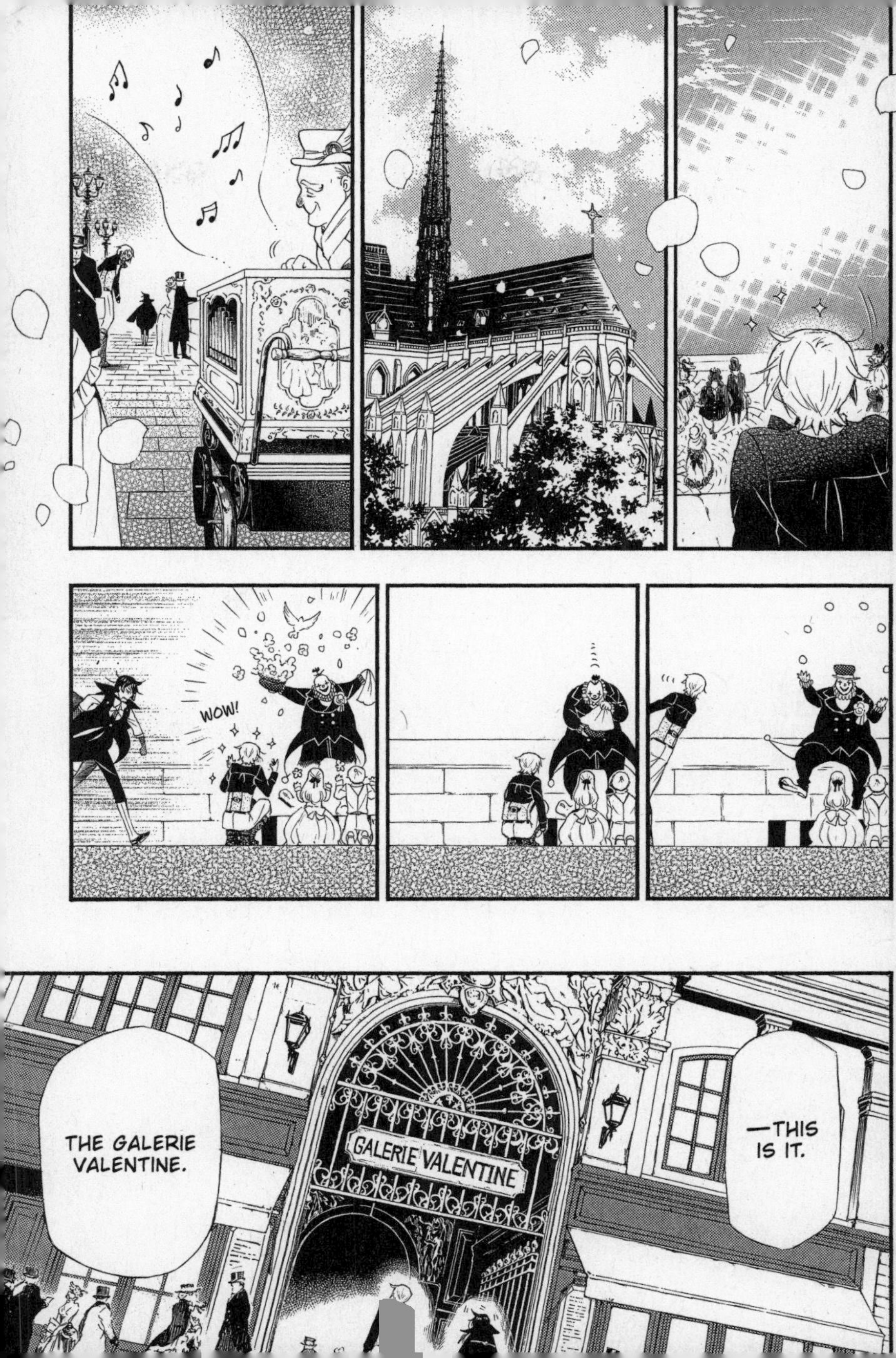
WOW!
—THIS IS IT.
GALERIE VALENTINE
THE GALERIE VALENTINE.

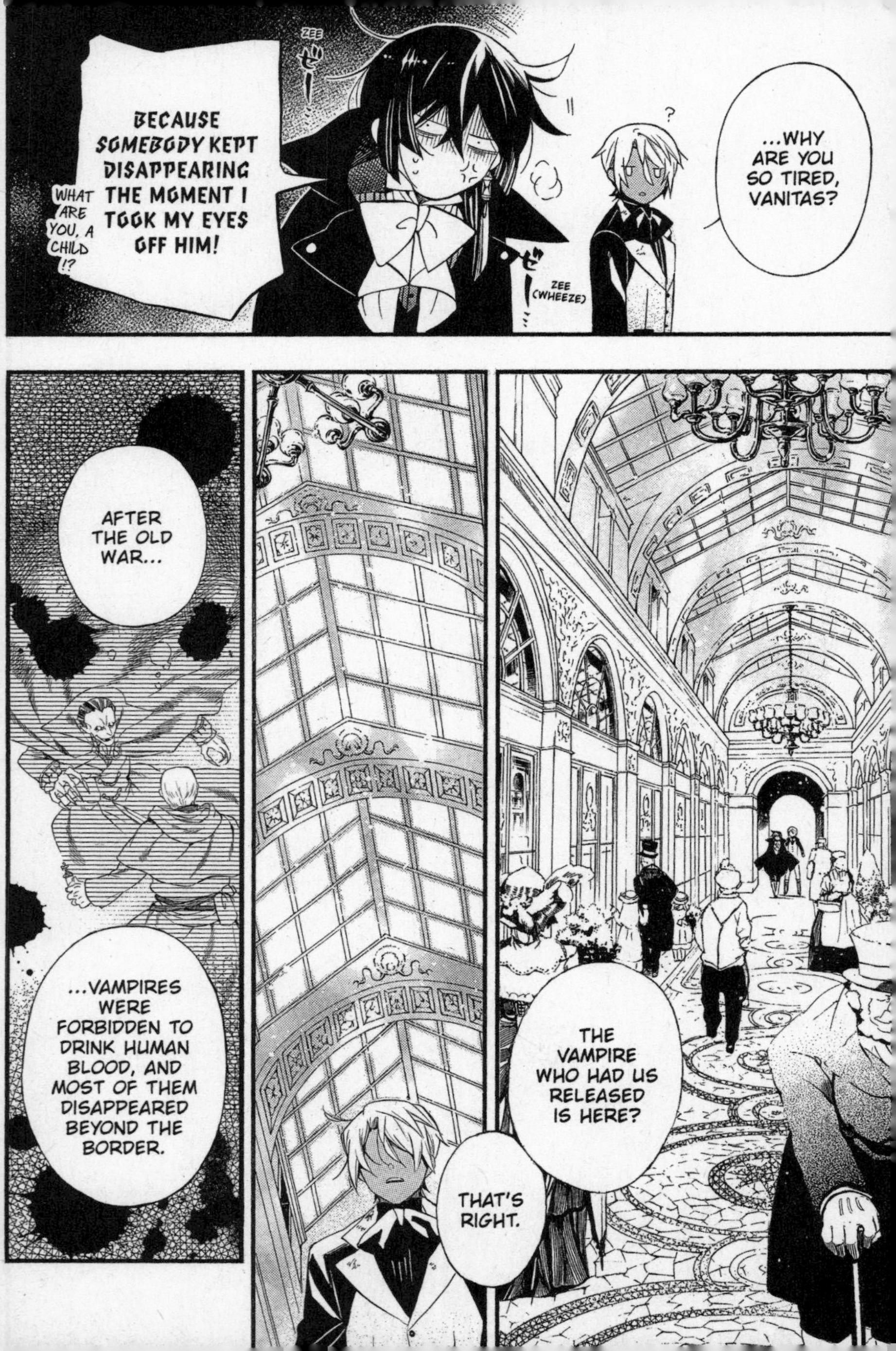
...WHY ARE YOU SO TIRED, VANITAS?
?
ZEE (WHEEZE)
ZEE
BECAUSE SOMEBODY KEPT DISAPPEARING THE MOMENT I TOOK MY EYES OFF HIM!
WHAT ARE YOU, A CHILD!?
THE VAMPIRE WHO HAD US RELEASED IS HERE?
THAT'S RIGHT.
AFTER THE OLD WAR...
...VAMPIRES WERE FORBIDDEN TO DRINK HUMAN BLOOD, AND MOST OF THEM DISAPPEARED BEYOND THE BORDER.

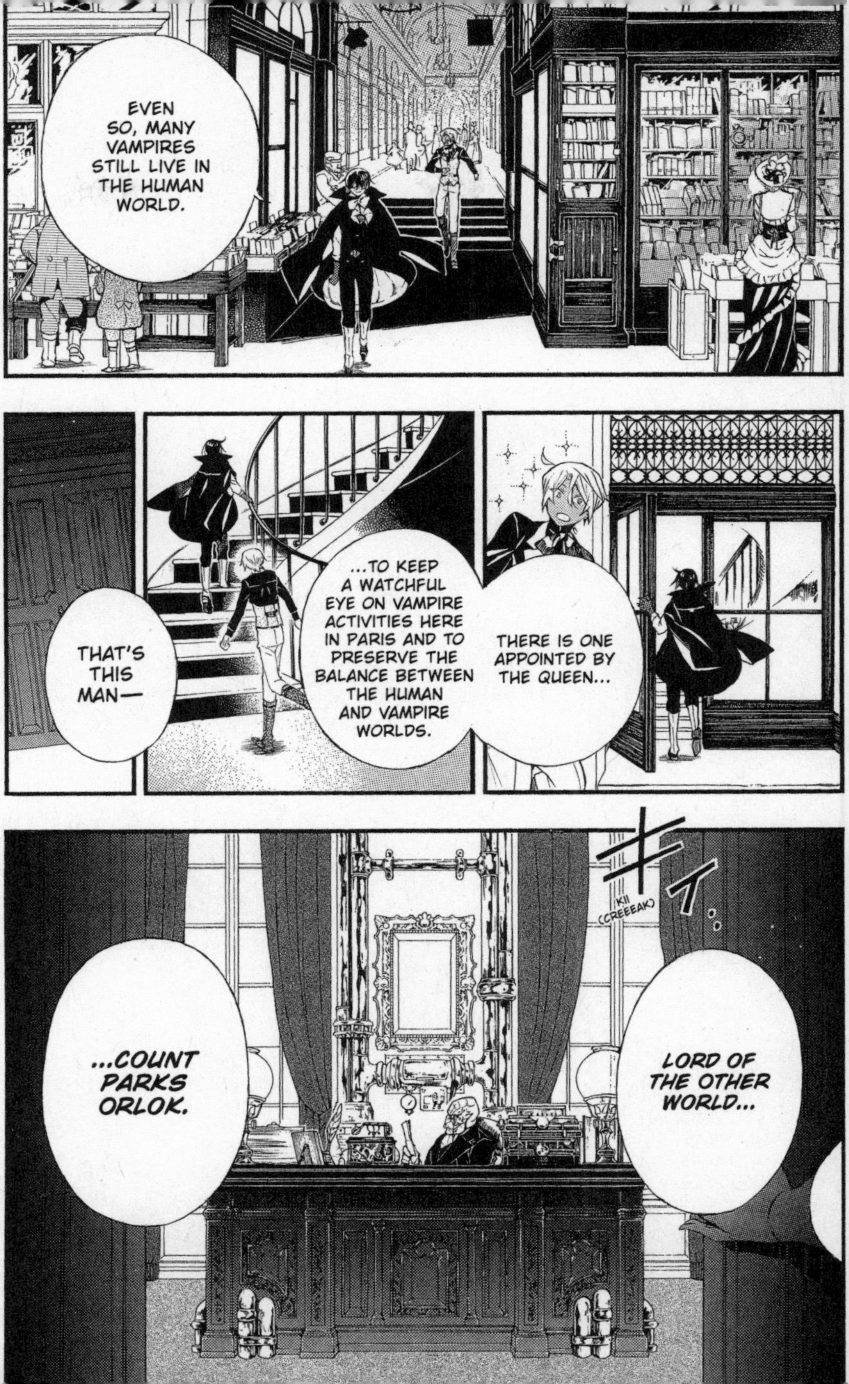
EVEN SO, MANY VAMPIRES STILL LIVE IN THE HUMAN WORLD.
THERE IS ONE APPOINTED BY THE QUEEN...
...TO KEEP A WATCHFUL EYE ON VAMPIRE ACTIVITIES HERE IN PARIS AND TO PRESERVE THE BALANCE BETWEEN THE HUMAN AND VAMPIRE WORLDS.
THAT'S THIS MAN—
KII (CREEEAK)
LORD OF THE OTHER WORLD...
...COUNT PARKS ORLOK.

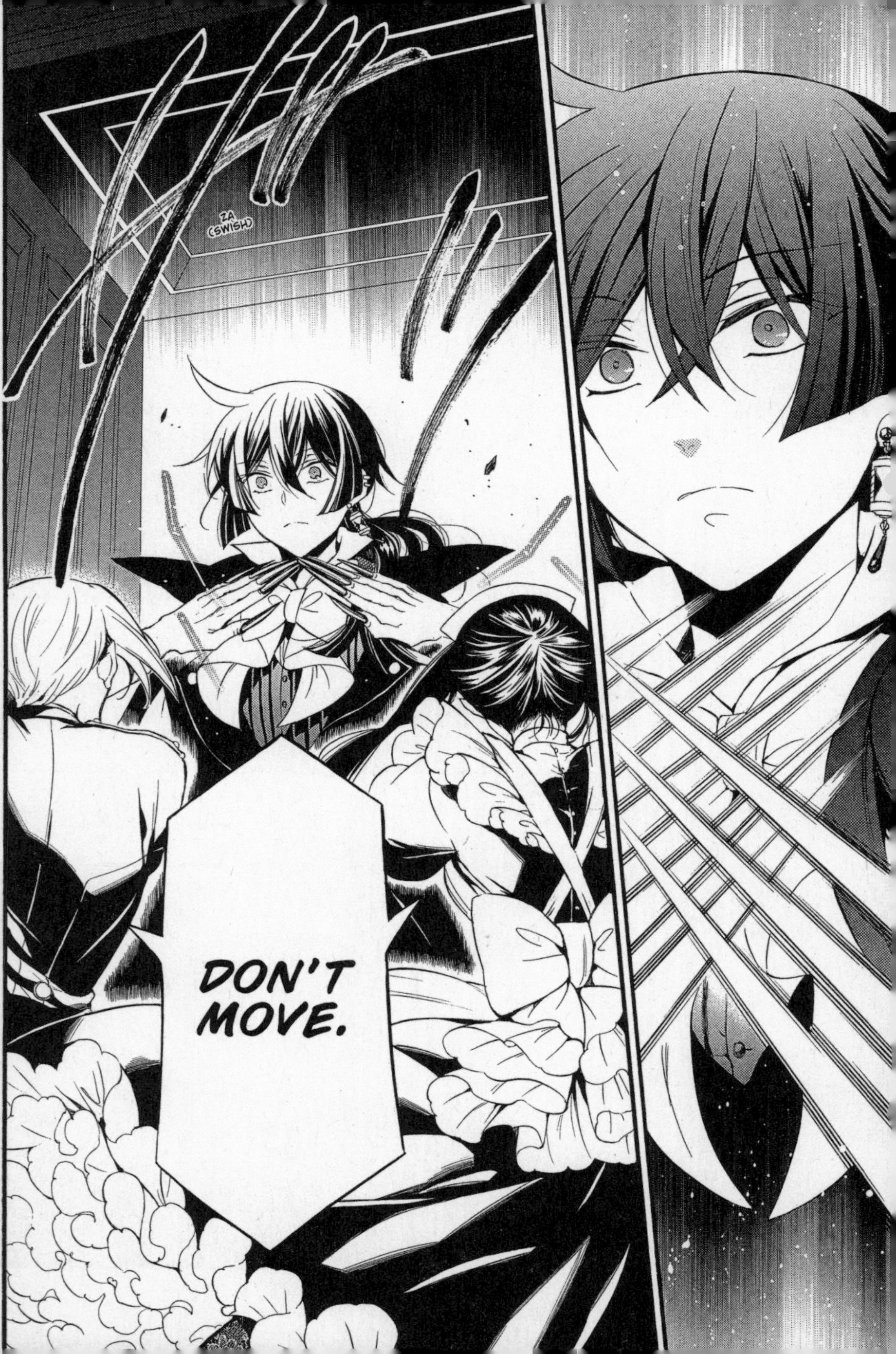
ZA (SWISH)
DON'T MOVE.

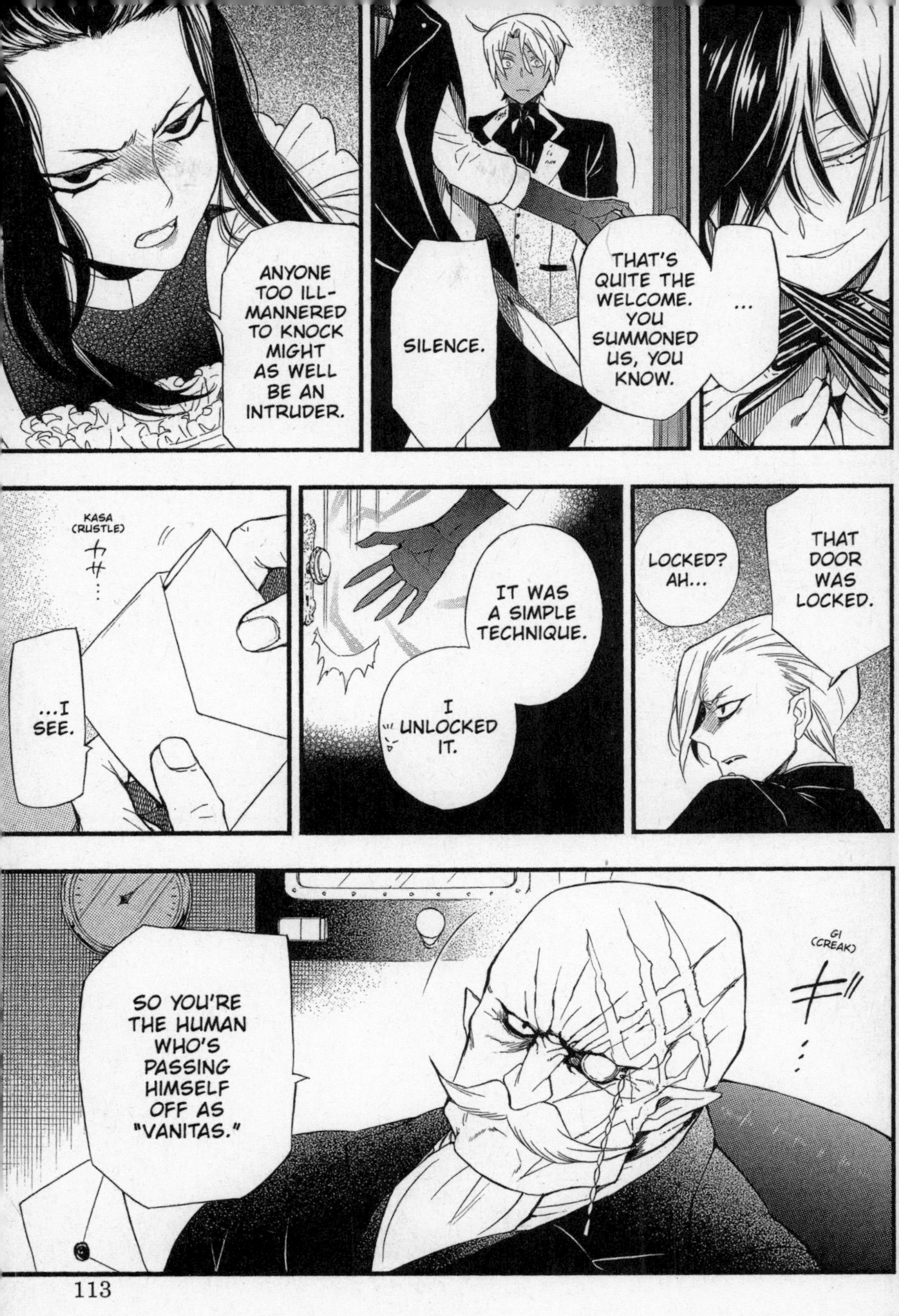
...
THAT'S QUITE THE WELCOME. YOU SUMMONED US, YOU KNOW.
SILENCE.
ANYONE TOO ILL-MANNERED TO KNOCK MIGHT AS WELL BE AN INTRUDER.
THAT DOOR WAS LOCKED.
LOCKED? AH...
IT WAS A SIMPLE TECHNIQUE.
I UNLOCKED IT.
KASA (RUSTLE)
...I SEE.
GI (CREAK)
SO YOU'RE THE HUMAN WHO'S PASSING HIMSELF OFF AS "VANITAS."

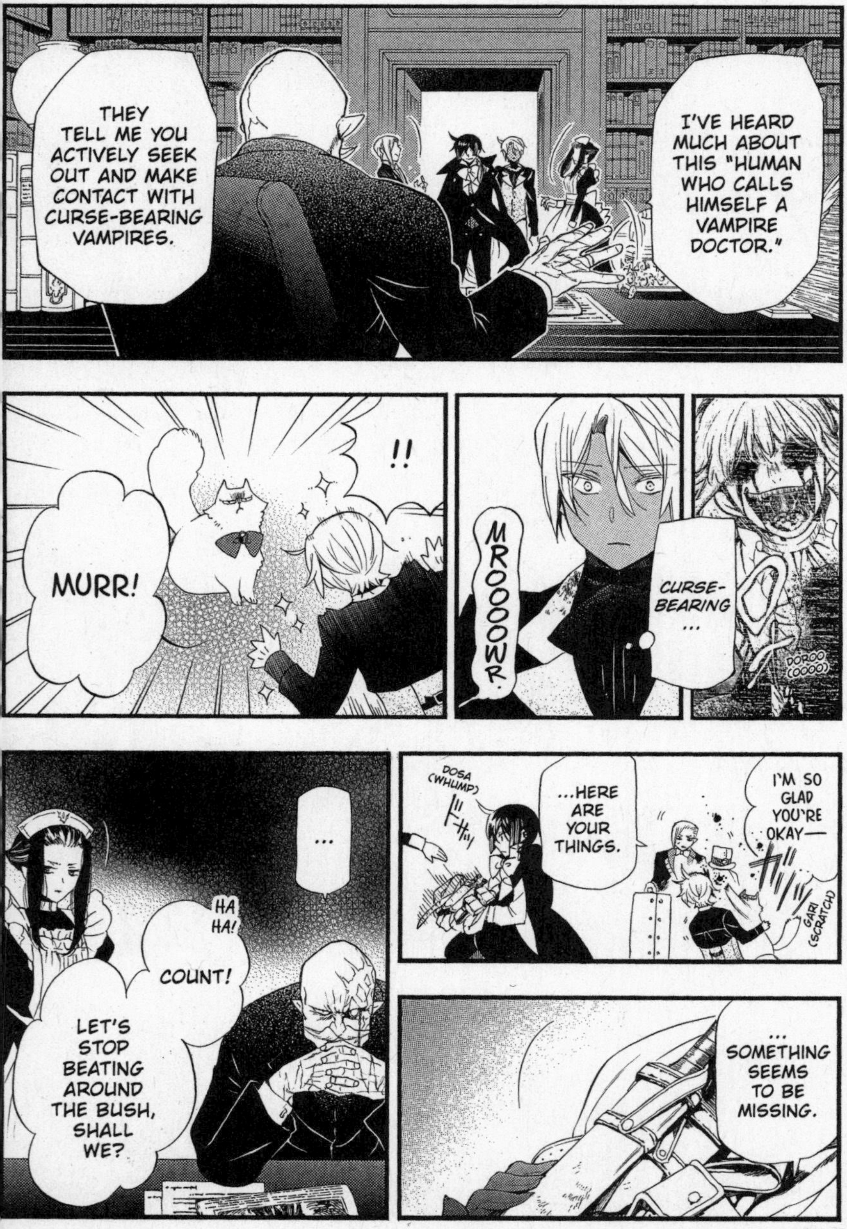
I'VE HEARD MUCH ABOUT THIS "HUMAN WHO CALLS HIMSELF A VAMPIRE DOCTOR."
THEY TELL ME YOU ACTIVELY SEEK OUT AND MAKE CONTACT WITH CURSE-BEARING VAMPIRES.
DOROO (OOOO)
CURSE-BEARING ...
MROOOOOWR.
!!
MURR!
I'M SO GLAD YOU'RE OKAY—
GARI (SCRATCH)
...HERE ARE YOUR THINGS.
DOSA (WHUMP)
... SOMETHING SEEMS TO BE MISSING.
...
HA HA!
COUNT!
LET'S STOP BEATING AROUND THE BUSH, SHALL WE?

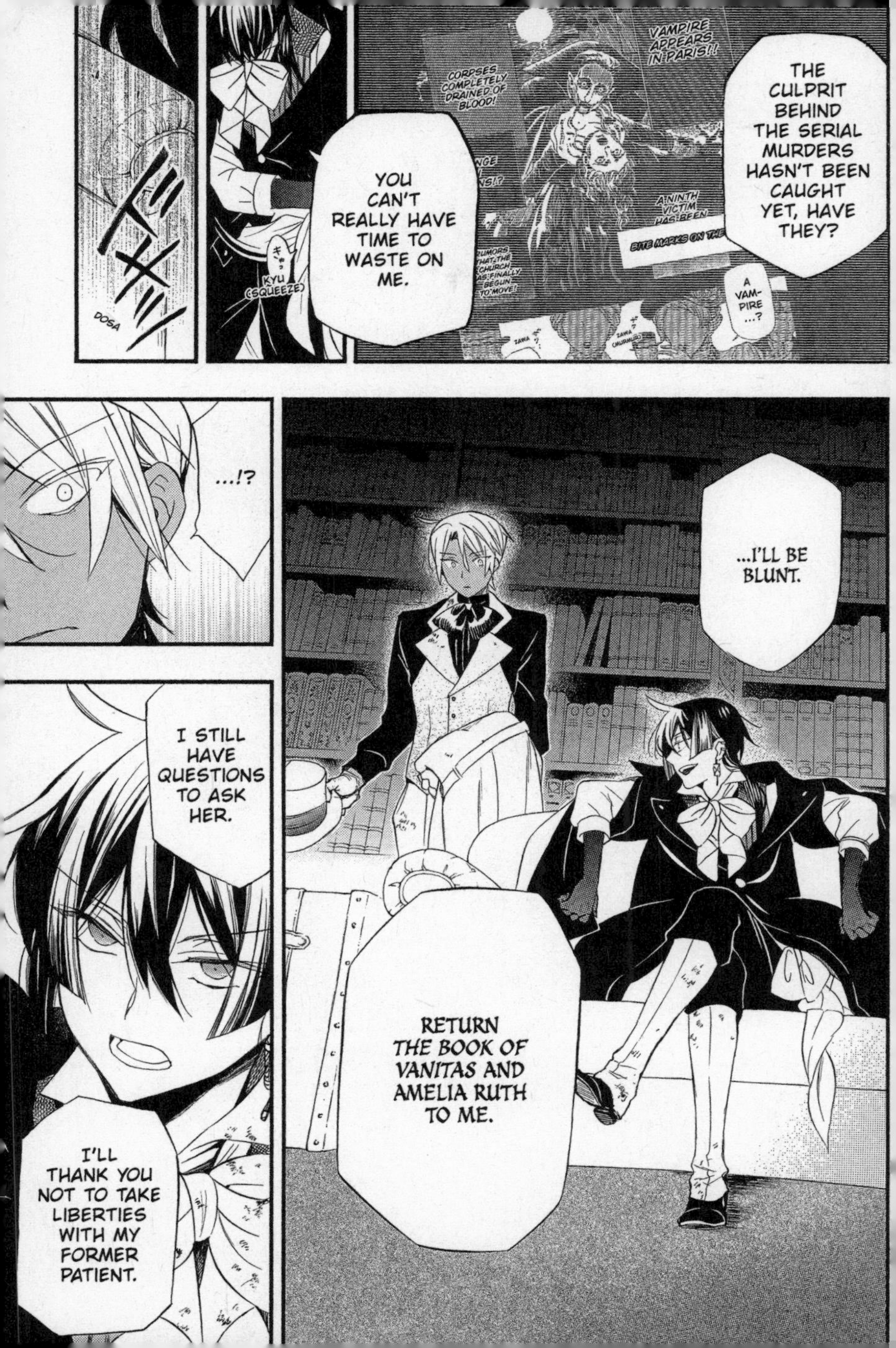

VAMPIRE APPEARS IN PARIS!!
THE CULPRIT BEHIND THE SERIAL MURDERS HASN'T BEEN CAUGHT YET, HAVE THEY?
CORPSES COMPLETELY DRAINED OF BLOOD!
A NINTH VICTIM HAS BEEN
BITE MARKS ON THE
RUMORS THAT THE CHURCH HAS FINALLY BEGUN TO MOVE!
A VAMPIRE ...?
ZAWA (MURMUR)
ZAWA
YOU CAN'T REALLY HAVE TIME TO WASTE ON ME.
KYU (SQUEEZE)
DOSA
...I'LL BE BLUNT.
RETURN THE BOOK OF VANITAS AND AMELIA RUTH TO ME.
...!?
I STILL HAVE QUESTIONS TO ASK HER.
I'LL THANK YOU NOT TO TAKE LIBERTIES WITH MY FORMER PATIENT.

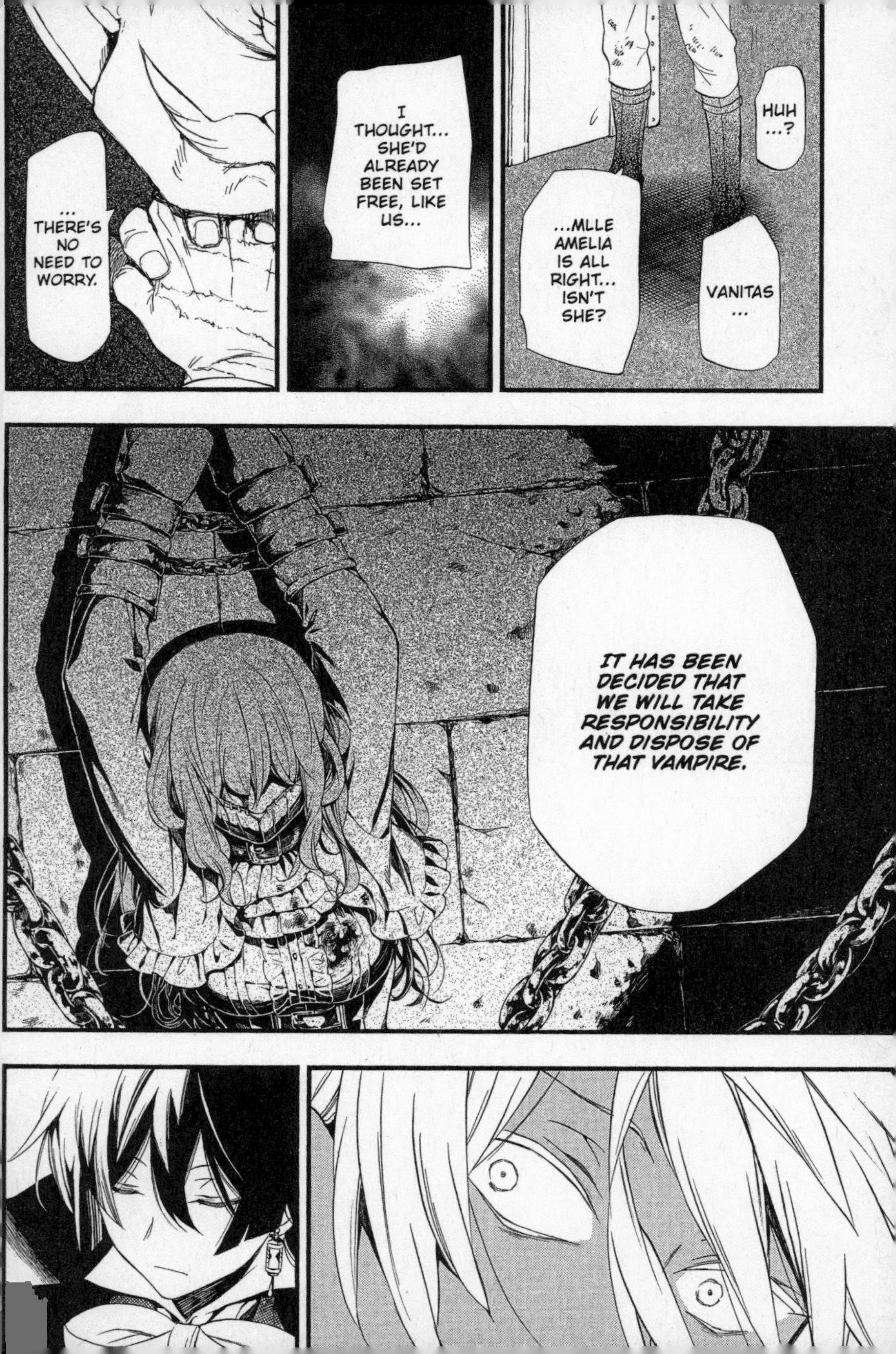
HUH ...?
VANITAS ...
...MLLE AMELIA IS ALL RIGHT... ISN'T SHE?
I THOUGHT... SHE'D ALREADY BEEN SET FREE, LIKE US...
... THERE'S NO NEED TO WORRY.
IT HAS BEEN DECIDED THAT WE WILL TAKE RESPONSIBILITY AND DISPOSE OF THAT VAMPIRE.

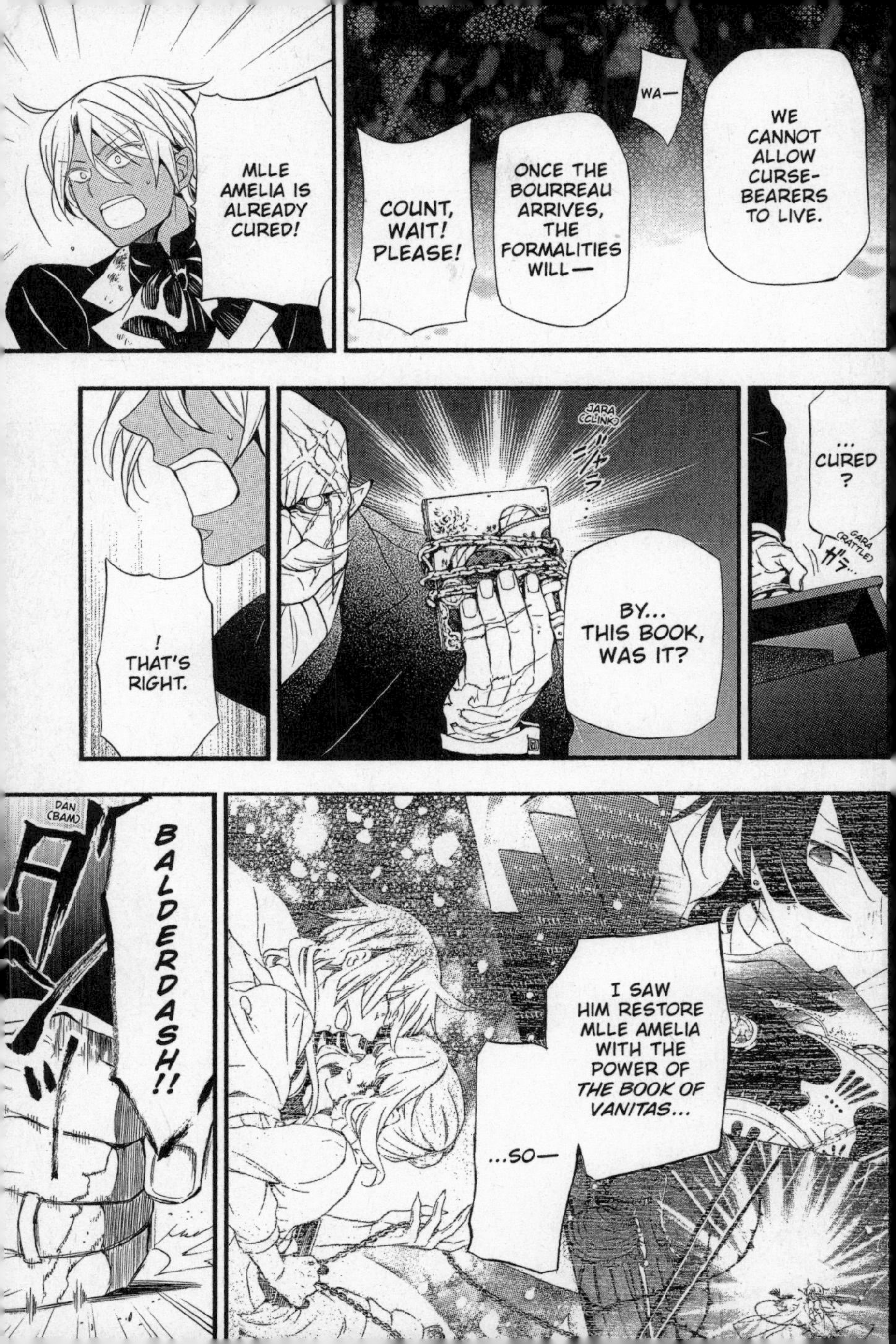
WA—
WE CANNOT ALLOW CURSE-BEARERS TO LIVE.
ONCE THE BOURREAU ARRIVES, THE FORMALITIES WILL—
COUNT, WAIT! PLEASE!
MLLE AMELIA IS ALREADY CURED!
...CURED?
GARA (RATTLE)
JARA (CLINK)
BY... THIS BOOK, WAS IT?
! THAT'S RIGHT.
I SAW HIM RESTORE MLLE AMELIA WITH THE POWER OF *THE BOOK OF VANITAS*...
...SO—
DAN (BAM)
BALDERDASH!!

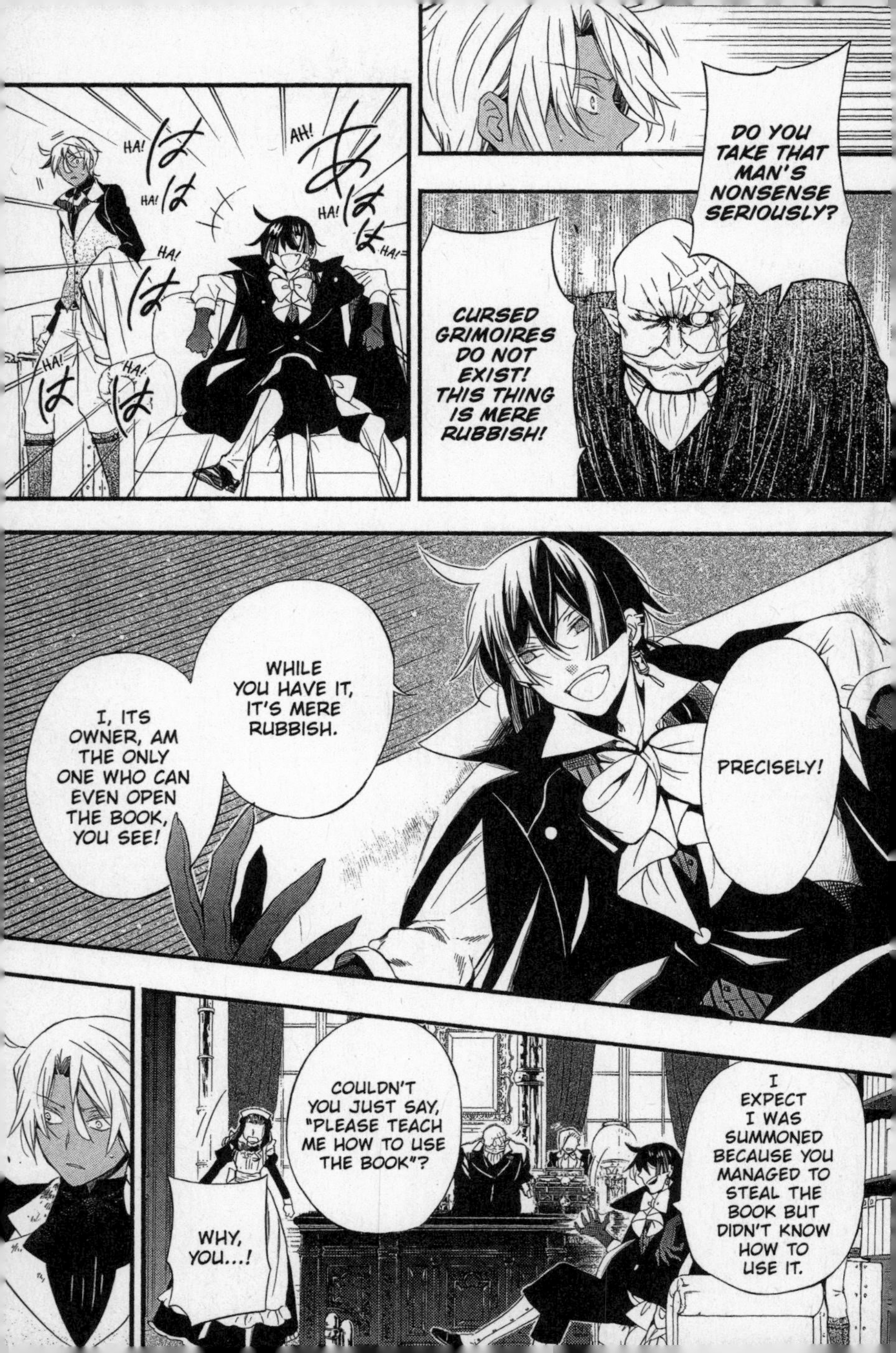
DO YOU TAKE THAT MAN'S NONSENSE SERIOUSLY?
CURSED GRIMOIRES DO NOT EXIST! THIS THING IS MERE RUBBISH!
AH! あ
HA! は
HA! は
HA! は
HA! は
HA! は
HA! は
PRECISELY!
WHILE YOU HAVE IT, IT'S MERE RUBBISH.
I, ITS OWNER, AM THE ONLY ONE WHO CAN EVEN OPEN THE BOOK, YOU SEE!
I EXPECT I WAS SUMMONED BECAUSE YOU MANAGED TO STEAL THE BOOK BUT DIDN'T KNOW HOW TO USE IT.
COULDN'T YOU JUST SAY, "PLEASE TEACH ME HOW TO USE THE BOOK"?
WHY, YOU...!

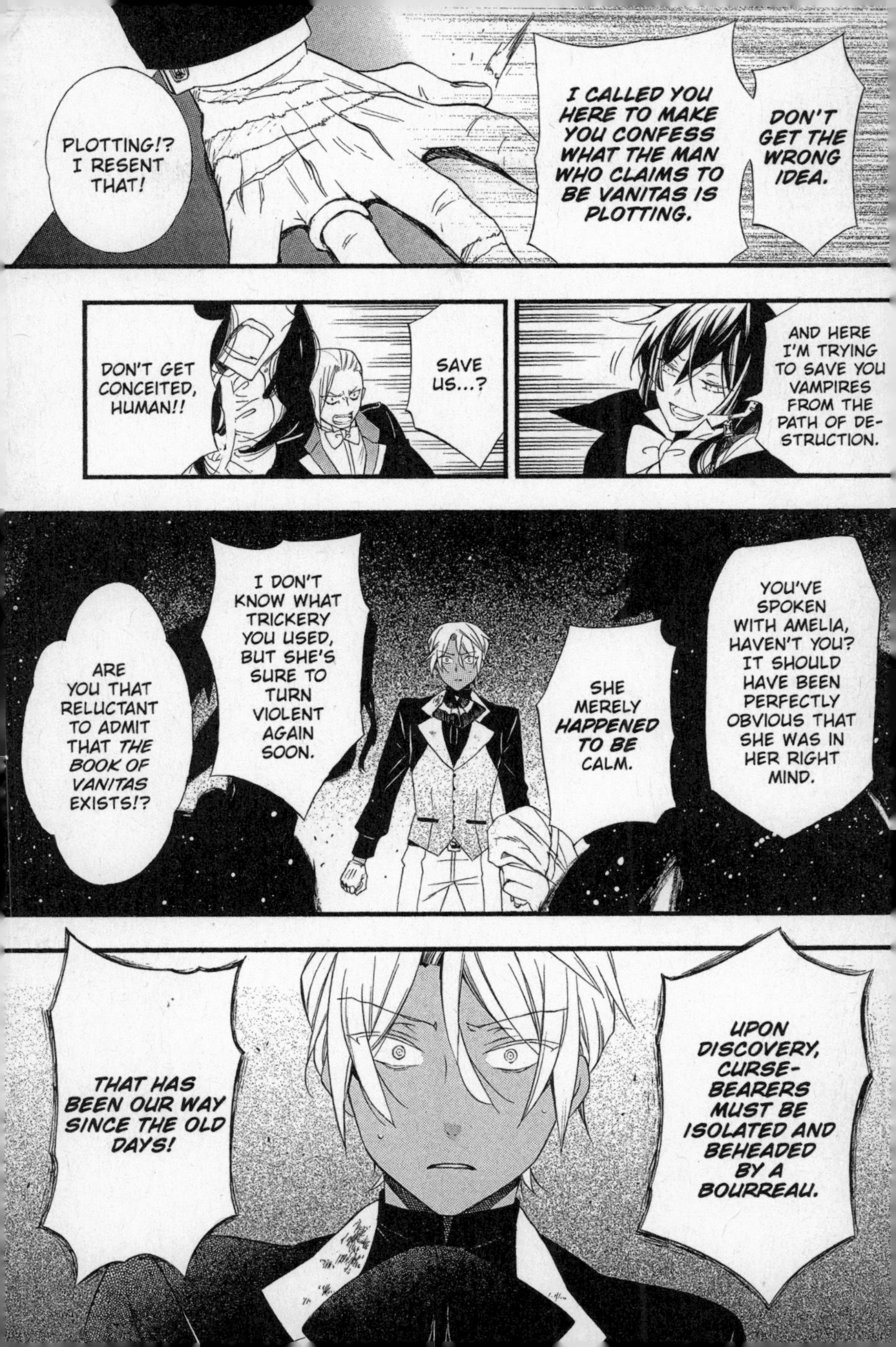

DON'T GET THE WRONG IDEA.
I CALLED YOU HERE TO MAKE YOU CONFESS WHAT THE MAN WHO CLAIMS TO BE VANITAS IS PLOTTING.
PLOTTING!? I RESENT THAT!
AND HERE I'M TRYING TO SAVE YOU VAMPIRES FROM THE PATH OF DE-STRUCTION.
SAVE US...?
DON'T GET CONCEITED, HUMAN!!
YOU'VE SPOKEN WITH AMELIA, HAVEN'T YOU? IT SHOULD HAVE BEEN PERFECTLY OBVIOUS THAT SHE WAS IN HER RIGHT MIND.
SHE MERELY *HAPPENED* TO BE CALM.
I DON'T KNOW WHAT TRICKERY YOU USED, BUT SHE'S SURE TO TURN VIOLENT AGAIN SOON.
ARE YOU THAT RELUCTANT TO ADMIT THAT *THE BOOK OF VANITAS* EXISTS!?
UPON DISCOVERY, CURSE-BEARERS MUST BE ISOLATED AND BEHEADED BY A BOURREAU.
THAT HAS BEEN OUR WAY SINCE THE OLD DAYS!

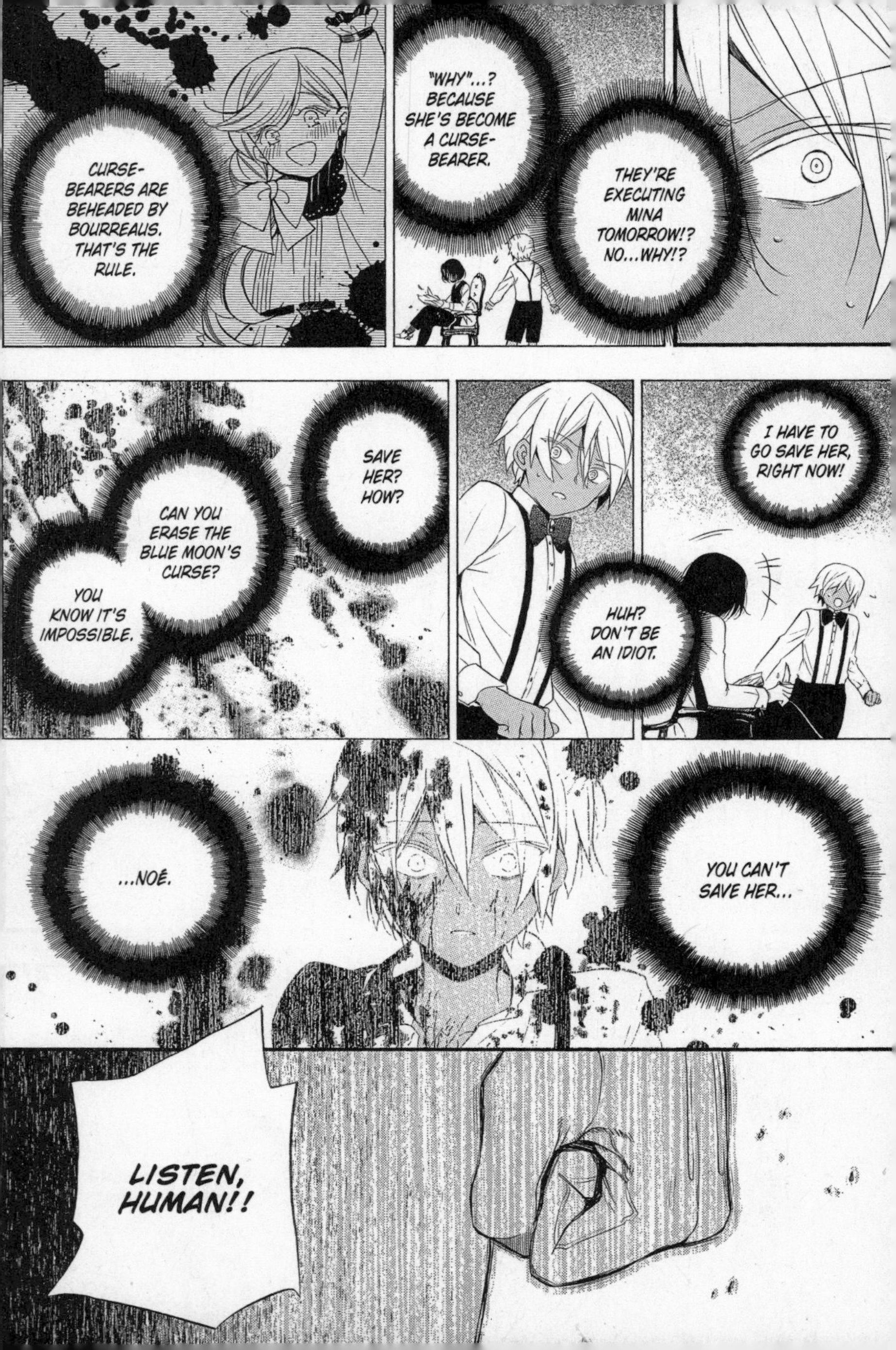
THEY'RE EXECUTING MINA TOMORROW!? NO...WHY!?
"WHY"...? BECAUSE SHE'S BECOME A CURSE-BEARER.
CURSE-BEARERS ARE BEHEADED BY BOURREAUS. THAT'S THE RULE.
I HAVE TO GO SAVE HER, RIGHT NOW!
HUH? DON'T BE AN IDIOT.
SAVE HER? HOW?
CAN YOU ERASE THE BLUE MOON'S CURSE?
YOU KNOW IT'S IMPOSSIBLE.
YOU CAN'T SAVE HER...
...NOÉ.
LISTEN, HUMAN!!

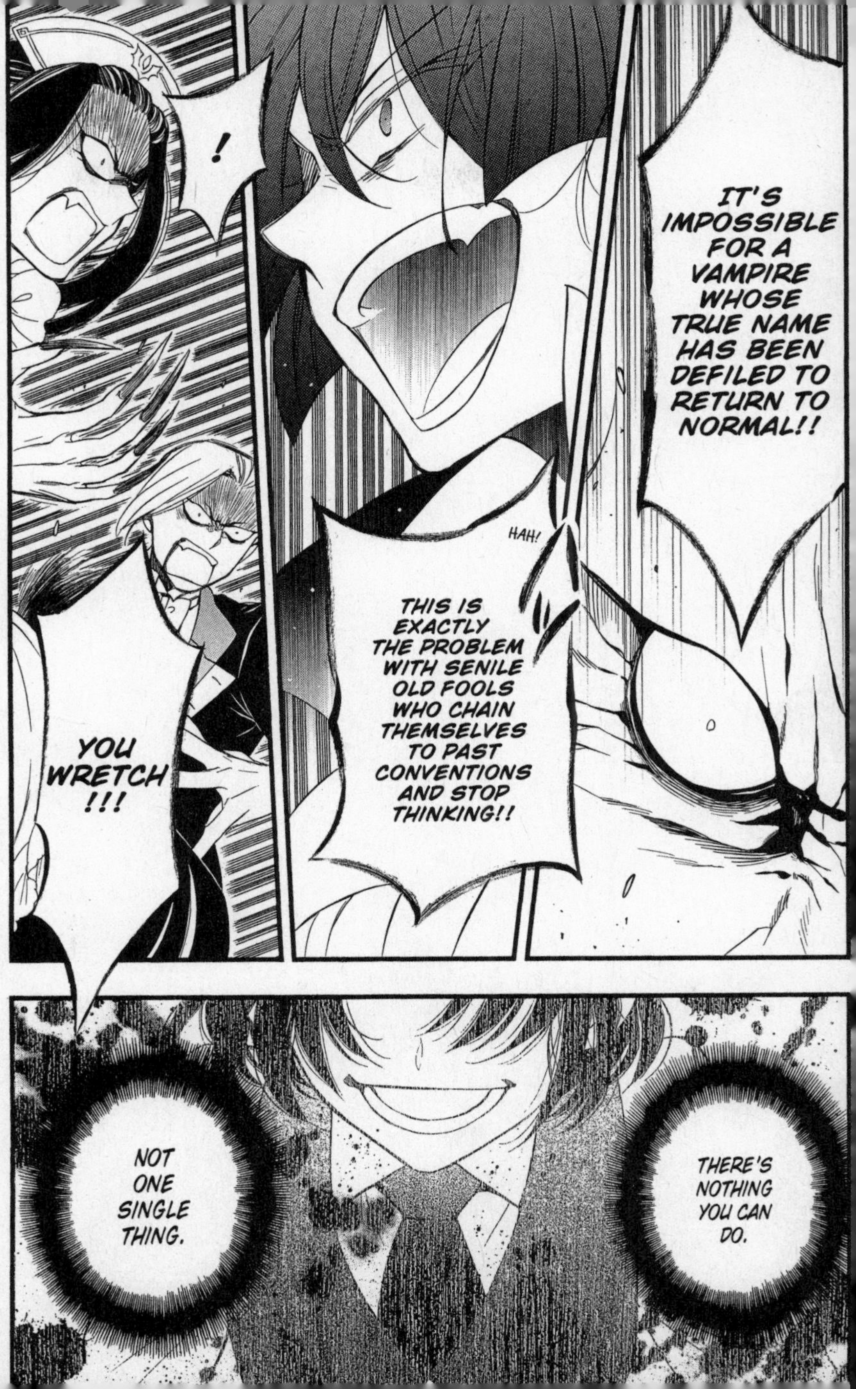
IT'S IMPOSSIBLE FOR A VAMPIRE WHOSE TRUE NAME HAS BEEN DEFILED TO RETURN TO NORMAL!!
HAH!
THIS IS EXACTLY THE PROBLEM WITH SENILE OLD FOOLS WHO CHAIN THEMSELVES TO PAST CONVENTIONS AND STOP THINKING!!
!
YOU WRETCH!!!
THERE'S NOTHING YOU CAN DO.
NOT ONE SINGLE THING.

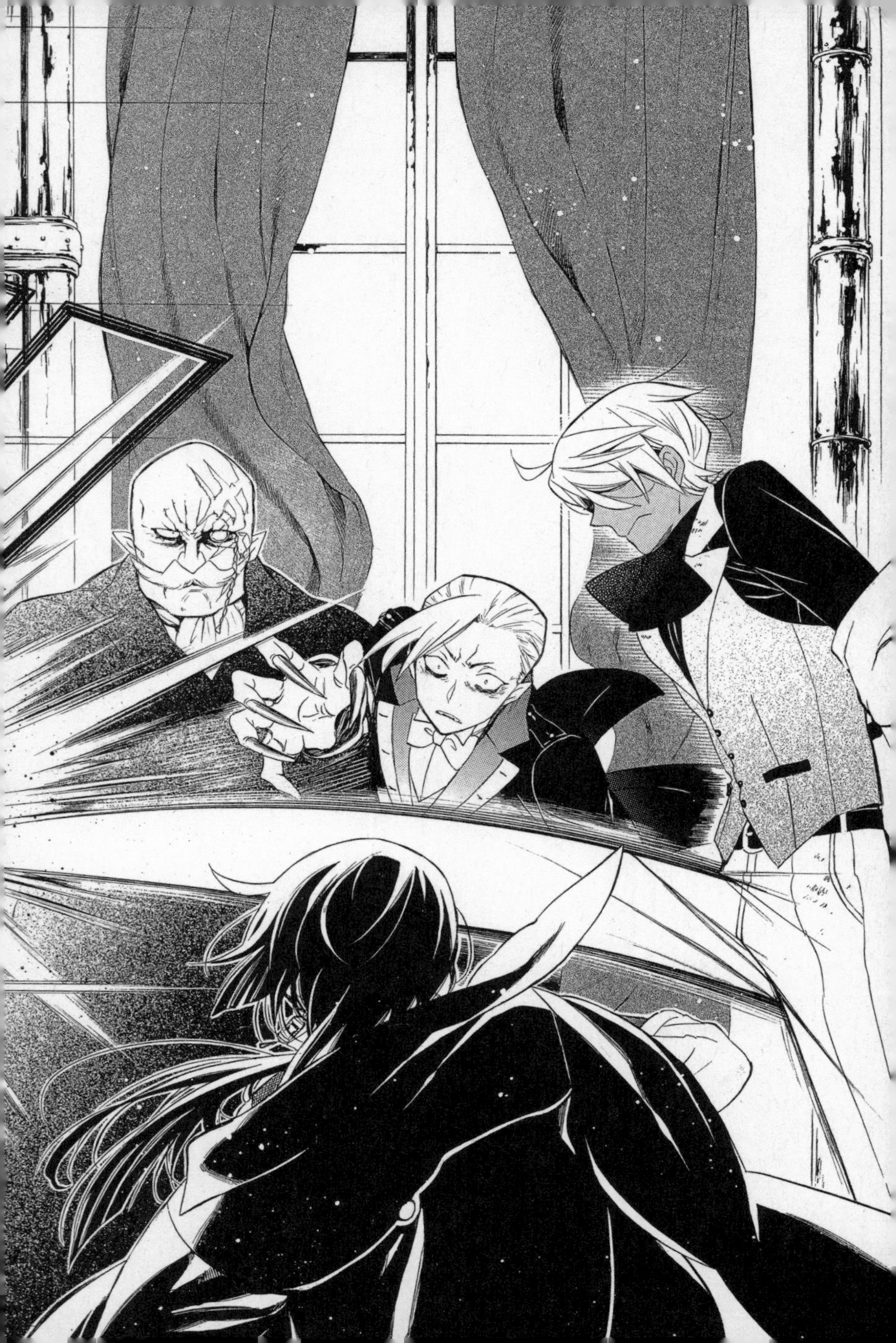

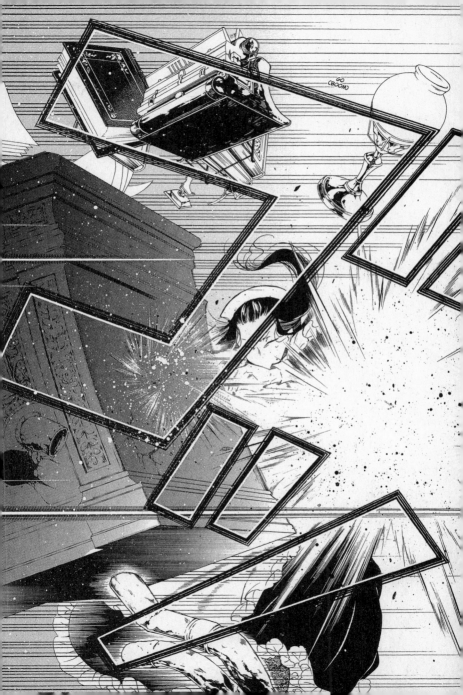

GO
(BOOM)

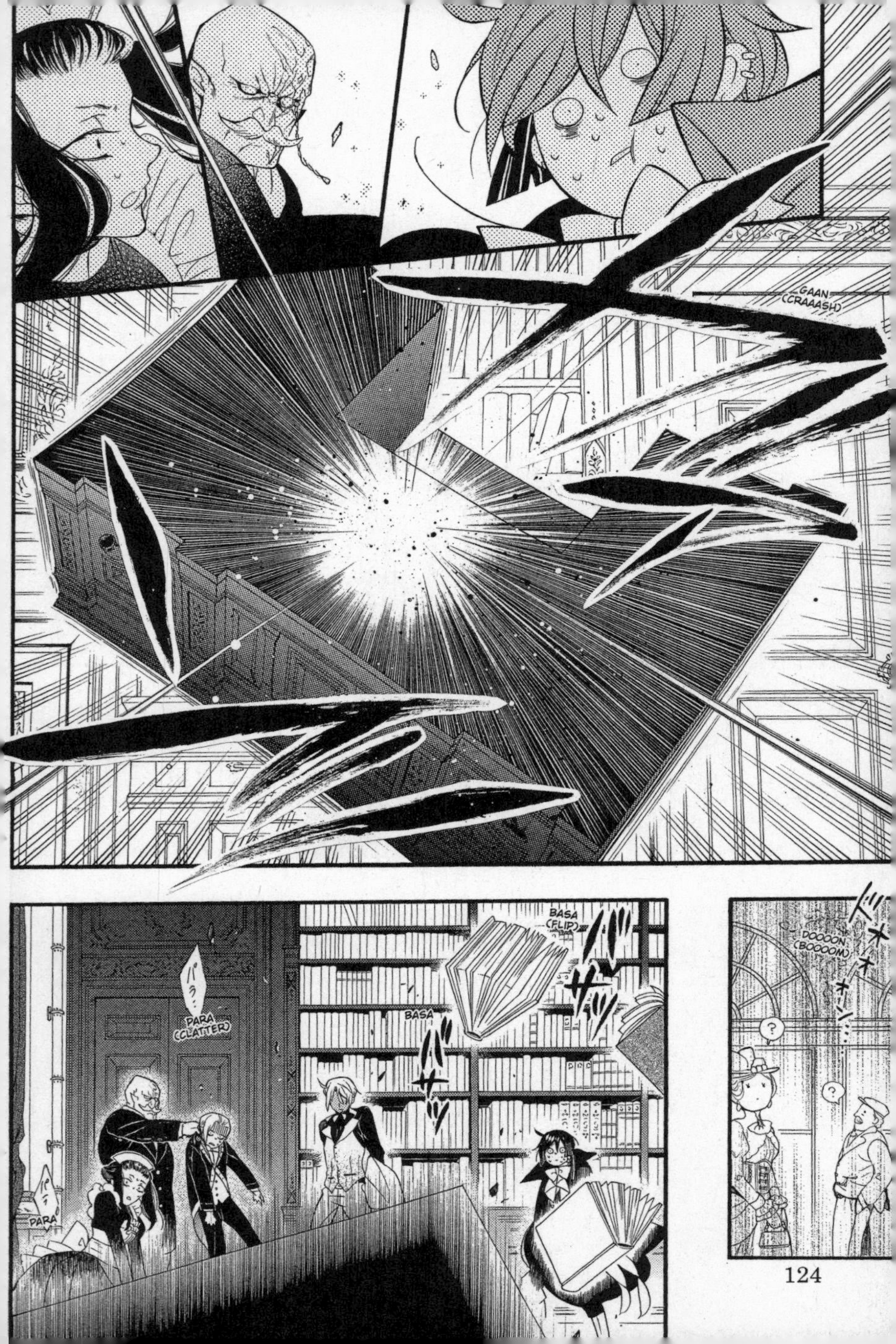
GAAN
(CRAAASH)
ドォオオーン…
DOOOON
(BOOOOM)
BASA
(FLIP)
バサッ
BASA
バサッ
パラ…
PARA
(CLATTER)
パラ
PARA

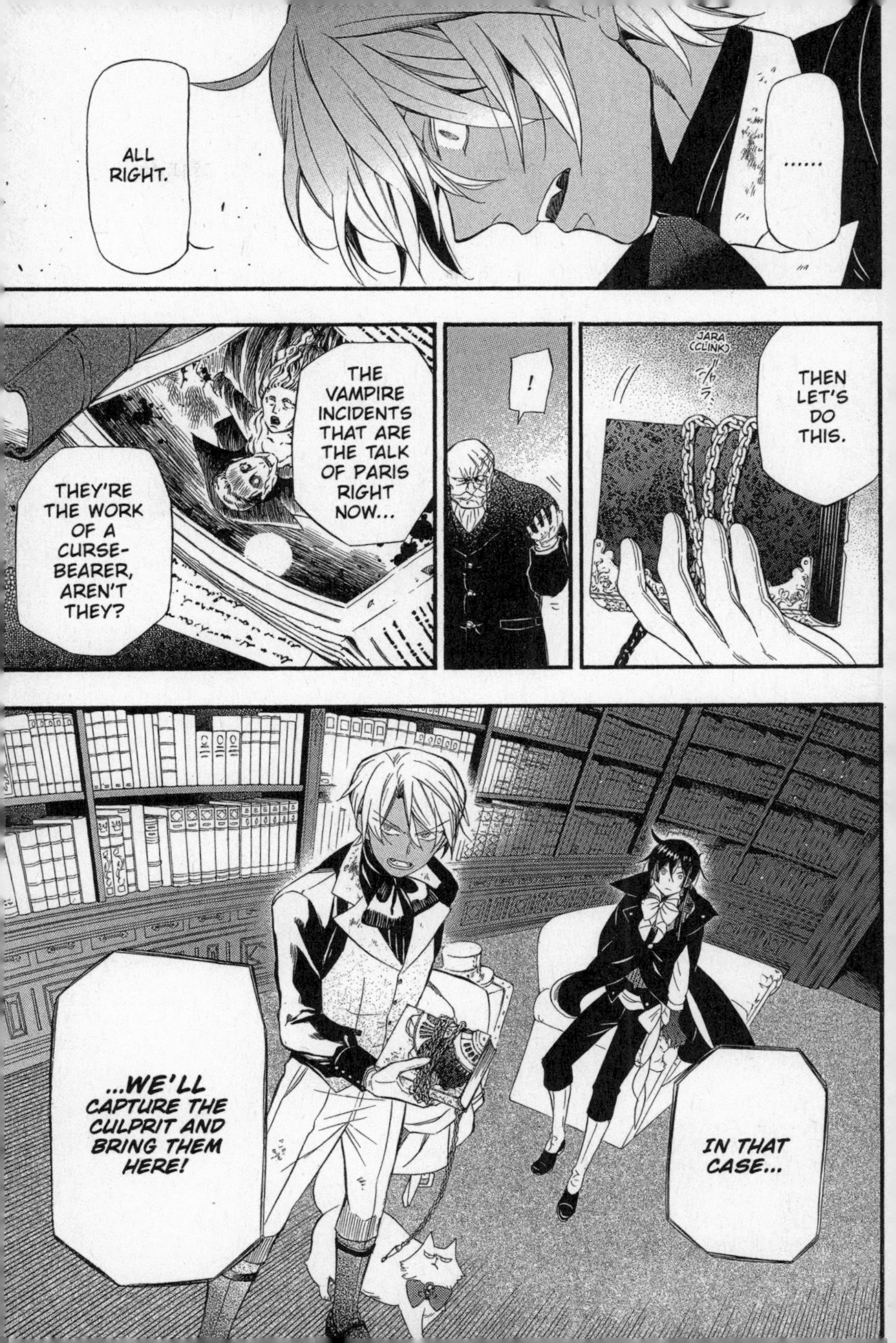
......
ALL RIGHT.
JARA (CLINK)
THEN LET'S DO THIS.
!
THE VAMPIRE INCIDENTS THAT ARE THE TALK OF PARIS RIGHT NOW...
THEY'RE THE WORK OF A CURSE-BEARER, AREN'T THEY?
IN THAT CASE...
...WE'LL CAPTURE THE CULPRIT AND BRING THEM HERE!

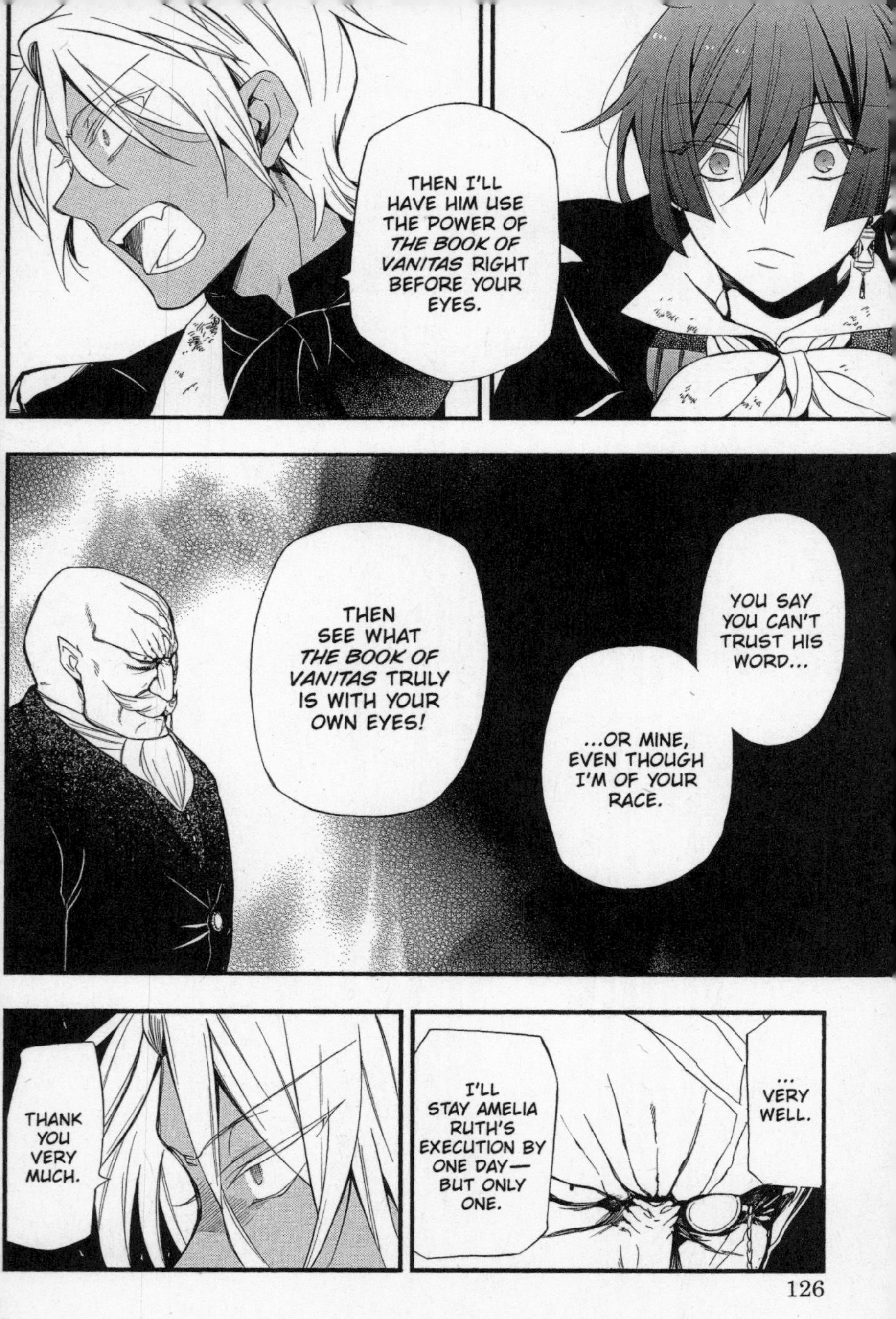
THEN I'LL HAVE HIM USE THE POWER OF *THE BOOK OF VANITAS* RIGHT BEFORE YOUR EYES.
YOU SAY YOU CAN'T TRUST HIS WORD...
...OR MINE, EVEN THOUGH I'M OF YOUR RACE.
THEN SEE WHAT *THE BOOK OF VANITAS* TRULY IS WITH YOUR OWN EYES!
...VERY WELL.
I'LL STAY AMELIA RUTH'S EXECUTION BY ONE DAY—BUT ONLY ONE.
THANK YOU VERY MUCH.

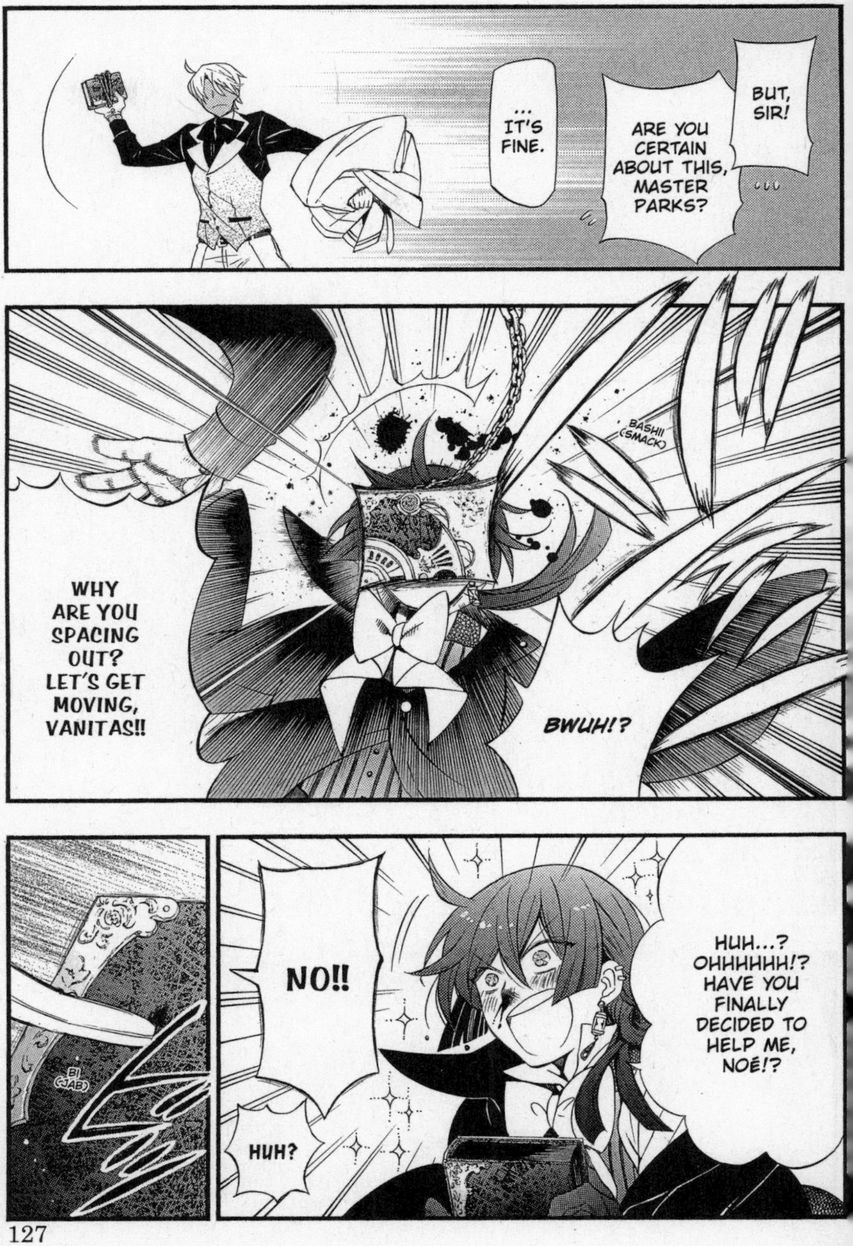
BUT, SIR!
...
ARE YOU CERTAIN ABOUT THIS, MASTER PARKS?
... IT'S FINE.
BASHI (SMACK)
BWUH!?
WHY ARE YOU SPACING OUT? LET'S GET MOVING, VANITAS!!
HUH...? OHHHHHH!? HAVE YOU FINALLY DECIDED TO HELP ME, NOÉ!?
NO!!
HUH?
BI (JAB)

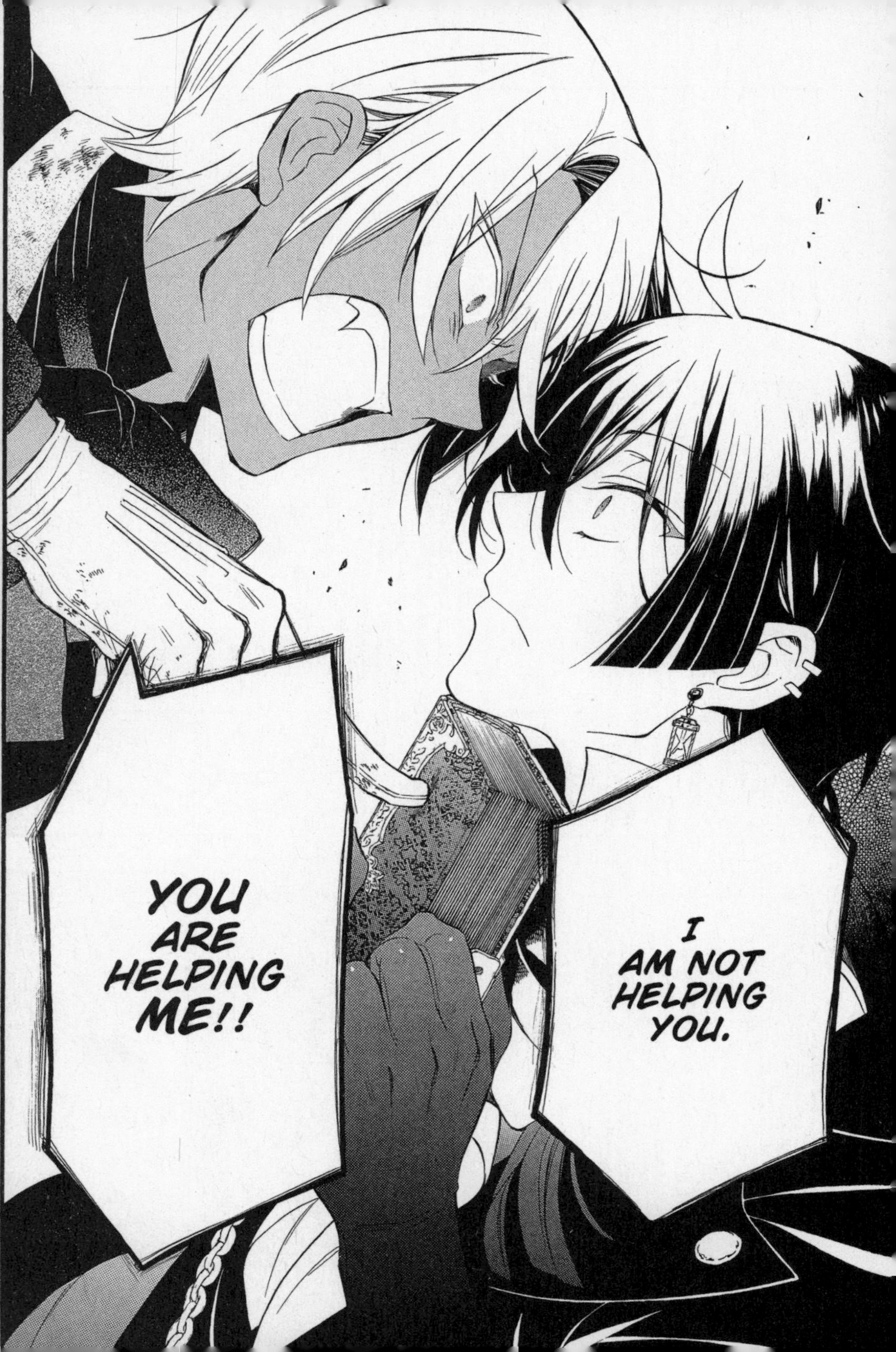
I AM NOT HELPING YOU.
YOU ARE HELPING ME!!

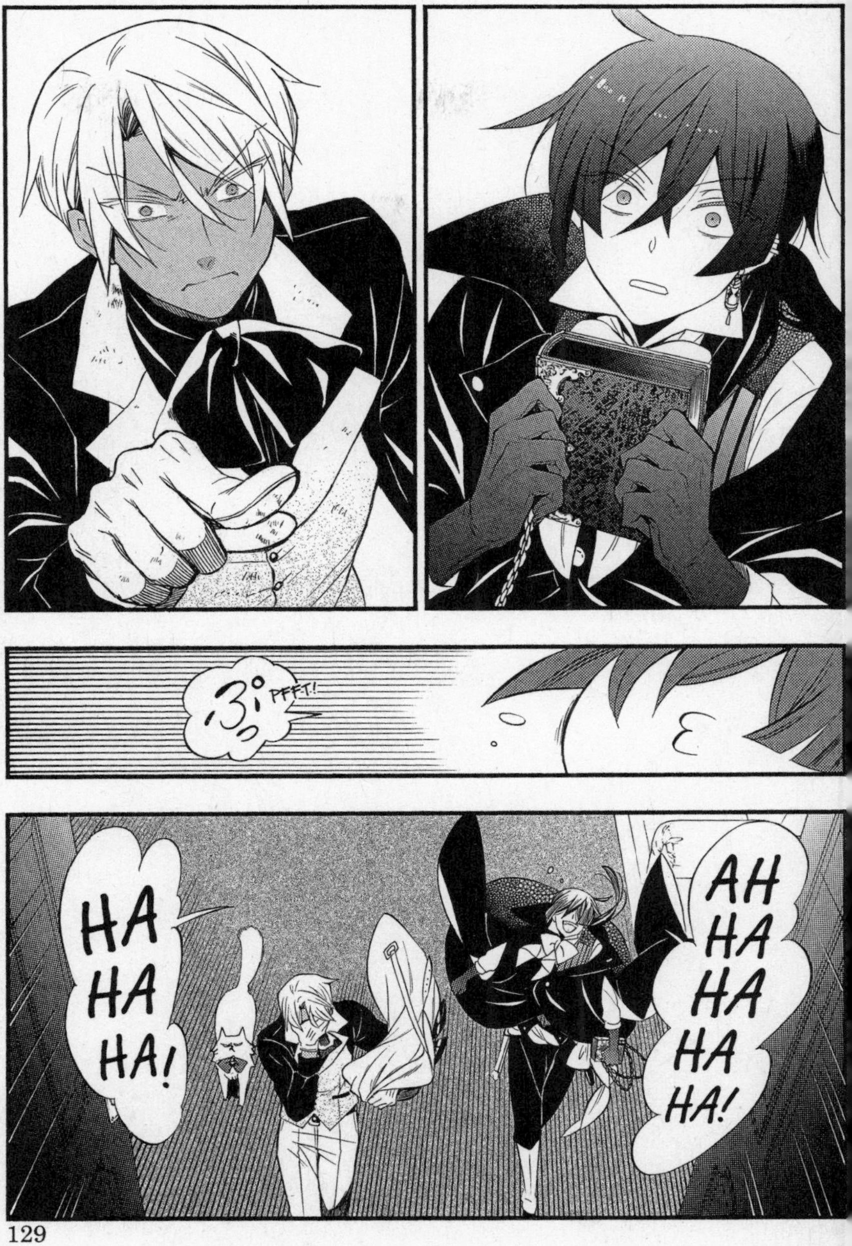
ぷ PFFT!
AH HA HA HA HA HA!
HA HA HA!

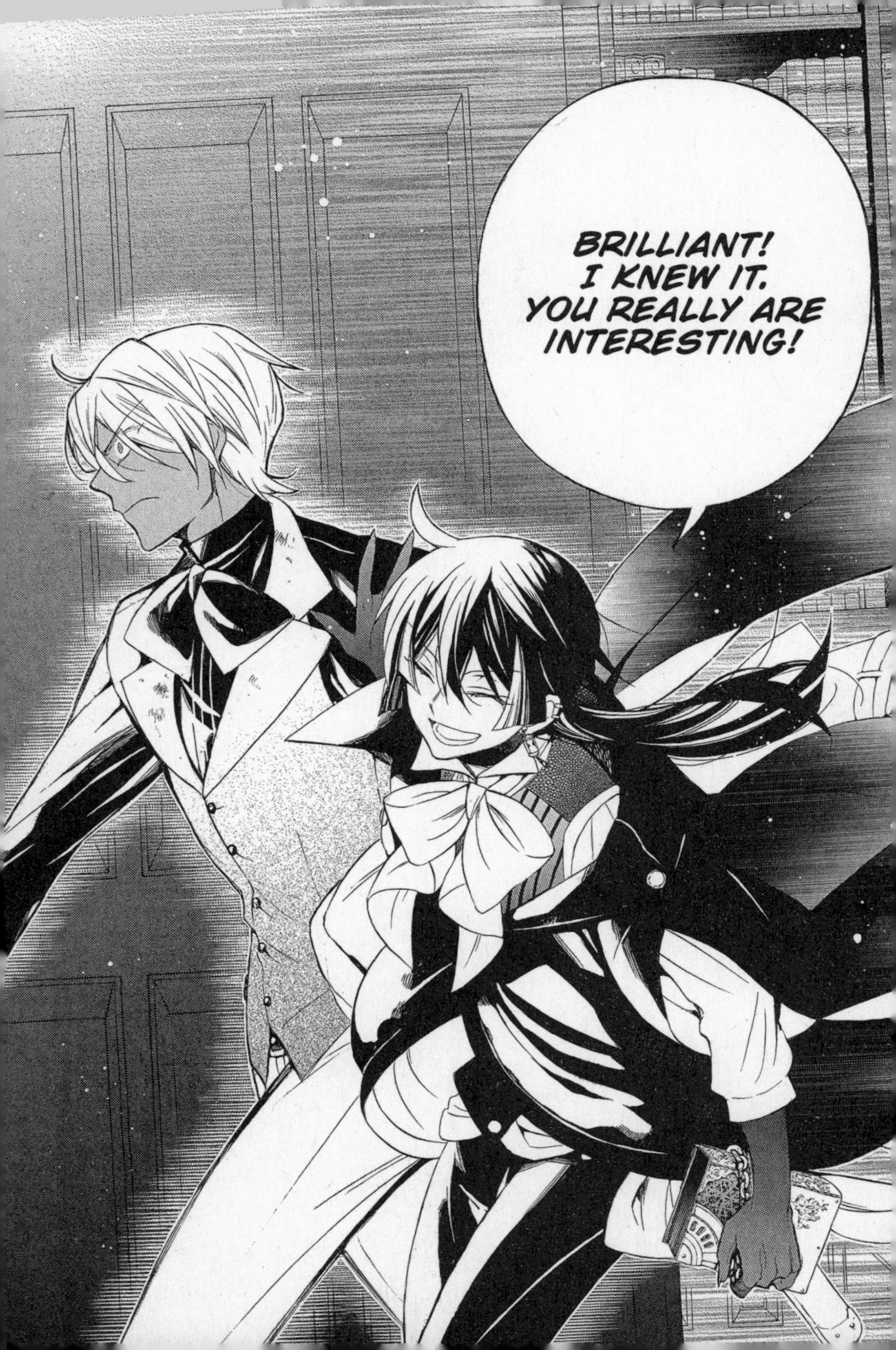
BRILLIANT! I KNEW IT. YOU REALLY ARE INTERESTING!

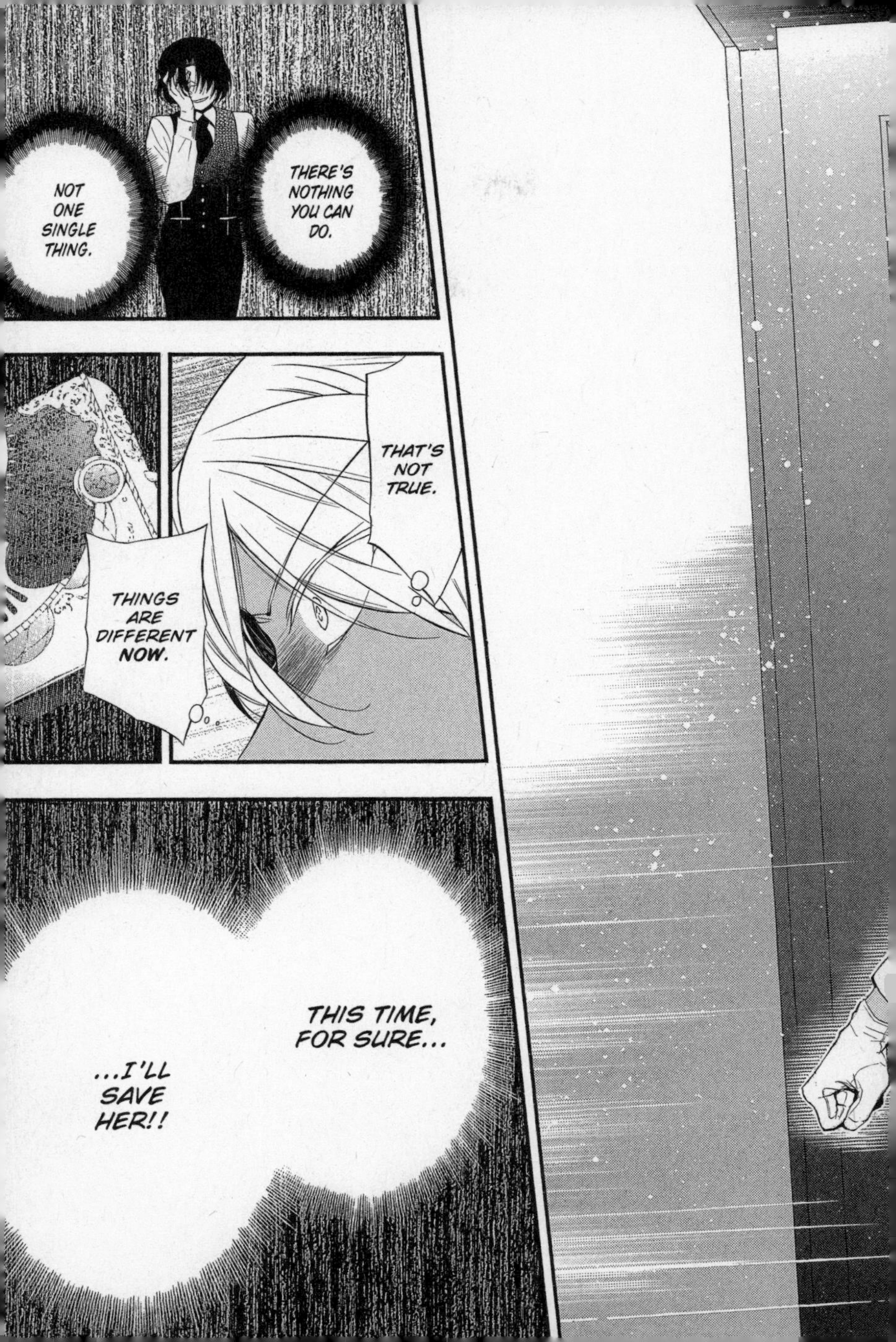
THERE'S NOTHING YOU CAN DO.
NOT ONE SINGLE THING.
THAT'S NOT TRUE.
THINGS ARE DIFFERENT NOW.
THIS TIME, FOR SURE...
...I'LL SAVE HER!!

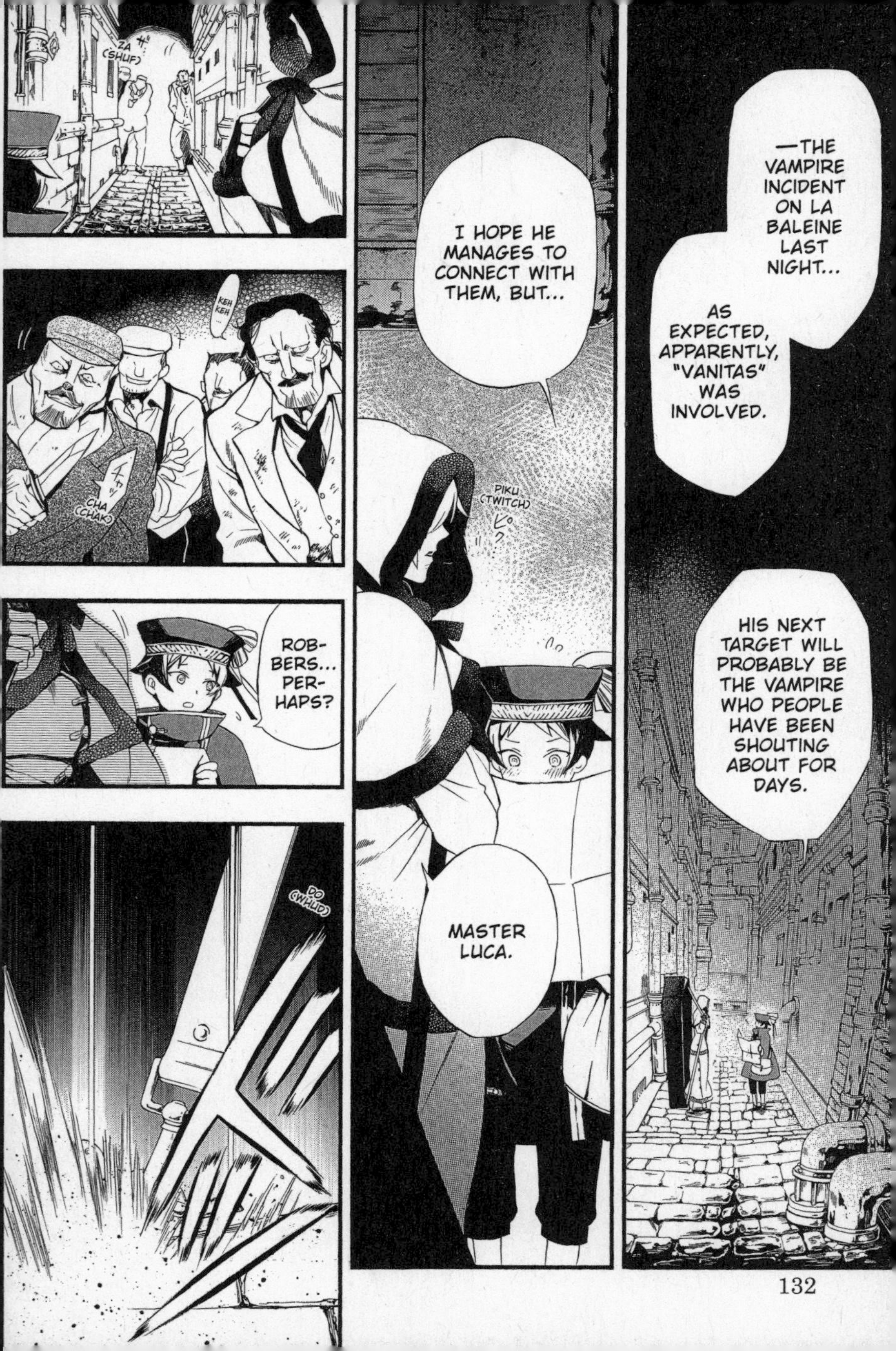
—THE VAMPIRE INCIDENT ON LA BALEINE LAST NIGHT...
AS EXPECTED, APPARENTLY, "VANITAS" WAS INVOLVED.
HIS NEXT TARGET WILL PROBABLY BE THE VAMPIRE WHO PEOPLE HAVE BEEN SHOUTING ABOUT FOR DAYS.
I HOPE HE MANAGES TO CONNECT WITH THEM, BUT...
PIKU (TWITCH)
MASTER LUCA.
ZA (SHUF)
KEH KEH...
CHA (CHAK)
ROBBERS... PERHAPS?
DO (WHUD)

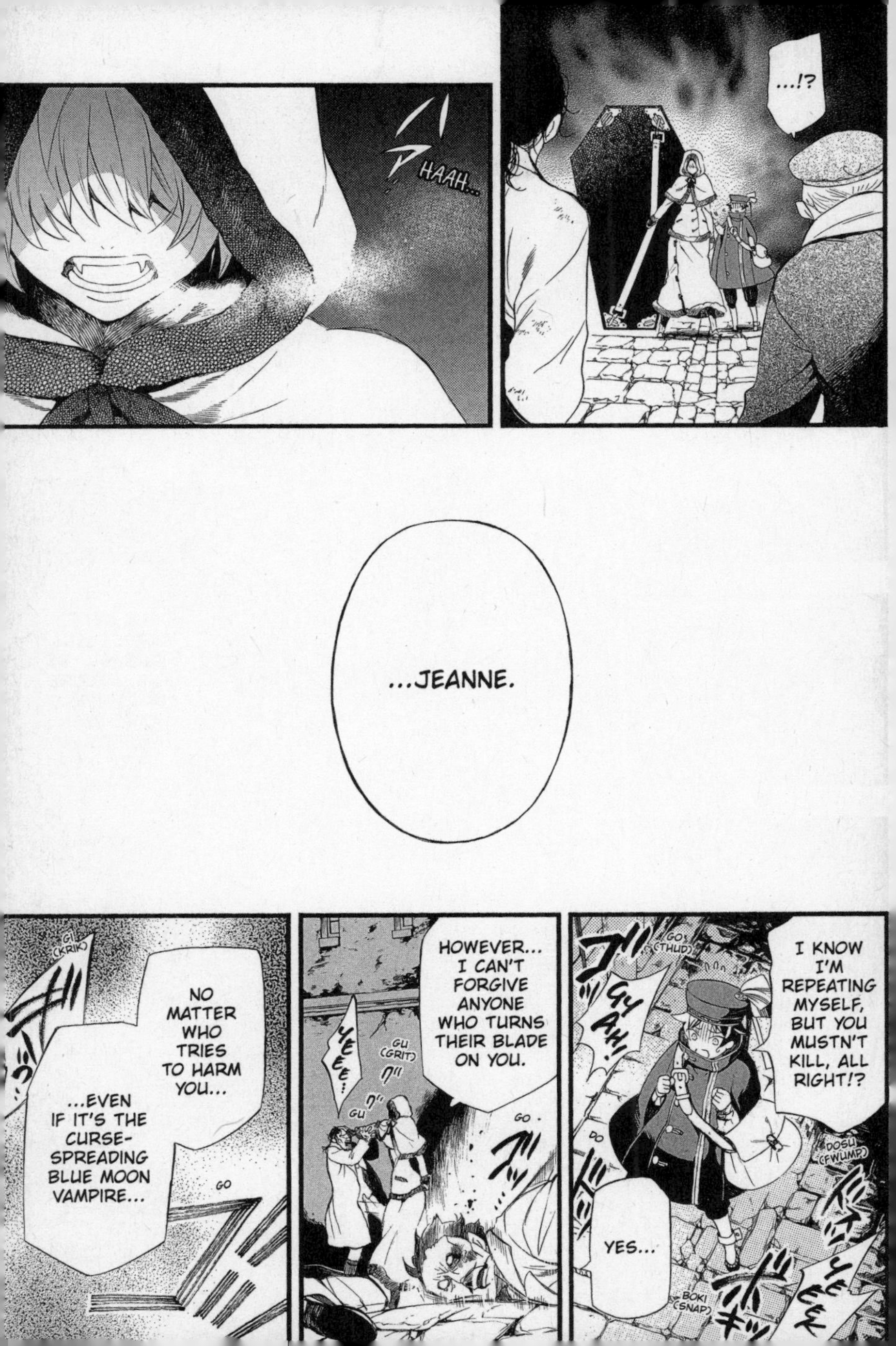
...!?
HAAH...
...JEANNE.
I KNOW I'M REPEATING MYSELF, BUT YOU MUSTN'T KILL, ALL RIGHT!?
GO (THUD)
GYAH!
DOSU (FWUMP)
DO
YES...
BOKI (SNAP)
YEEEK
HOWEVER... I CAN'T FORGIVE ANYONE WHO TURNS THEIR BLADE ON YOU.
YEEEE...!
GU (GRIT)
GU
GO
NO MATTER WHO TRIES TO HARM YOU...
...EVEN IF IT'S THE CURSE-SPREADING BLUE MOON VAMPIRE...
GI (KRIK)
GO

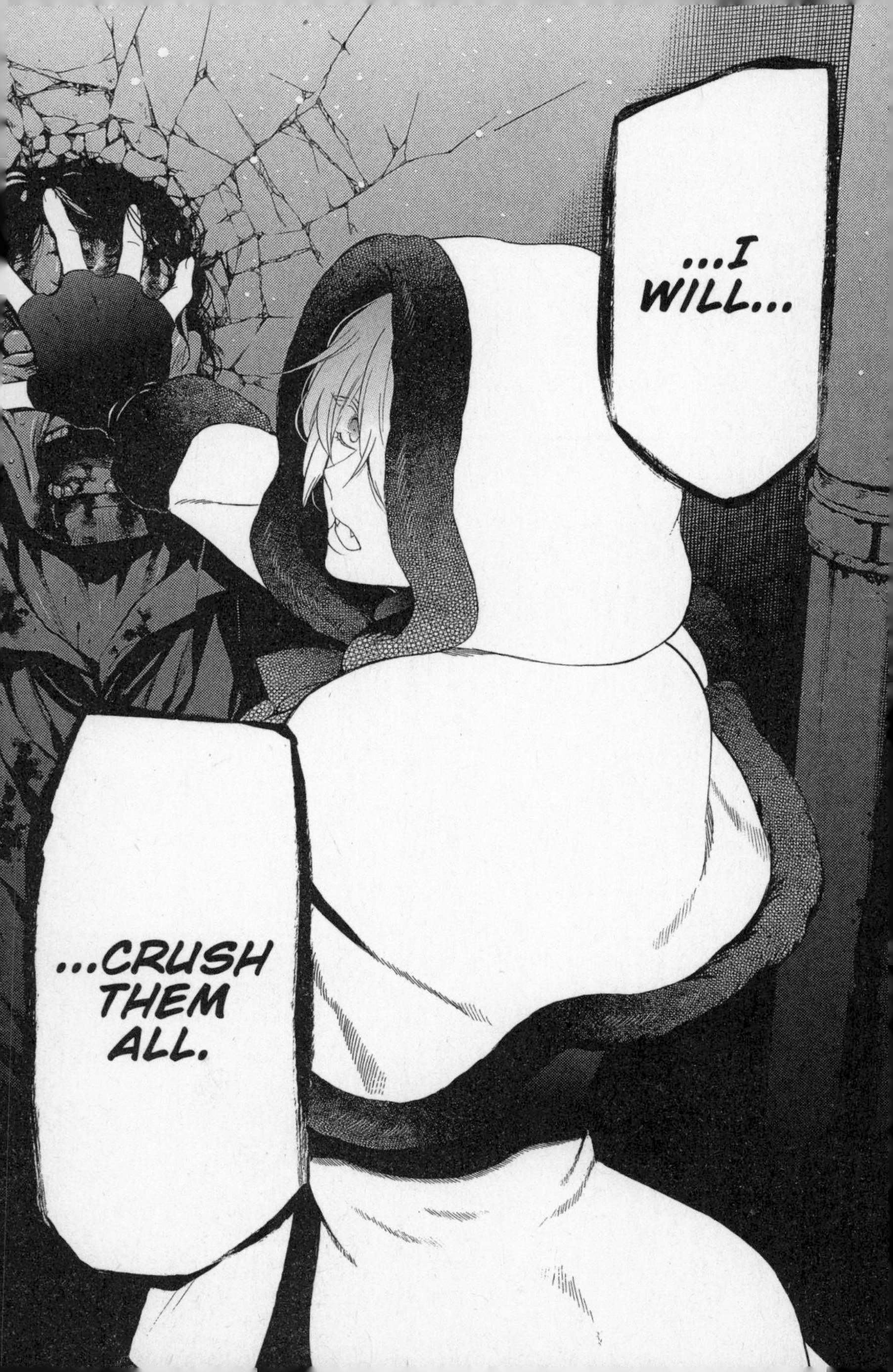
...I WILL...
...CRUSH THEM ALL.

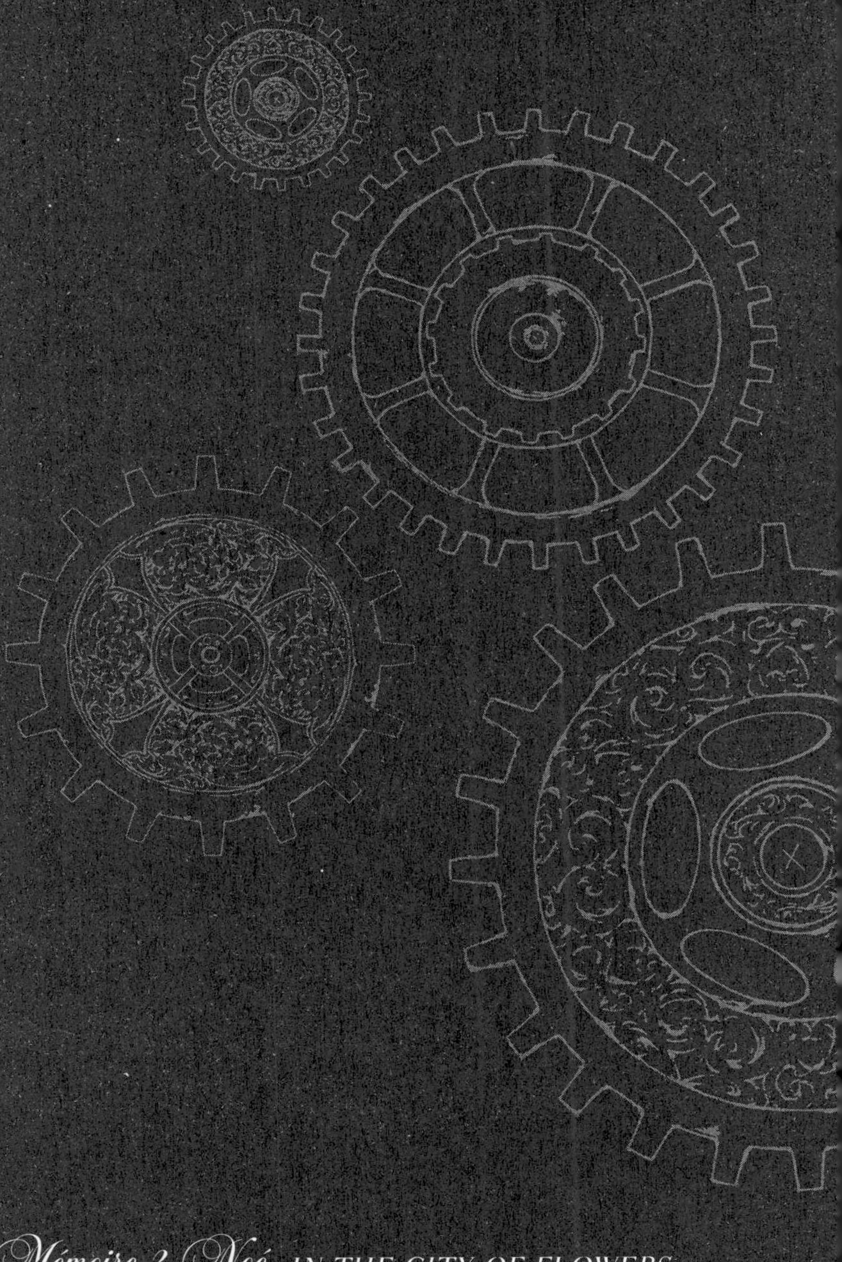

Mémoire 2 Noé IN THE CITY OF FLOWERS

Les Mémoires de Vanitas

THE CASE STUDY OF
VANITAS

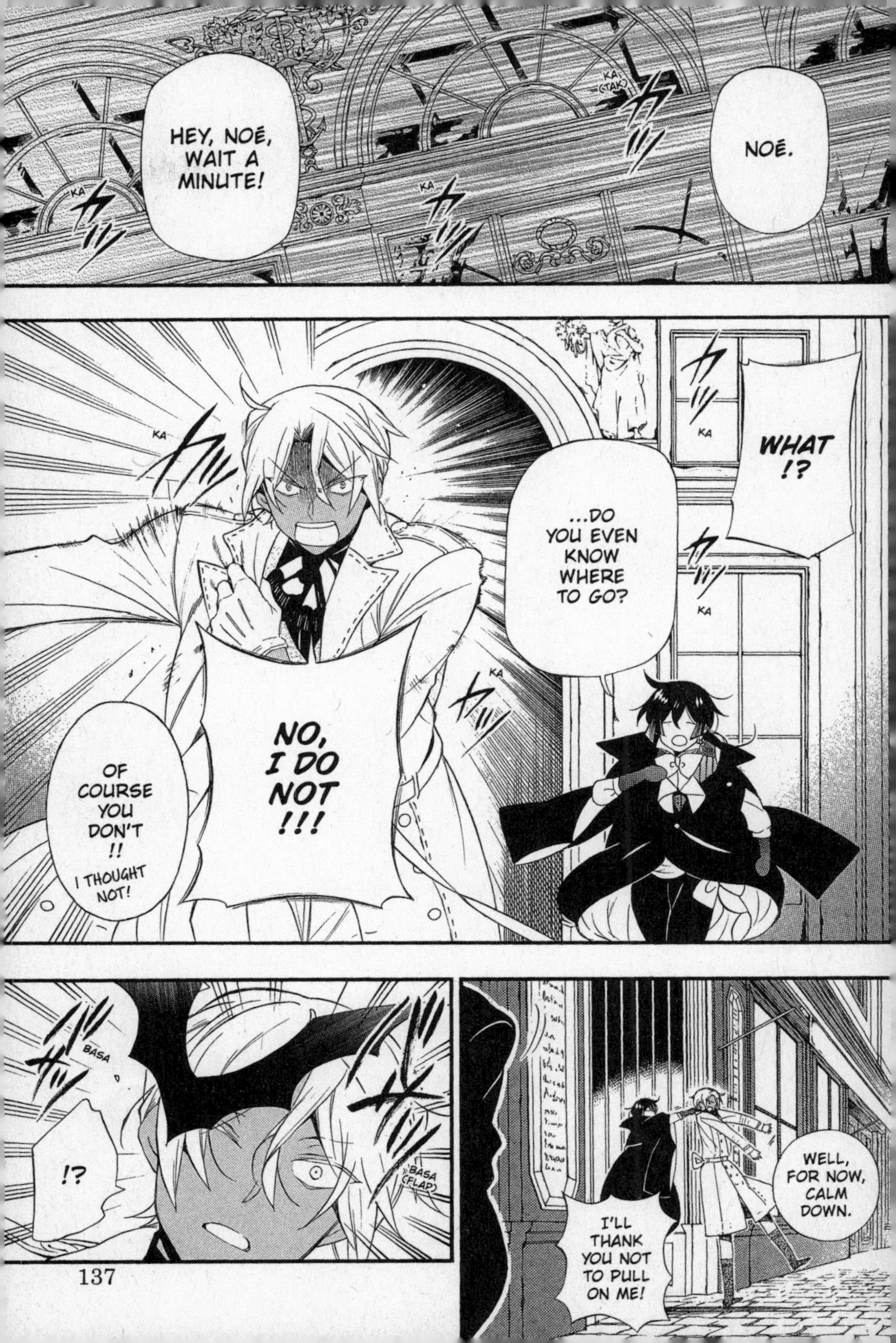
NOÉ.
KA (TAK)
HEY, NOÉ, WAIT A MINUTE!
KA
KA
WHAT !?
KA
KA
...DO YOU EVEN KNOW WHERE TO GO?
KA
NO, I DO NOT !!!
KA
OF COURSE YOU DON'T !!
I THOUGHT NOT!
WELL, FOR NOW, CALM DOWN.
I'LL THANK YOU NOT TO PULL ON ME!
BASA
!?
BASA (FLAP)

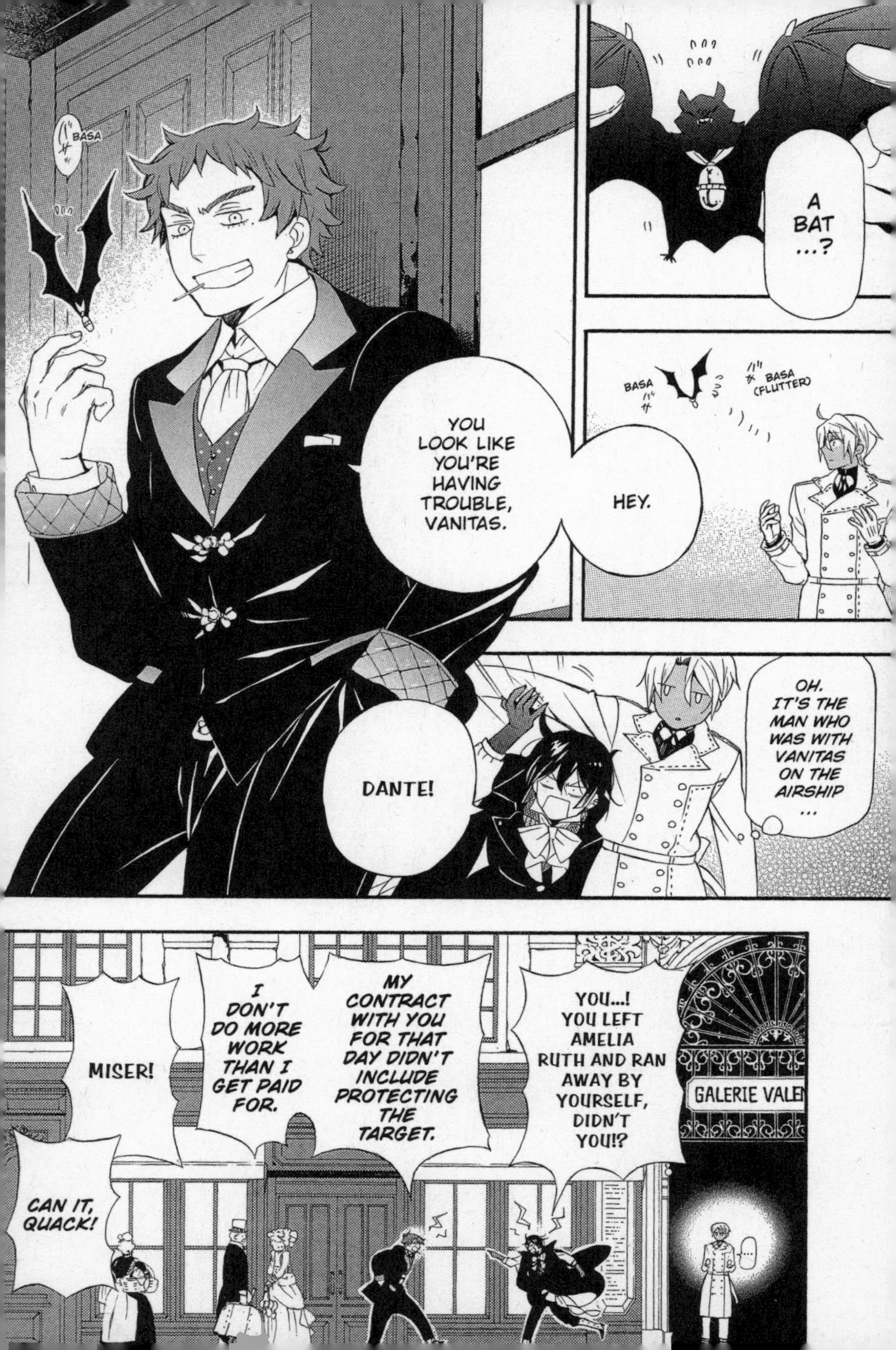

A BAT ...?
BASA
BASA (FLUTTER)
HEY.
YOU LOOK LIKE YOU'RE HAVING TROUBLE, VANITAS.
OH. IT'S THE MAN WHO WAS WITH VANITAS ON THE AIRSHIP ...
DANTE!
BASA
YOU...! YOU LEFT AMELIA RUTH AND RAN AWAY BY YOURSELF, DIDN'T YOU!?
GALERIE VALEN
MY CONTRACT WITH YOU FOR THAT DAY DIDN'T INCLUDE PROTECTING THE TARGET.
I DON'T DO MORE WORK THAN I GET PAID FOR.
MISER!
CAN IT, QUACK!
....

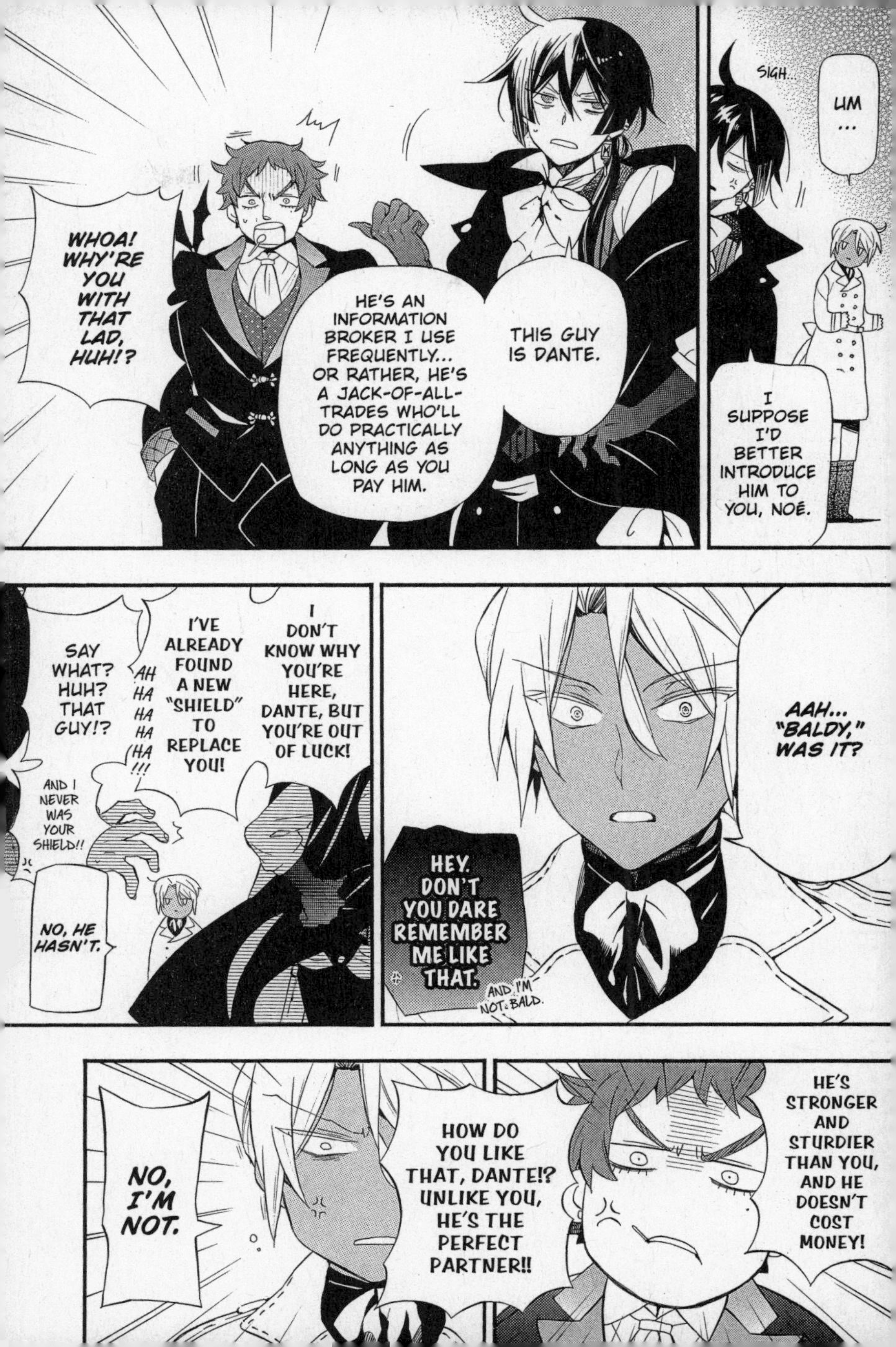

SIGH...
UM ...
I SUPPOSE I'D BETTER INTRODUCE HIM TO YOU, NOÉ.
THIS GUY IS DANTE.
HE'S AN INFORMATION BROKER I USE FREQUENTLY... OR RATHER, HE'S A JACK-OF-ALL-TRADES WHO'LL DO PRACTICALLY ANYTHING AS LONG AS YOU PAY HIM.
WHOA! WHY'RE YOU WITH THAT LAD, HUH!?
AAH... "BALDY," WAS IT?
HEY. DON'T YOU DARE REMEMBER ME LIKE THAT.
AND I'M NOT BALD.
I DON'T KNOW WHY YOU'RE HERE, DANTE, BUT YOU'RE OUT OF LUCK!
I'VE ALREADY FOUND A NEW "SHIELD" TO REPLACE YOU!
AH HA HA HA HA!!!
SAY WHAT? HUH? THAT GUY!?
AND I NEVER WAS YOUR SHIELD!!
NO, HE HASN'T.
HE'S STRONGER AND STURDIER THAN YOU, AND HE DOESN'T COST MONEY!
HOW DO YOU LIKE THAT, DANTE!? UNLIKE YOU, HE'S THE PERFECT PARTNER!!
NO, I'M NOT.

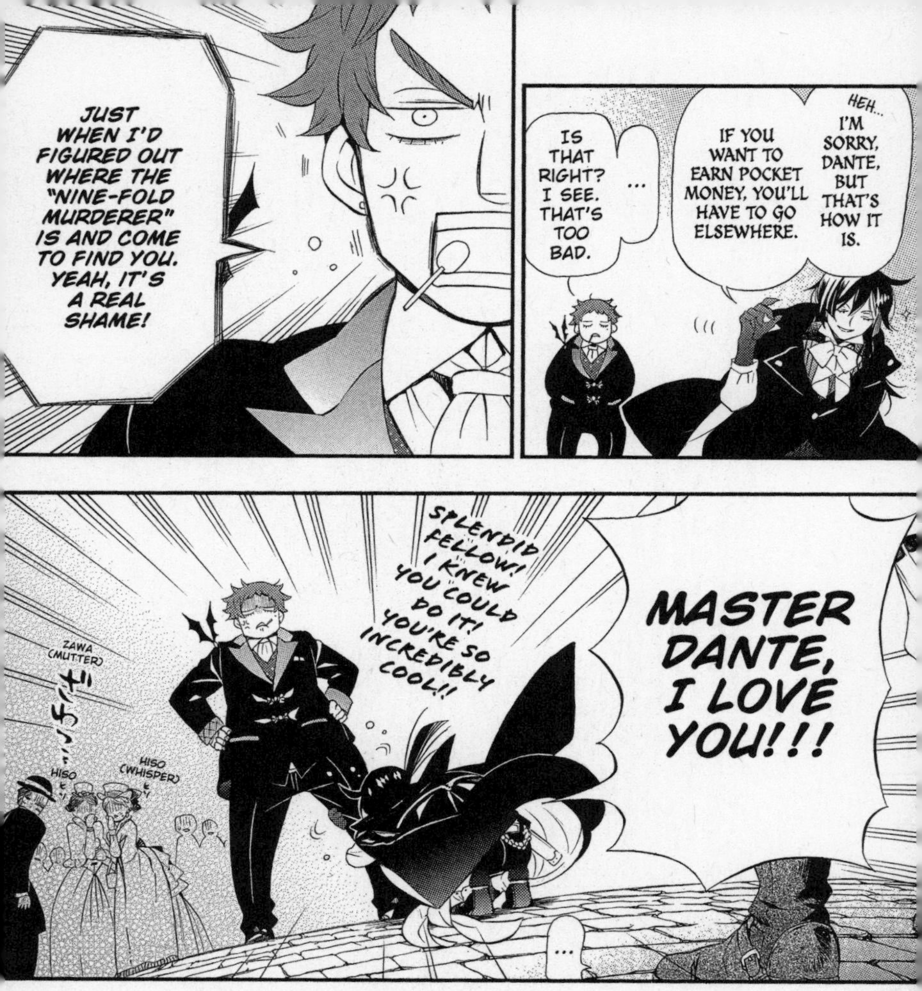
HEH... I'M SORRY, DANTE, BUT THAT'S HOW IT IS.
IF YOU WANT TO EARN POCKET MONEY, YOU'LL HAVE TO GO ELSEWHERE.
...
IS THAT RIGHT? I SEE. THAT'S TOO BAD.
JUST WHEN I'D FIGURED OUT WHERE THE "NINE-FOLD MURDERER" IS AND COME TO FIND YOU. YEAH, IT'S A REAL SHAME!
MASTER DANTE, I LOVE YOU!!!
...
SPLENDID FELLOW! I KNEW YOU COULD DO IT! YOU'RE SO INCREDIBLY COOL!!
ZAWA (MUTTER)
HISO (WHISPER)
HISO

MÉMOIRE 3

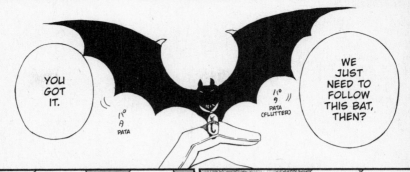

WE JUST NEED TO FOLLOW THIS BAT, THEN?

YOU GOT.

パタ PATA

パタ 9 PATA (FLUTTER)

MY FRIEND IS TAILING THE "NINE-FOLD MURDERER" AS WE SPEAK.

THIS LITTLE GUY WILL TAKE YOU TO THAT FRIEND.

I SEE.

... RRGH ...

YOU COMPLETELY SKINNED ME FOR THAT INFORMATION, BALDY!!

SHADDUP! YOU THOUGHT INFO EVEN OLD ORLOK DOESN'T HAVE WAS GONNA BE CHEAP!?

PE ペッ

PE ペッ

PE ペッ

PE ペッ

PE (PTOOIE)

キョロ KYORO

キョロ KYORO (PEEK)

...IT WILL BE FASTER TO GO OVER THE TOP.

HUH?

ガシ (GRAB)

WHAAAAA!?

!?

ピョーン PYOON (BOING)

ピョン PYON

ピョン PYON

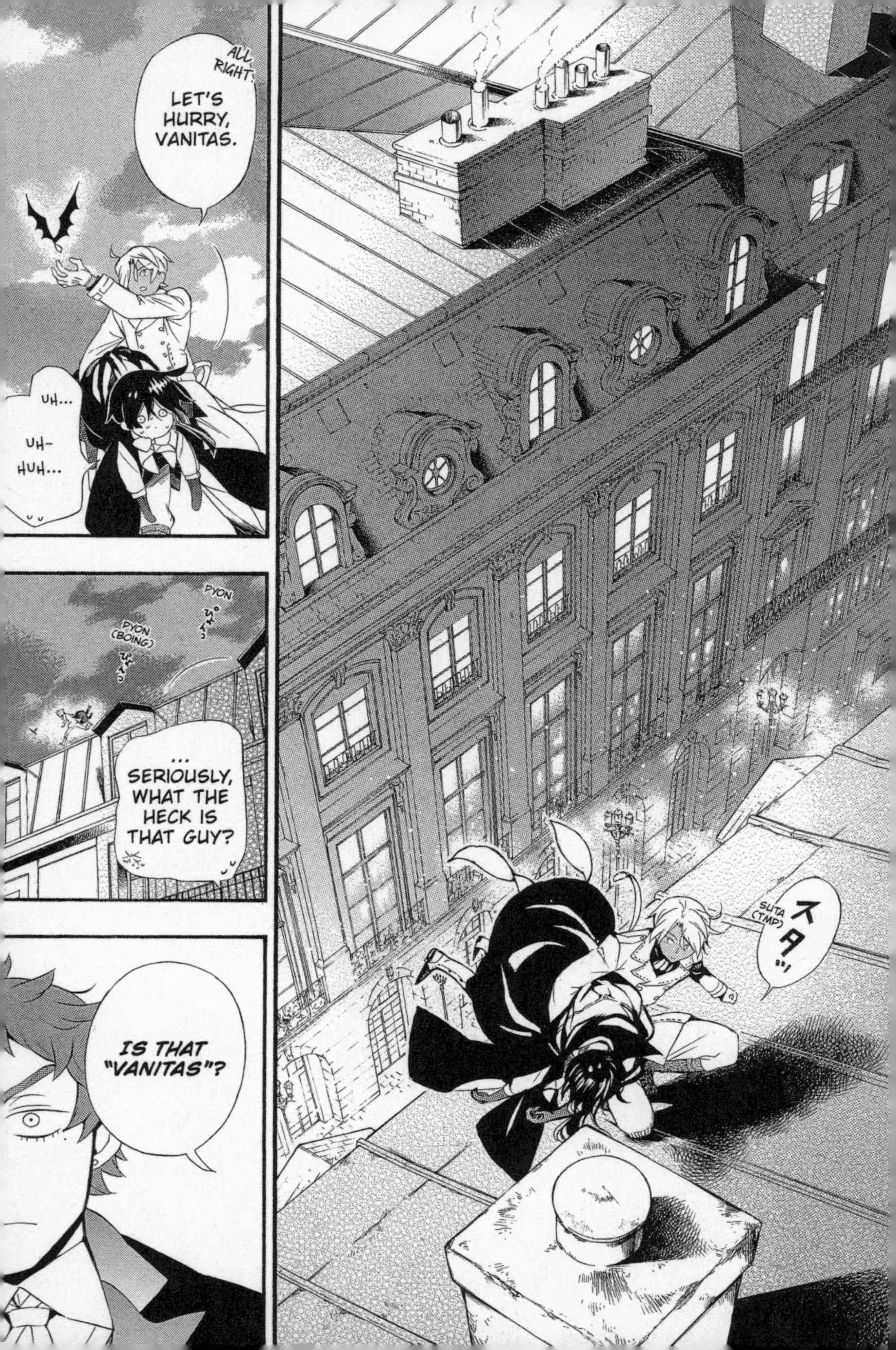
SUTA (TMP)
スタッ
ALL RIGHT.
LET'S HURRY, VANITAS.
UH... UH-HUH...
PYON
ぴょん
PYON (BOING)
ぴょん
...SERIOUSLY, WHAT THE HECK IS THAT GUY?
IS THAT "VANITAS"?

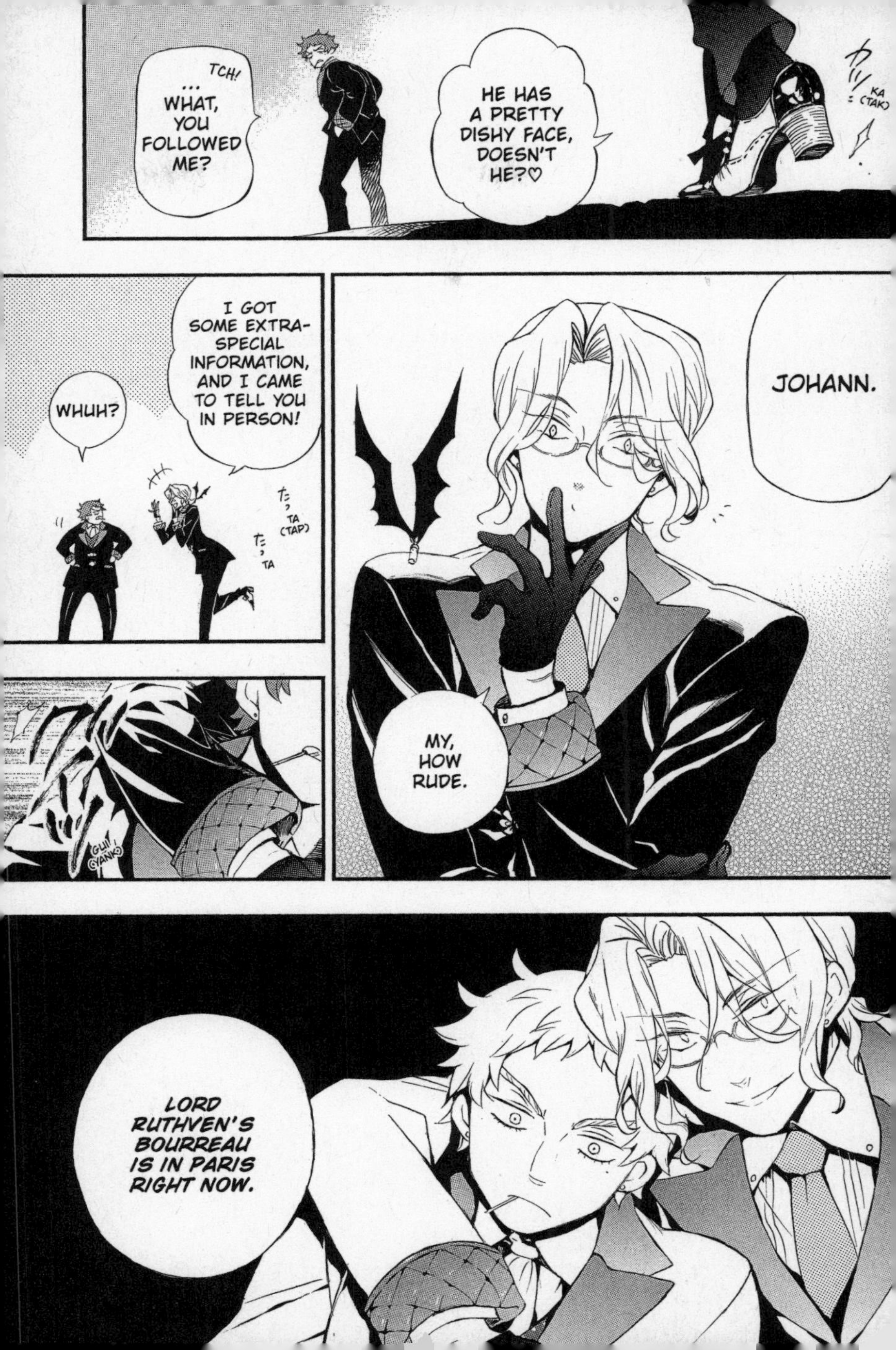
カッ
KA (TAK)
HE HAS A PRETTY DISHY FACE, DOESN'T HE?♡
TCH! ... WHAT, YOU FOLLOWED ME?
JOHANN.
MY, HOW RUDE.
I GOT SOME EXTRA-SPECIAL INFORMATION, AND I CAME TO TELL YOU IN PERSON!
WHUH?
たっ
TA (TAP)
たっ
TA
GUI (YANK)
LORD RUTHVEN'S BOURREAU IS IN PARIS RIGHT NOW.

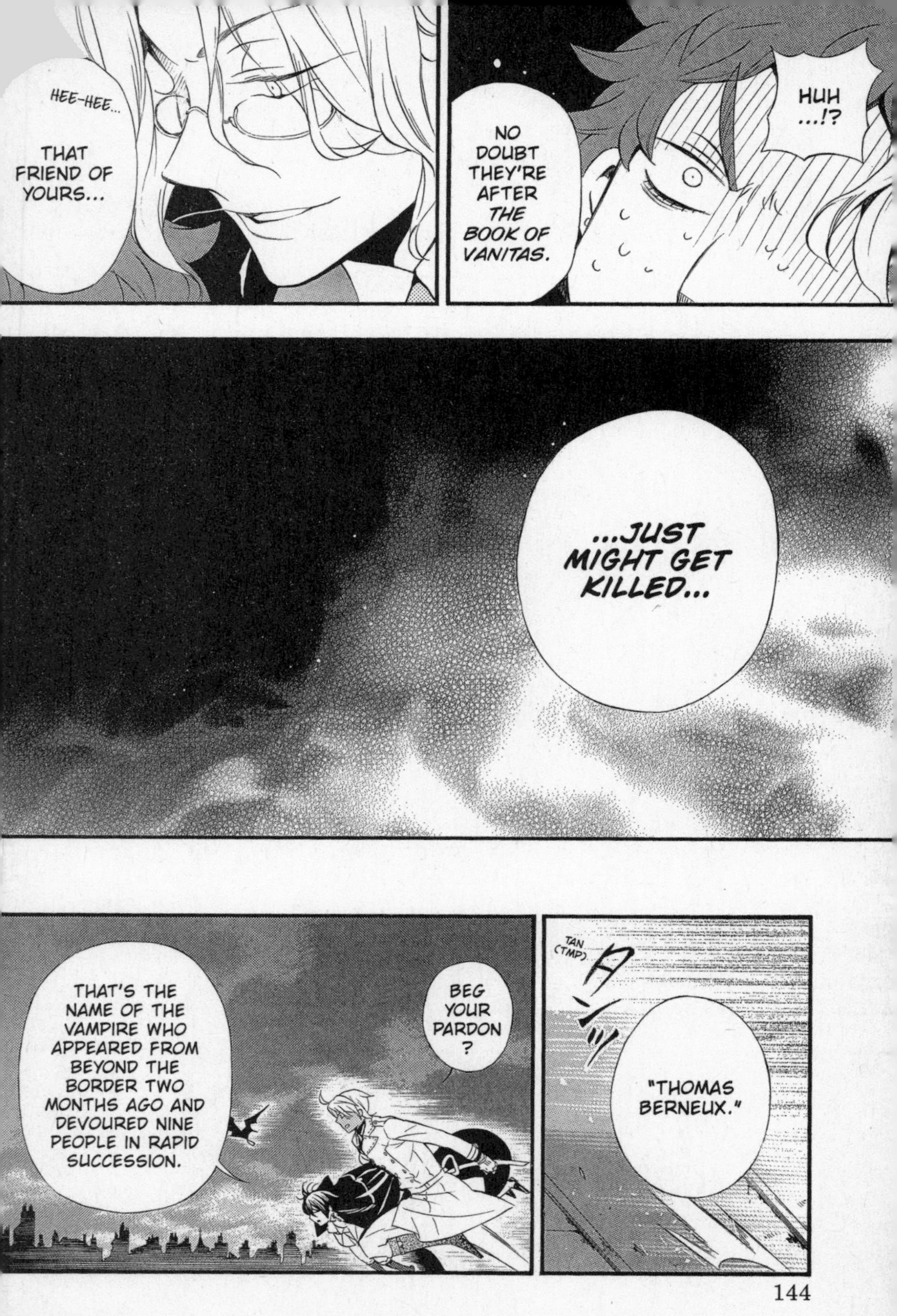
HUH ...!?
NO DOUBT THEY'RE AFTER *THE BOOK OF VANITAS.*
HEE-HEE...
THAT FRIEND OF YOURS...
...JUST MIGHT GET KILLED...
TAN (TMP)
"THOMAS BERNEUX."
BEG YOUR PARDON ?
THAT'S THE NAME OF THE VAMPIRE WHO APPEARED FROM BEYOND THE BORDER TWO MONTHS AGO AND DEVOURED NINE PEOPLE IN RAPID SUCCESSION.

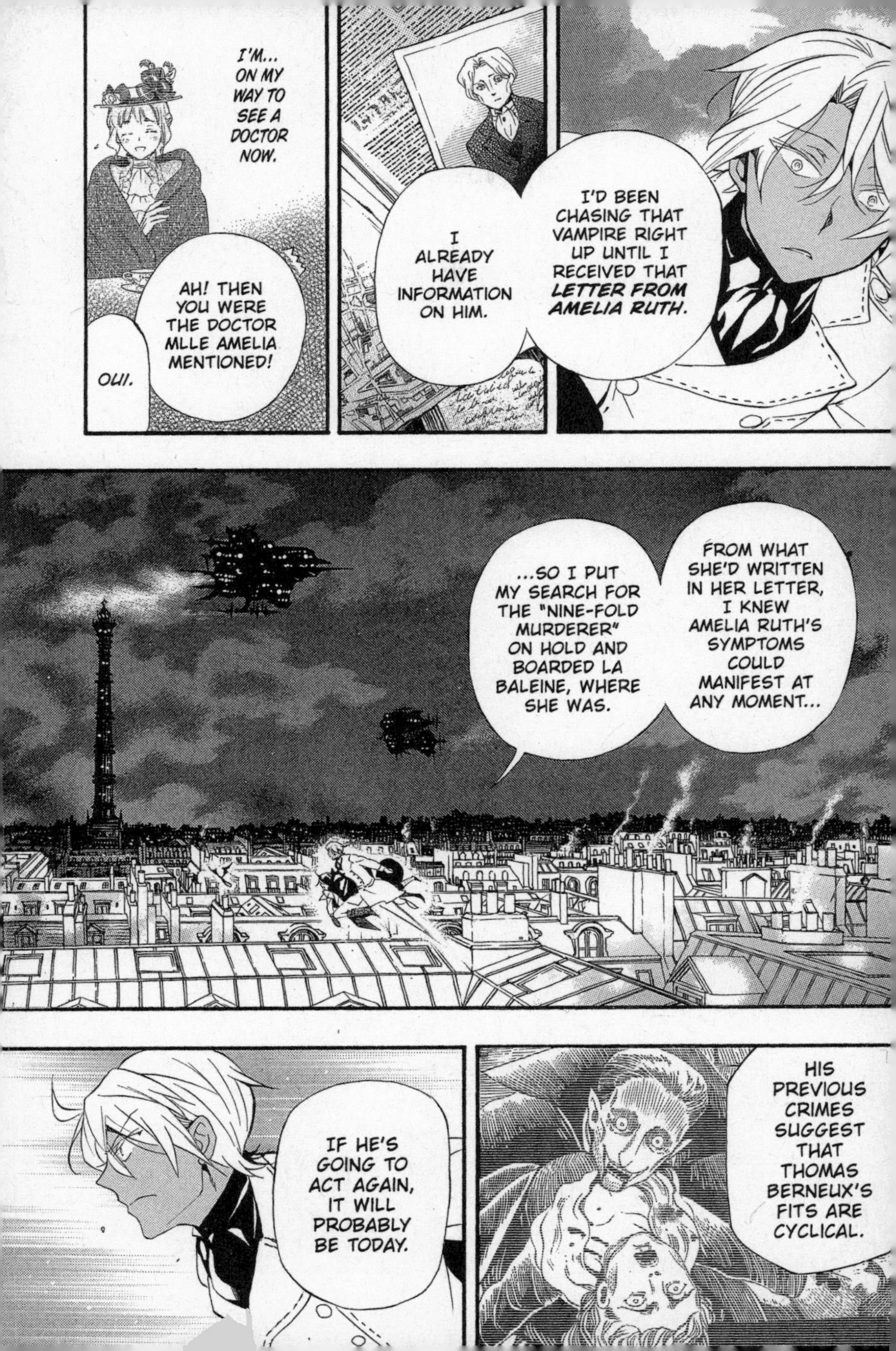
I'D BEEN CHASING THAT VAMPIRE RIGHT UP UNTIL I RECEIVED THAT *LETTER FROM AMELIA RUTH*.
I ALREADY HAVE INFORMATION ON HIM.
I'M... ON MY WAY TO SEE A DOCTOR NOW.
AH! THEN YOU WERE THE DOCTOR MLLE AMELIA MENTIONED!
OUI.
FROM WHAT SHE'D WRITTEN IN HER LETTER, I KNEW AMELIA RUTH'S SYMPTOMS COULD MANIFEST AT ANY MOMENT...
...SO I PUT MY SEARCH FOR THE "NINE-FOLD MURDERER" ON HOLD AND BOARDED LA BALEINE, WHERE SHE WAS.
HIS PREVIOUS CRIMES SUGGEST THAT THOMAS BERNEUX'S FITS ARE CYCLICAL.
IF HE'S GOING TO ACT AGAIN, IT WILL PROBABLY BE TODAY.

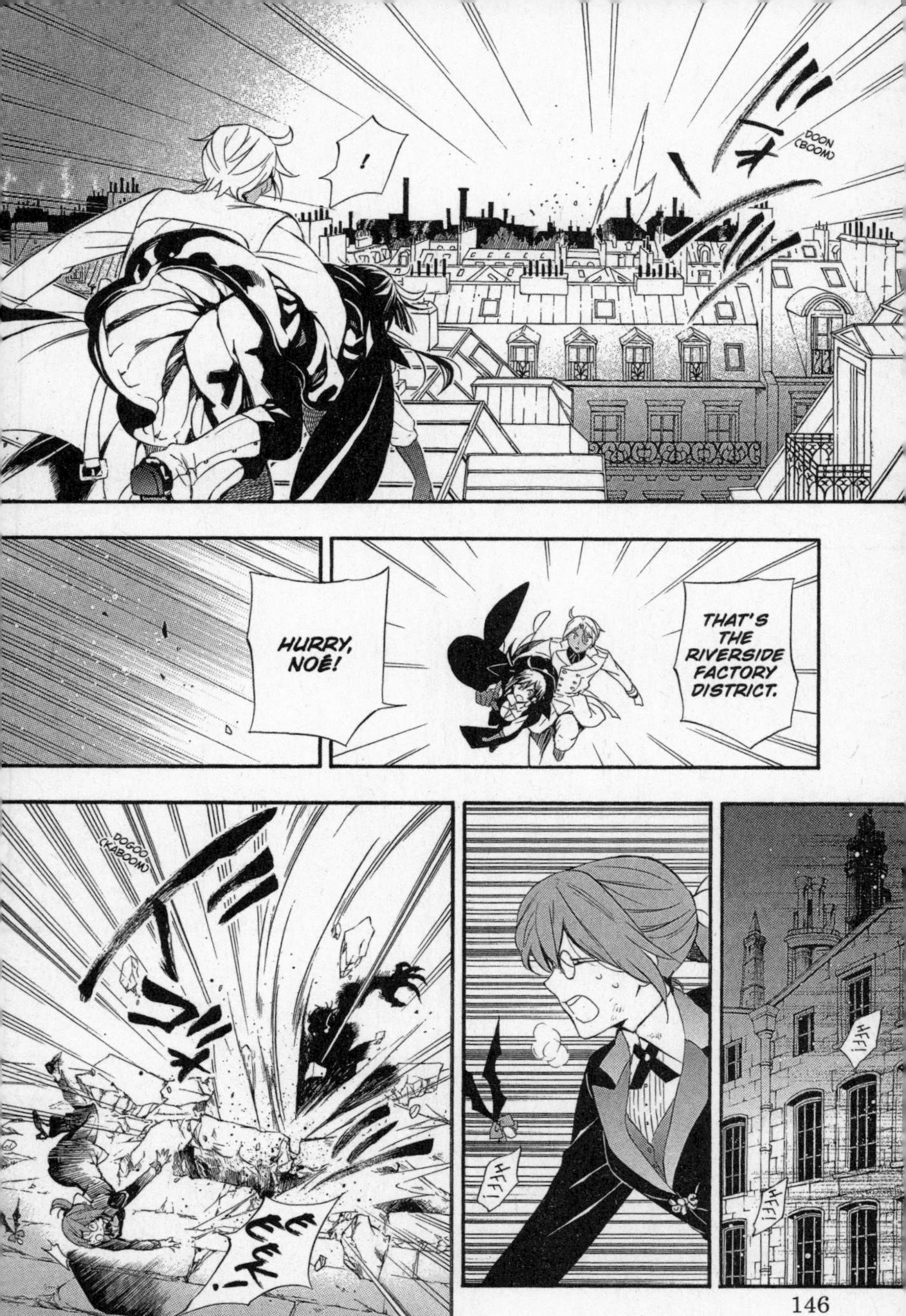

!
DOON (BOOM)
THAT'S THE RIVERSIDE FACTORY DISTRICT.
HURRY, NOÉ!
HFF!
HFF!
HFF!
DOGOO (KABOOM)
EEEK!

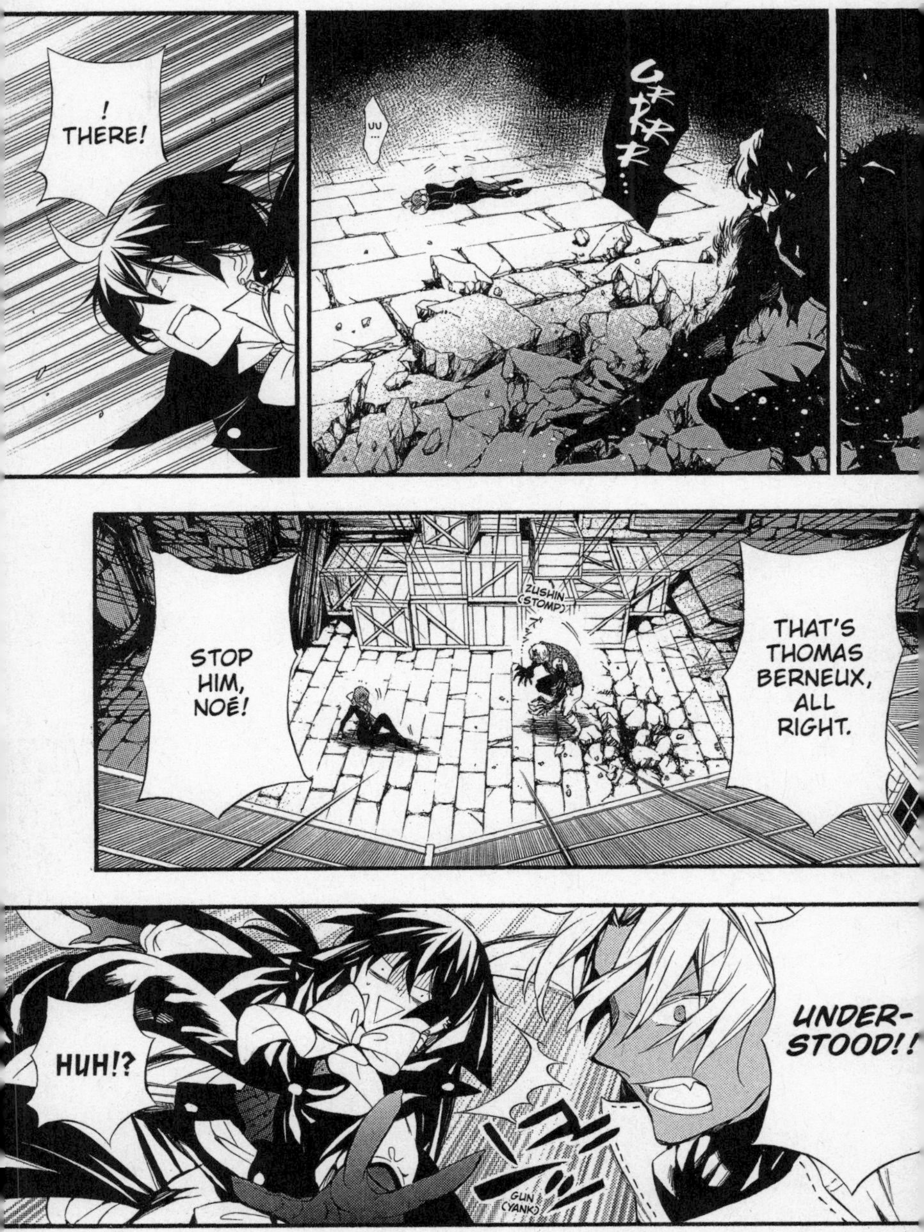
GRRRR...
UU...
! THERE!
THAT'S THOMAS BERNEUX, ALL RIGHT.
ZUSHIN (STOMP)
STOP HIM, NOÉ!
UNDER-STOOD!!
GUN (YANK)
HUH!?

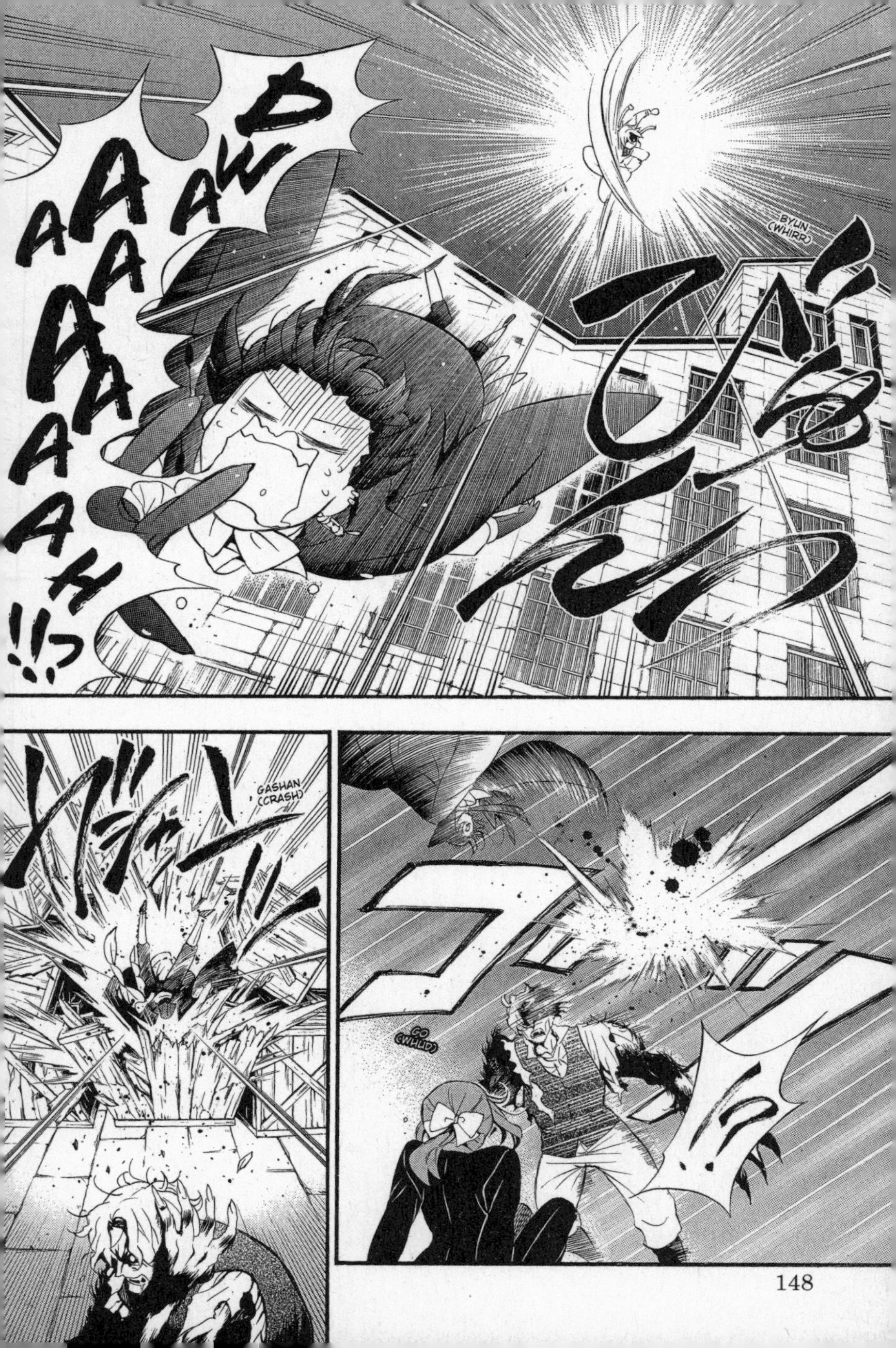
DAW AW
AAAAAAAAAH!!
BYUN (WHIRR)
GO (WHUD)
GASHAN (CRASH)

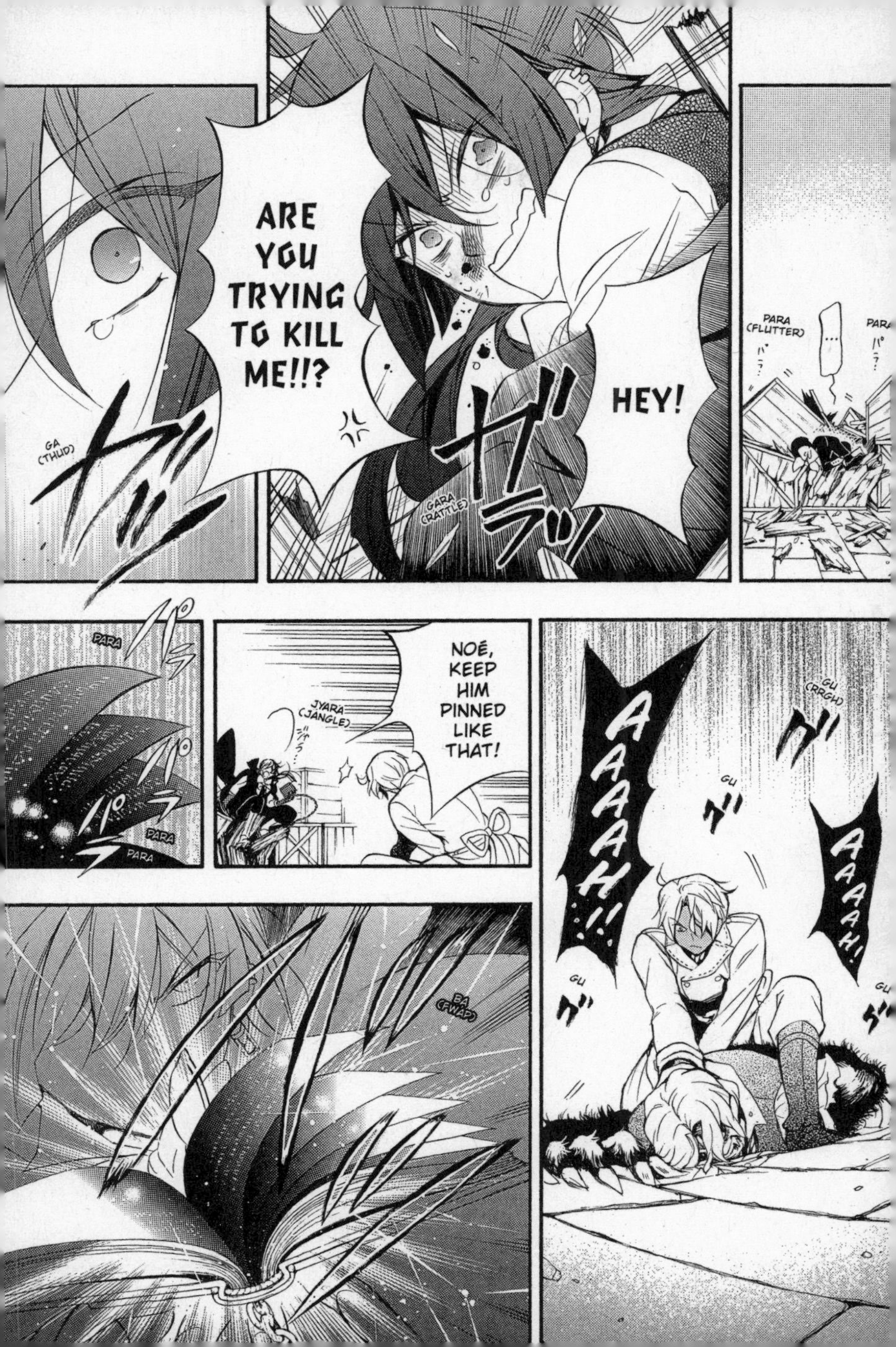
PARA (FLUTTER)
...
PARA
HEY!
ARE YOU TRYING TO KILL ME!!?
GARA (RATTLE)
GA (THUD)
AAAAAH!
GU (RRGH)
GU
AAAAAH!!
GU
GU
NOÉ, KEEP HIM PINNED LIKE THAT!
JYARA (JANGLE)
PARA
PARA
PARA
BA (FWAP)

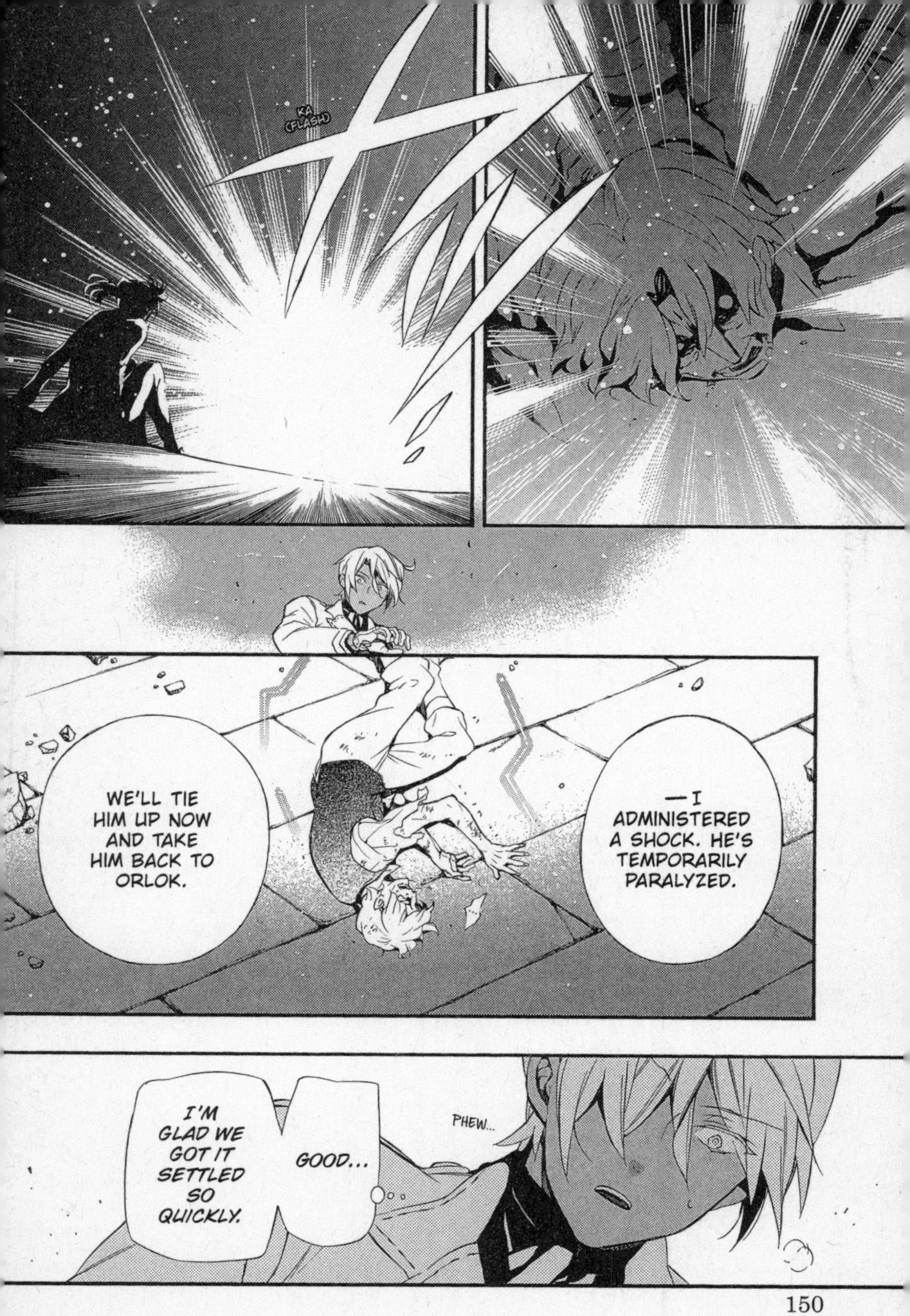
KA (FLASH)
—I ADMINISTERED A SHOCK. HE'S TEMPORARILY PARALYZED.
WE'LL TIE HIM UP NOW AND TAKE HIM BACK TO ORLOK.
PHEW...
GOOD...
I'M GLAD WE GOT IT SETTLED SO QUICKLY.

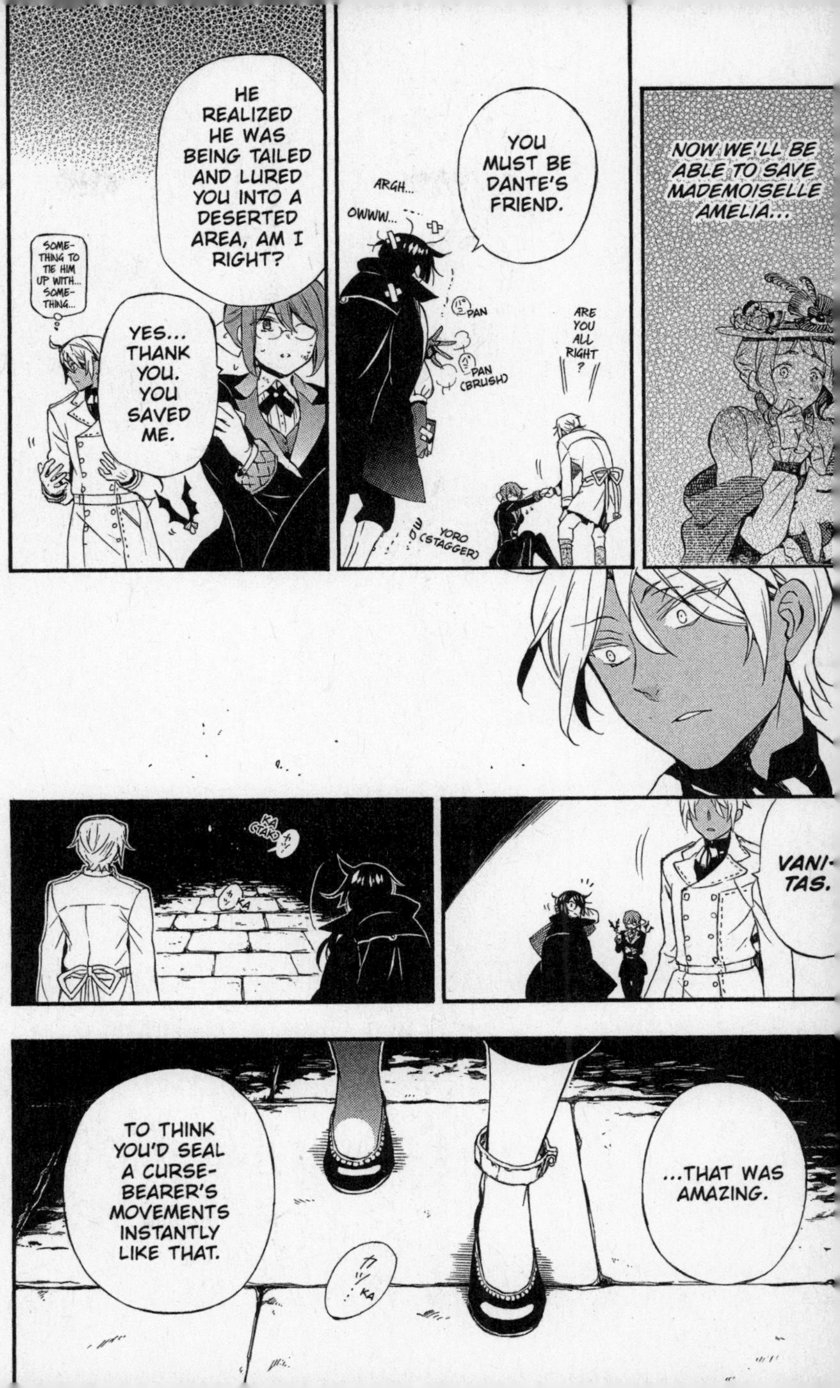
NOW WE'LL BE ABLE TO SAVE MADEMOISELLE AMELIA...
YOU MUST BE DANTE'S FRIEND.
ARGH...
OWWW...
PAN
PAN (BRUSH)
ARE YOU ALL RIGHT?
YORO (STAGGER)
HE REALIZED HE WAS BEING TAILED AND LURED YOU INTO A DESERTED AREA, AM I RIGHT?
YES... THANK YOU. YOU SAVED ME.
SOME-THING TO TIE HIM UP WITH... SOME-THING...
VANI-TAS.
KA (TAK)
KA
...THAT WAS AMAZING.
TO THINK YOU'D SEAL A CURSE-BEARER'S MOVEMENTS INSTANTLY LIKE THAT.
KA

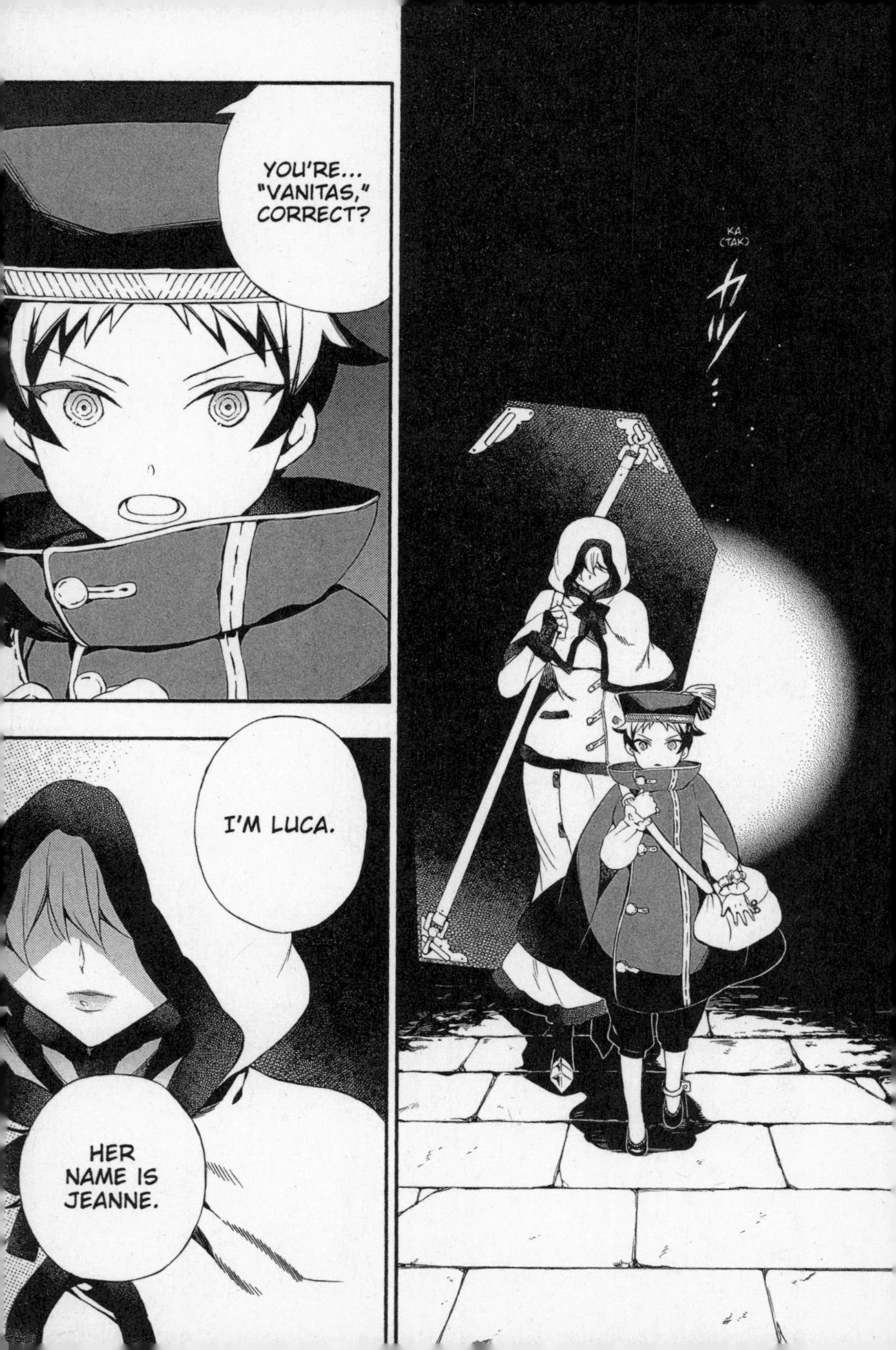
KA (TAK)
カッ…
YOU'RE… "VANITAS," CORRECT?
I'M LUCA.
HER NAME IS JEANNE.

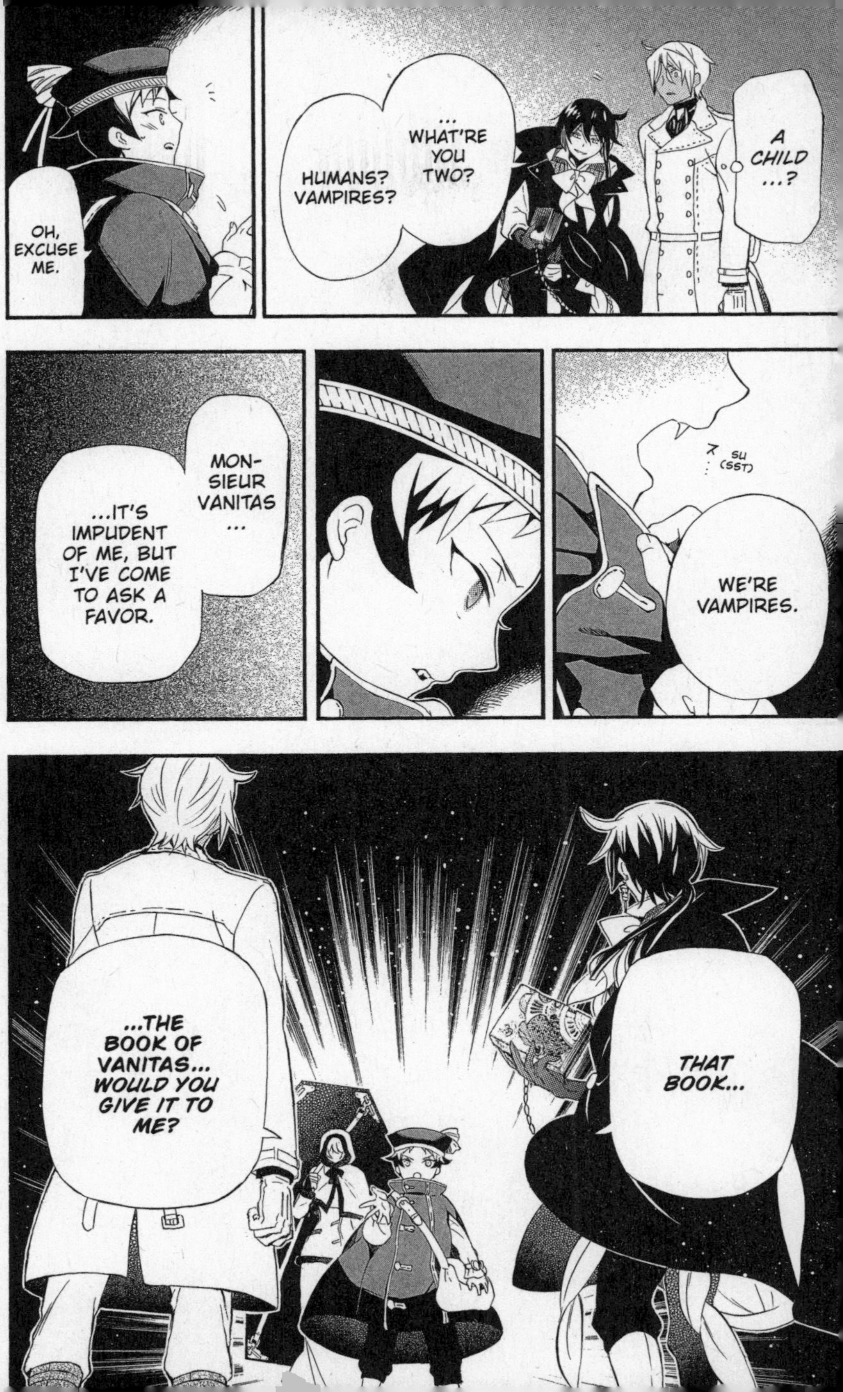
A CHILD ...?
... WHAT'RE YOU TWO?
HUMANS? VAMPIRES?
OH, EXCUSE ME.
SU (SST)
WE'RE VAMPIRES.
MON-SIEUR VANITAS ...
...IT'S IMPUDENT OF ME, BUT I'VE COME TO ASK A FAVOR.
THAT BOOK...
...THE BOOK OF VANITAS... WOULD YOU GIVE IT TO ME?

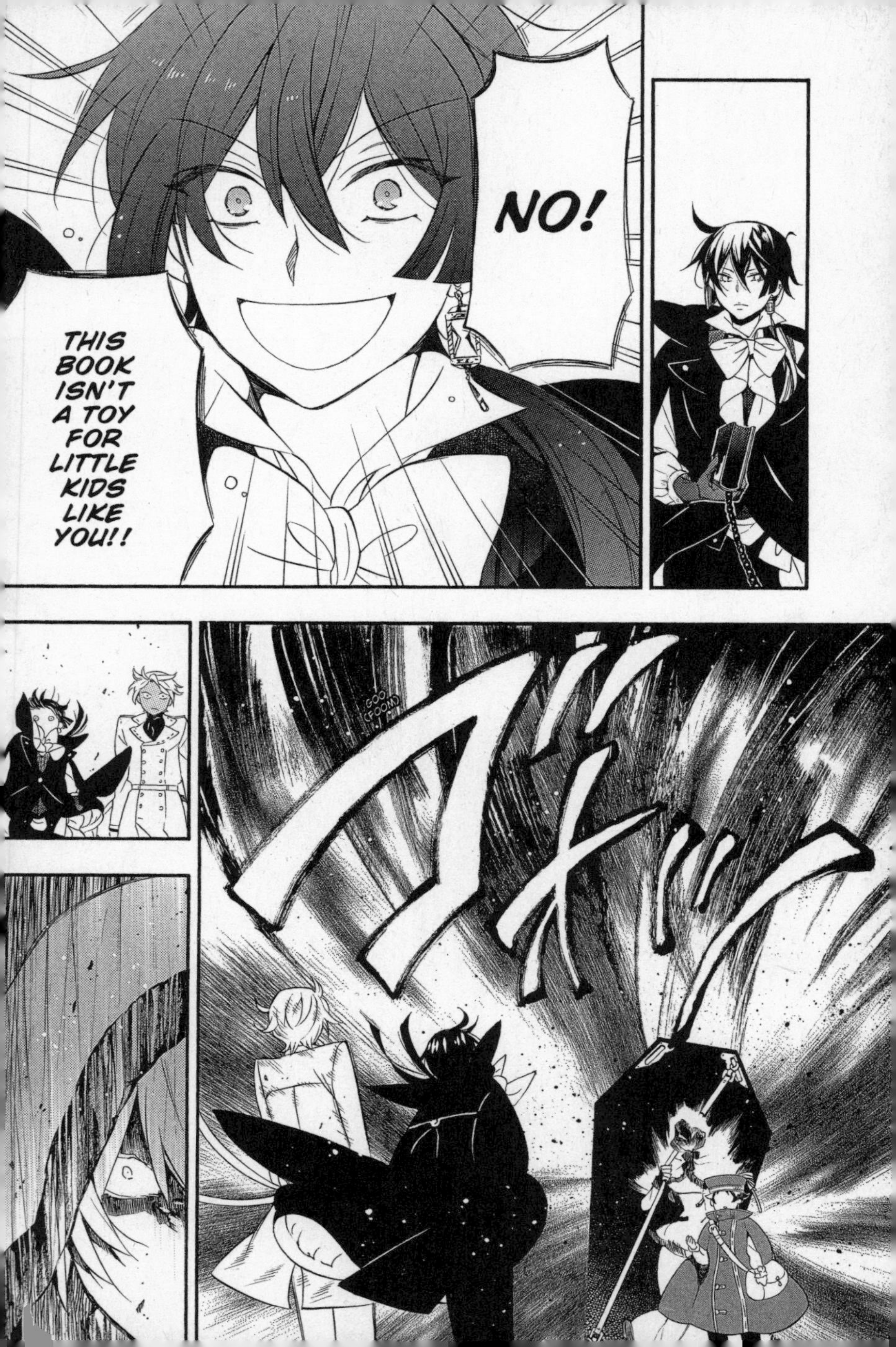
NO!
THIS BOOK ISN'T A TOY FOR LITTLE KIDS LIKE YOU!!
GOO (FOOM)

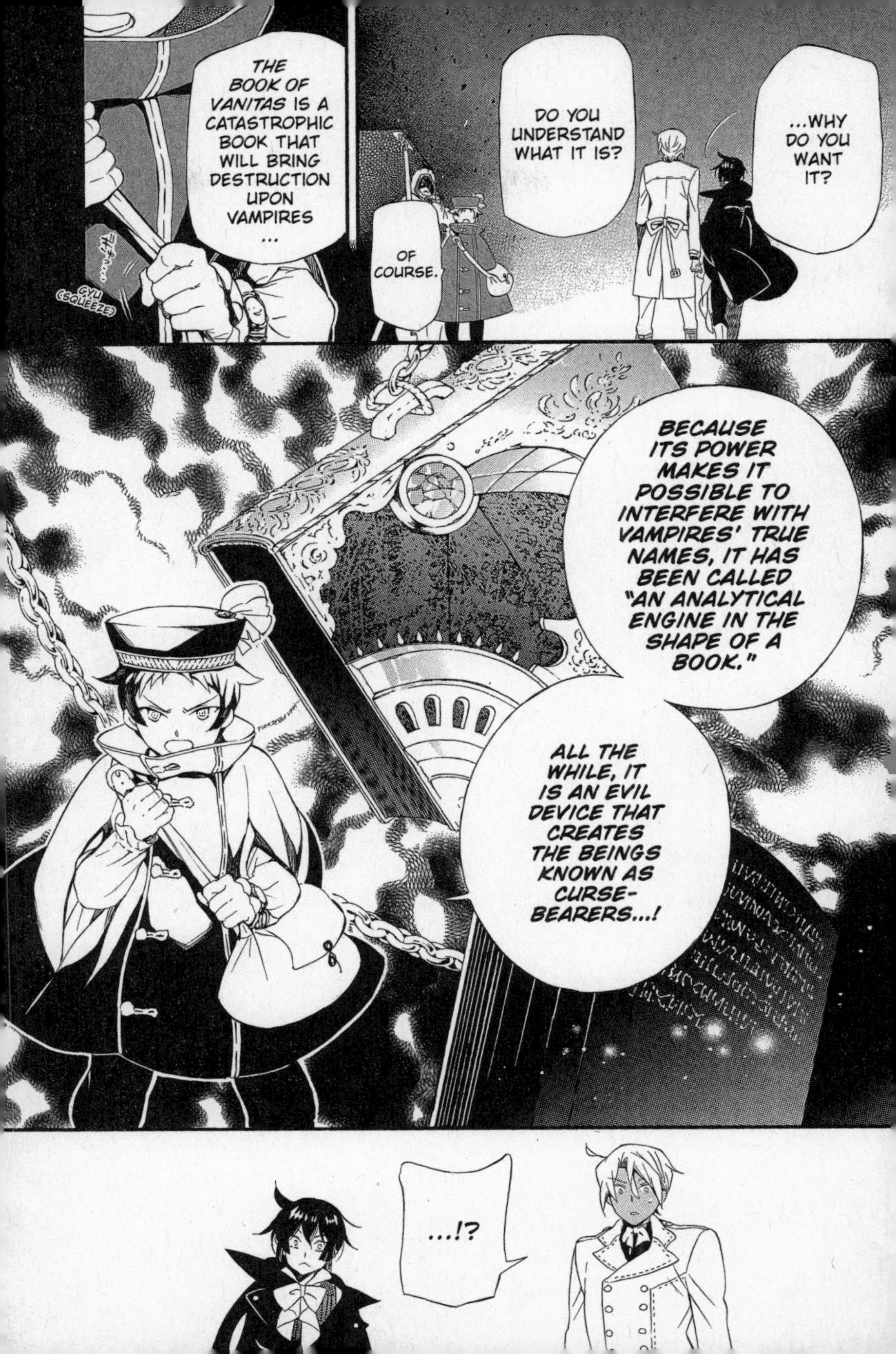
...WHY DO YOU WANT IT?
DO YOU UNDERSTAND WHAT IT IS?
OF COURSE.
THE BOOK OF VANITAS IS A CATASTROPHIC BOOK THAT WILL BRING DESTRUCTION UPON VAMPIRES ...
GYU (SQUEEZE)
BECAUSE ITS POWER MAKES IT POSSIBLE TO INTERFERE WITH VAMPIRES' TRUE NAMES, IT HAS BEEN CALLED "AN ANALYTICAL ENGINE IN THE SHAPE OF A BOOK."
ALL THE WHILE, IT IS AN EVIL DEVICE THAT CREATES THE BEINGS KNOWN AS CURSE-BEARERS...!
...!?

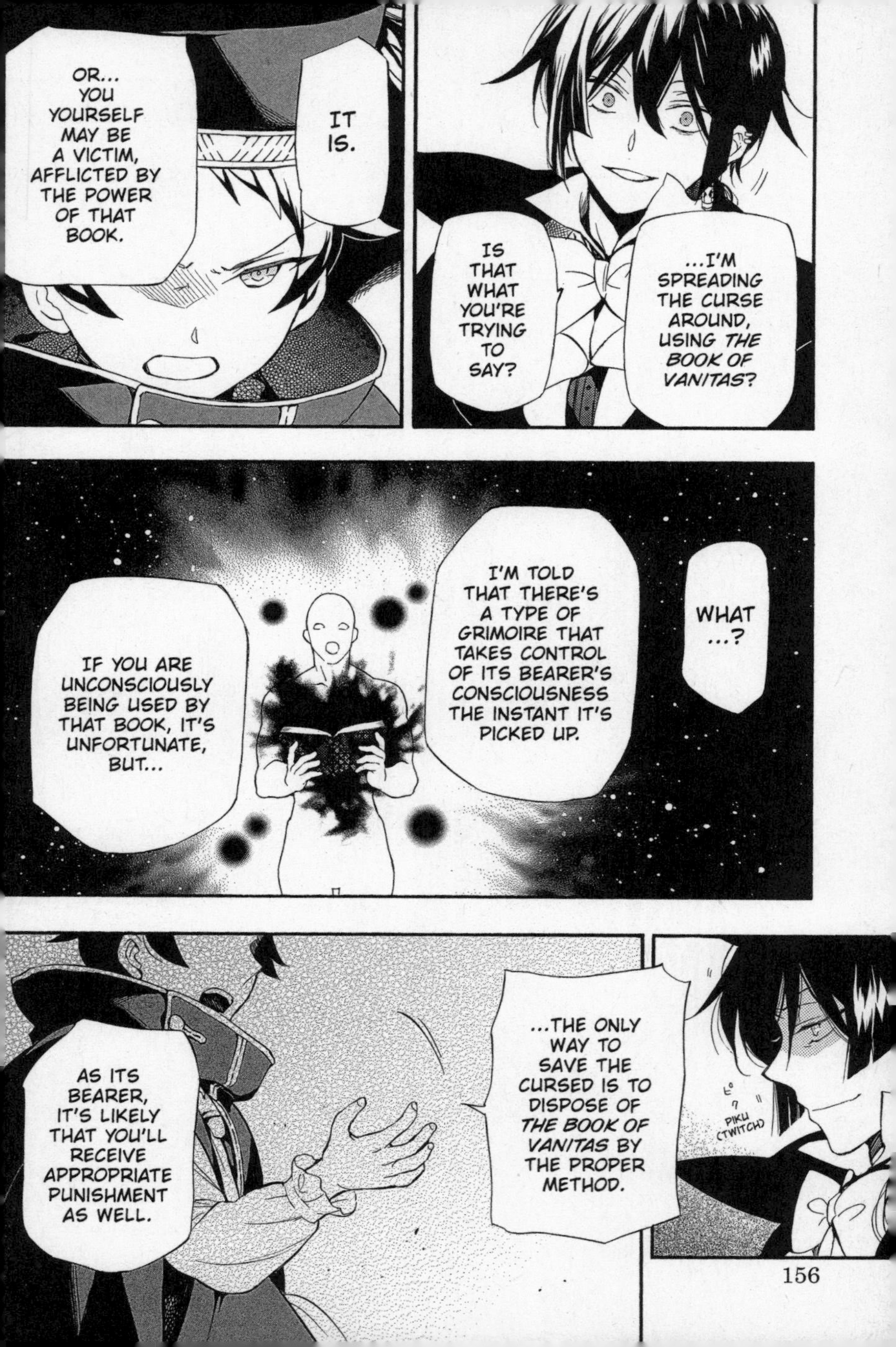
...I'M SPREADING THE CURSE AROUND, USING *THE BOOK OF VANITAS*?
IS THAT WHAT YOU'RE TRYING TO SAY?
IT IS.
OR... YOU YOURSELF MAY BE A VICTIM, AFFLICTED BY THE POWER OF THAT BOOK.
WHAT...?
I'M TOLD THAT THERE'S A TYPE OF GRIMOIRE THAT TAKES CONTROL OF ITS BEARER'S CONSCIOUSNESS THE INSTANT IT'S PICKED UP.
IF YOU ARE UNCONSCIOUSLY BEING USED BY THAT BOOK, IT'S UNFORTUNATE, BUT...
ピク
PIKU (TWITCH)
...THE ONLY WAY TO SAVE THE CURSED IS TO DISPOSE OF *THE BOOK OF VANITAS* BY THE PROPER METHOD.
AS ITS BEARER, IT'S LIKELY THAT YOU'LL RECEIVE APPROPRIATE PUNISHMENT AS WELL.

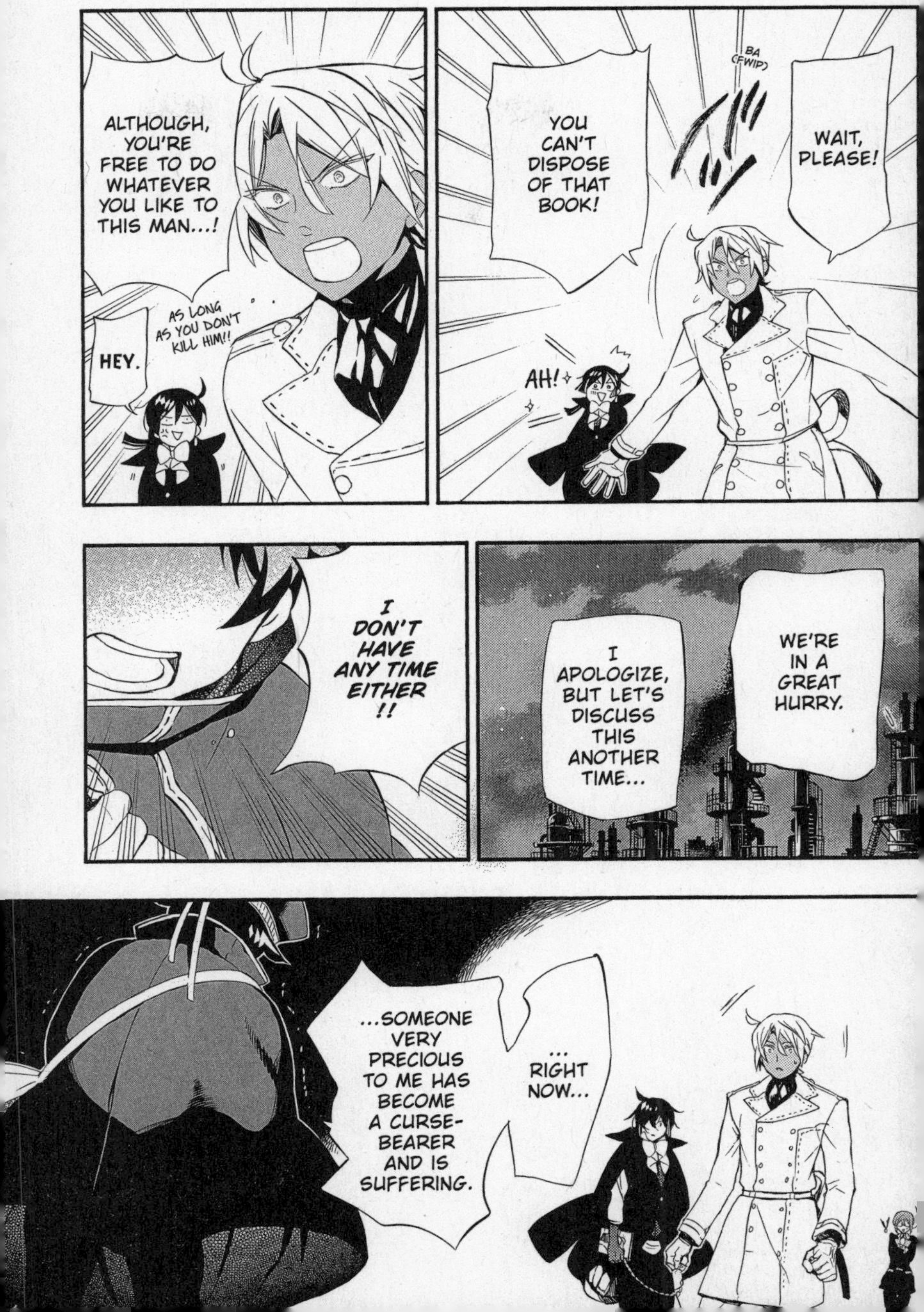
WAIT, PLEASE!
BA (FWIP)
YOU CAN'T DISPOSE OF THAT BOOK!
AH!
ALTHOUGH, YOU'RE FREE TO DO WHATEVER YOU LIKE TO THIS MAN...!
AS LONG AS YOU DON'T KILL HIM!!
HEY.
WE'RE IN A GREAT HURRY.
I APOLOGIZE, BUT LET'S DISCUSS THIS ANOTHER TIME...
I DON'T HAVE ANY TIME EITHER!!
...RIGHT NOW...
...SOMEONE VERY PRECIOUS TO ME HAS BECOME A CURSE-BEARER AND IS SUFFERING.

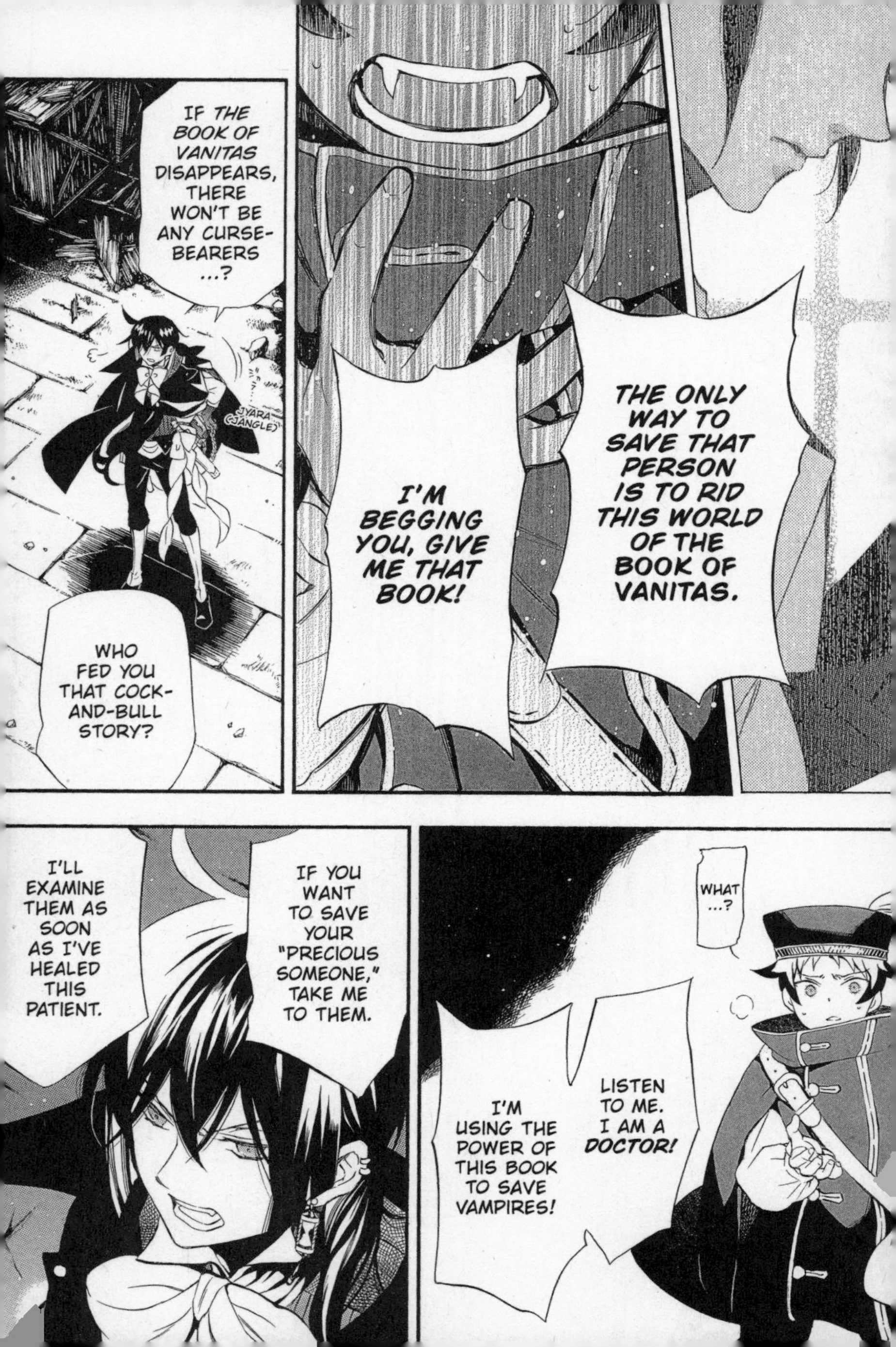
THE ONLY WAY TO SAVE THAT PERSON IS TO RID THIS WORLD OF THE BOOK OF VANITAS.
I'M BEGGING YOU, GIVE ME THAT BOOK!
IF *THE BOOK OF VANITAS* DISAPPEARS, THERE WON'T BE ANY CURSE-BEARERS ...?
JYARA (JANGLE)
WHO FED YOU THAT COCK-AND-BULL STORY?
WHAT ...?
LISTEN TO ME. I AM A *DOCTOR!*
I'M USING THE POWER OF THIS BOOK TO SAVE VAMPIRES!
IF YOU WANT TO SAVE YOUR "PRECIOUS SOMEONE," TAKE ME TO THEM.
I'LL EXAMINE THEM AS SOON AS I'VE HEALED THIS PATIENT.

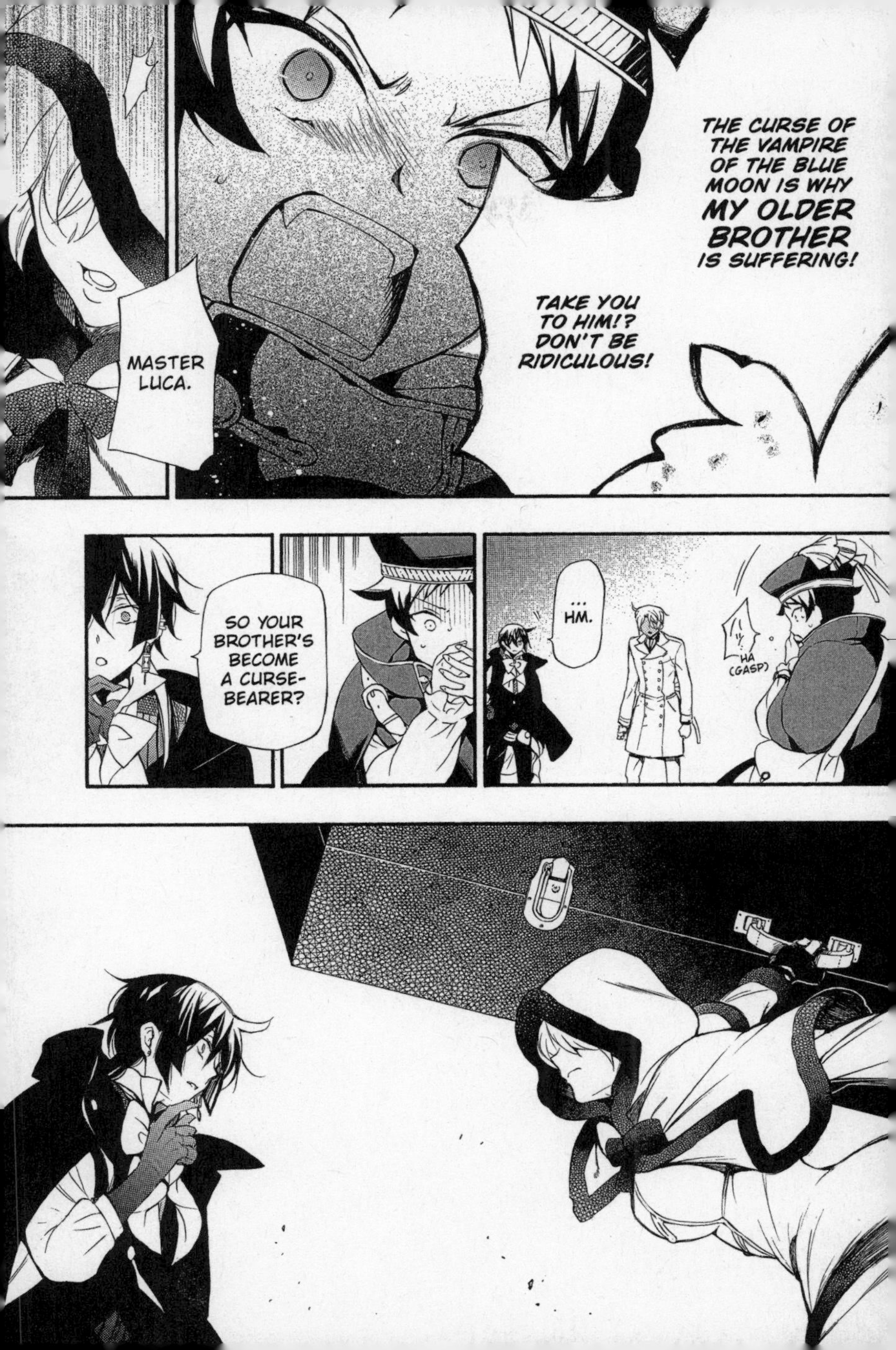

THE CURSE OF THE VAMPIRE OF THE BLUE MOON IS WHY MY OLDER BROTHER IS SUFFERING!
TAKE YOU TO HIM!? DON'T BE RIDICULOUS!
MASTER LUCA.
HA (GASP)
... HM.
SO YOUR BROTHER'S BECOME A CURSE-BEARER?

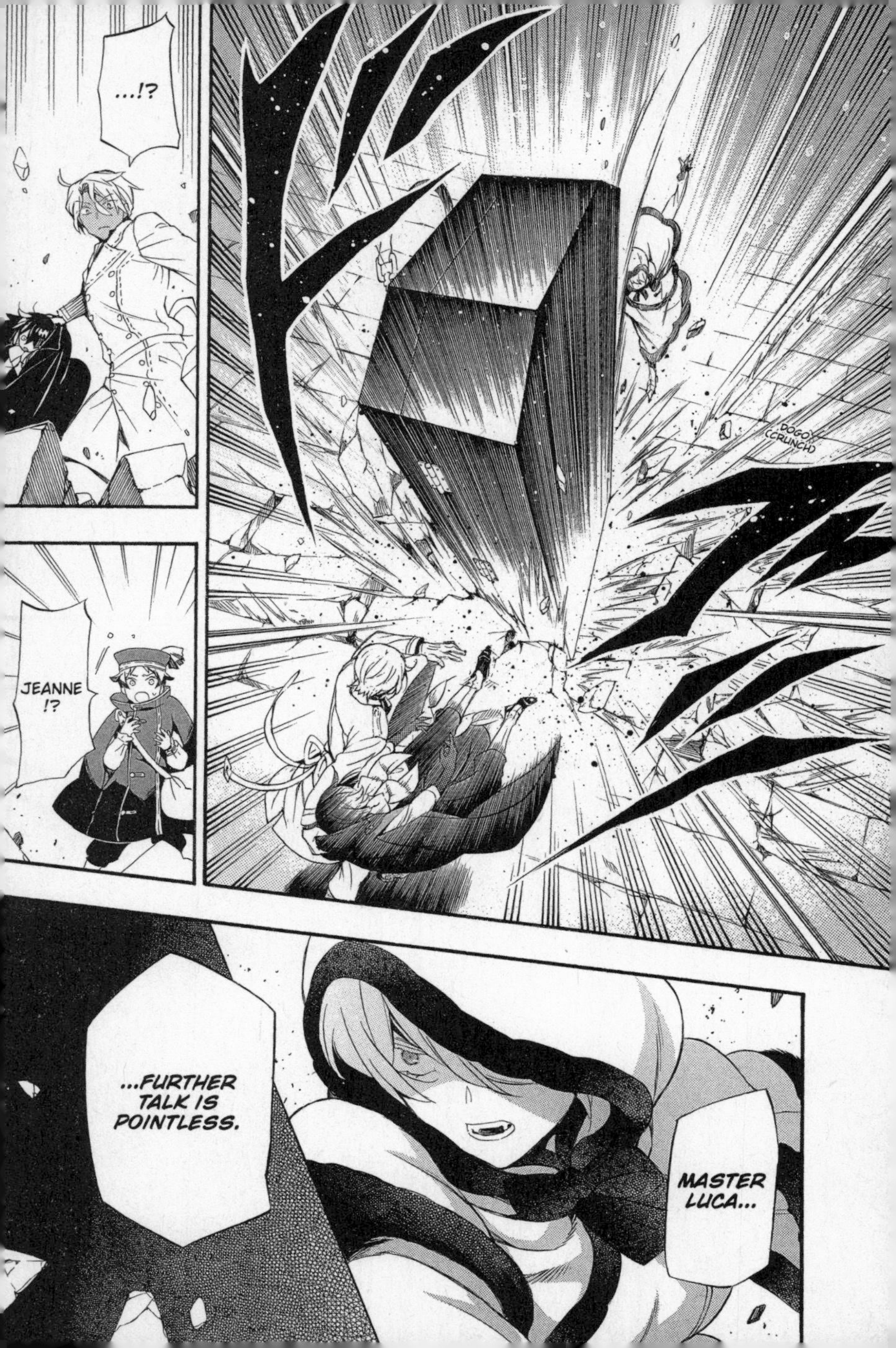
DOGO (CRUNCH)
...!?
JEANNE !?
MASTER LUCA...
...FURTHER TALK IS POINTLESS.

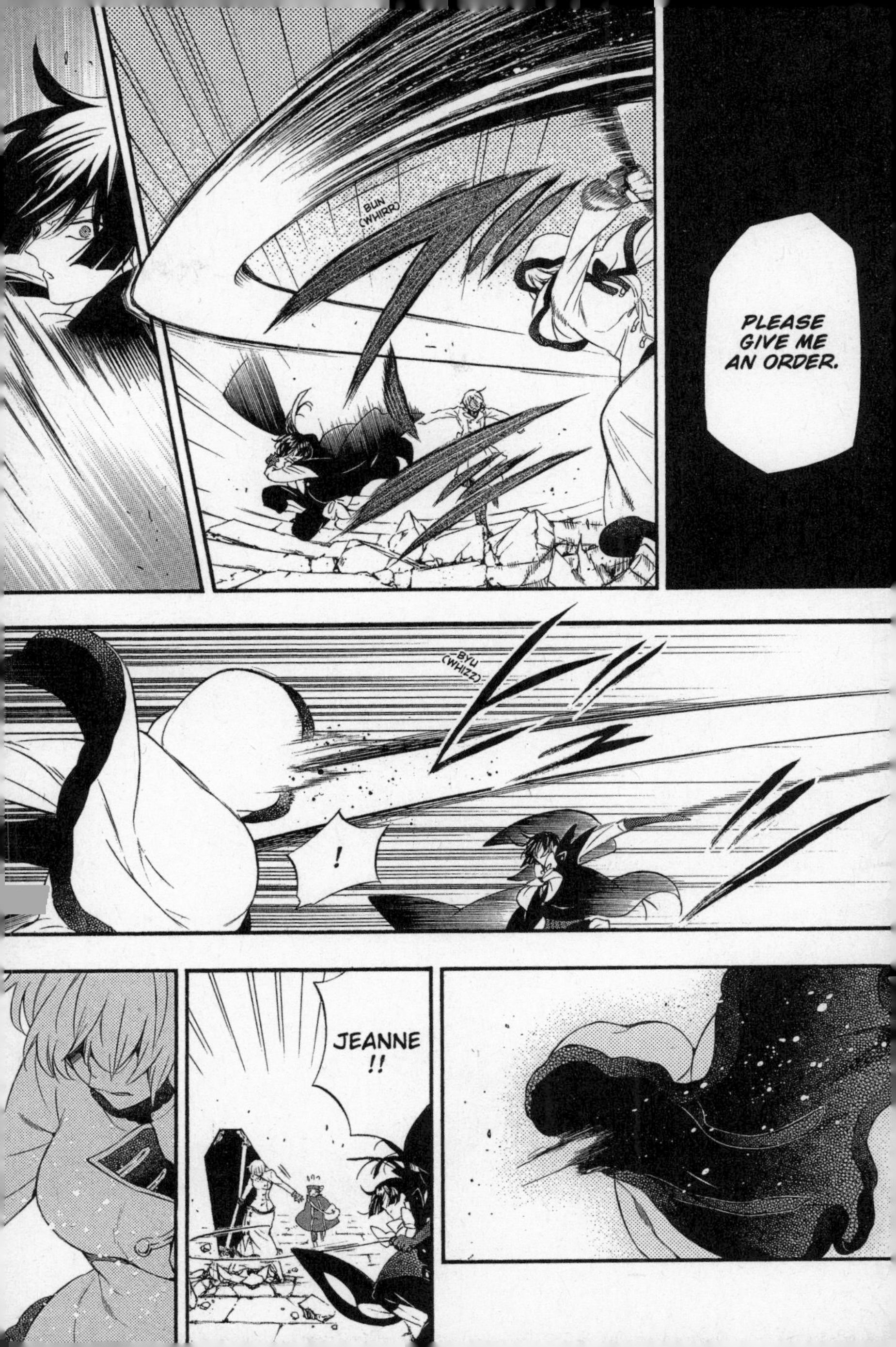
PLEASE GIVE ME AN ORDER.
BUN (WHIRR)
BYU (WHIZZ)
!
JEANNE !!

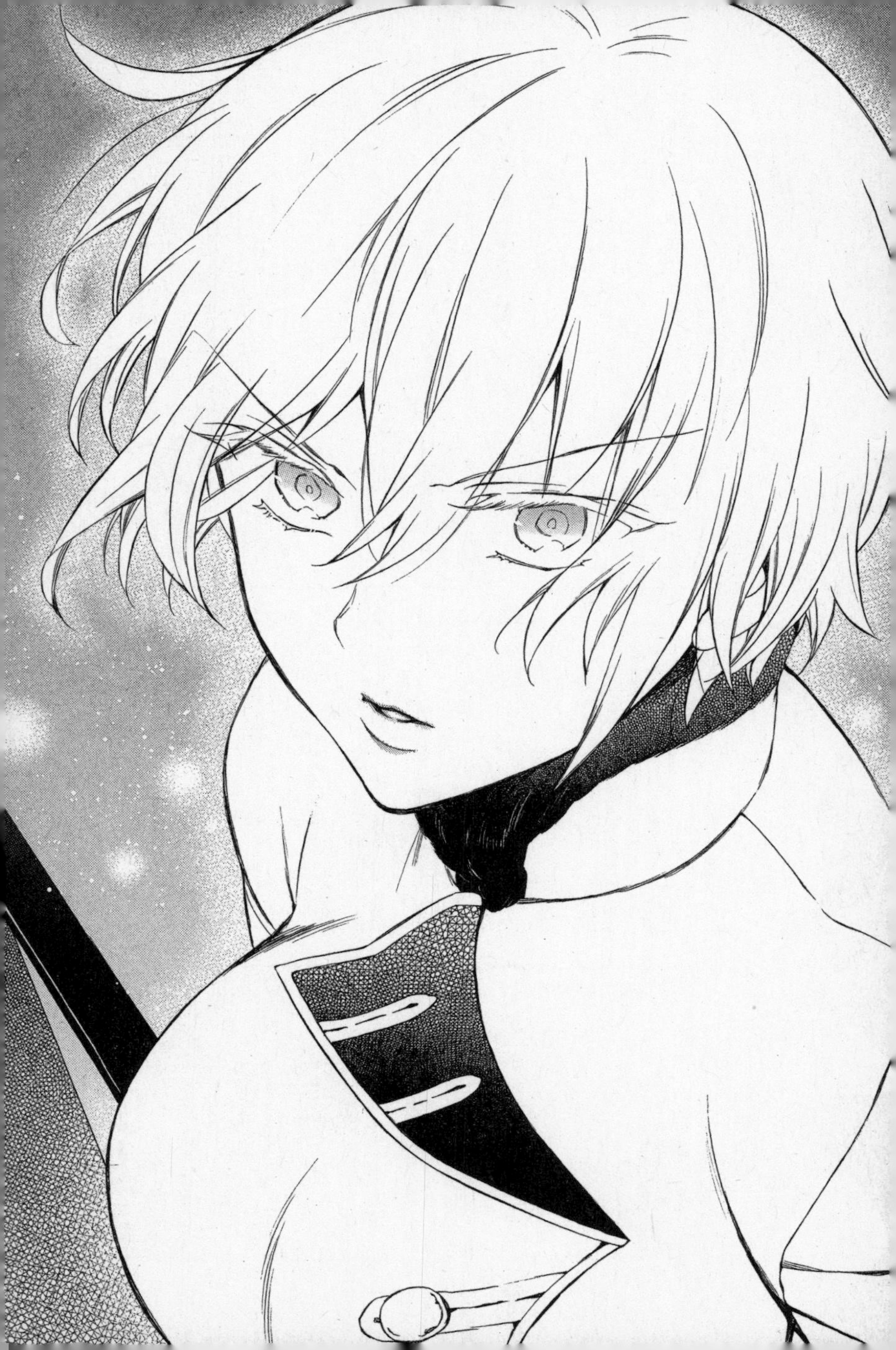

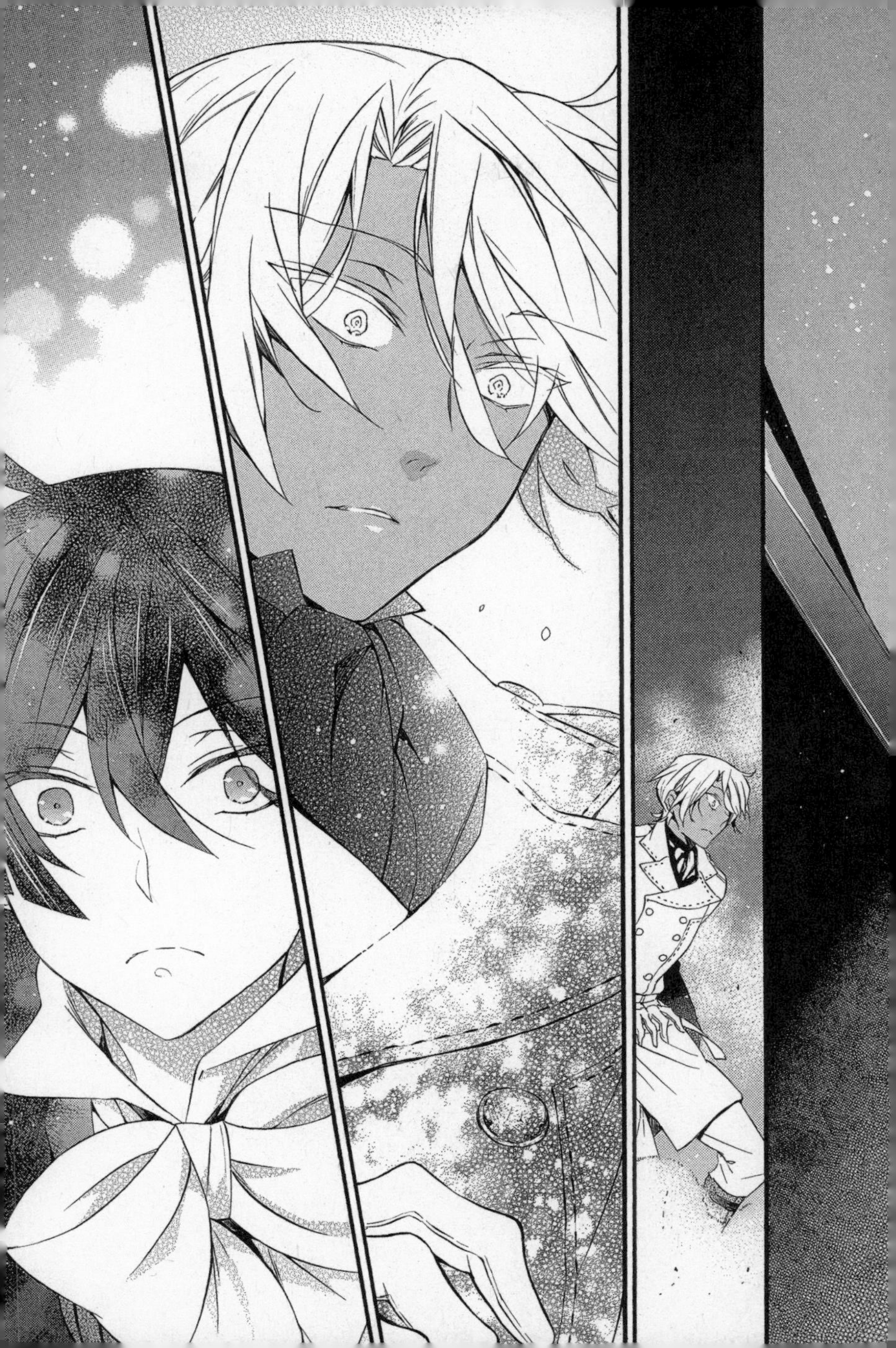

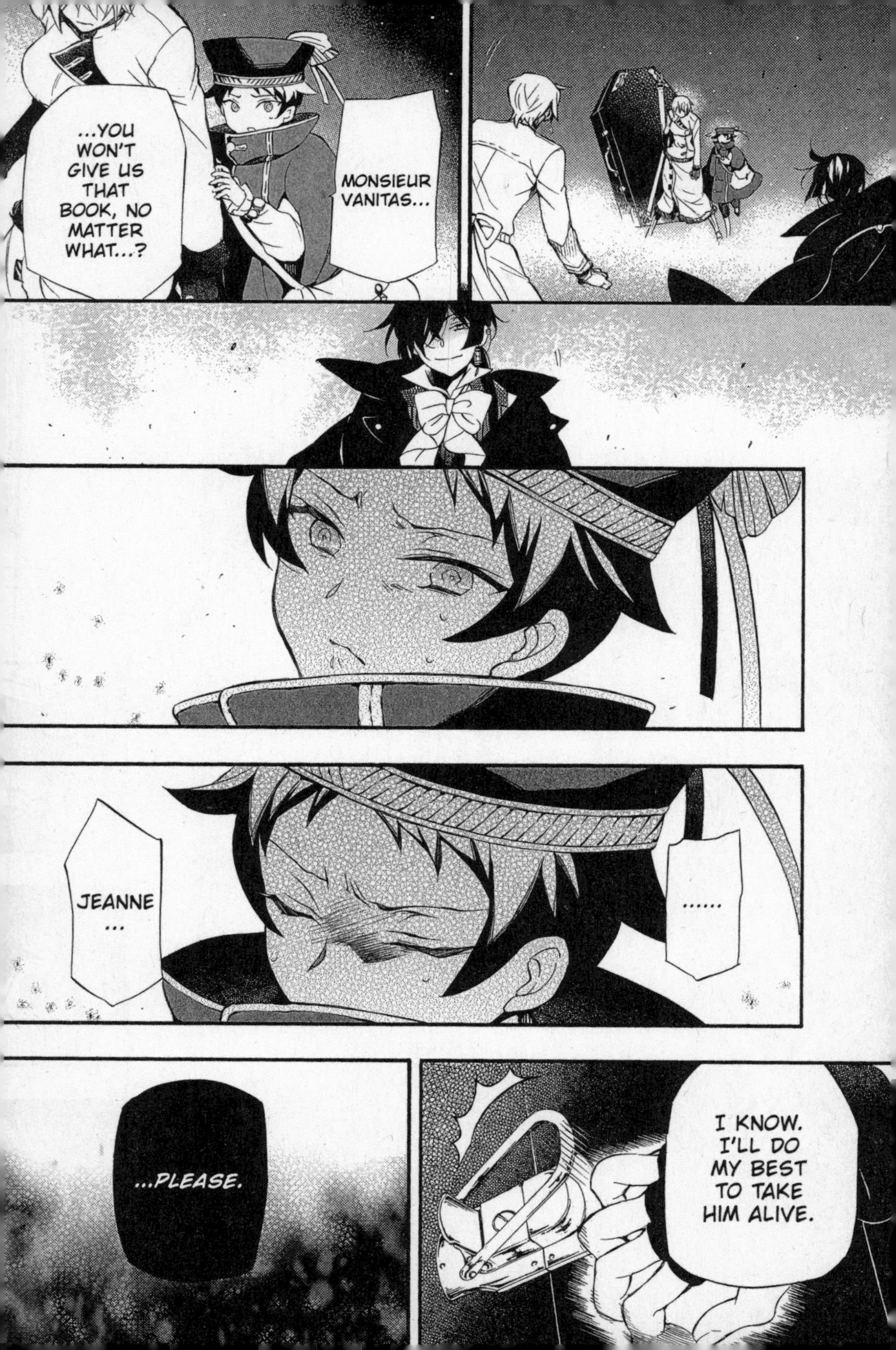
MONSIEUR VANITAS...
...YOU WON'T GIVE US THAT BOOK, NO MATTER WHAT...?
......
JEANNE ...
I KNOW. I'LL DO MY BEST TO TAKE HIM ALIVE.
...PLEASE.

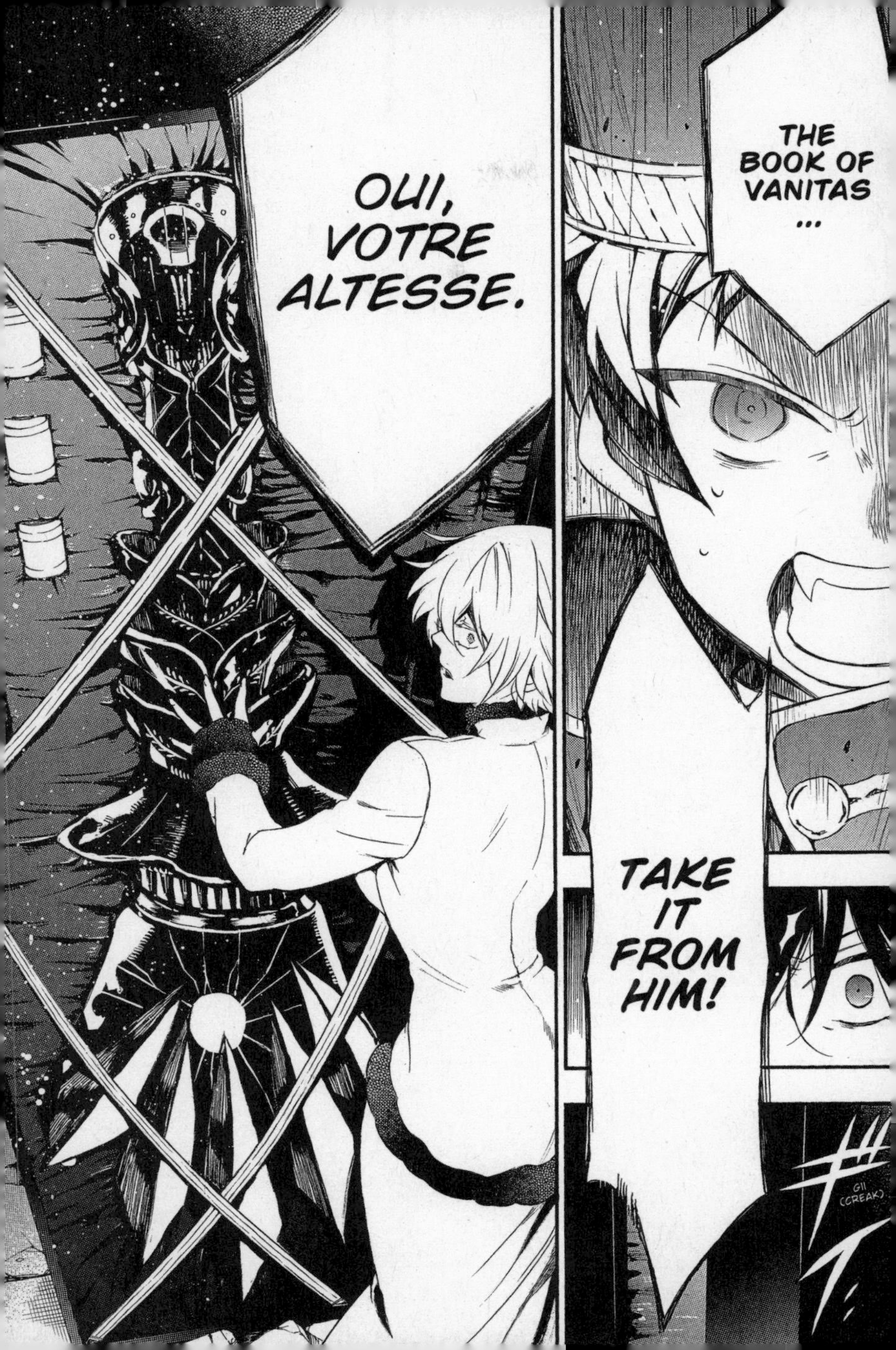
THE BOOK OF VANITAS...
TAKE IT FROM HIM!
GII (CREAK)
OUI, VOTRE ALTESSE.

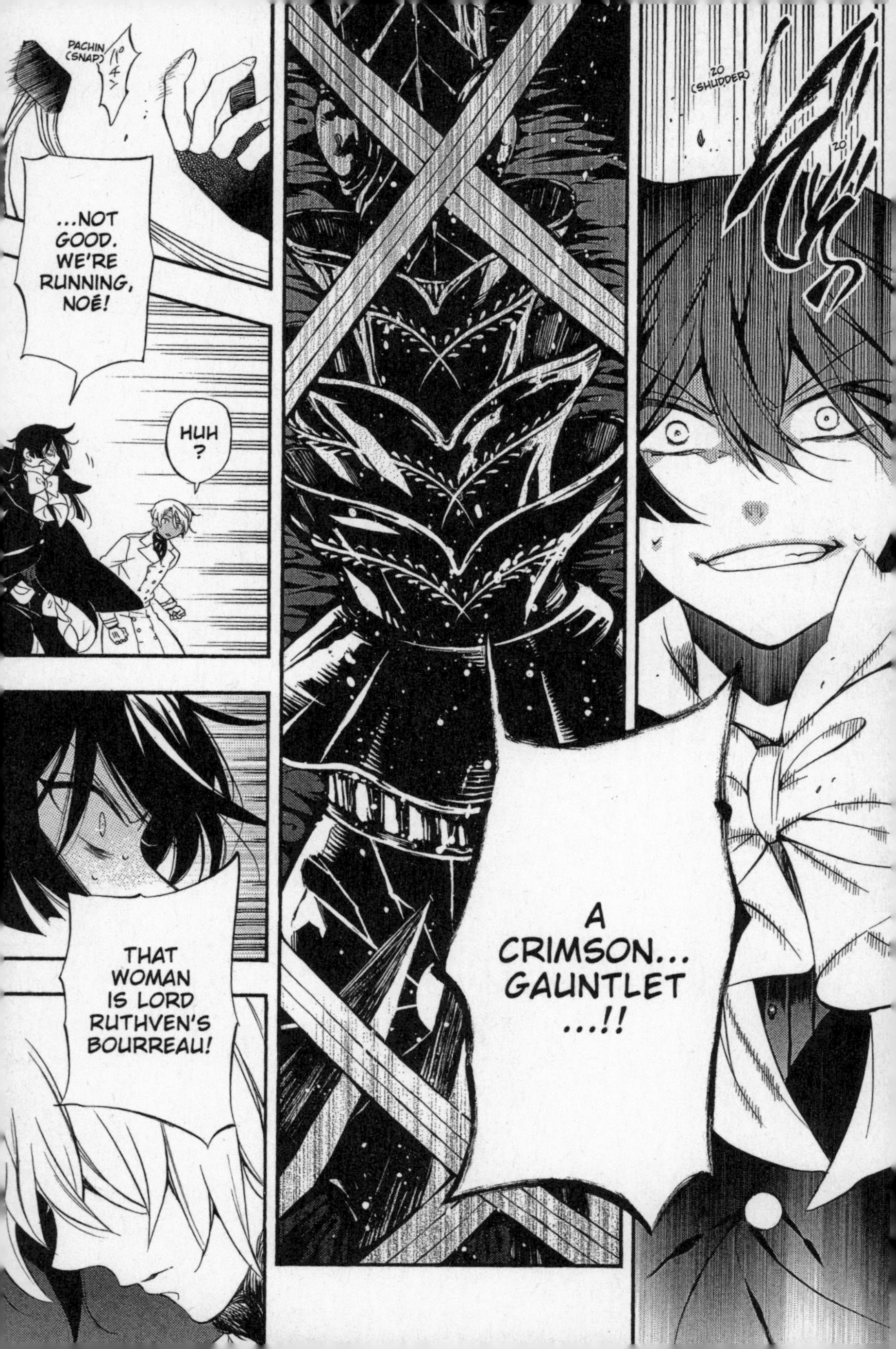
ZO (SHUDDER)
ZO
A CRIMSON... GAUNTLET ...!!
PACHIN (SNAP)
パチン
...NOT GOOD. WE'RE RUNNING, NOÉ!
HUH?
THAT WOMAN IS LORD RUTHVEN'S BOURREAU!

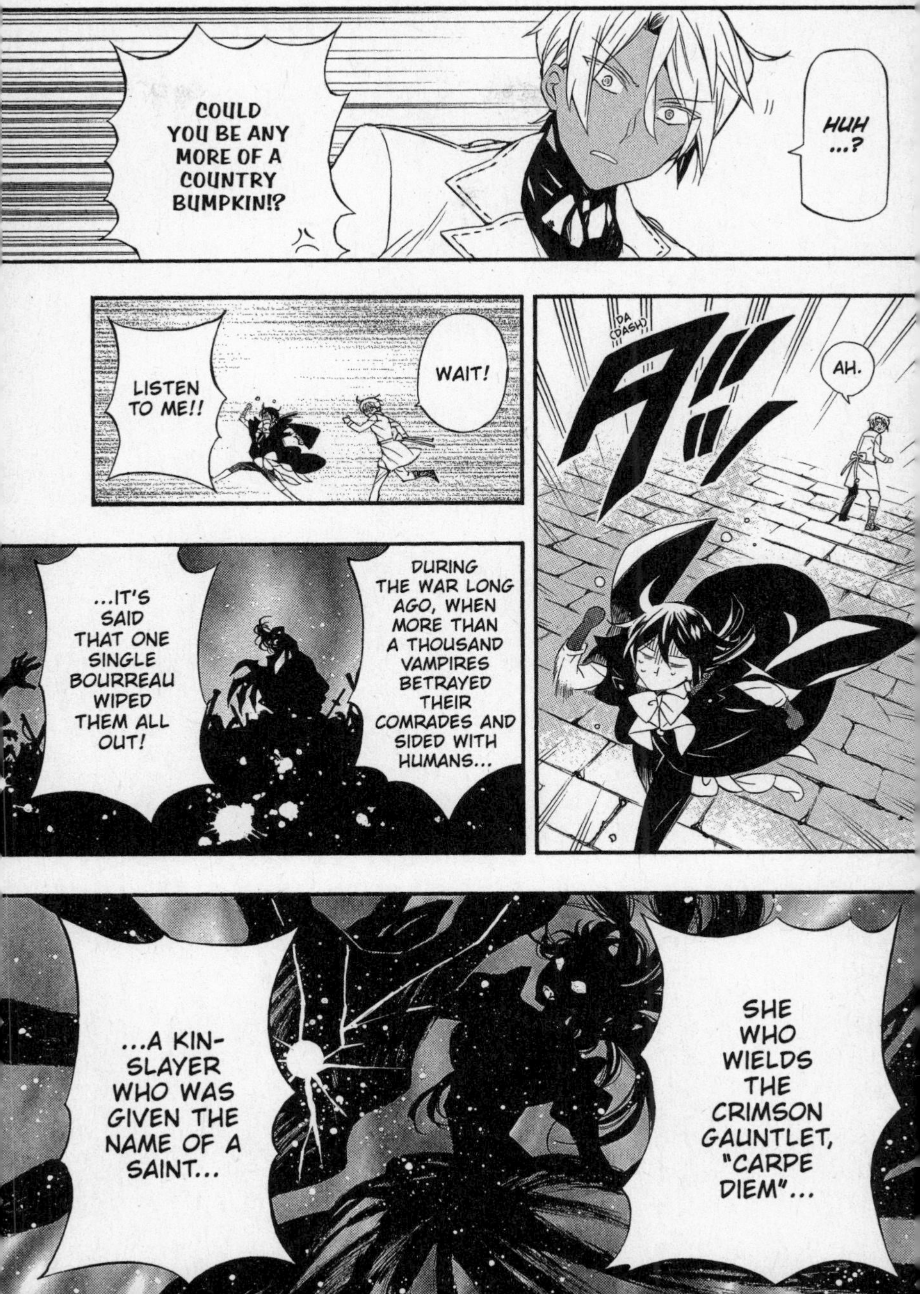
HUH ...?
COULD YOU BE ANY MORE OF A COUNTRY BUMPKIN!?
DA (DASH)
AH.
WAIT!
LISTEN TO ME!!
DURING THE WAR LONG AGO, WHEN MORE THAN A THOUSAND VAMPIRES BETRAYED THEIR COMRADES AND SIDED WITH HUMANS...
...IT'S SAID THAT ONE SINGLE BOURREAU WIPED THEM ALL OUT!
SHE WHO WIELDS THE CRIMSON GAUNTLET, "CARPE DIEM"...
...A KIN-SLAYER WHO WAS GIVEN THE NAME OF A SAINT...

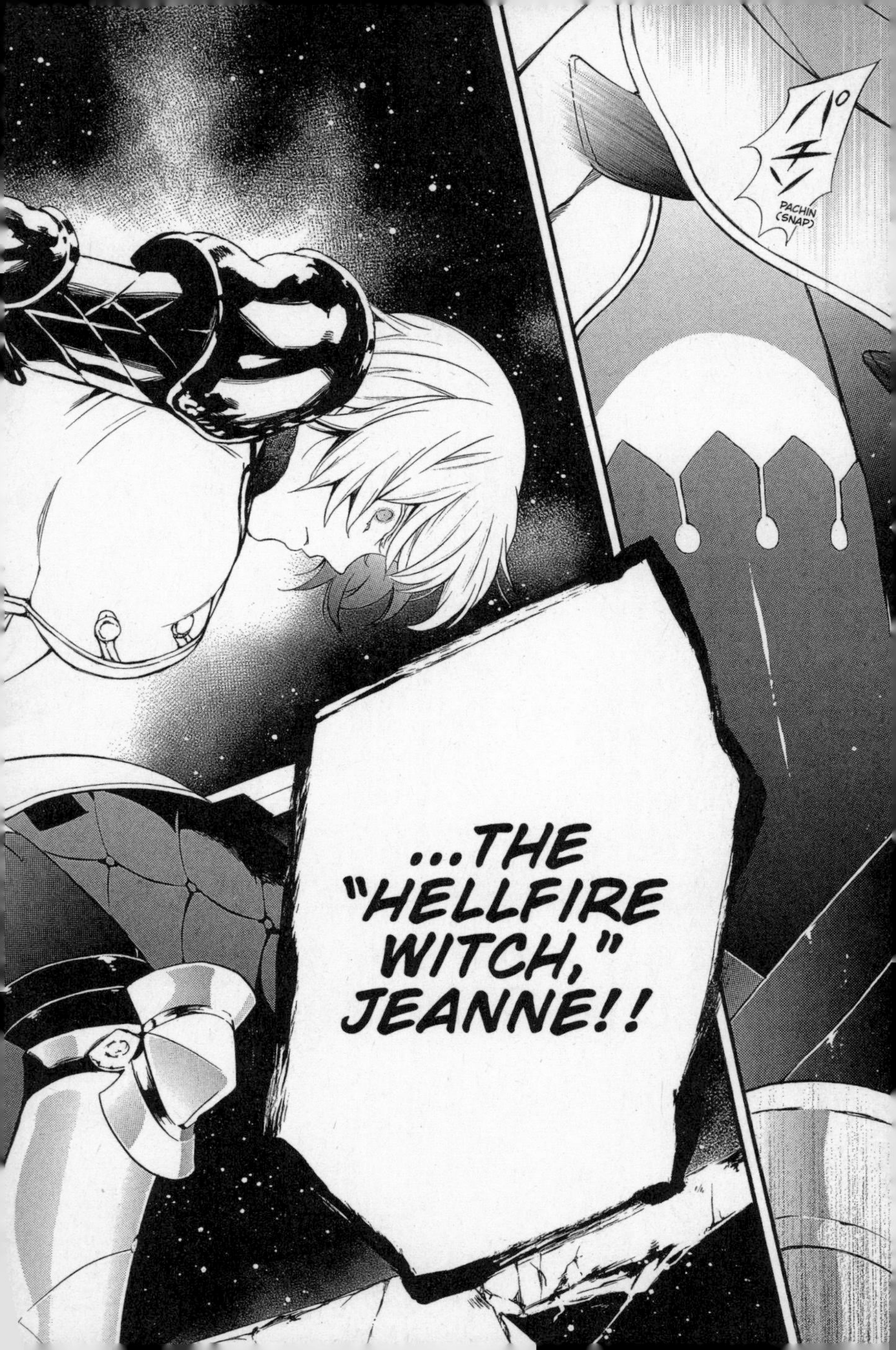
パチン
PACHIN (SNAP)
..."THE "HELLFIRE WITCH," JEANNE!!

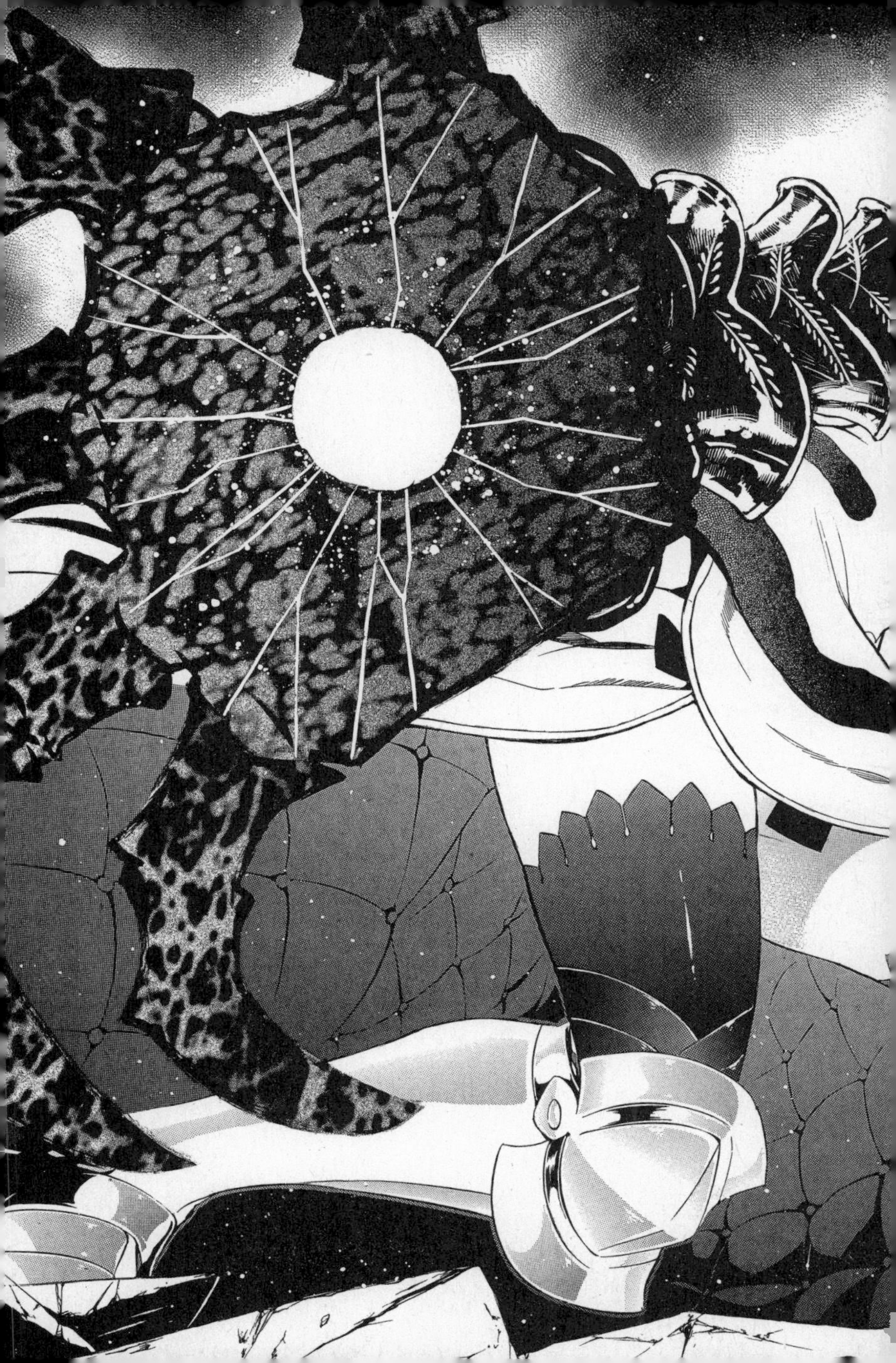

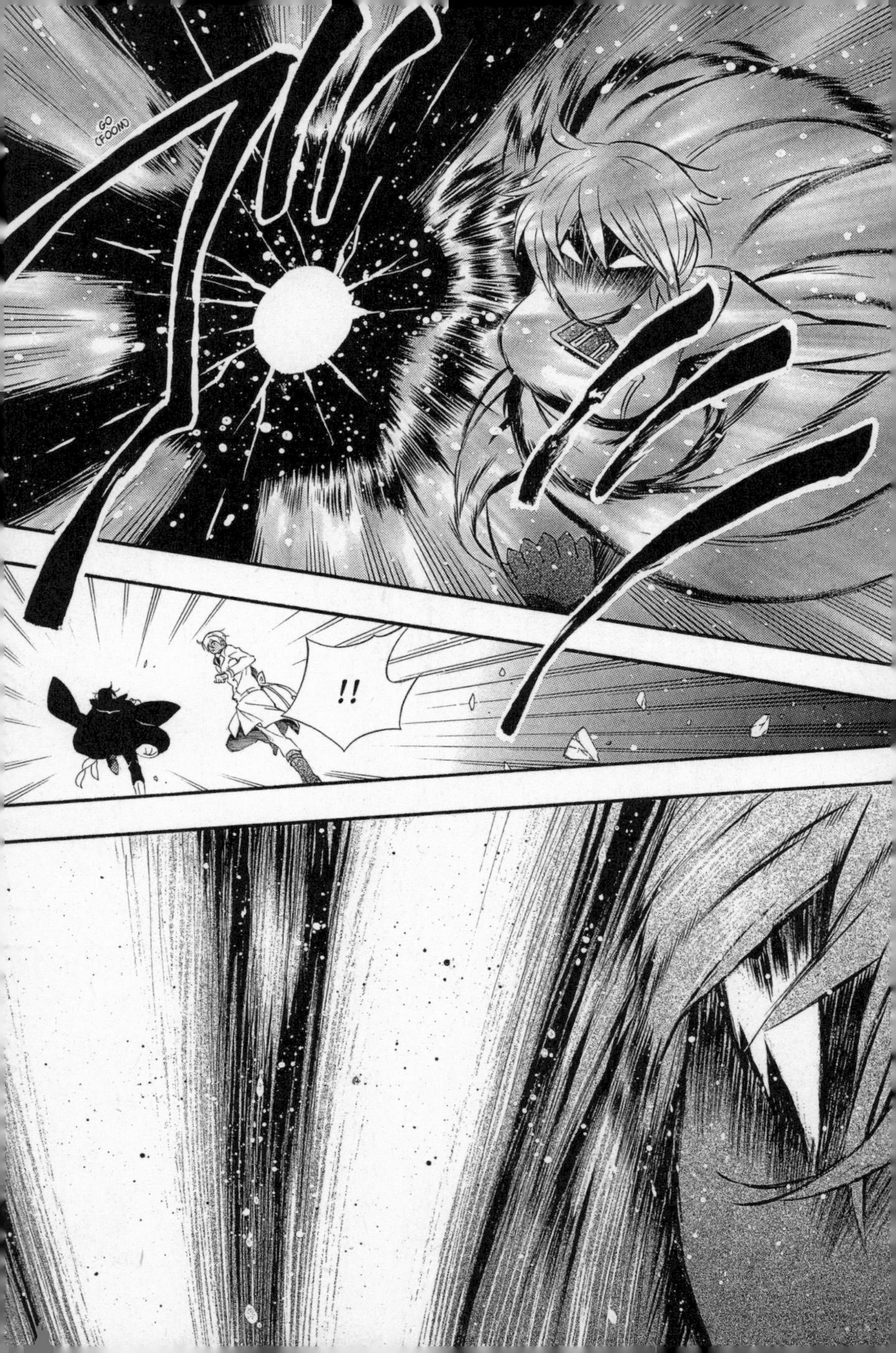
GO (FOOM)
!!

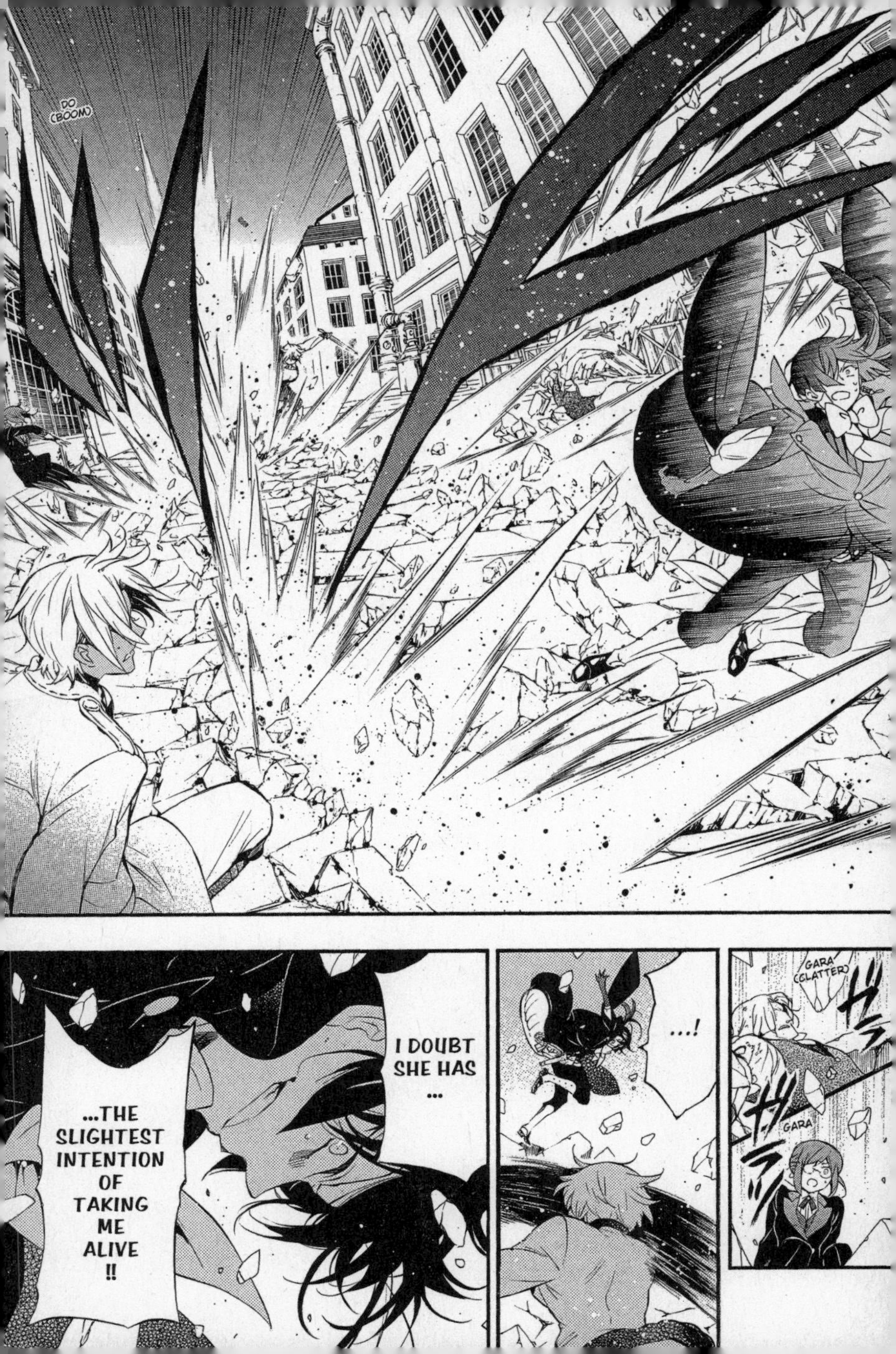
DO (BOOM)
GARA (CLATTER)
GARA
...!
I DOUBT SHE HAS ...
...THE SLIGHTEST INTENTION OF TAKING ME ALIVE !!

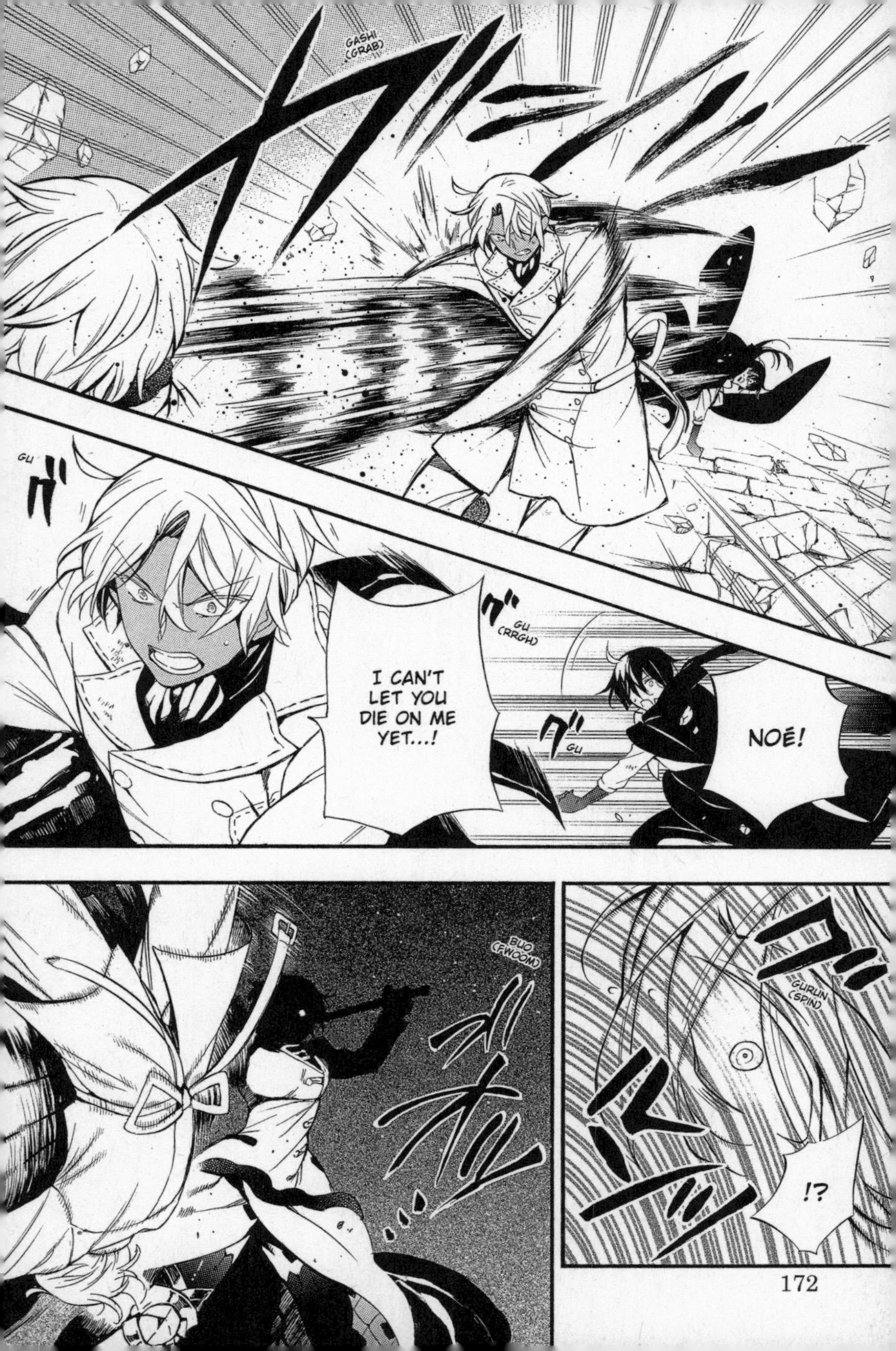
GASHI (GRAB)
NOÉ!
GU
GU (RRGH)
I CAN'T LET YOU DIE ON ME YET...!
GU
GURUN (SPIN)
!?
BUO (FWOOM)

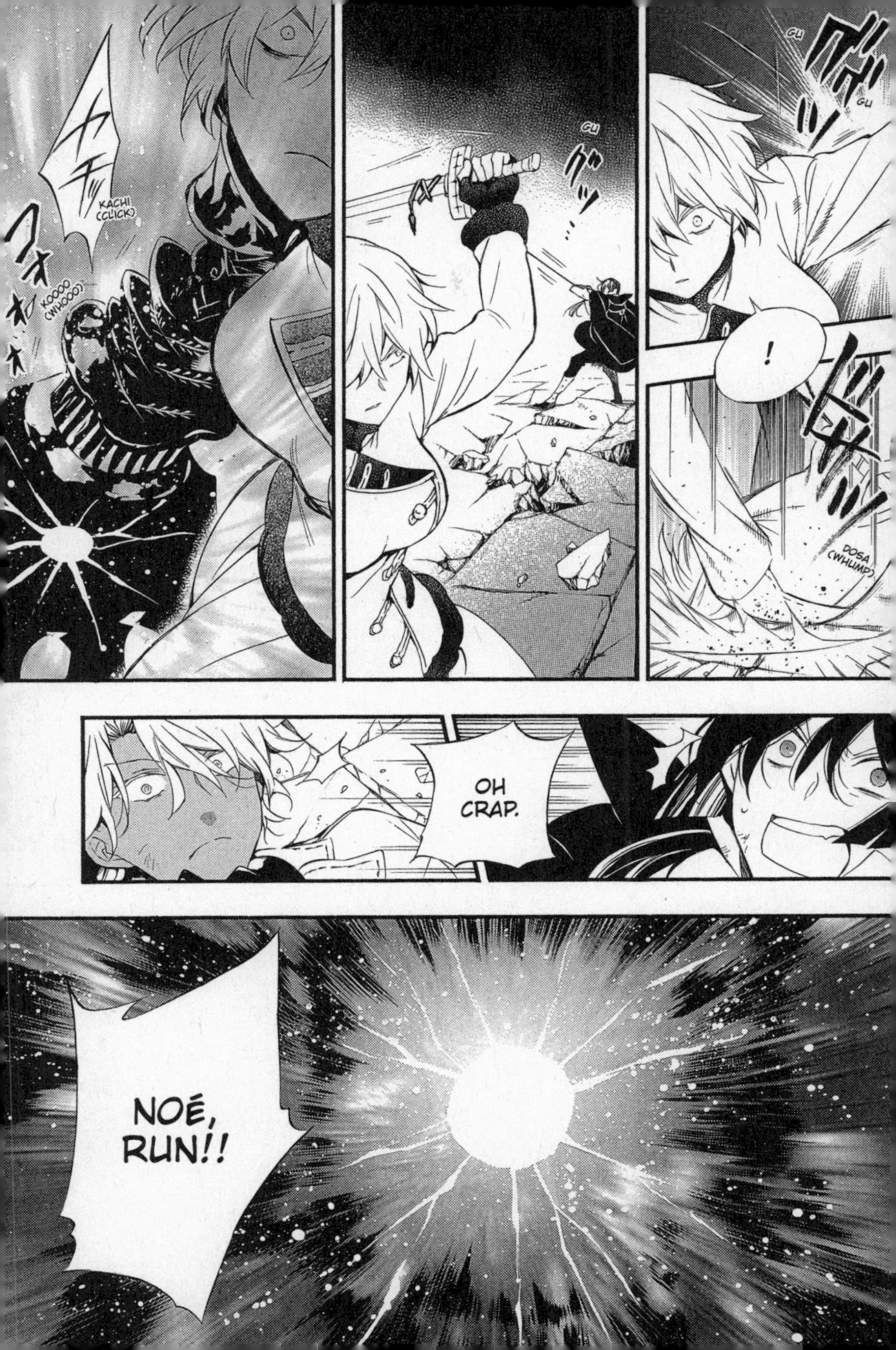
GU
GU
!
DOSA (WHUMP)
GU
KACHI (CLICK)
KOOOO (WHOOO)
OH CRAP.
NOÉ, RUN!!

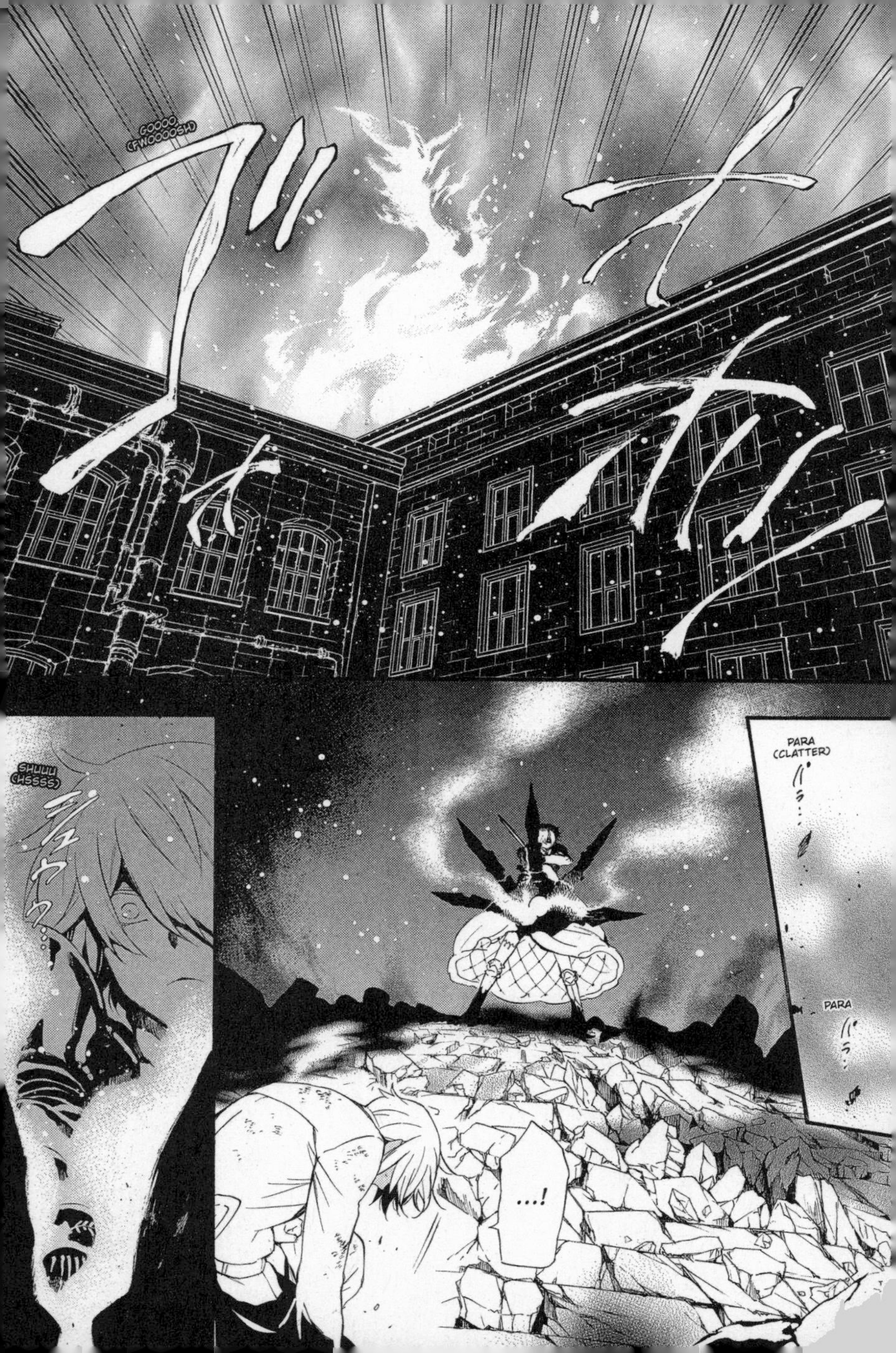
GOOOO (FWOOOOSH)
PARA (CLATTER)
PARA
...!
SHUUU (HSSSS)

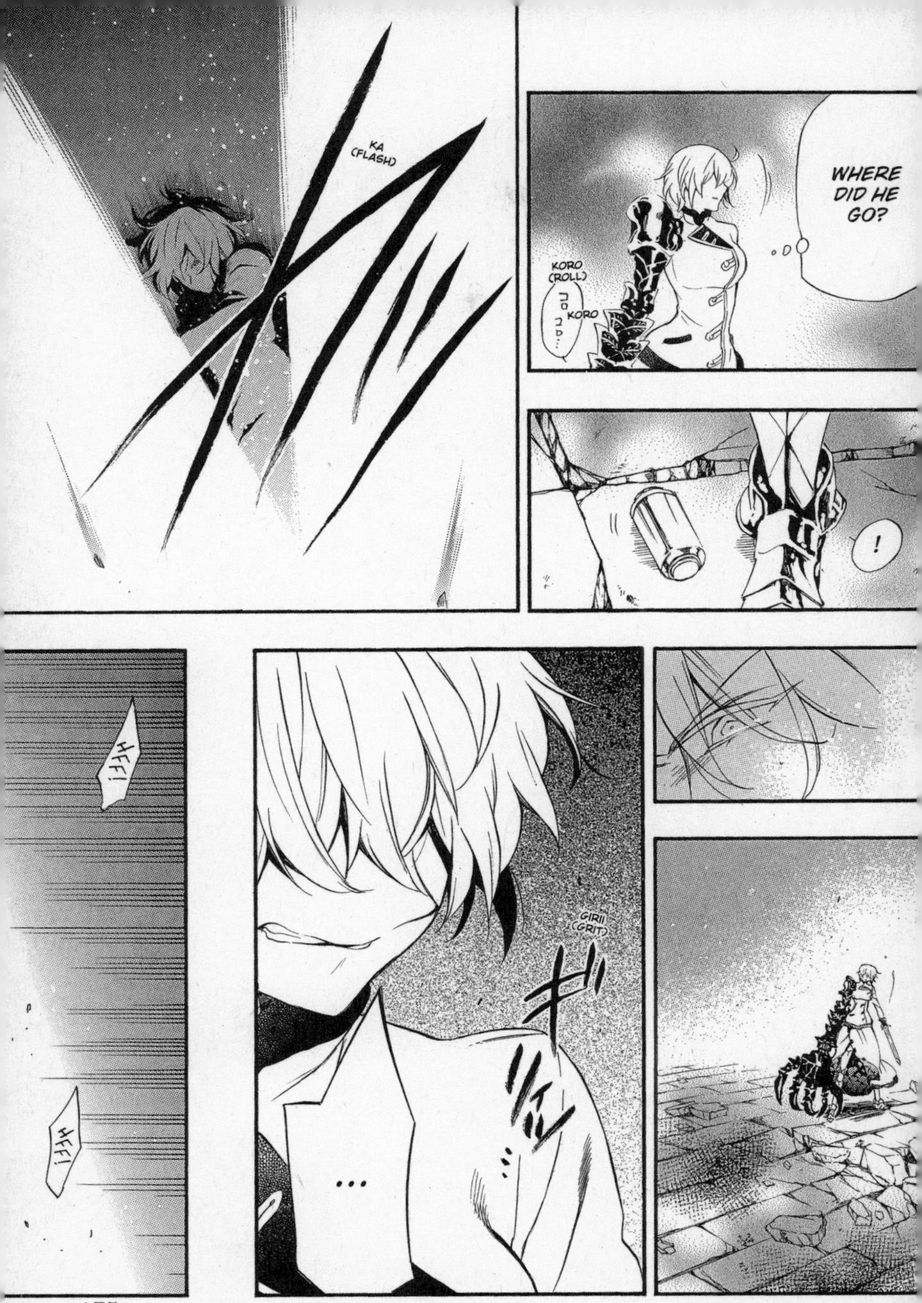
WHERE DID HE GO?
KORO (ROLL)
KORO
!
KA (FLASH)
GIRII (GRIT)
...
HFF!
HFF!

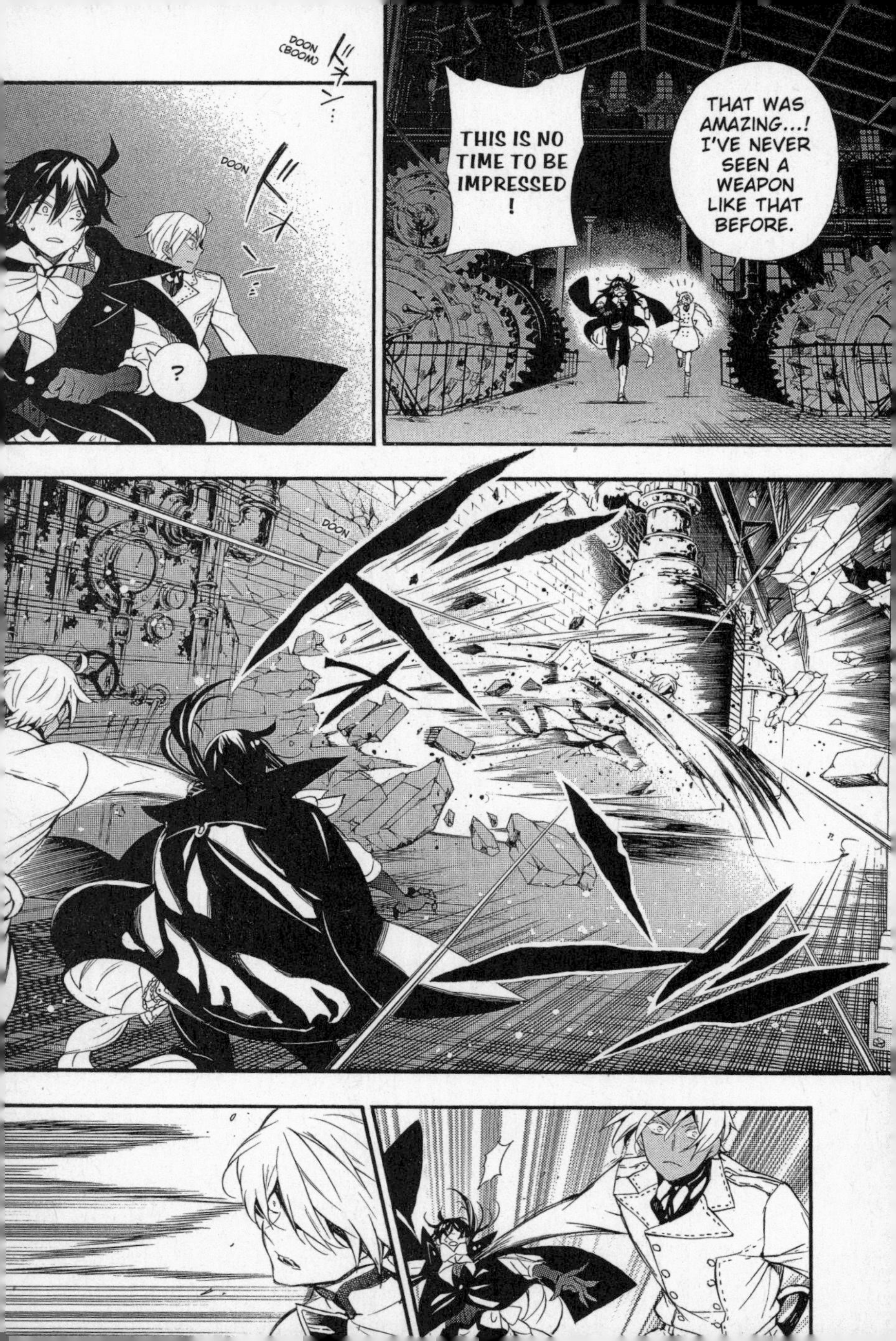
THAT WAS AMAZING...! I'VE NEVER SEEN A WEAPON LIKE THAT BEFORE.
THIS IS NO TIME TO BE IMPRESSED!
DOON (BOOM)
ドオン…
DOON
ドオン
?
DOON

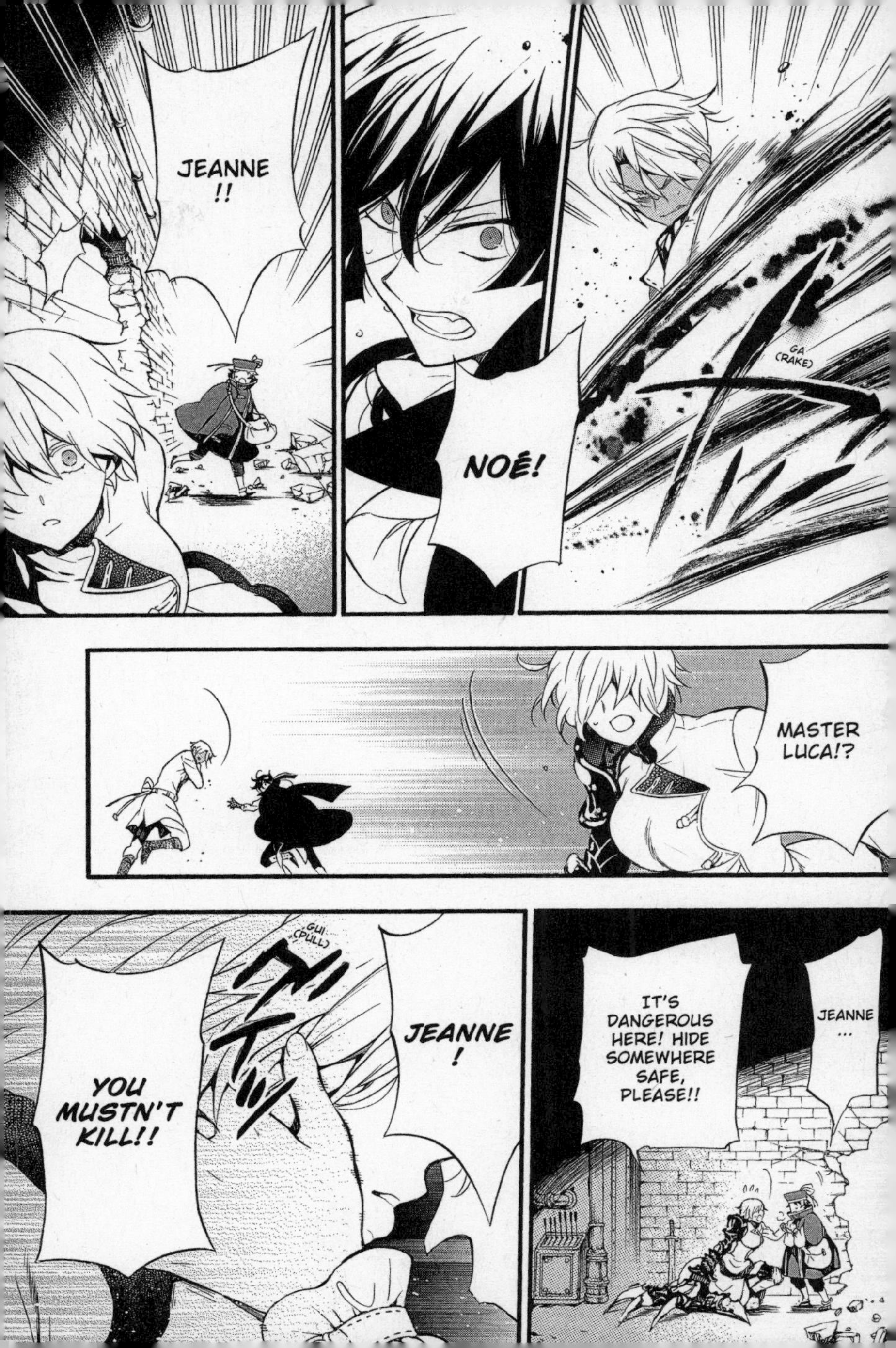
GA (RAKE)
NOÉ!
JEANNE !!
MASTER LUCA!?
JEANNE ...
IT'S DANGEROUS HERE! HIDE SOMEWHERE SAFE, PLEASE!!
JEANNE !
GUI (PULL)
YOU MUSTN'T KILL!!

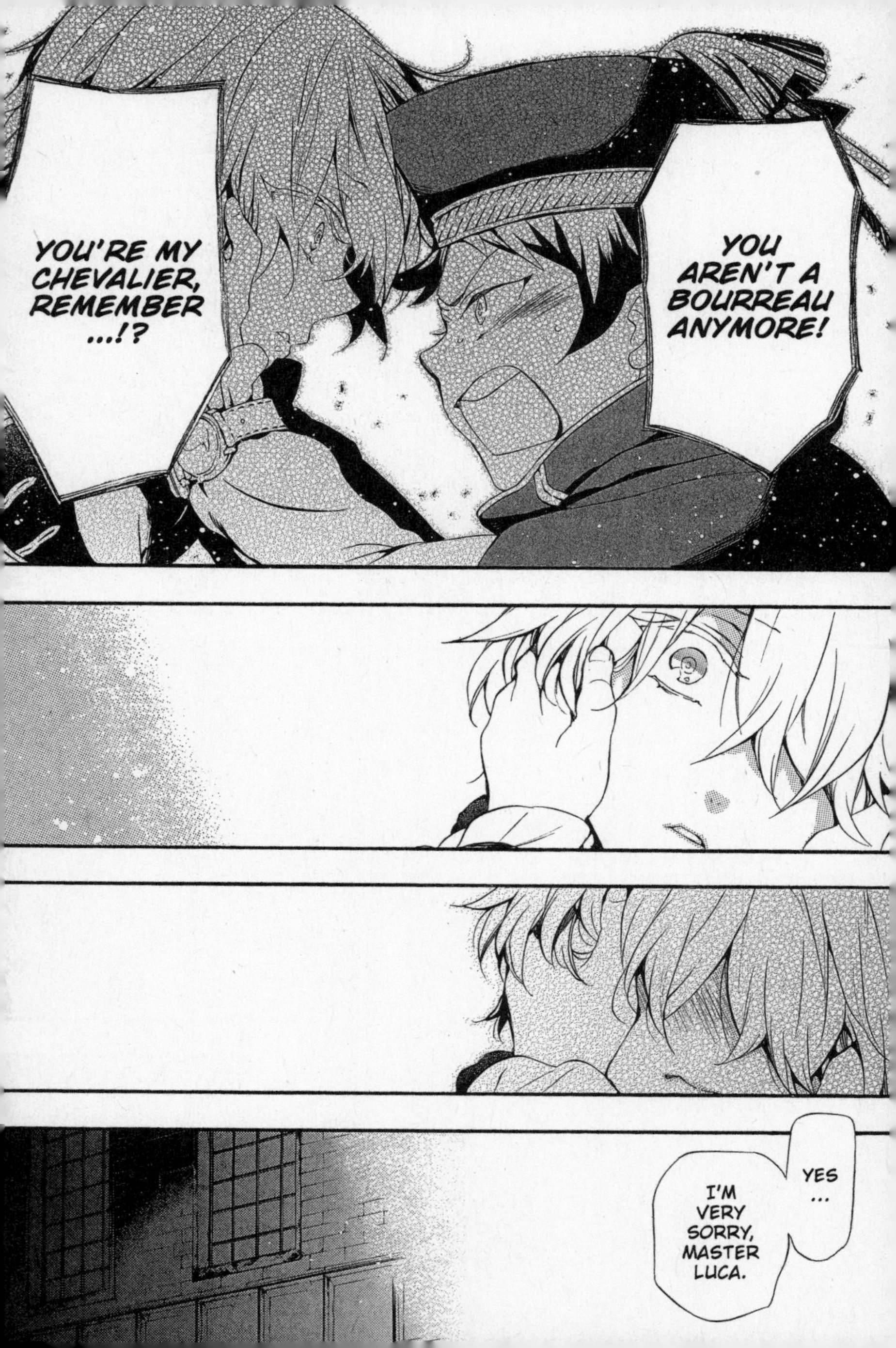
YOU AREN'T A BOURREAU ANYMORE!
YOU'RE MY CHEVALIER, REMEMBER ...!?
YES ...
I'M VERY SORRY, MASTER LUCA.

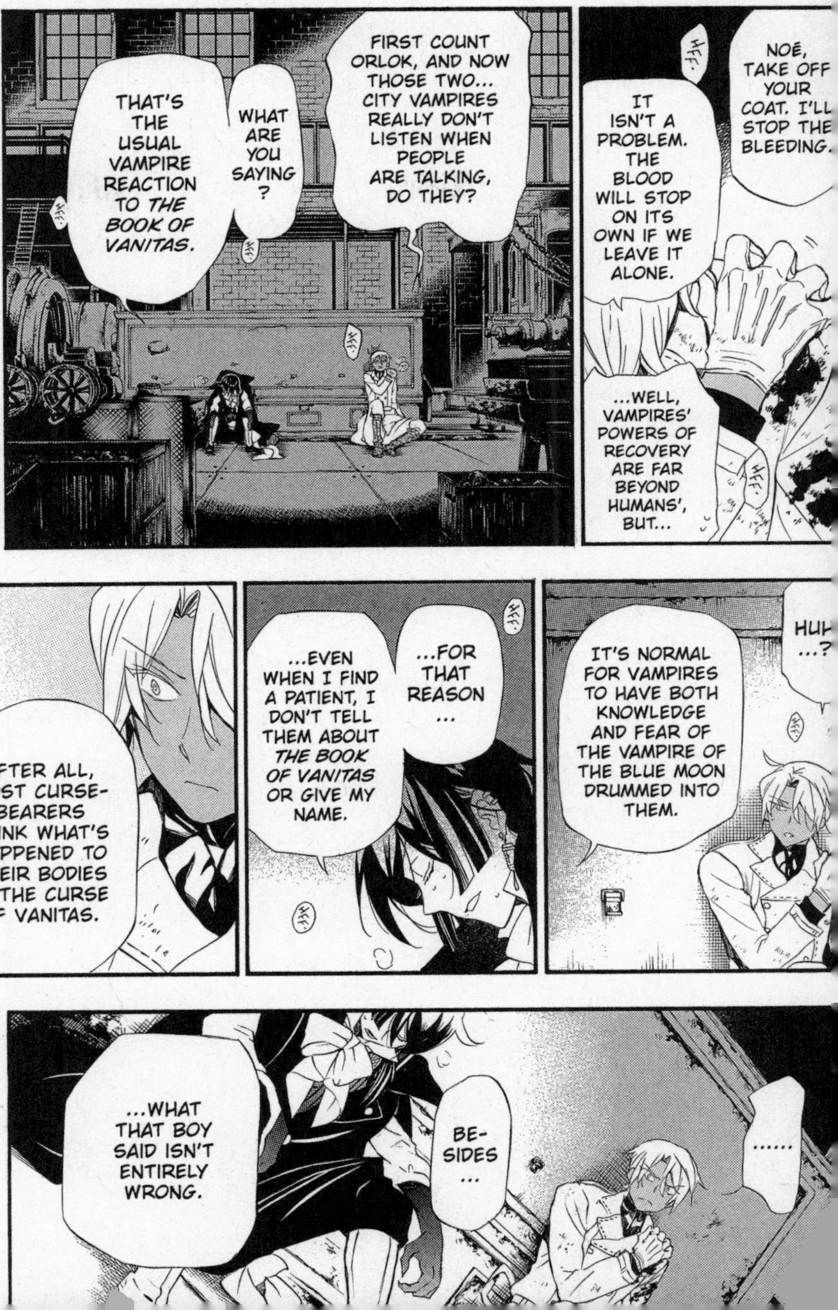
NOÉ, TAKE OFF YOUR COAT. I'LL STOP THE BLEEDING.
HFF.
IT ISN'T A PROBLEM. THE BLOOD WILL STOP ON ITS OWN IF WE LEAVE IT ALONE.
...WELL, VAMPIRES' POWERS OF RECOVERY ARE FAR BEYOND HUMANS', BUT...
HFF.
FIRST COUNT ORLOK, AND NOW THOSE TWO... CITY VAMPIRES REALLY DON'T LISTEN WHEN PEOPLE ARE TALKING, DO THEY?
HFF.
WHAT ARE YOU SAYING?
HFF.
THAT'S THE USUAL VAMPIRE REACTION TO *THE BOOK OF VANITAS*.
HFF.
HUH...?
HFF.
IT'S NORMAL FOR VAMPIRES TO HAVE BOTH KNOWLEDGE AND FEAR OF THE VAMPIRE OF THE BLUE MOON DRUMMED INTO THEM.
HFF.
...FOR THAT REASON...
...EVEN WHEN I FIND A PATIENT, I DON'T TELL THEM ABOUT *THE BOOK OF VANITAS* OR GIVE MY NAME.
HFF.
AFTER ALL, MOST CURSE-BEARERS THINK WHAT'S HAPPENED TO THEIR BODIES IS THE CURSE OF VANITAS.
......
BESIDES...
...WHAT THAT BOY SAID ISN'T ENTIRELY WRONG.

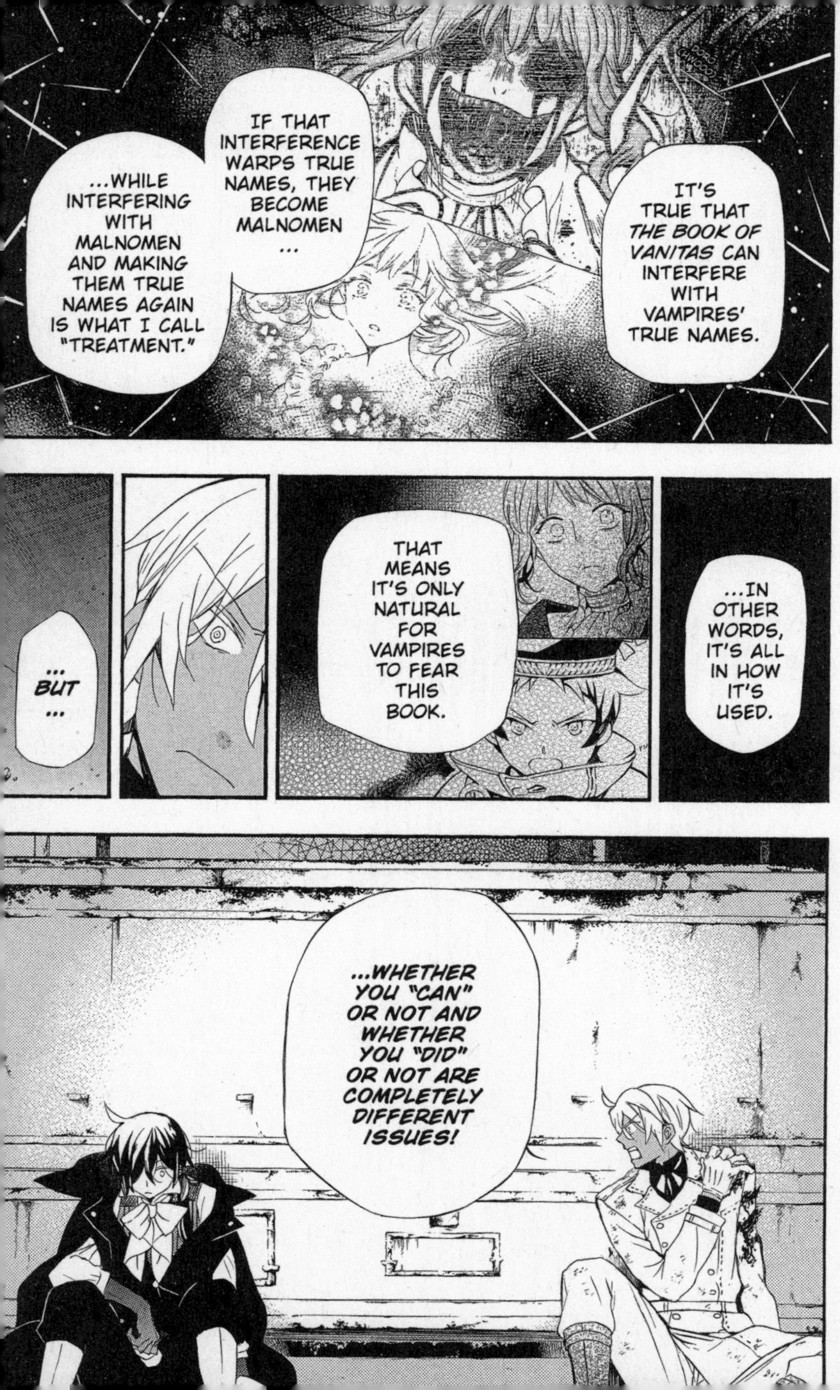
IT'S TRUE THAT *THE BOOK OF VANITAS* CAN INTERFERE WITH VAMPIRES' TRUE NAMES.
IF THAT INTERFERENCE WARPS TRUE NAMES, THEY BECOME MALNOMEN...
...WHILE INTERFERING WITH MALNOMEN AND MAKING THEM TRUE NAMES AGAIN IS WHAT I CALL "TREATMENT."
...IN OTHER WORDS, IT'S ALL IN HOW IT'S USED.
THAT MEANS IT'S ONLY NATURAL FOR VAMPIRES TO FEAR THIS BOOK.
...BUT...
...WHETHER YOU "CAN" OR NOT AND WHETHER YOU "DID" OR NOT ARE COMPLETELY DIFFERENT ISSUES!

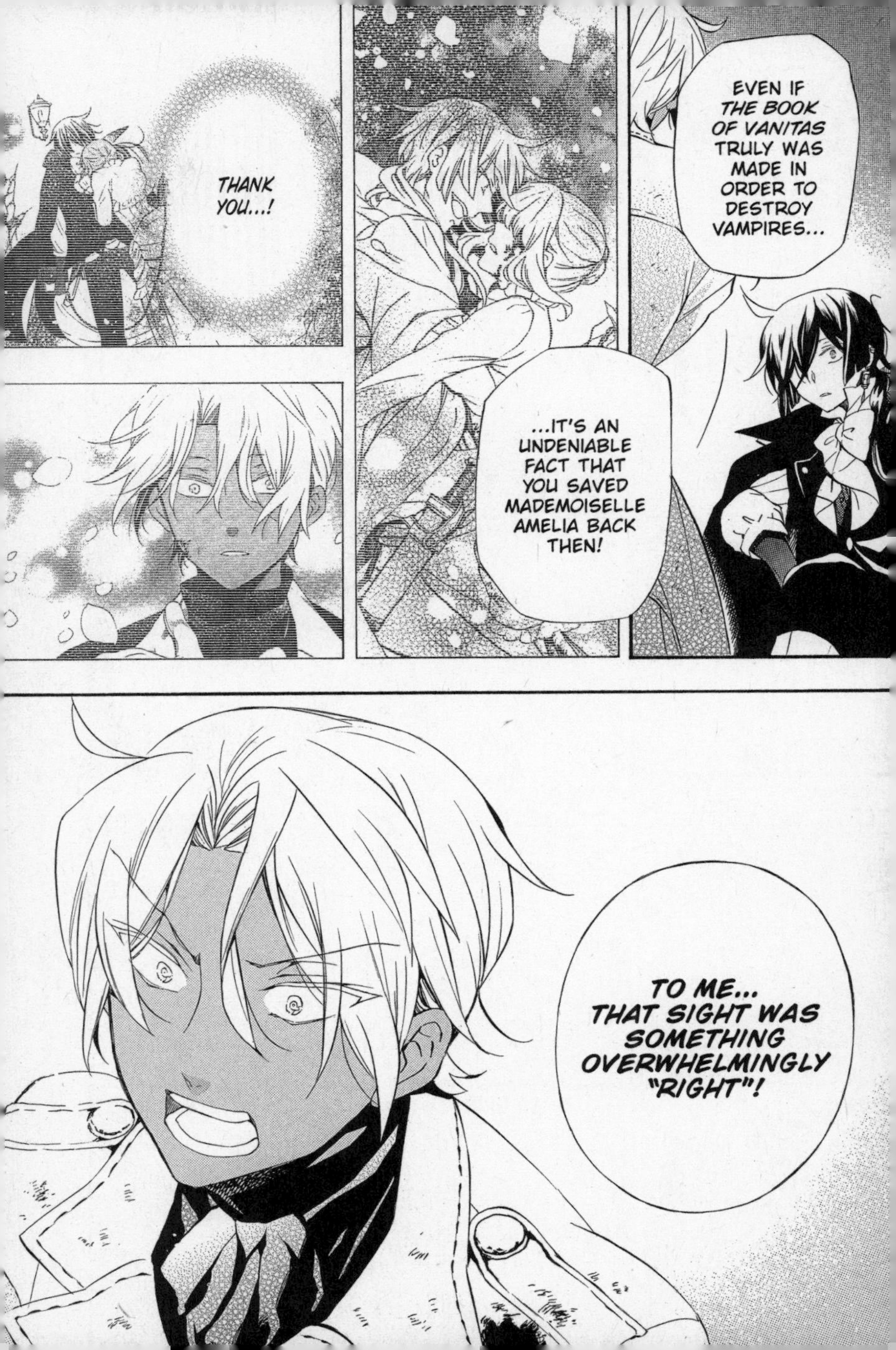
EVEN IF *THE BOOK OF VANITAS* TRULY WAS MADE IN ORDER TO DESTROY VAMPIRES...
...IT'S AN UNDENIABLE FACT THAT YOU SAVED MADEMOISELLE AMELIA BACK THEN!
THANK YOU...!
TO ME... THAT SIGHT WAS SOMETHING OVERWHELMINGLY "RIGHT"!

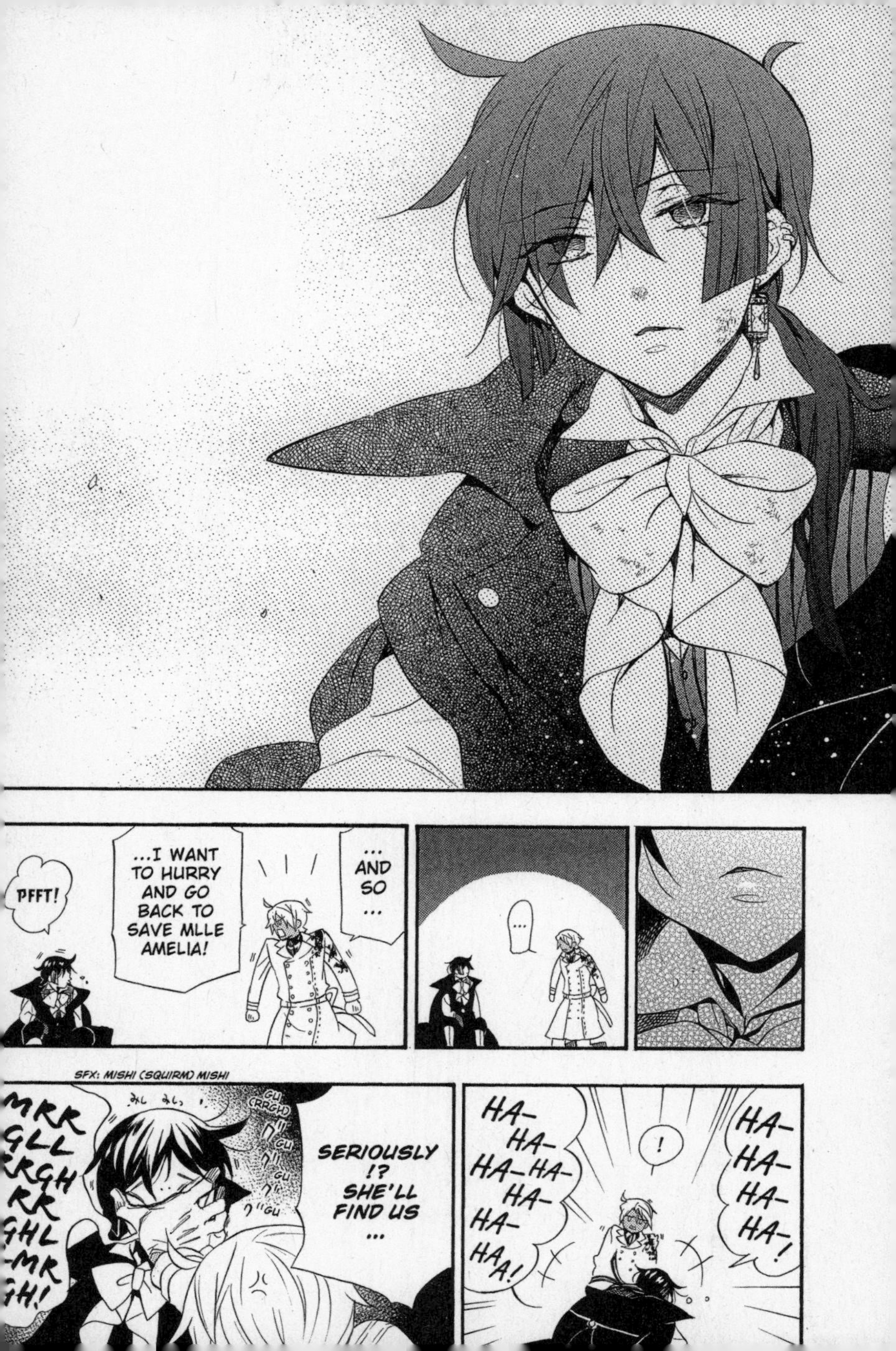

...
... AND SO ...
...I WANT TO HURRY AND GO BACK TO SAVE MLLE AMELIA!
PFFT!
HA-HA-HA-HA-!
!
HA-HA-HA-HA-HA-HA-HA-HAA!
SFX: MISHI (SQUIRM) MISHI
SERIOUSLY!? SHE'LL FIND US ...
GU (RRGH) GU GU GU GU
MRR GLL RGH RR GHL -MR GH!

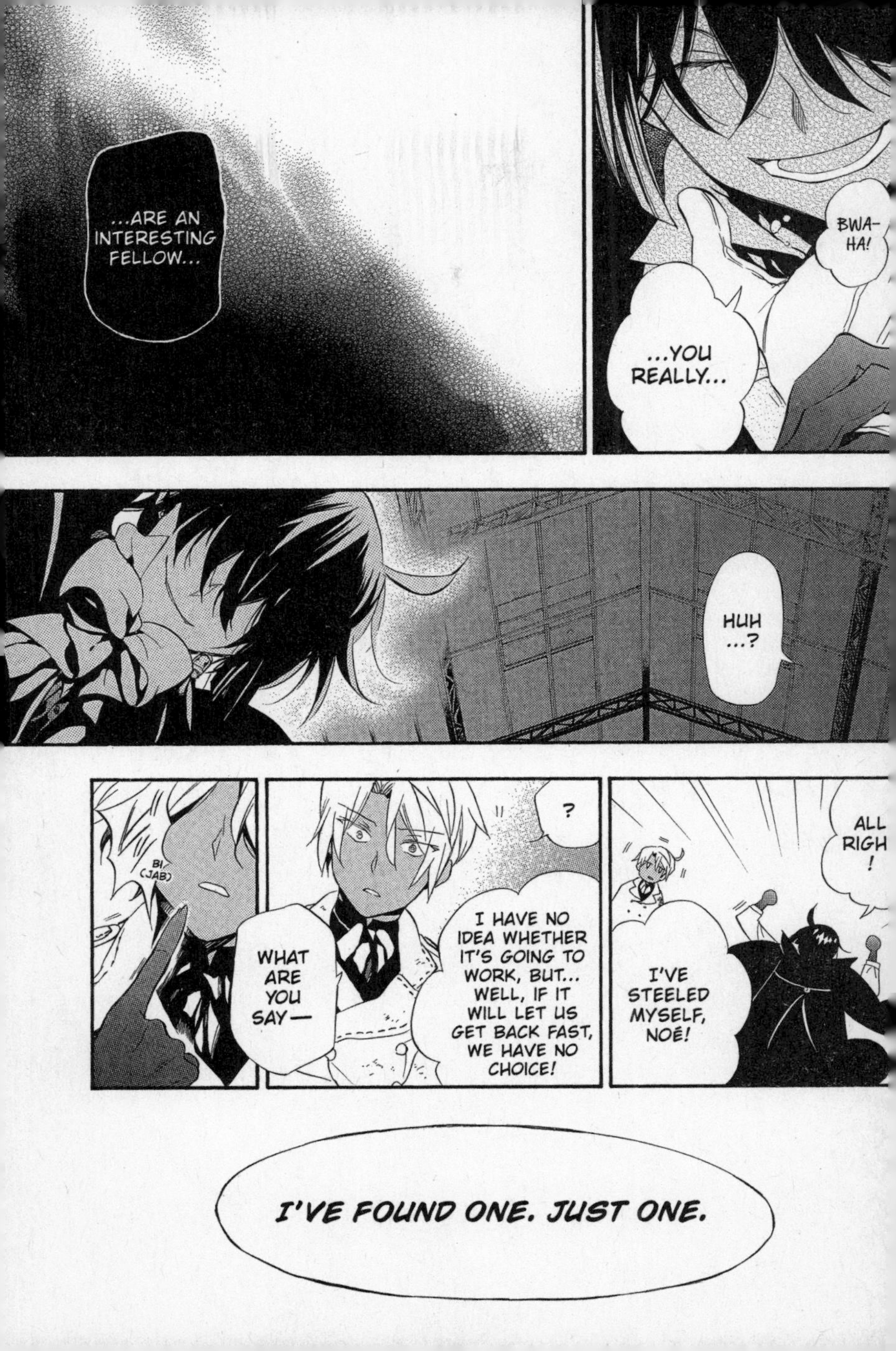
BWA-HA!
...YOU REALLY...
...ARE AN INTERESTING FELLOW...
HUH ...?
ALL RIGH!
I'VE STEELED MYSELF, NOÉ!
?
I HAVE NO IDEA WHETHER IT'S GOING TO WORK, BUT... WELL, IF IT WILL LET US GET BACK FAST, WE HAVE NO CHOICE!
BI (JAB)
WHAT ARE YOU SAY—
I'VE FOUND ONE. JUST ONE.

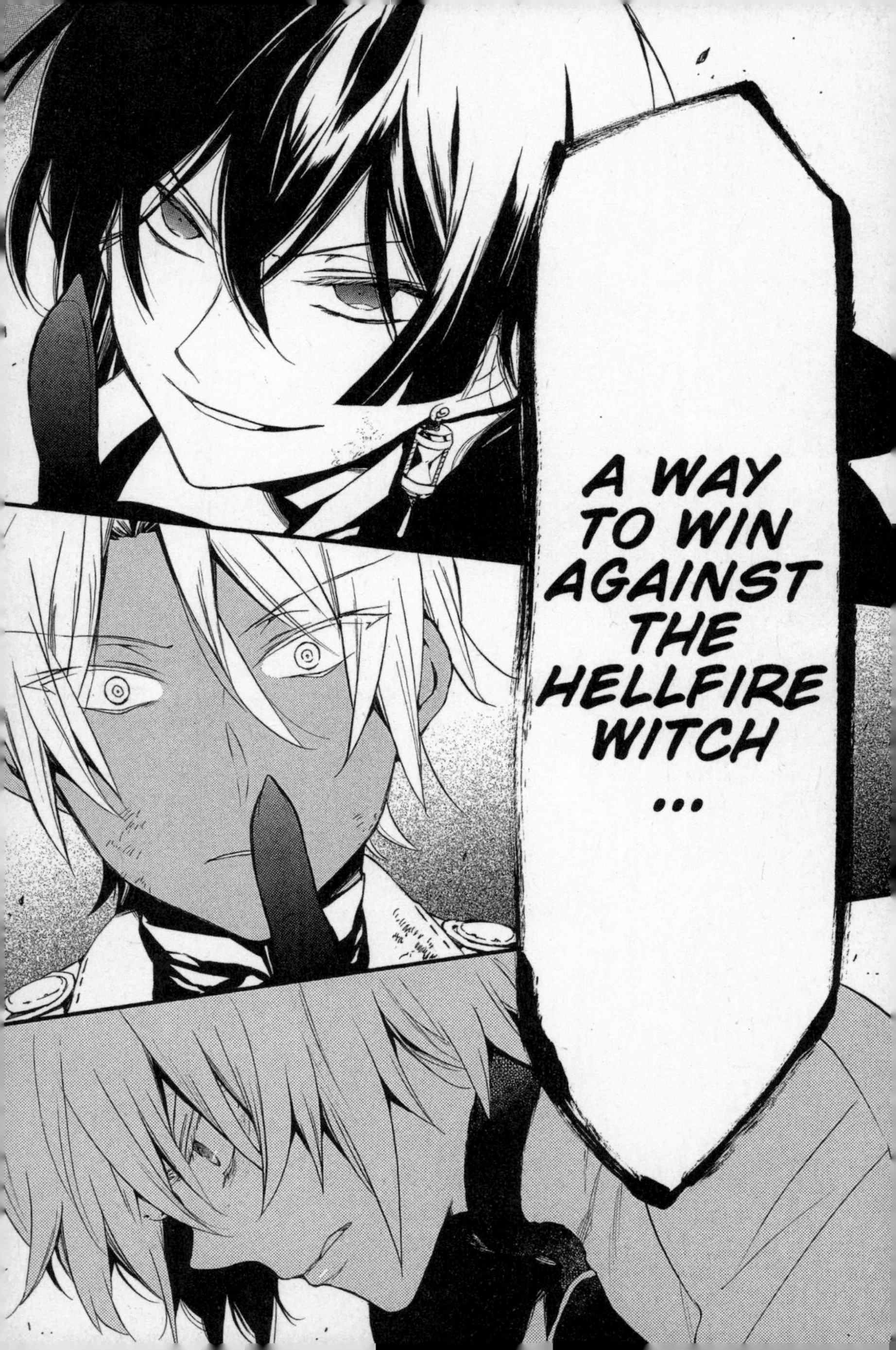
A WAY TO WIN AGAINST THE HELLFIRE WITCH...

Mémoire 3 Jeanne THE HELLFIRE WITCH

Les Mémoires de Vanitas

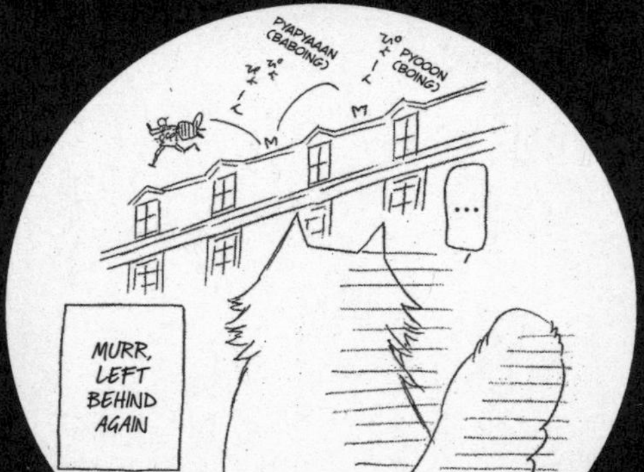

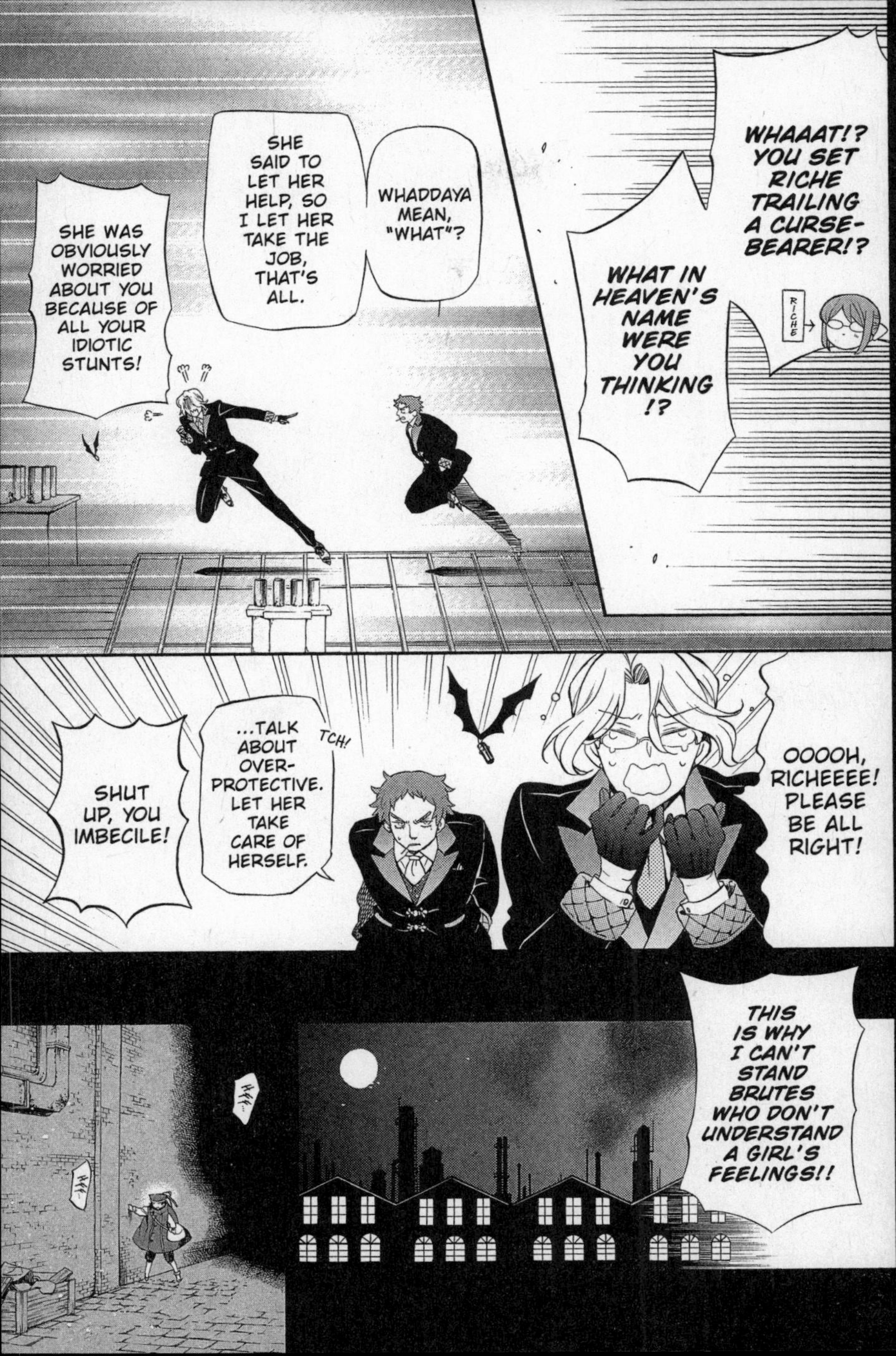
WHAAAT!? YOU SET RICHE TRAILING A CURSE-BEARER!?
WHAT IN HEAVEN'S NAME WERE YOU THINKING !?
RICHE
WHADDAYA MEAN, "WHAT"?
SHE SAID TO LET HER HELP, SO I LET HER TAKE THE JOB, THAT'S ALL.
SHE WAS OBVIOUSLY WORRIED ABOUT YOU BECAUSE OF ALL YOUR IDIOTIC STUNTS!
OOOOH, RICHEEEE! PLEASE BE ALL RIGHT!
TCH!
...TALK ABOUT OVER-PROTECTIVE. LET HER TAKE CARE OF HERSELF.
SHUT UP, YOU IMBECILE!
THIS IS WHY I CAN'T STAND BRUTES WHO DON'T UNDERSTAND A GIRL'S FEELINGS!!

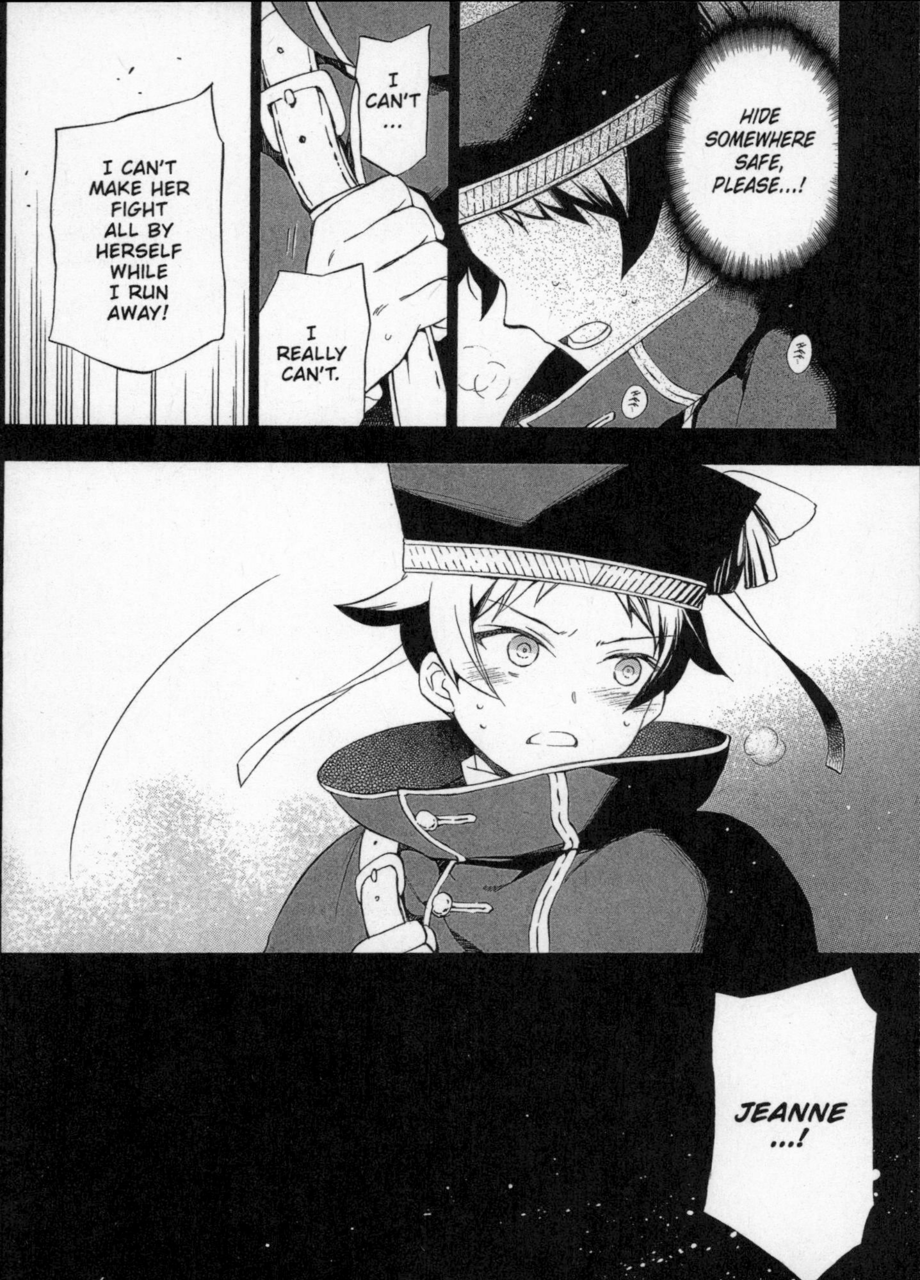
HIDE SOMEWHERE SAFE, PLEASE...!
I CAN'T...
I REALLY CAN'T.
I CAN'T MAKE HER FIGHT ALL BY HERSELF WHILE I RUN AWAY!
JEANNE...!

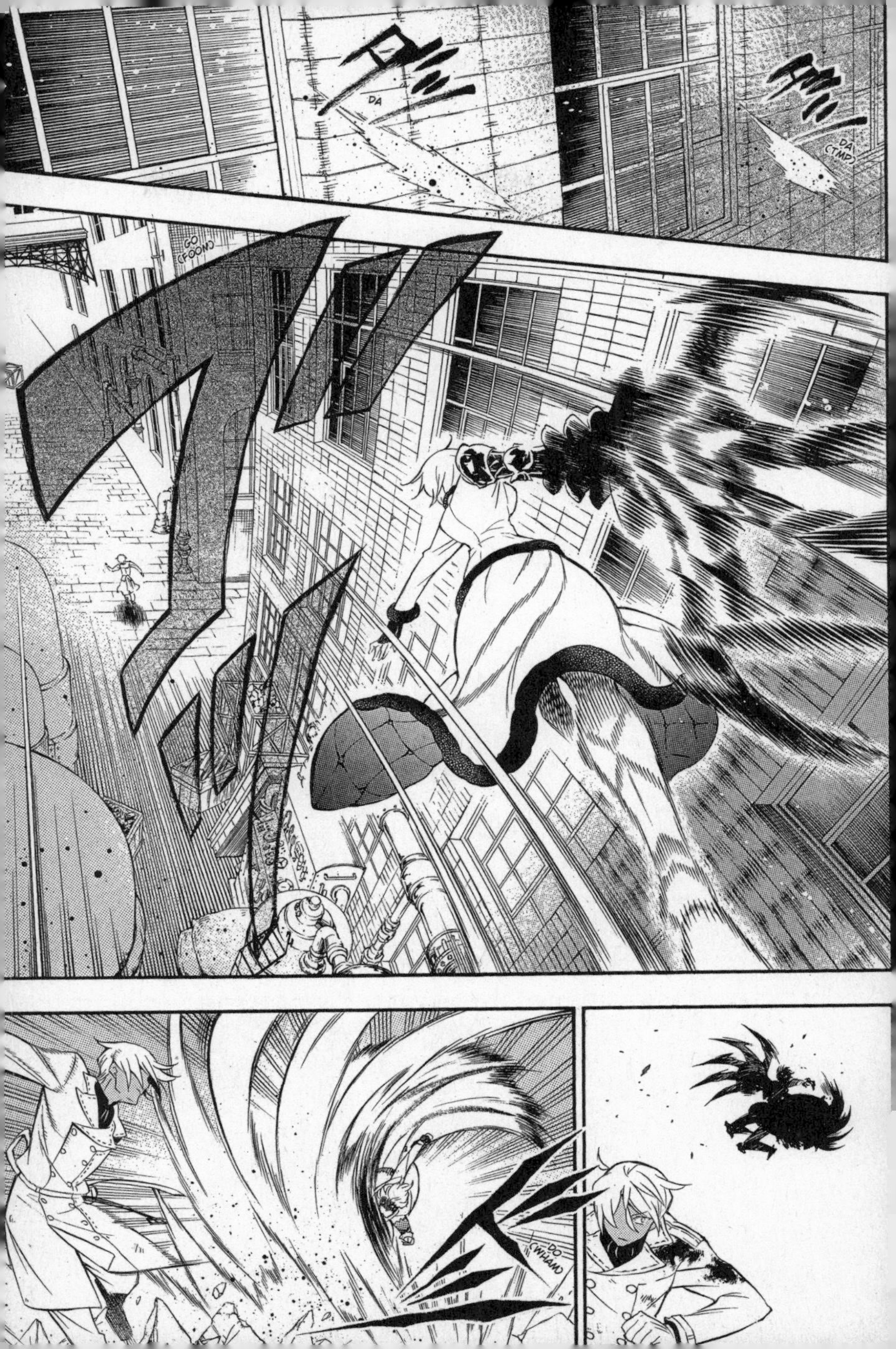
DA
(TMP)
DA
GO
(FOOM)
DO
(WHAM)

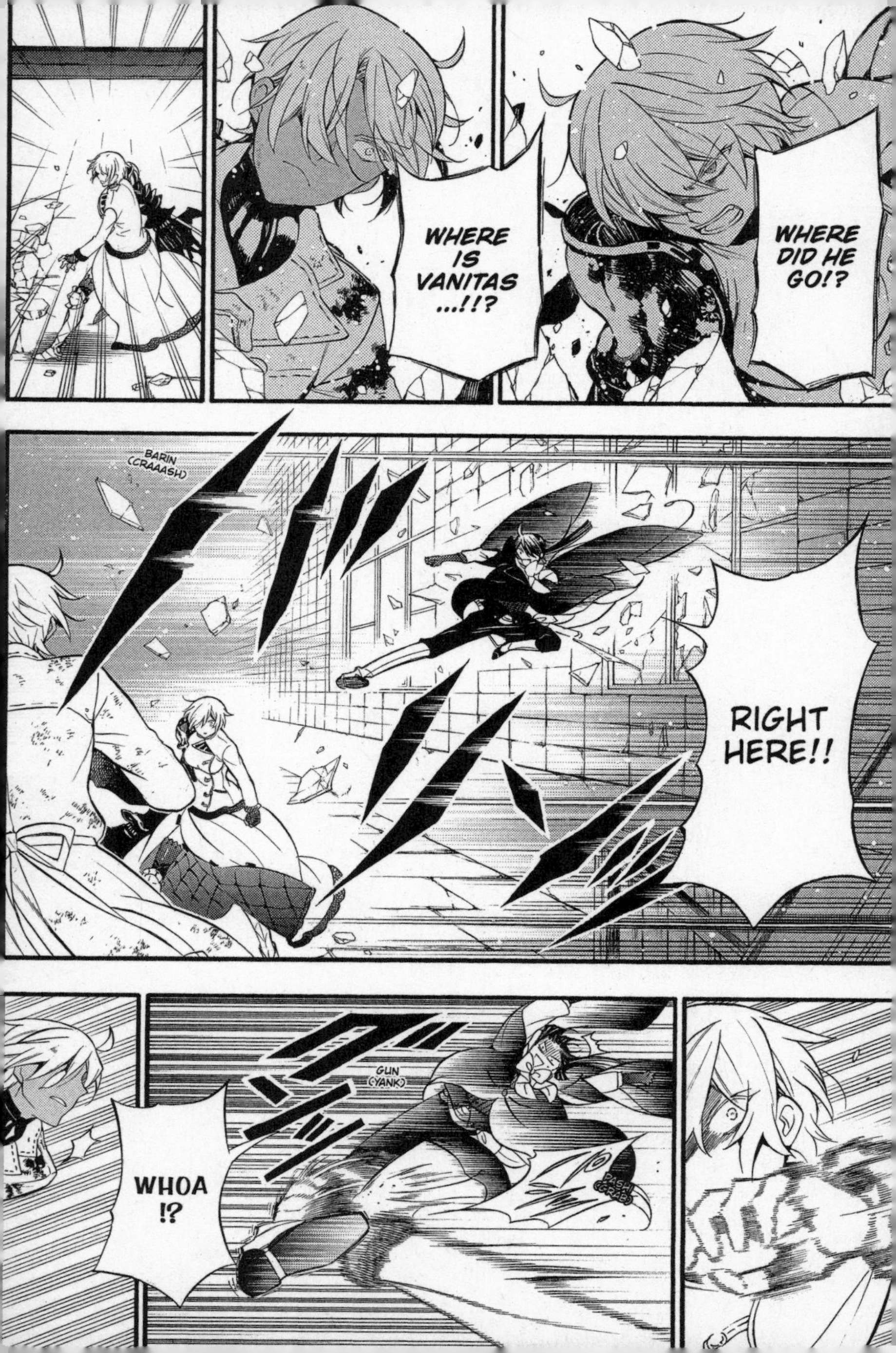
WHERE DID HE GO!?
WHERE IS VANITAS ...!!?
RIGHT HERE!!
BARIN (CRAAASH)
GUN (YANK)
PASHI (GRAB)
WHOA !?

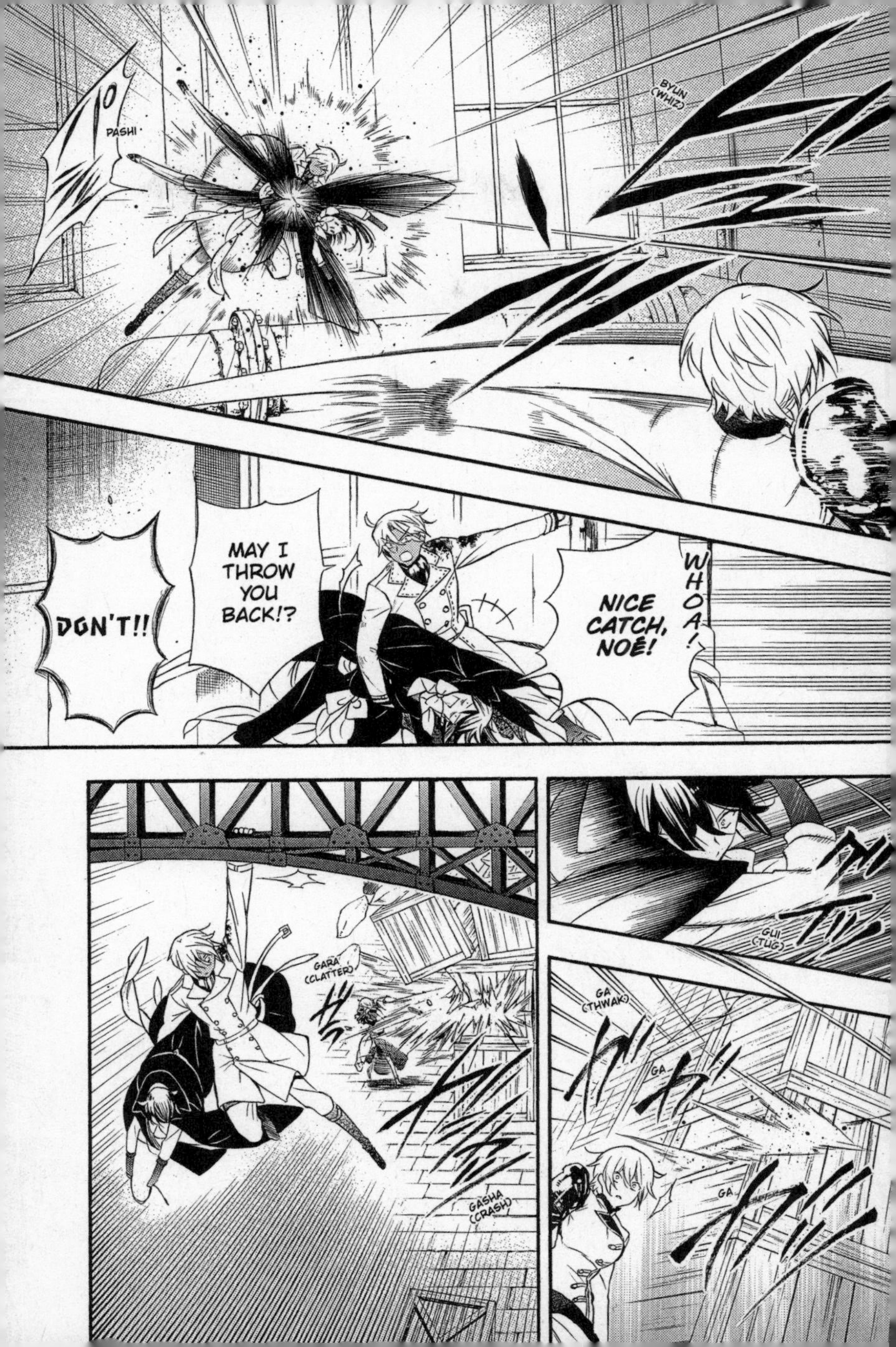
BYUN (WHIZ)
PASHI
WHOA!
NICE CATCH, NOÉ!
MAY I THROW YOU BACK!?
DON'T!!
GUI (TUG)
GA (THWAK)
GA
GA
GARA (CLATTER)
GASHA (CRASH)

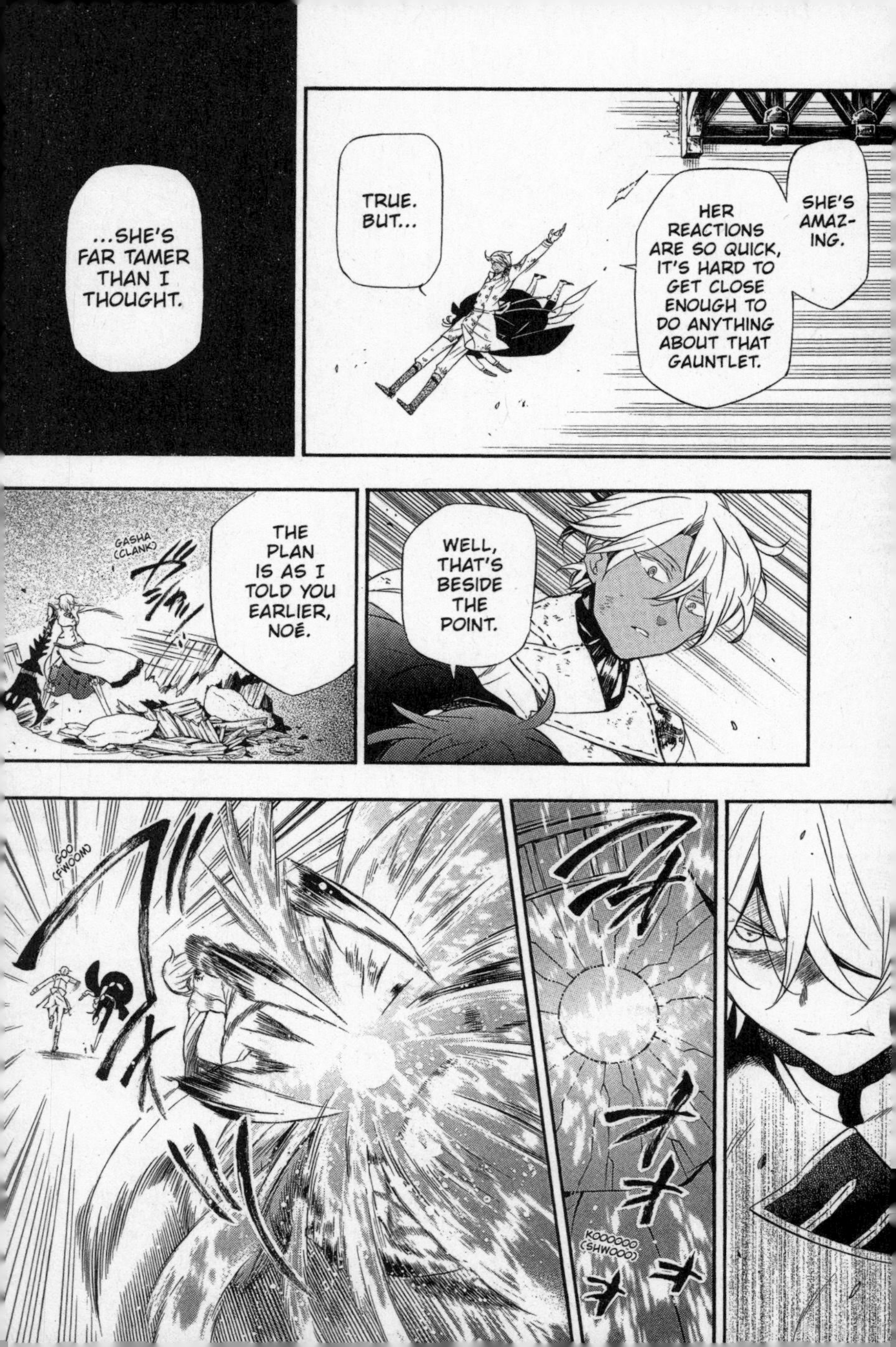
SHE'S AMAZ-ING.
HER REACTIONS ARE SO QUICK, IT'S HARD TO GET CLOSE ENOUGH TO DO ANYTHING ABOUT THAT GAUNTLET.
TRUE. BUT...
...SHE'S FAR TAMER THAN I THOUGHT.
WELL, THAT'S BESIDE THE POINT.
THE PLAN IS AS I TOLD YOU EARLIER, NOÉ.
GASHA (CLANK)
KOOOOOO (SHWOOO)
GOO (FWOOM)

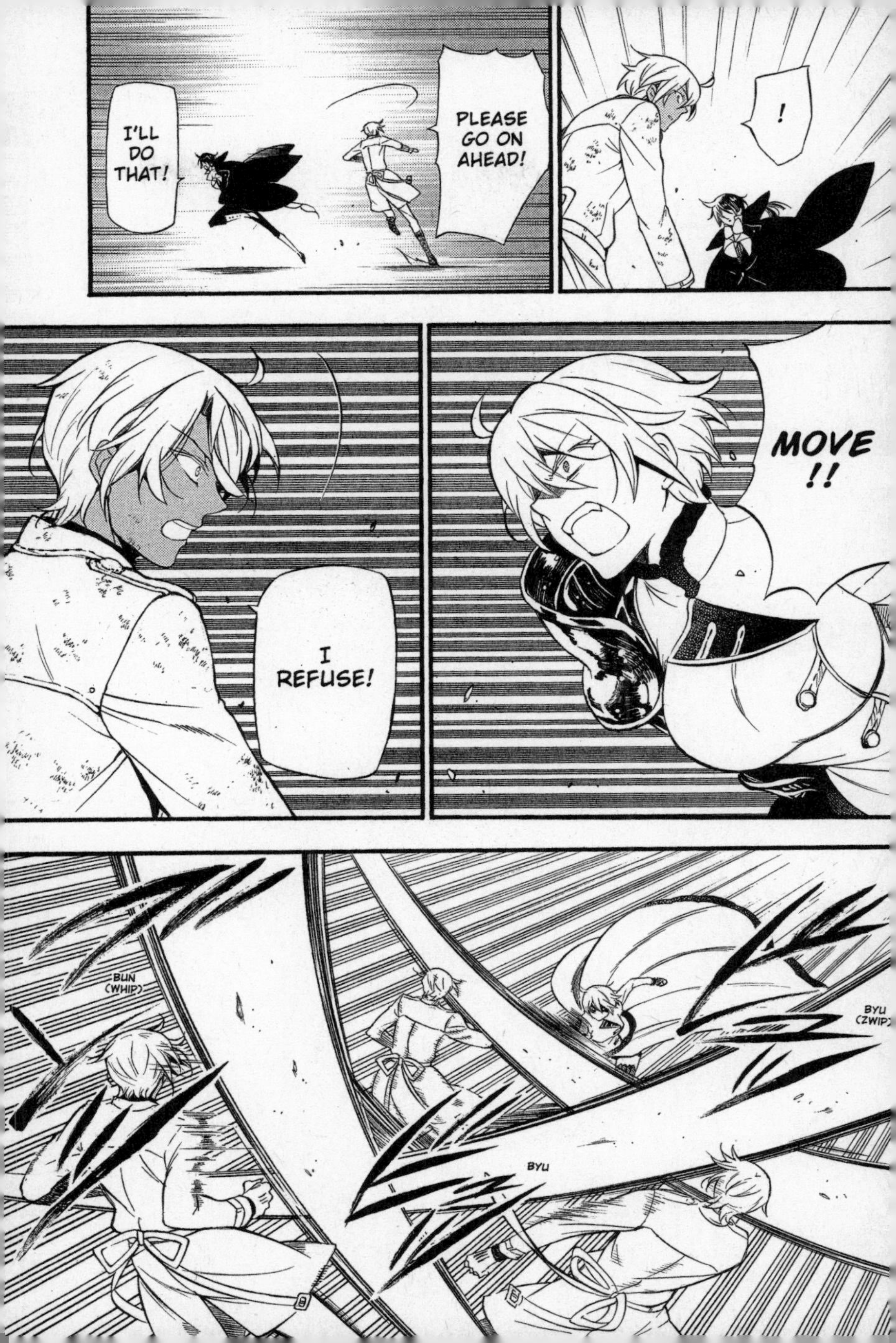
!
PLEASE GO ON AHEAD!
I'LL DO THAT!
MOVE!!
I REFUSE!
BYU (ZWIP)
BYU
BUN (WHIP)

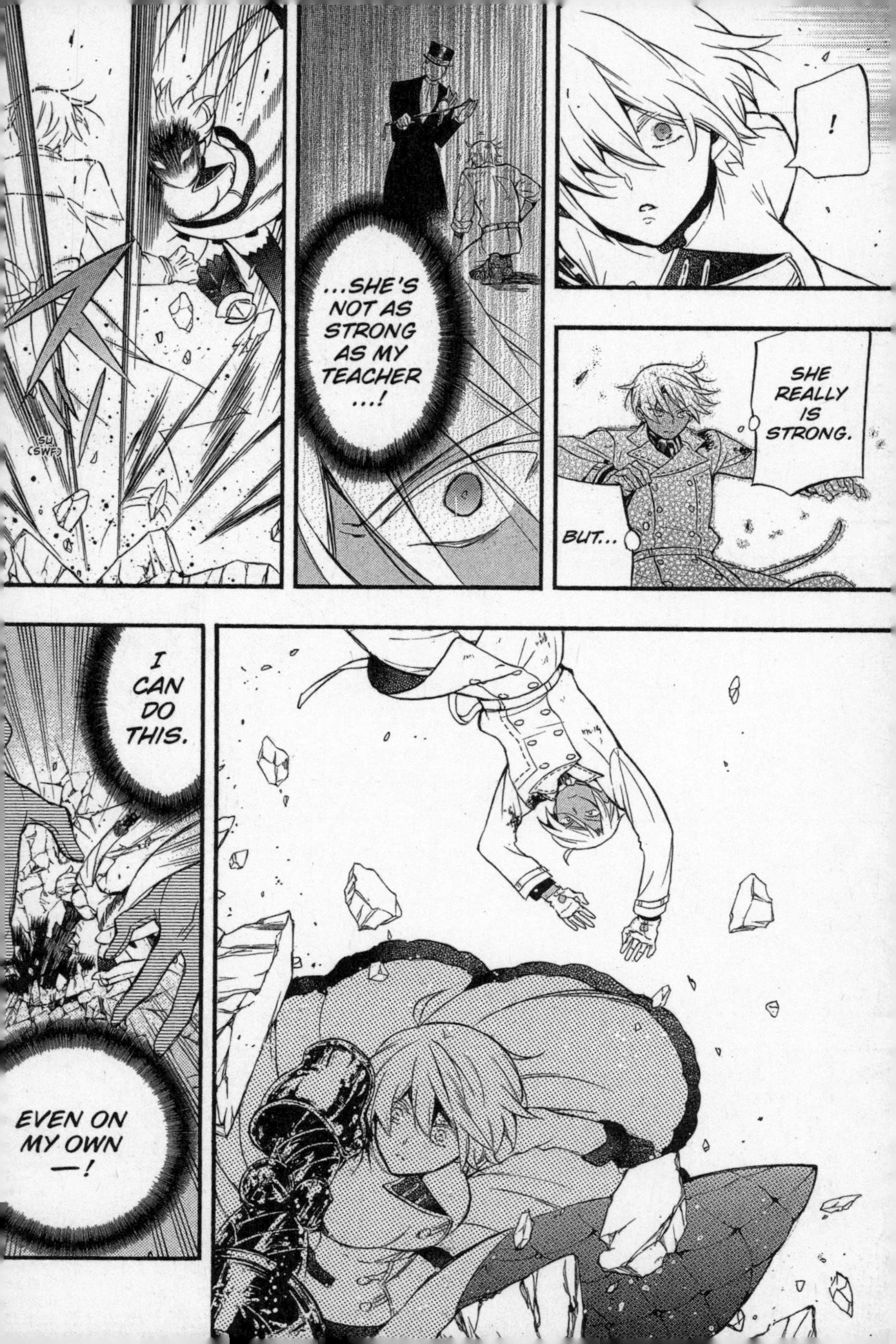
!
SHE REALLY IS STRONG.
BUT...
...SHE'S NOT AS STRONG AS MY TEACHER...!
SU (SWF)
I CAN DO THIS.
EVEN ON MY OWN—!

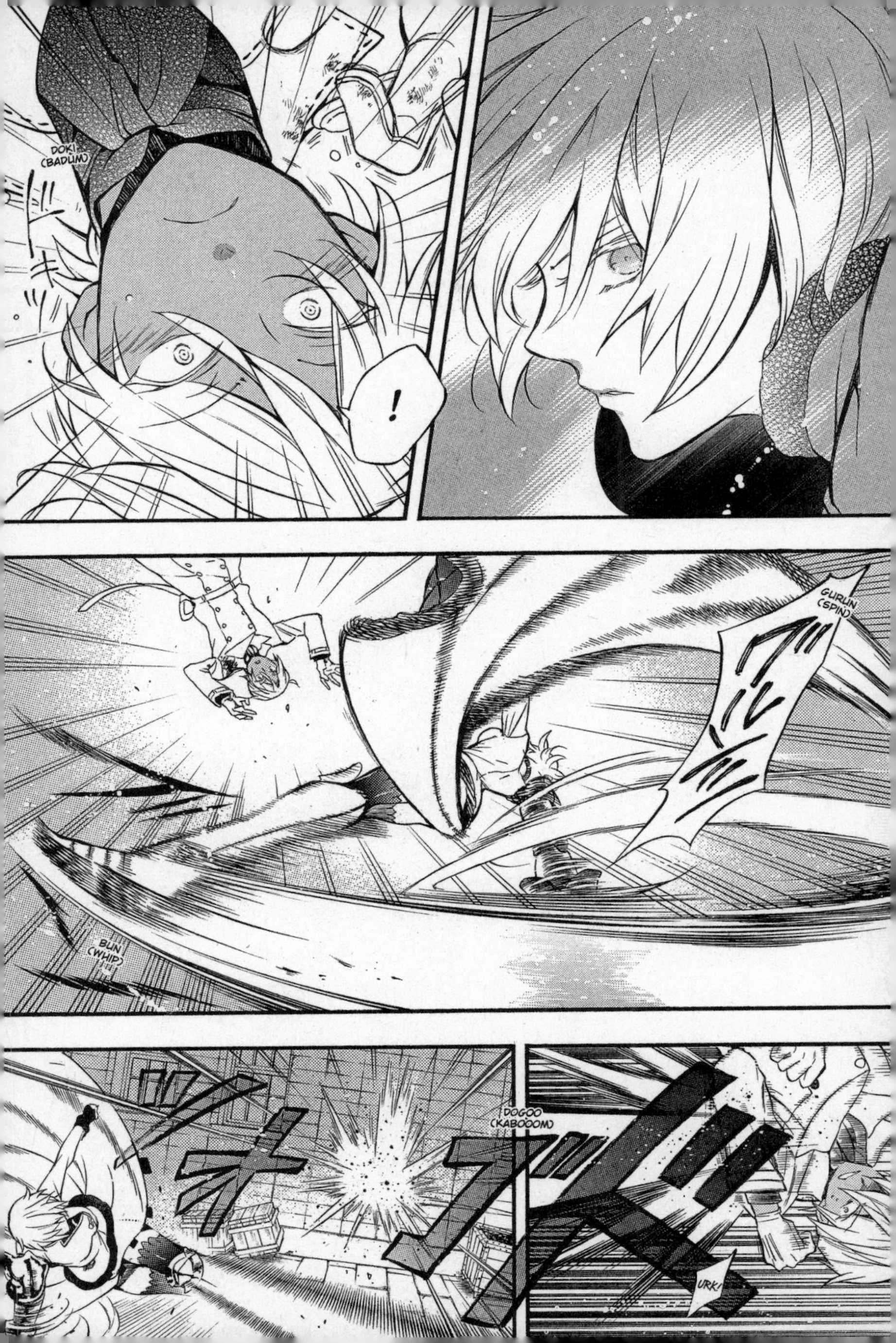
DOKI
(BADUM)
!
GURUN
(SPIN)
BUN
(WHIP)
DOGOO
(KABOOOM)
URK!

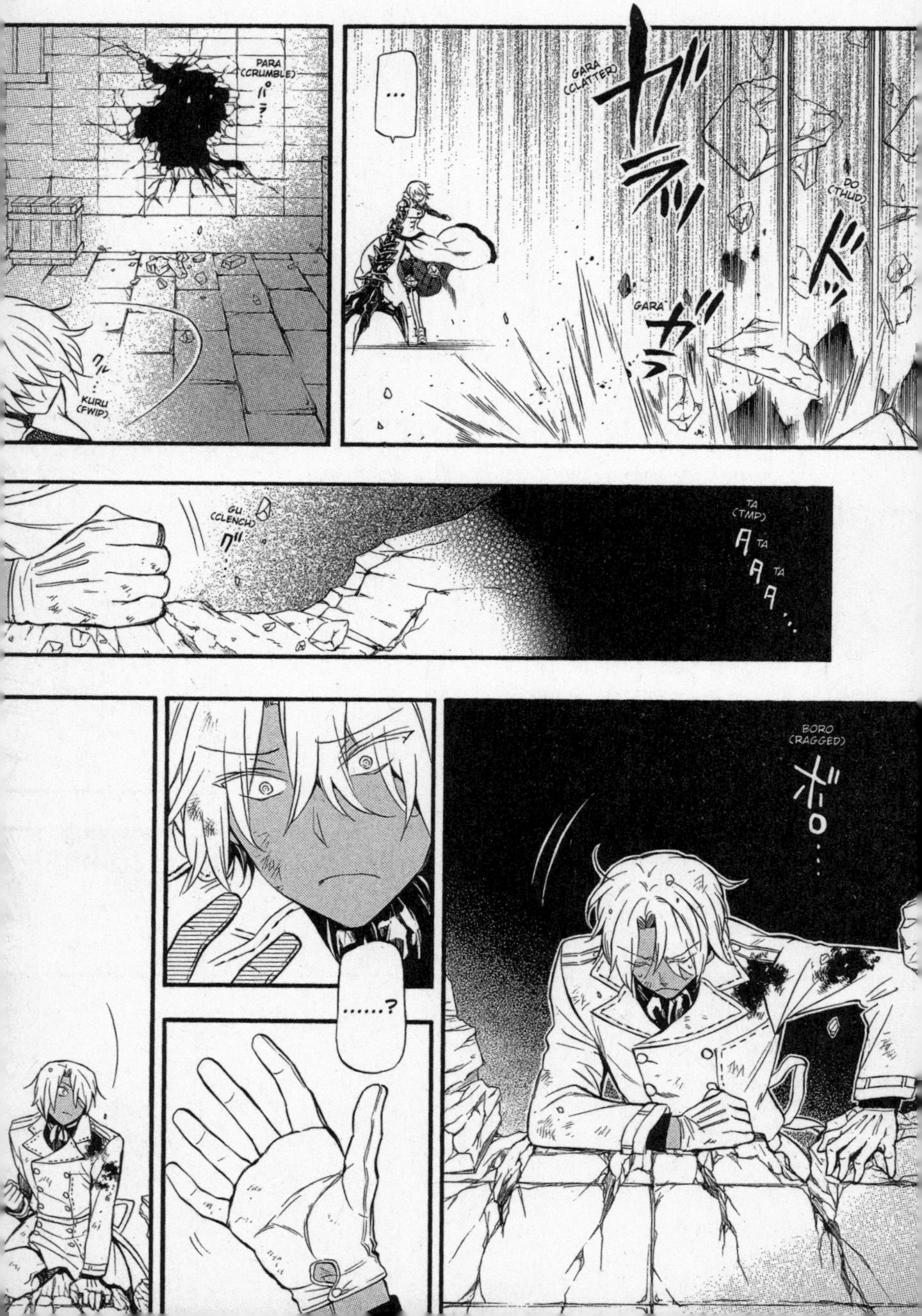
GARA (CLATTER)
DO (THUD)
GARA
...
PARA (CRUMBLE)
KURU (FWIP)
TA (TMP) TA TA TA...
GU (CLENCH)
BORO (RAGGED)
......?

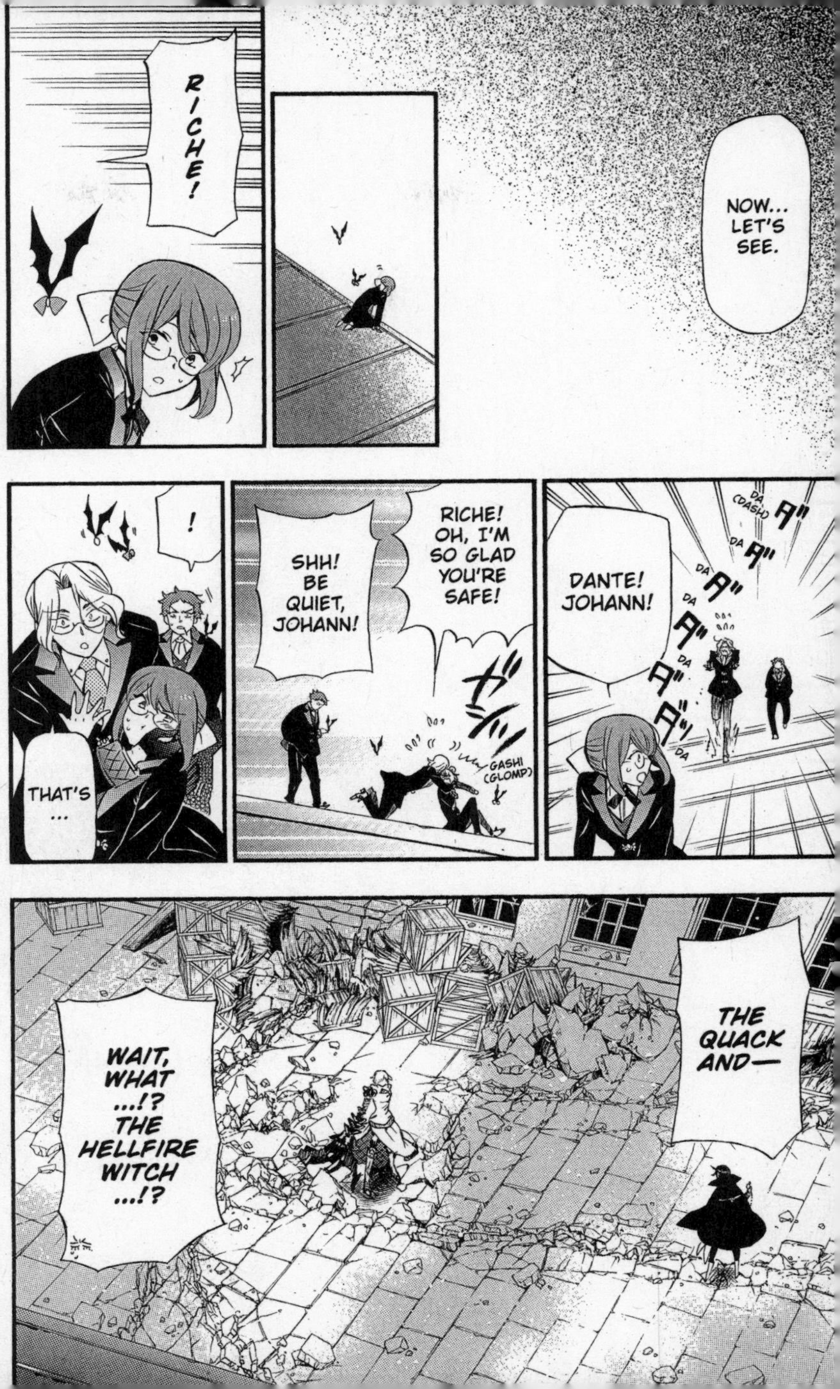
NOW... LET'S SEE.
RICHE!
DA (DASH) DA DA DA DA DA DA
DANTE! JOHANN!
RICHE! OH, I'M SO GLAD YOU'RE SAFE!
GASHI (GLOMP)
SHH! BE QUIET, JOHANN!
!
THAT'S ...
THE QUACK AND—
WAIT, WHAT ...!? THE HELLFIRE WITCH ...!?

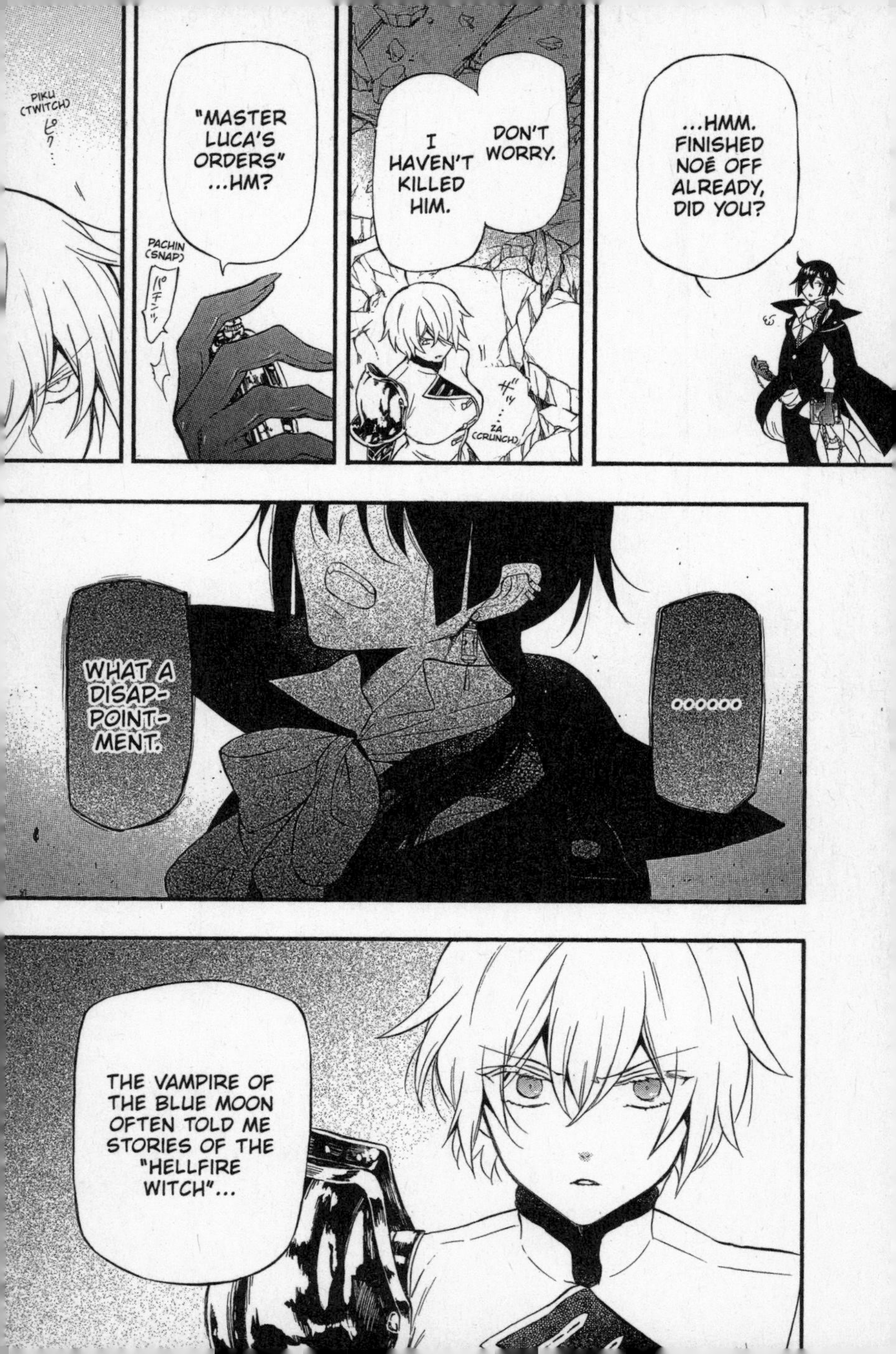
...HMM. FINISHED NOÉ OFF ALREADY, DID YOU?
DON'T WORRY.
I HAVEN'T KILLED HIM.
ZA (CRUNCH)
"MASTER LUCA'S ORDERS" ...HM?
PACHIN (SNAP)
PIKU (TWITCH)
......
WHAT A DISAP-POINT-MENT.
THE VAMPIRE OF THE BLUE MOON OFTEN TOLD ME STORIES OF THE "HELLFIRE WITCH"...

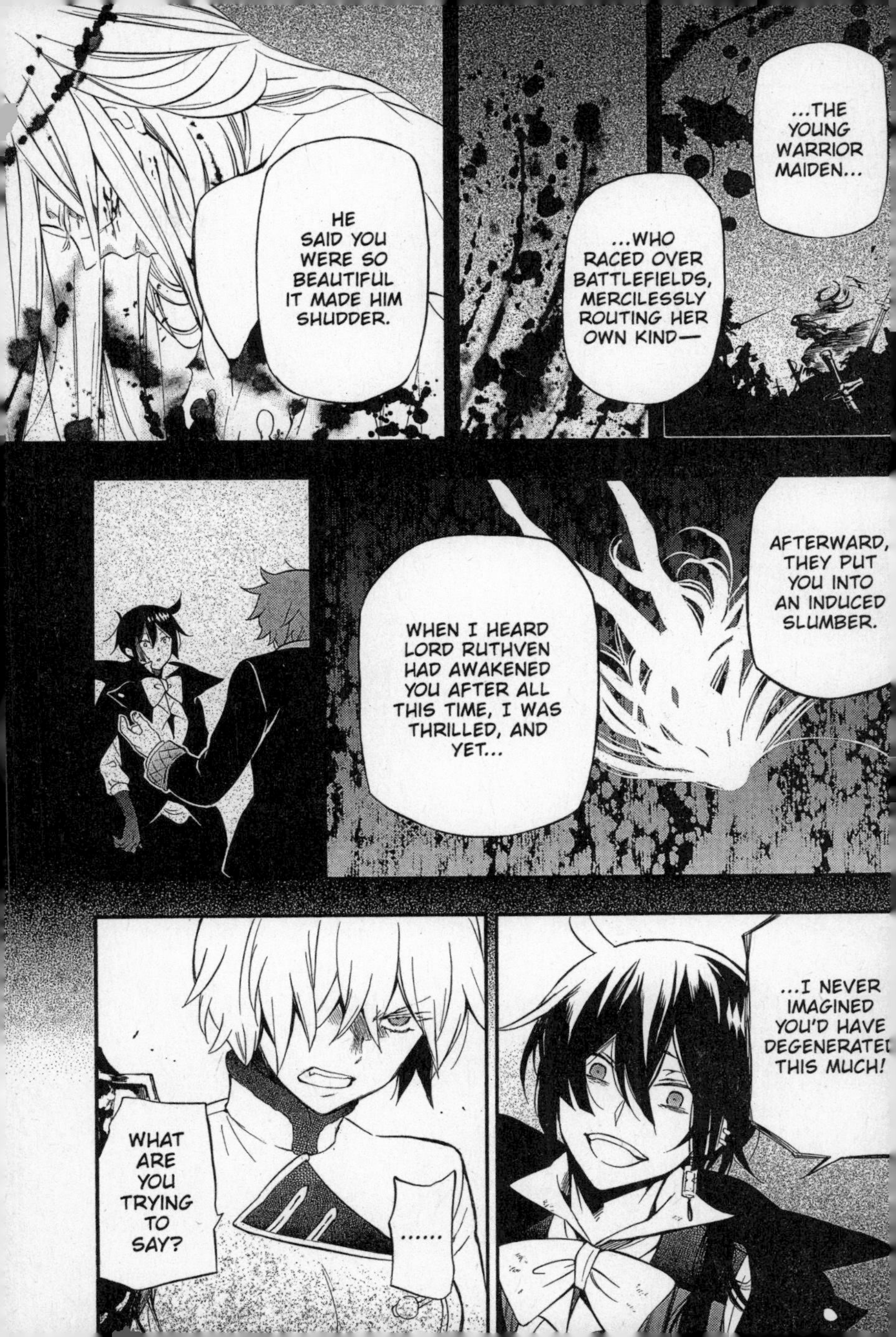
...THE YOUNG WARRIOR MAIDEN...
...WHO RACED OVER BATTLEFIELDS, MERCILESSLY ROUTING HER OWN KIND—
HE SAID YOU WERE SO BEAUTIFUL IT MADE HIM SHUDDER.
AFTERWARD, THEY PUT YOU INTO AN INDUCED SLUMBER.
WHEN I HEARD LORD RUTHVEN HAD AWAKENED YOU AFTER ALL THIS TIME, I WAS THRILLED, AND YET...
...I NEVER IMAGINED YOU'D HAVE DEGENERATED THIS MUCH!
......
WHAT ARE YOU TRYING TO SAY?

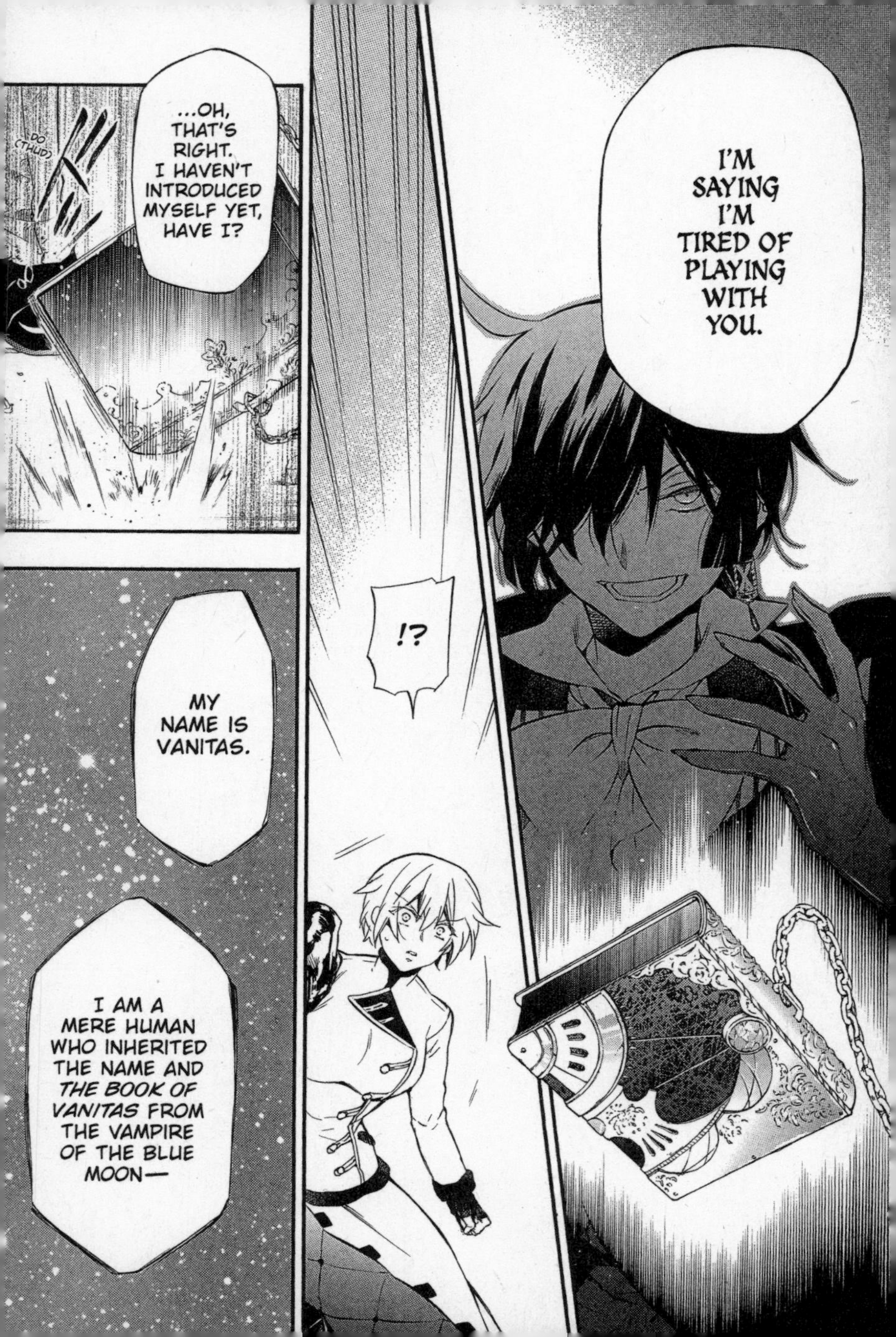
I'M SAYING I'M TIRED OF PLAYING WITH YOU.
!?
...OH, THAT'S RIGHT. I HAVEN'T INTRODUCED MYSELF YET, HAVE I?
DO (THUD)
MY NAME IS VANITAS.
I AM A MERE HUMAN WHO INHERITED THE NAME AND *THE BOOK OF VANITAS* FROM THE VAMPIRE OF THE BLUE MOON—

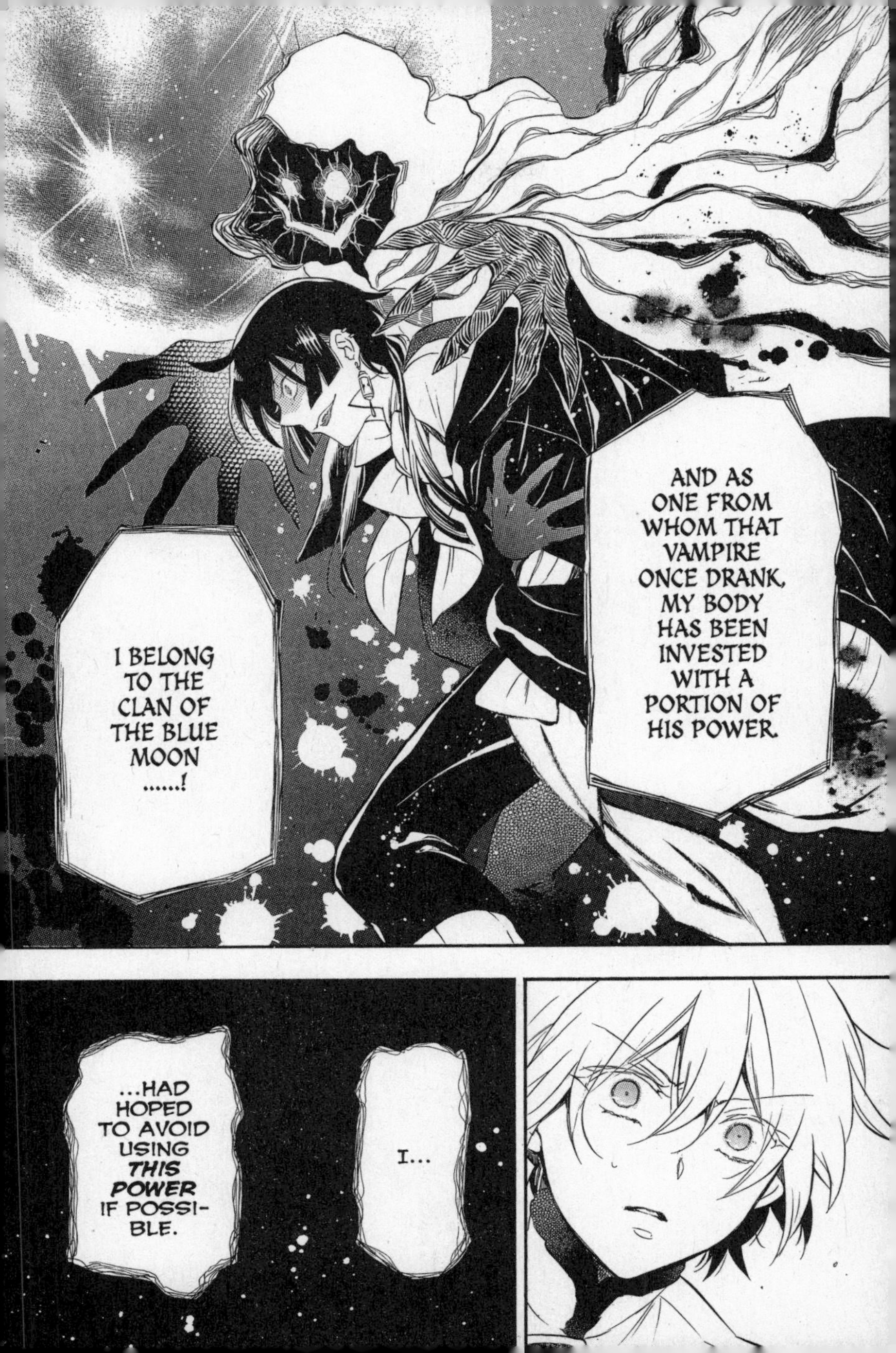
AND AS ONE FROM WHOM THAT VAMPIRE ONCE DRANK, MY BODY HAS BEEN INVESTED WITH A PORTION OF HIS POWER.
I BELONG TO THE CLAN OF THE BLUE MOON ......!
I...
...HAD HOPED TO AVOID USING THIS POWER IF POSSI-BLE.

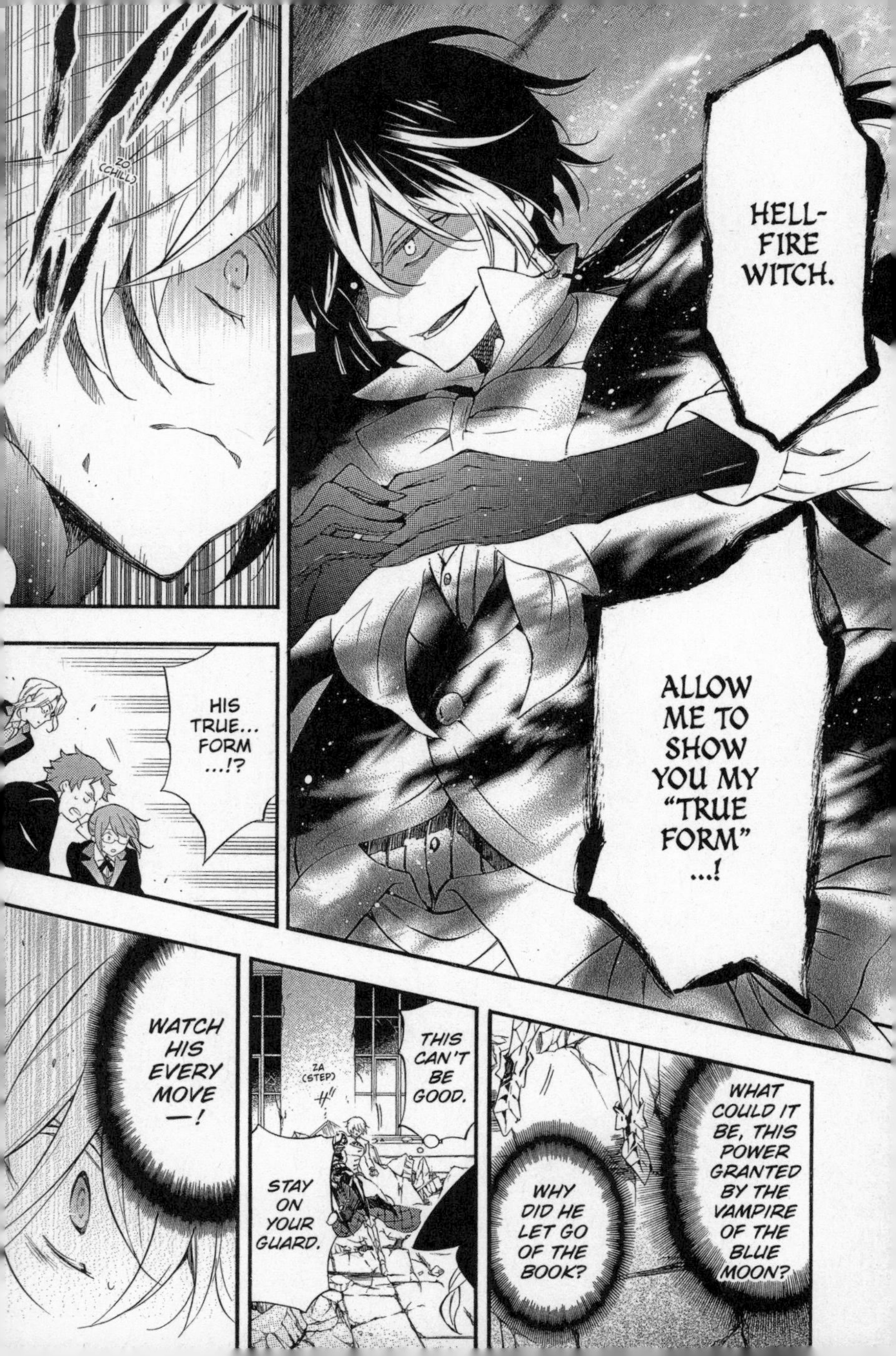
HELL-FIRE WITCH.
ALLOW ME TO SHOW YOU MY "TRUE FORM"...!
ZO (CHILL)
HIS TRUE... FORM...!?
WHAT COULD IT BE, THIS POWER GRANTED BY THE VAMPIRE OF THE BLUE MOON?
WHY DID HE LET GO OF THE BOOK?
THIS CAN'T BE GOOD.
ZA (STEP)
STAY ON YOUR GUARD.
WATCH HIS EVERY MOVE—!

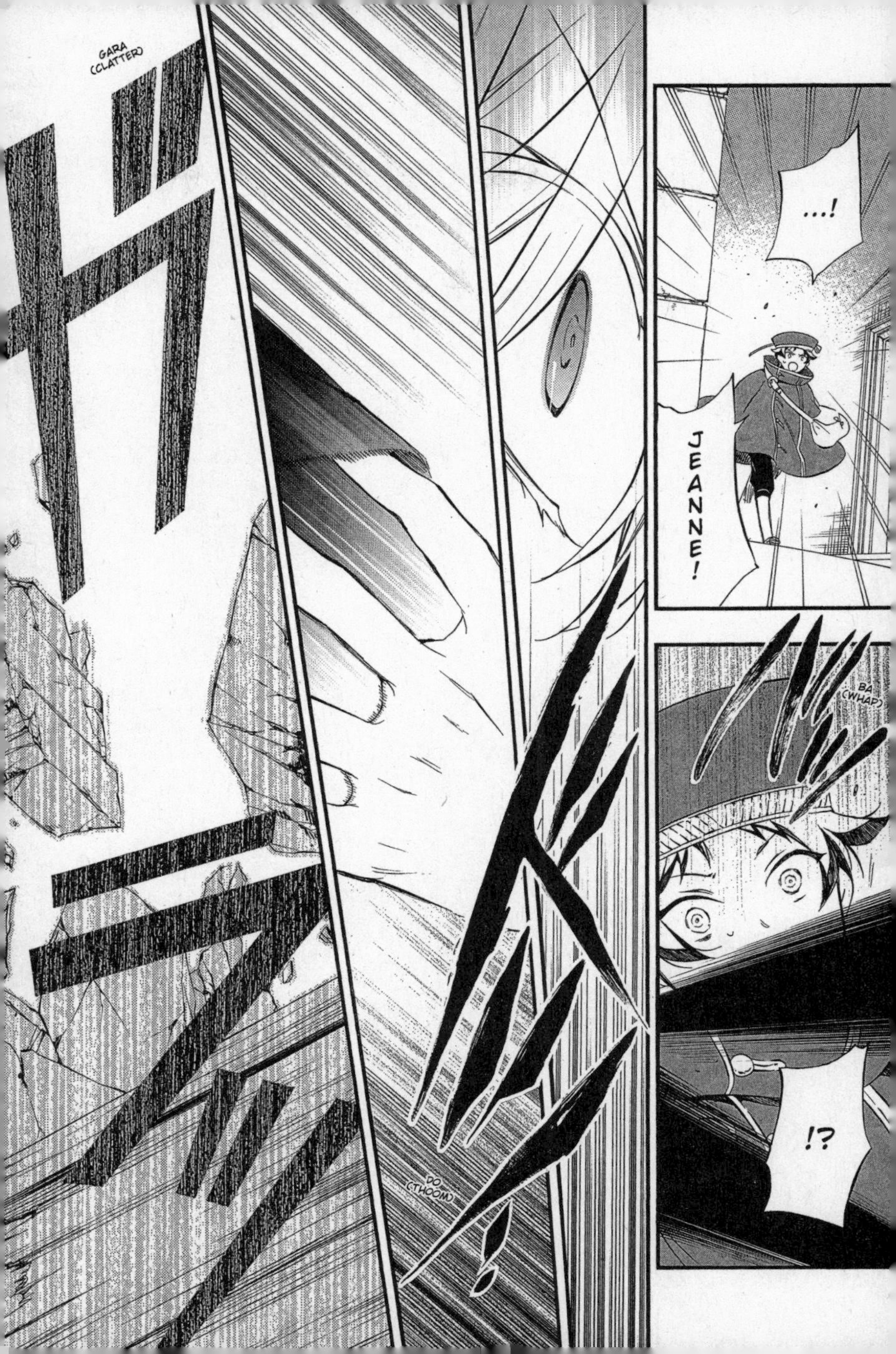
...!
JEANNE!
BA (WHAP)
!?
DO (THOOM)
GARA (CLATTER)

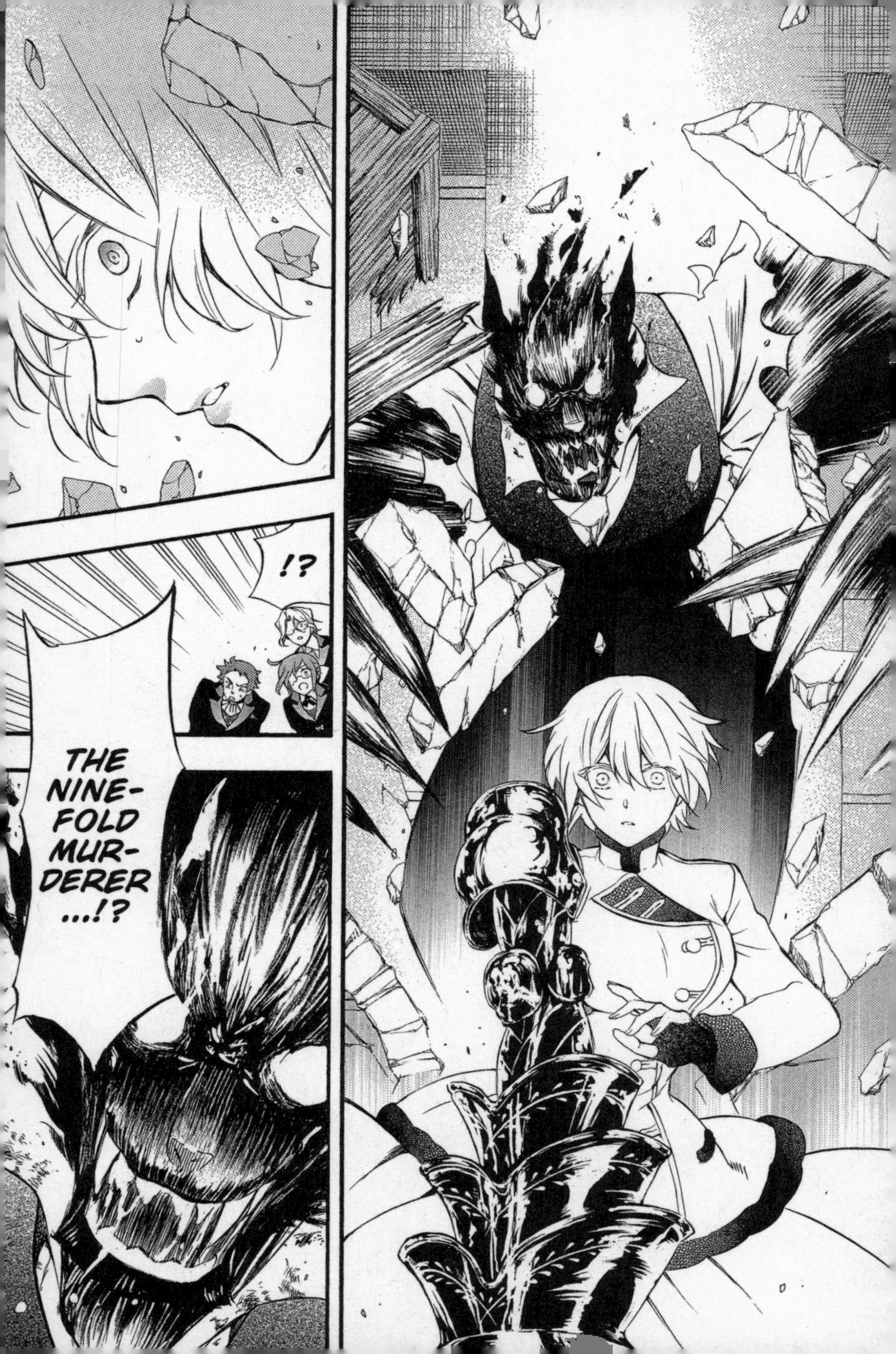
!?
THE NINE-FOLD MUR-DERER ...!?

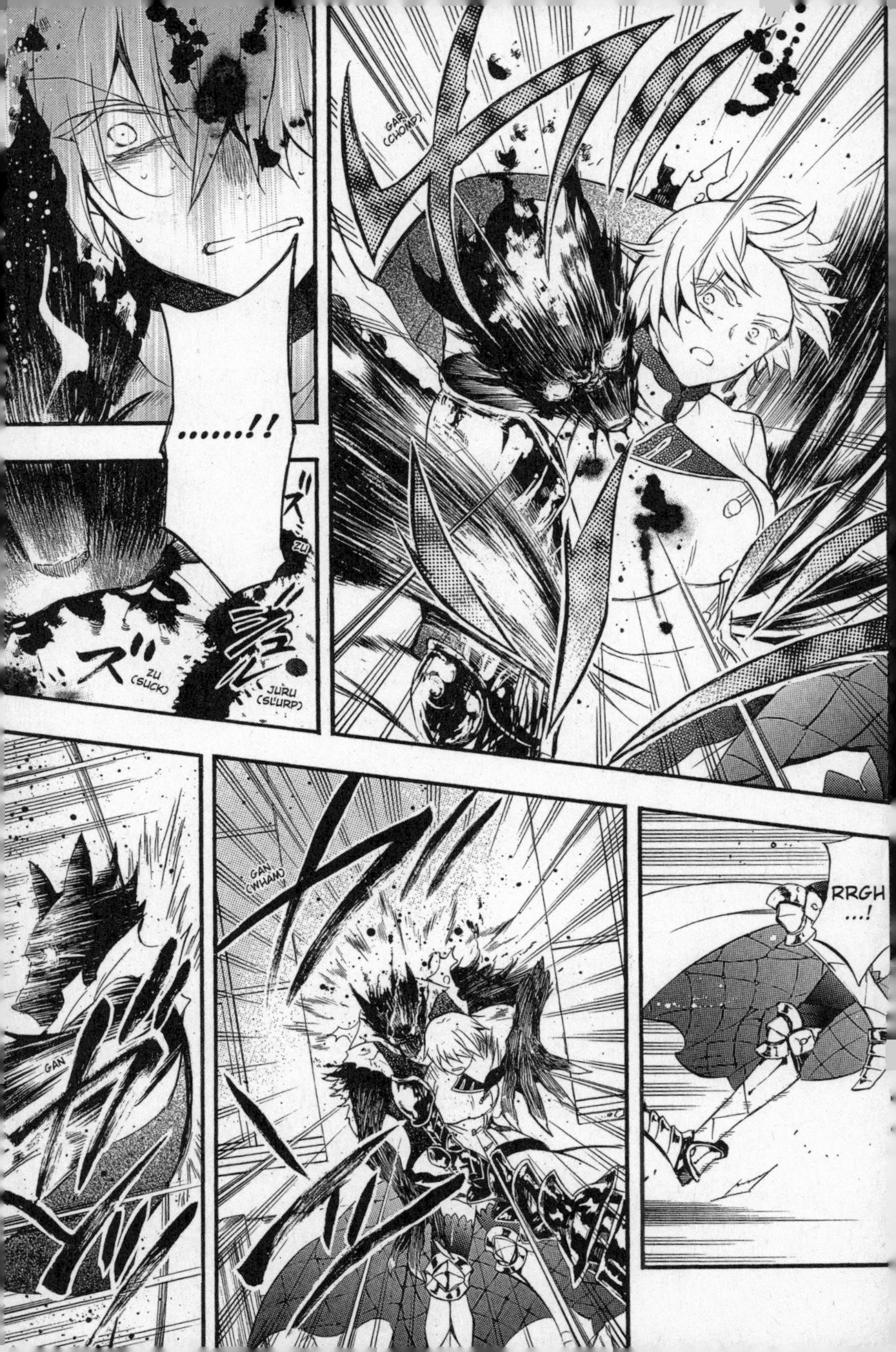
GARI (CHOMP)
......!!
ZU
ZU (SUCK)
JURU (SLURP)
RRGH ...!
GAN (WHAM)
GAN

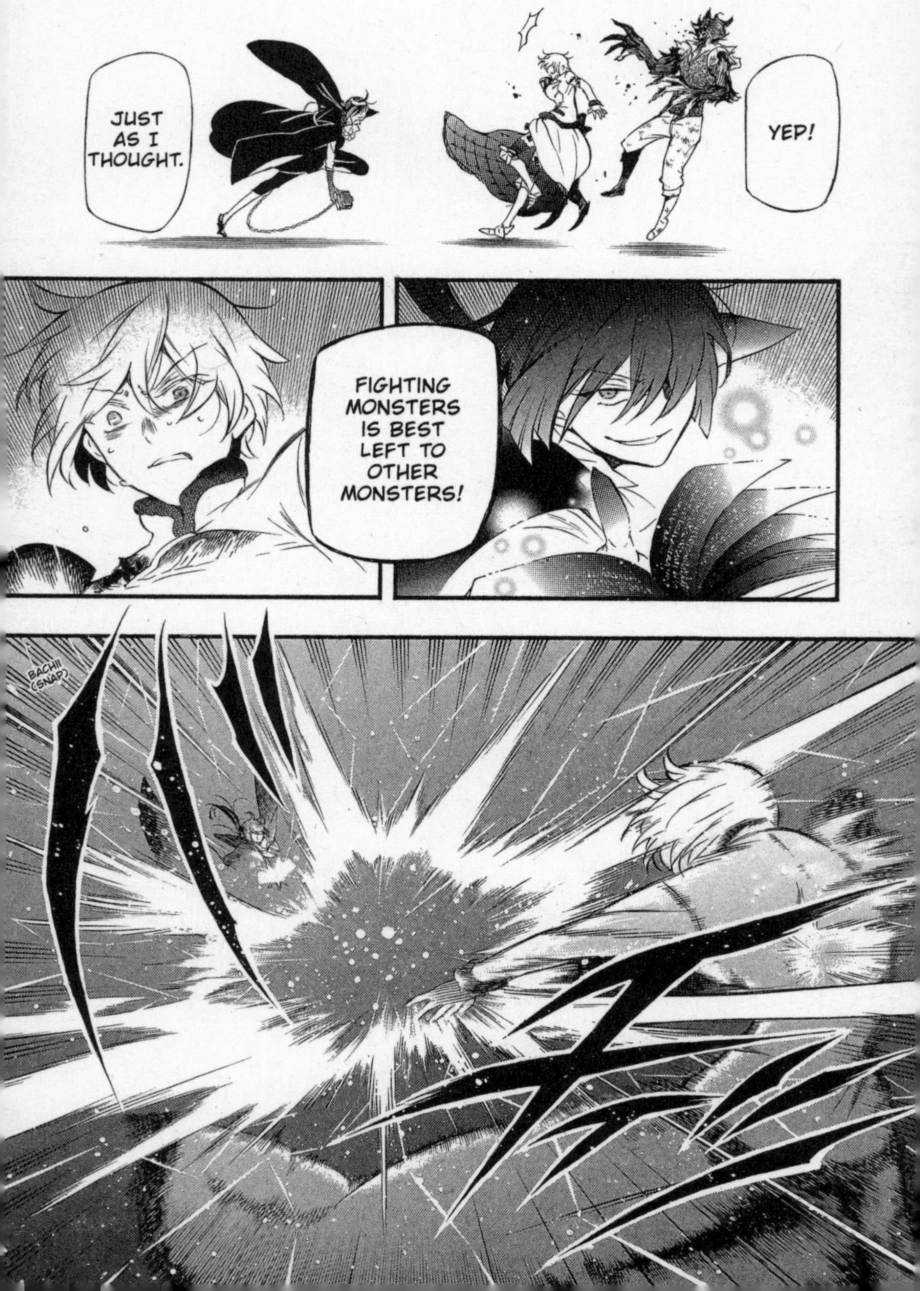
YEP!
JUST AS I THOUGHT.
FIGHTING MONSTERS IS BEST LEFT TO OTHER MONSTERS!
BACHII (SNAP)

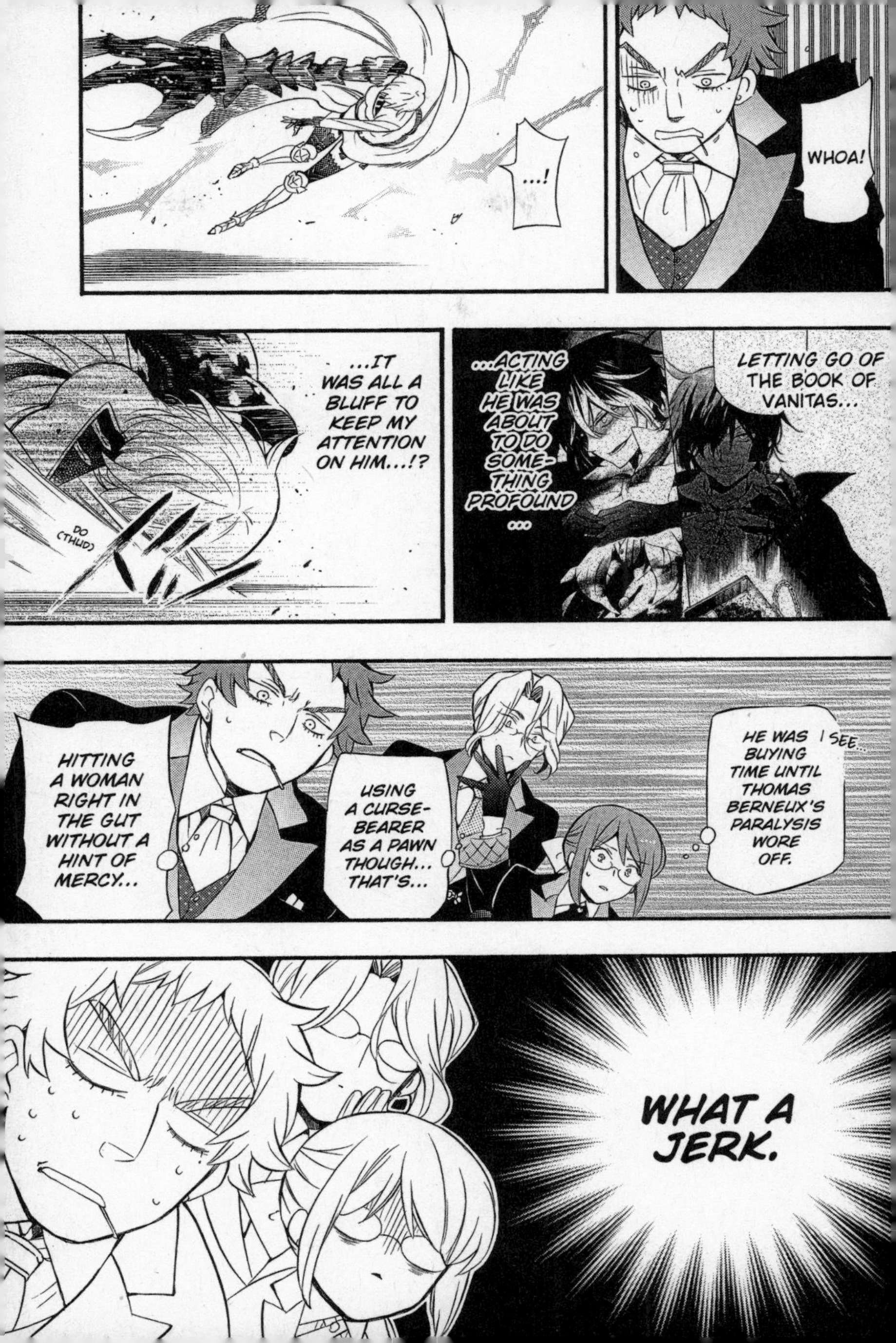
WHOA!
...!
LETTING GO OF THE BOOK OF VANITAS...
...ACTING LIKE HE WAS ABOUT TO DO SOMETHING PROFOUND...
...IT WAS ALL A BLUFF TO KEEP MY ATTENTION ON HIM...!?
DO (THUD)
I SEE...
HE WAS BUYING TIME UNTIL THOMAS BERNEUX'S PARALYSIS WORE OFF.
USING A CURSE-BEARER AS A PAWN THOUGH... THAT'S...
HITTING A WOMAN RIGHT IN THE GUT WITHOUT A HINT OF MERCY...
WHAT A JERK.

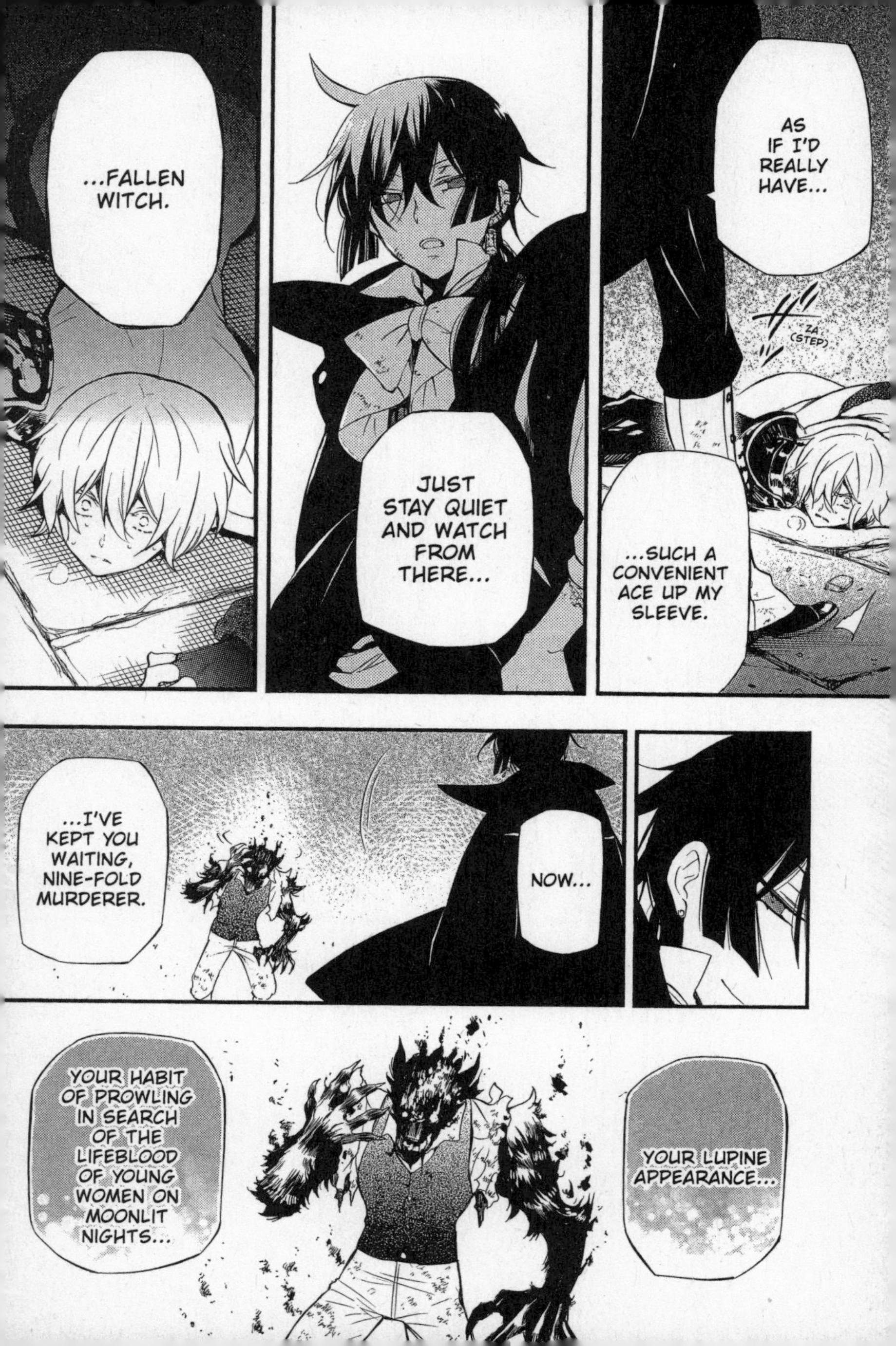
AS IF I'D REALLY HAVE...
ZA (STEP)
...SUCH A CONVENIENT ACE UP MY SLEEVE.
JUST STAY QUIET AND WATCH FROM THERE...
...FALLEN WITCH.
NOW...
...I'VE KEPT YOU WAITING, NINE-FOLD MURDERER.
YOUR LUPINE APPEARANCE...
YOUR HABIT OF PROWLING IN SEARCH OF THE LIFEBLOOD OF YOUNG WOMEN ON MOONLIT NIGHTS...

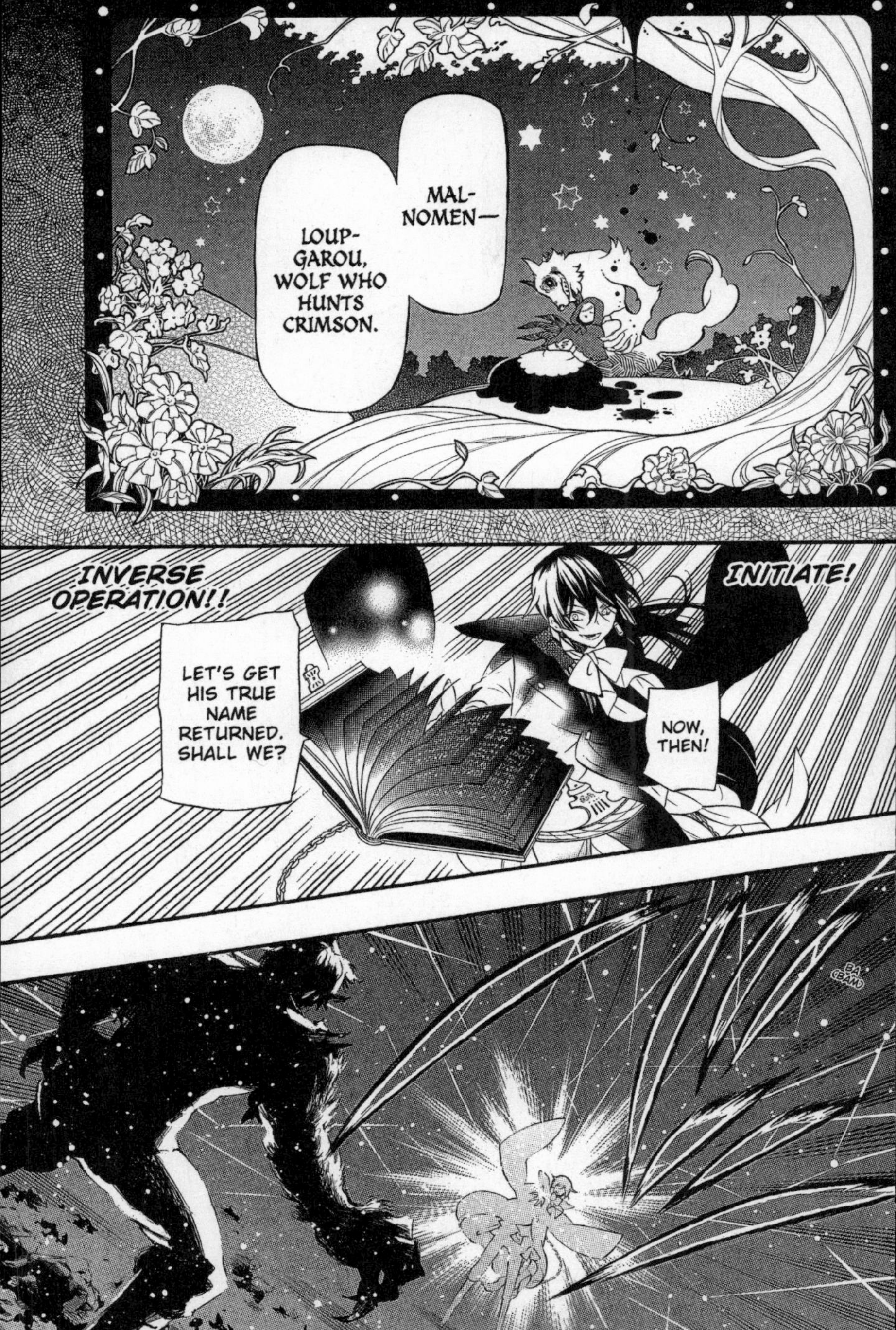
MAL-NOMEN—
LOUP-GAROU, WOLF WHO HUNTS CRIMSON.
NOW, THEN!
LET'S GET HIS TRUE NAME RETURNED. SHALL WE?
INVERSE OPERATION!!
INITIATE!
BA (BAM)

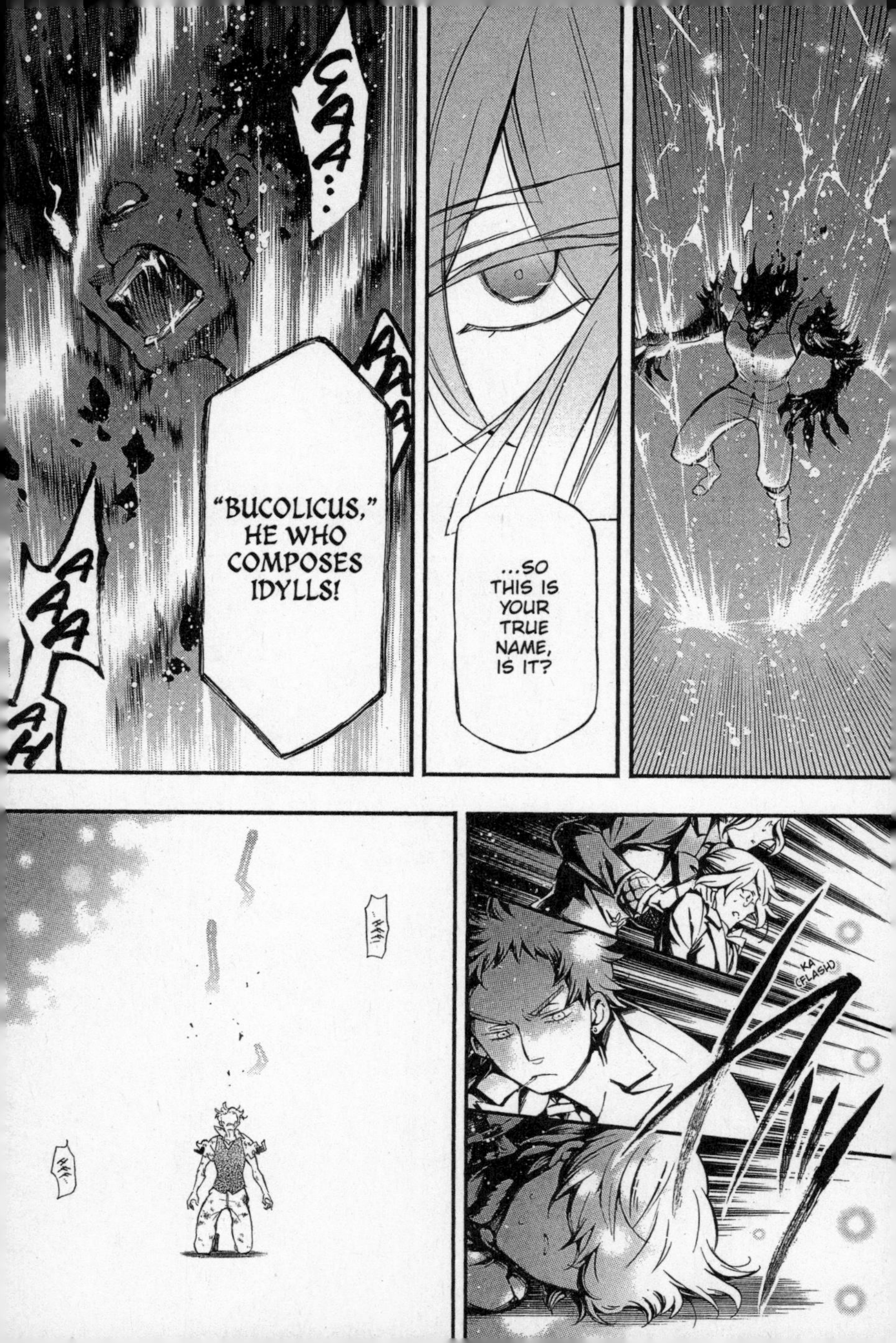
...SO THIS IS YOUR TRUE NAME, IS IT?
GAAA...
AAA
"BUCOLICUS," HE WHO COMPOSES IDYLLS!
AAAAH
KA (FLASH)
...HFF...
HFF...

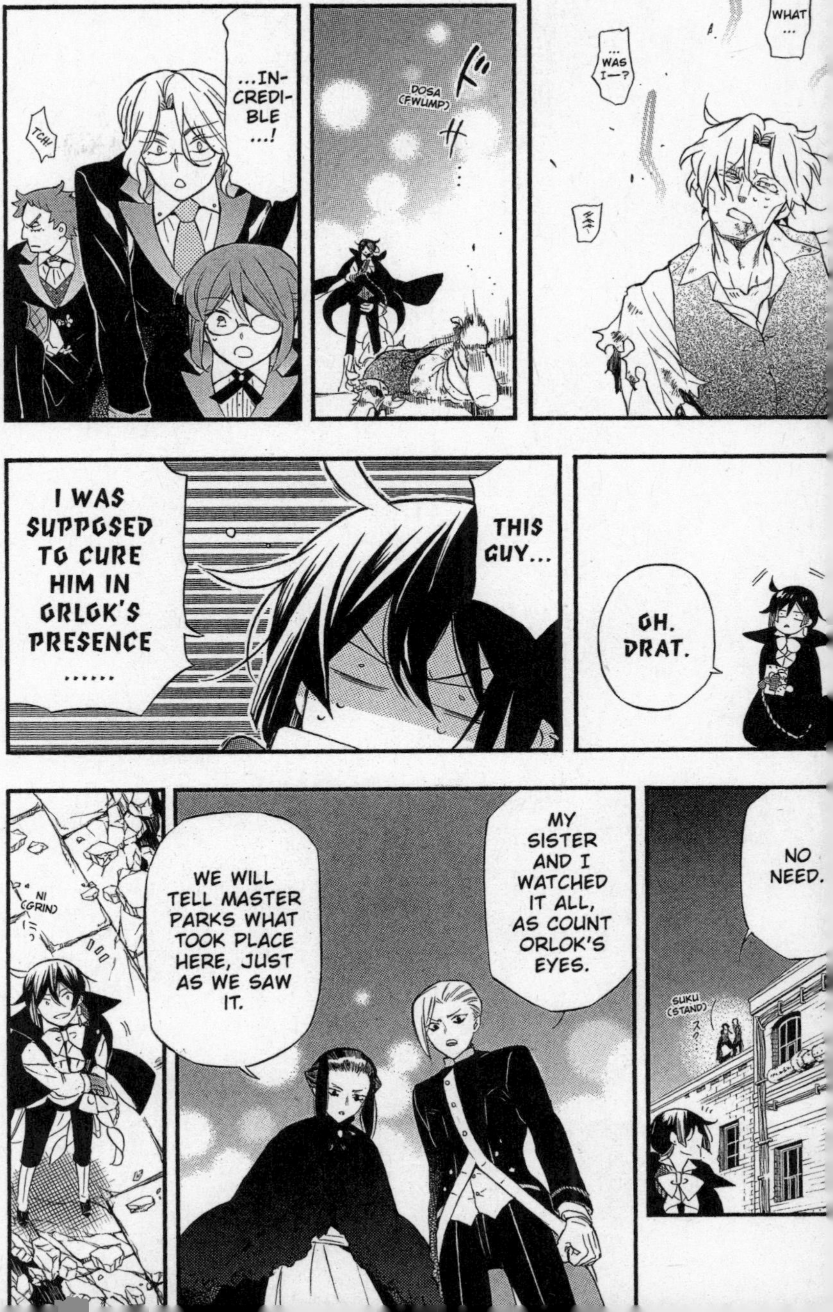
WHAT...
...WAS I—?
DOSA (FWUMP)
...IN-CREDIBLE...!
TCH!
OH. DRAT.
THIS GUY...
I WAS SUPPOSED TO CURE HIM IN ORLOK'S PRESENCE ......
NO NEED.
SUKU (STAND)
MY SISTER AND I WATCHED IT ALL, AS COUNT ORLOK'S EYES.
WE WILL TELL MASTER PARKS WHAT TOOK PLACE HERE, JUST AS WE SAW IT.
NI (GRIN)

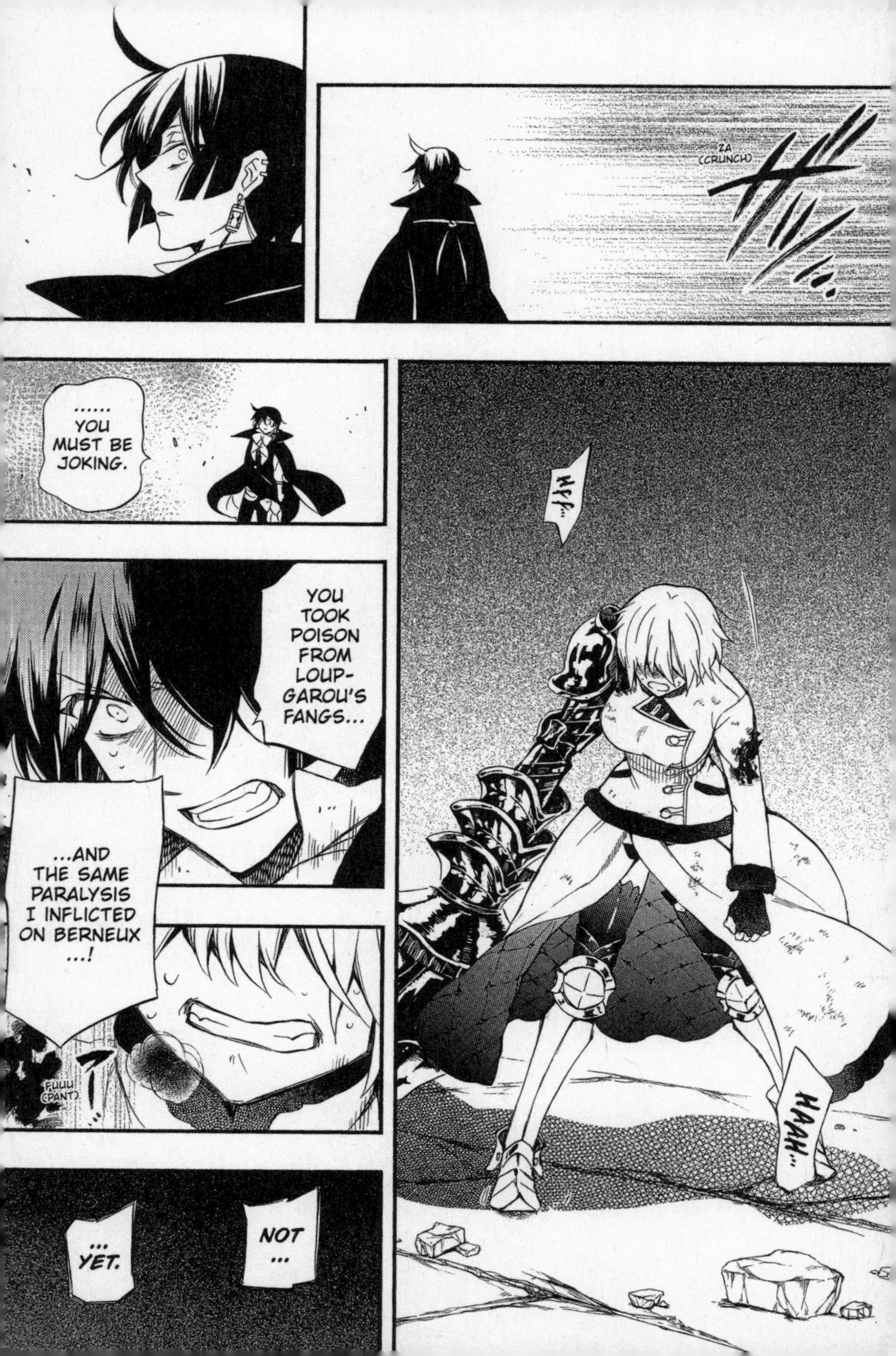
ZA (CRUNCH)
HFF...
HAAH...
...... YOU MUST BE JOKING.
YOU TOOK POISON FROM LOUP-GAROU'S FANGS...
...AND THE SAME PARALYSIS I INFLICTED ON BERNEUX ...!
FUUU (PANT)
NOT ...
... YET.

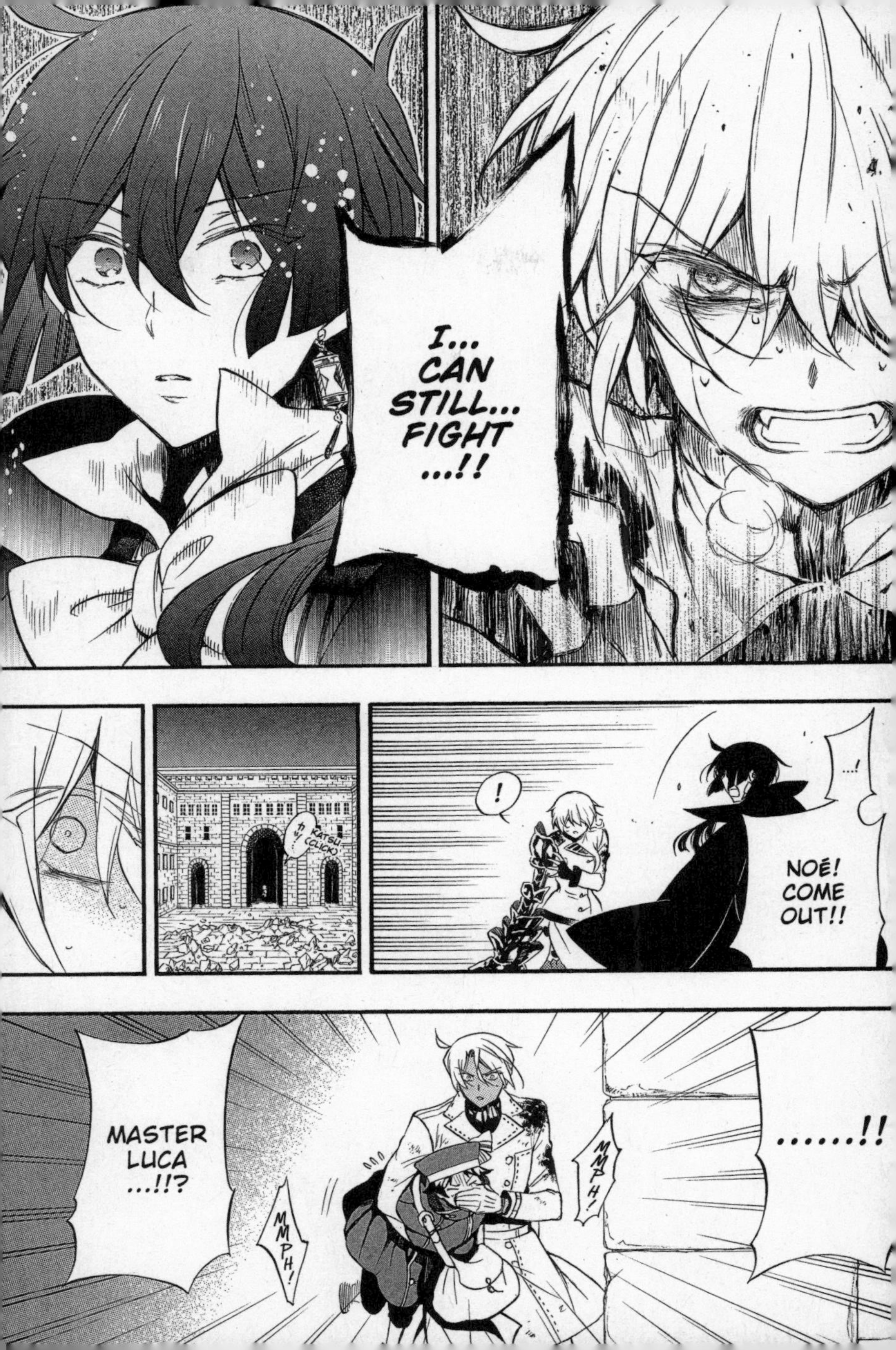
I... CAN STILL... FIGHT ...!!
...!
NOÉ! COME OUT!!
!
KATSU (CLICK)
......!!
MMPH!
MMPH!
MASTER LUCA ...!!?

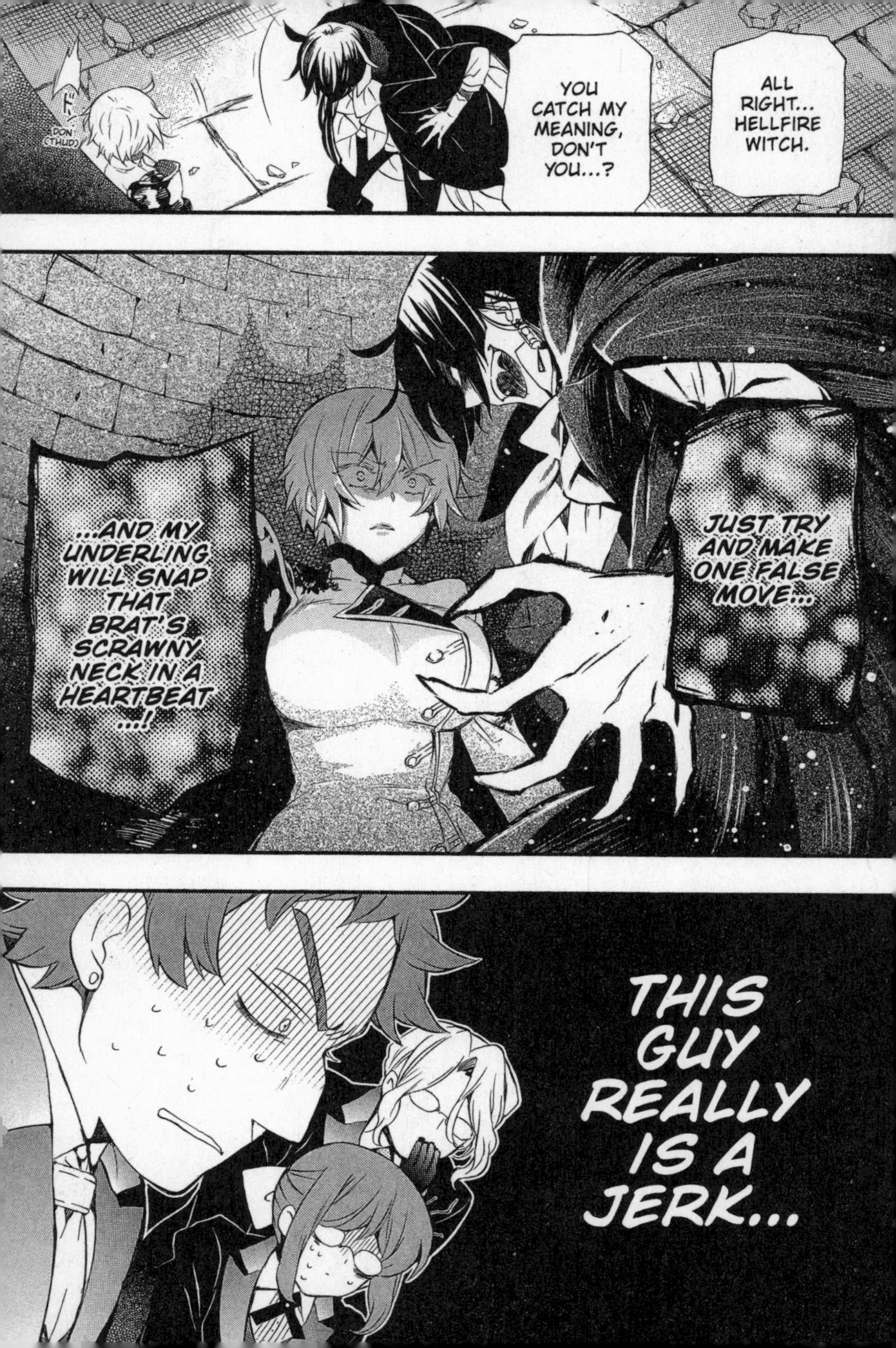
ALL RIGHT... HELLFIRE WITCH.
YOU CATCH MY MEANING, DON'T YOU...?
DON (THUD)
JUST TRY AND MAKE ONE FALSE MOVE...
...AND MY UNDERLING WILL SNAP THAT BRAT'S SCRAWNY NECK IN A HEARTBEAT...!
THIS GUY REALLY IS A JERK...

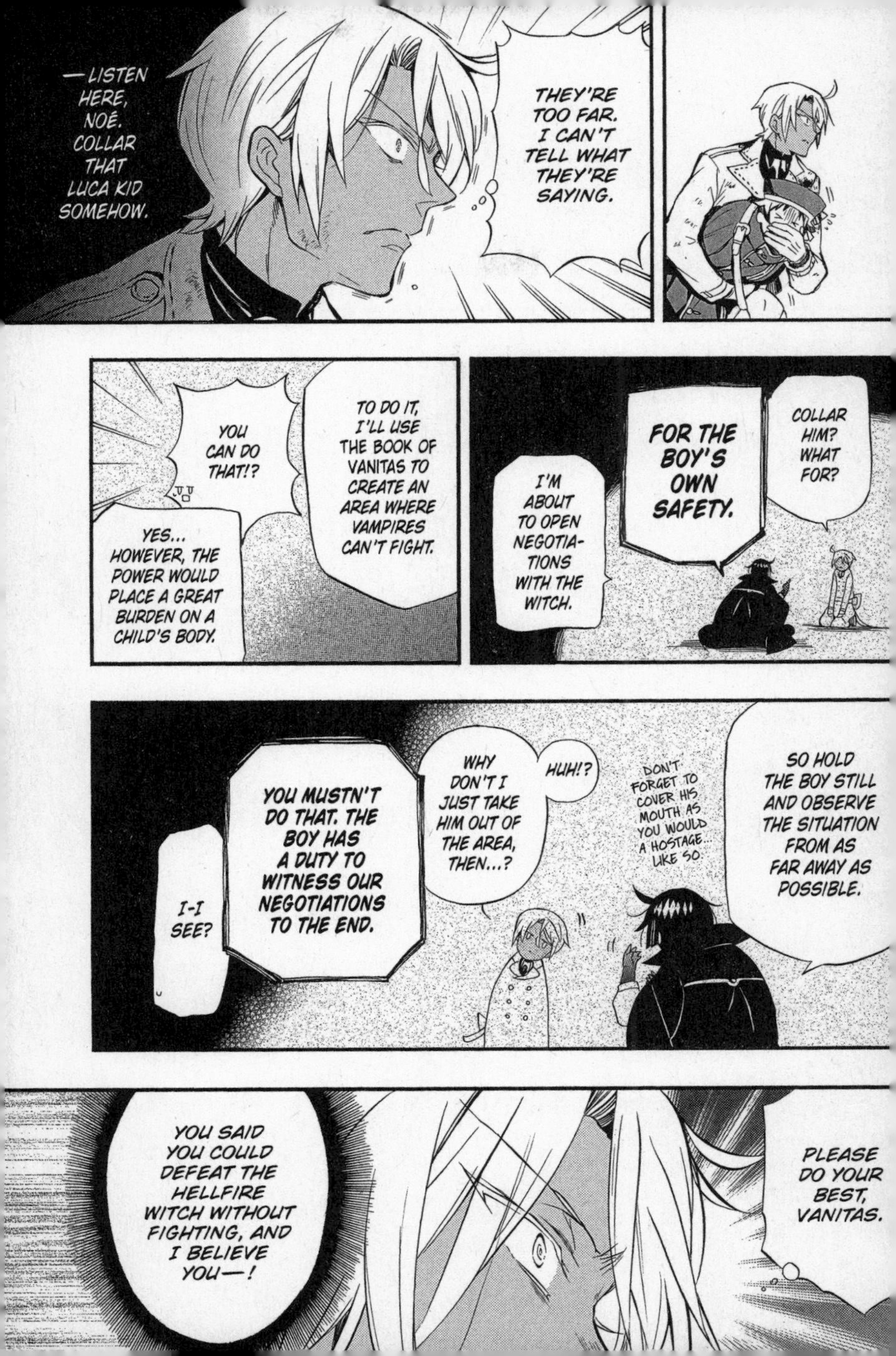

THEY'RE TOO FAR. I CAN'T TELL WHAT THEY'RE SAYING.
—LISTEN HERE, NOÉ. COLLAR THAT LUCA KID SOMEHOW.
COLLAR HIM? WHAT FOR?
FOR THE BOY'S OWN SAFETY.
I'M ABOUT TO OPEN NEGOTIA-TIONS WITH THE WITCH.
TO DO IT, I'LL USE THE BOOK OF VANITAS TO CREATE AN AREA WHERE VAMPIRES CAN'T FIGHT.
YOU CAN DO THAT!?
YES... HOWEVER, THE POWER WOULD PLACE A GREAT BURDEN ON A CHILD'S BODY.
SO HOLD THE BOY STILL AND OBSERVE THE SITUATION FROM AS FAR AWAY AS POSSIBLE.
DON'T FORGET TO COVER HIS MOUTH AS YOU WOULD A HOSTAGE... LIKE SO.
HUH!?
WHY DON'T I JUST TAKE HIM OUT OF THE AREA, THEN...?
YOU MUSTN'T DO THAT. THE BOY HAS A DUTY TO WITNESS OUR NEGOTIATIONS TO THE END.
I-I SEE?
PLEASE DO YOUR BEST, VANITAS.
YOU SAID YOU COULD DEFEAT THE HELLFIRE WITCH WITHOUT FIGHTING, AND I BELIEVE YOU—!

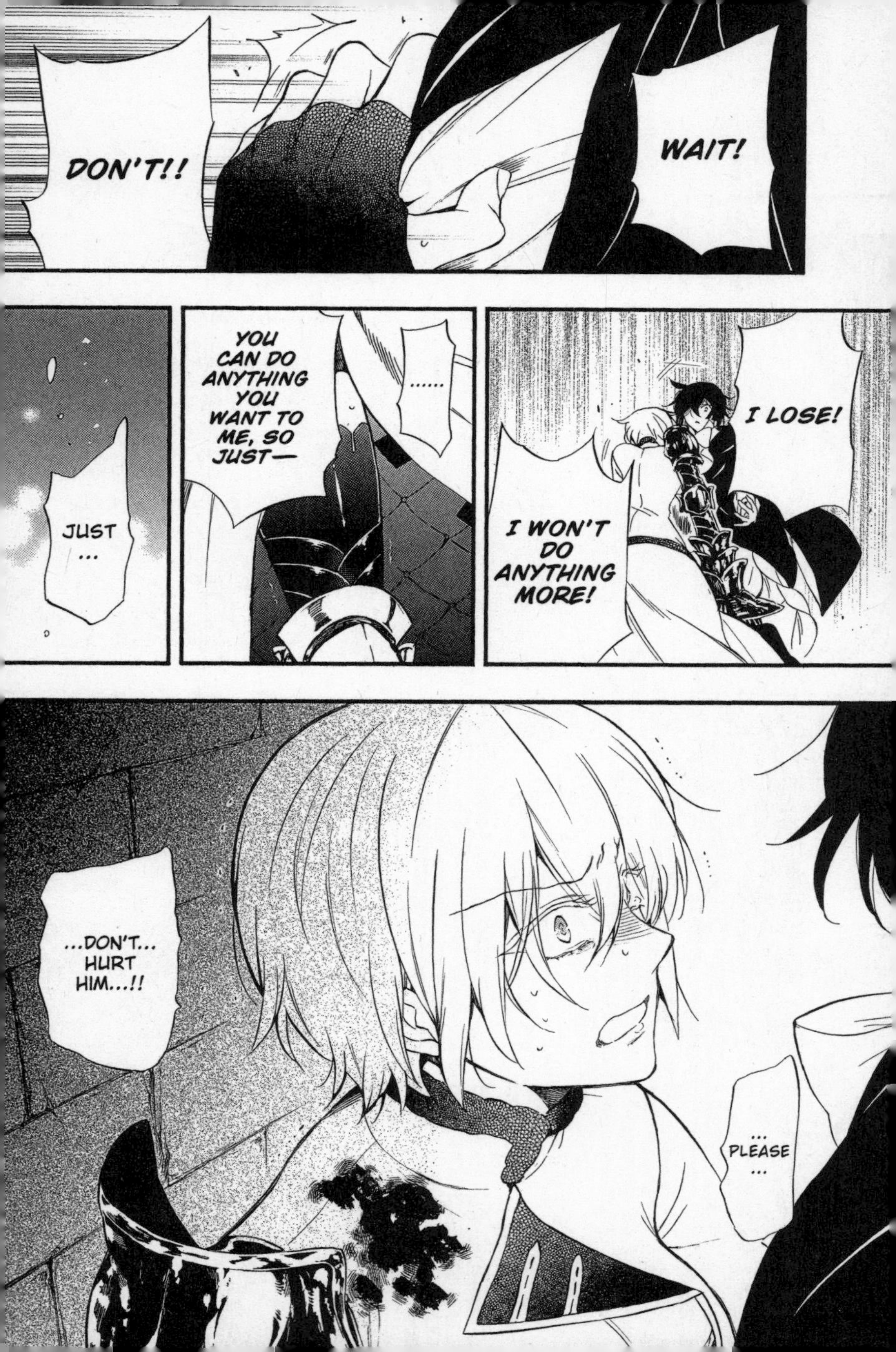
WAIT!
DON'T!!
I LOSE!
I WON'T DO ANYTHING MORE!
......
YOU CAN DO ANYTHING YOU WANT TO ME, SO JUST—
JUST ...
... PLEASE ...
...DON'T... HURT HIM...!!

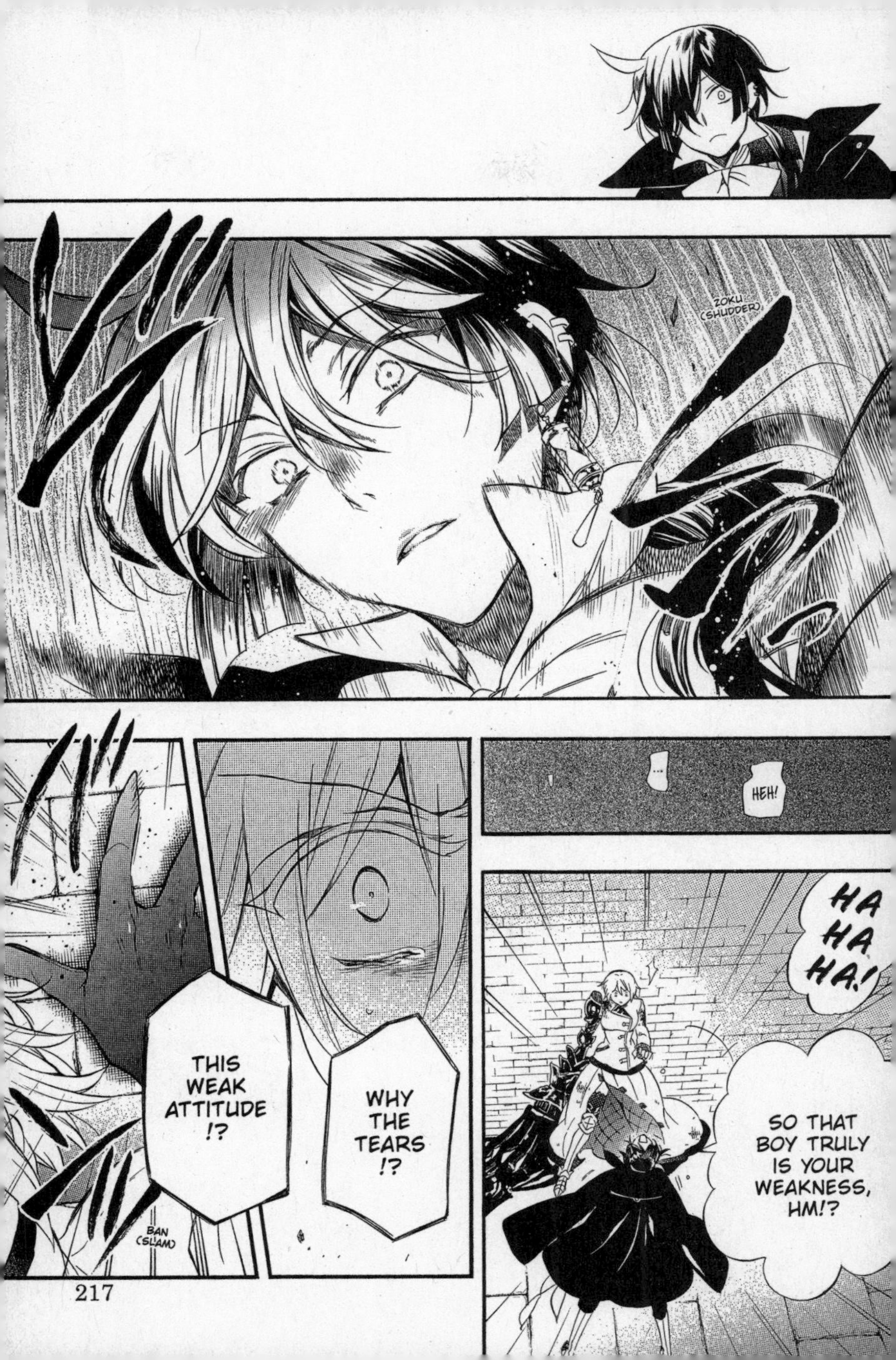
ZOKU (SHUDDER)
...
HEH!
HA HA HA!
SO THAT BOY TRULY IS YOUR WEAKNESS, HM!?
WHY THE TEARS !?
THIS WEAK ATTITUDE !?
BAN (SLAM)

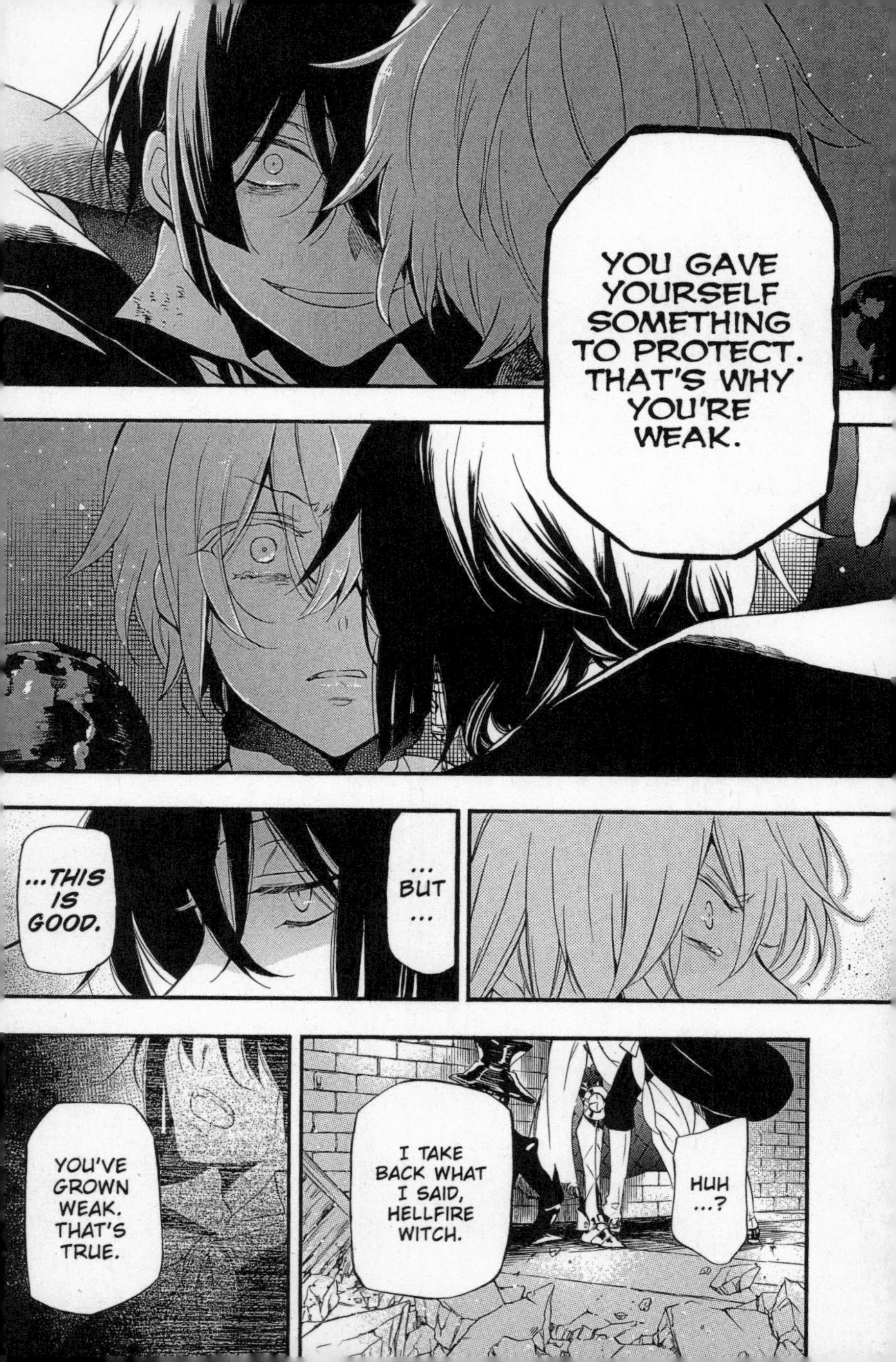
YOU GAVE YOURSELF SOMETHING TO PROTECT. THAT'S WHY YOU'RE WEAK.
... BUT ...
...THIS IS GOOD.
HUH ...?
I TAKE BACK WHAT I SAID, HELLFIRE WITCH.
YOU'VE GROWN WEAK. THAT'S TRUE.

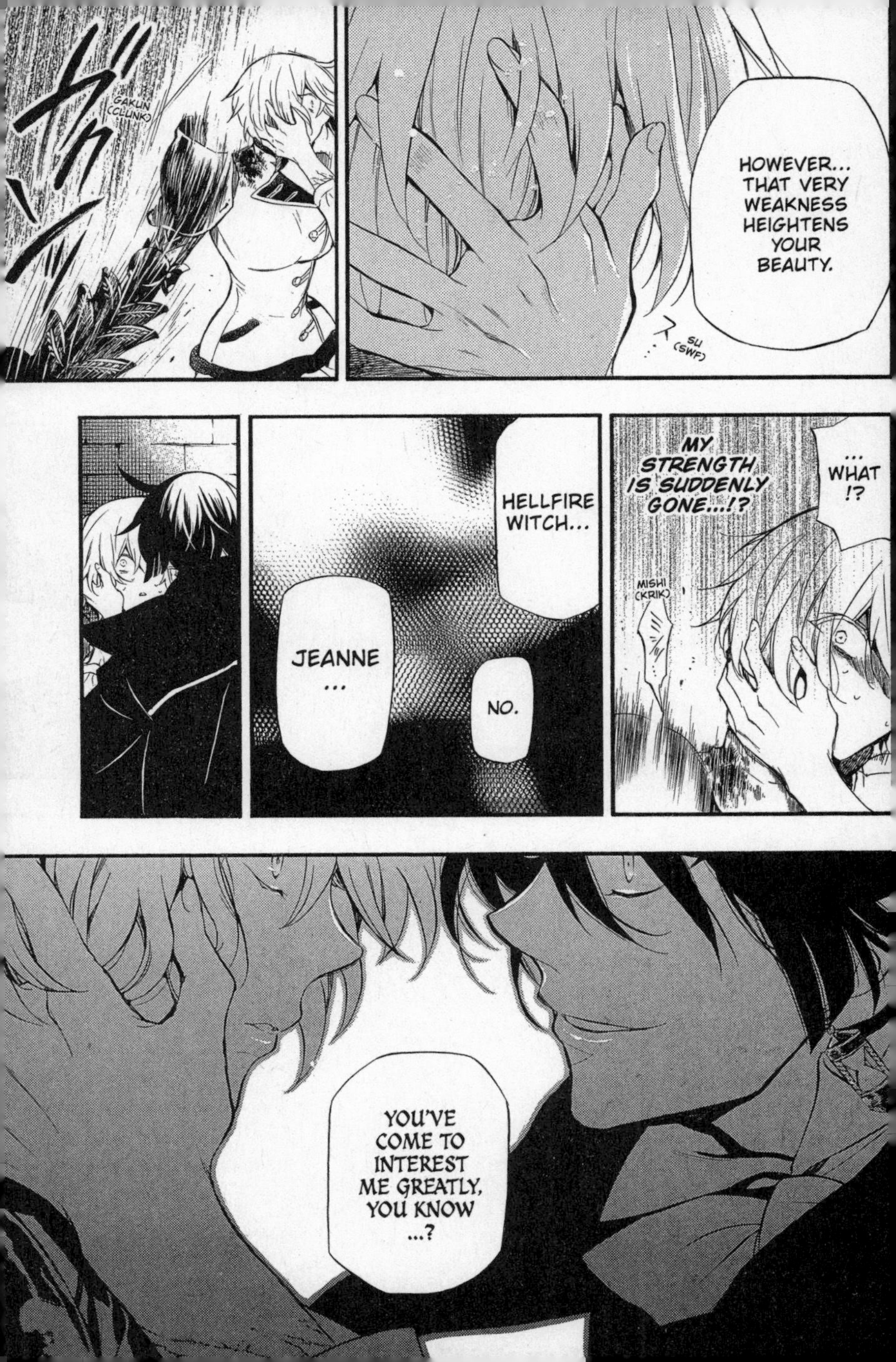
HOWEVER... THAT VERY WEAKNESS HEIGHTENS YOUR BEAUTY.
SU (SWF)
GAKUN (CLUNK)
... WHAT !?
MY STRENGTH IS SUDDENLY GONE...!?
MISHI (KRIK)
HELLFIRE WITCH...
JEANNE ...
NO.
YOU'VE COME TO INTEREST ME GREATLY, YOU KNOW ...?

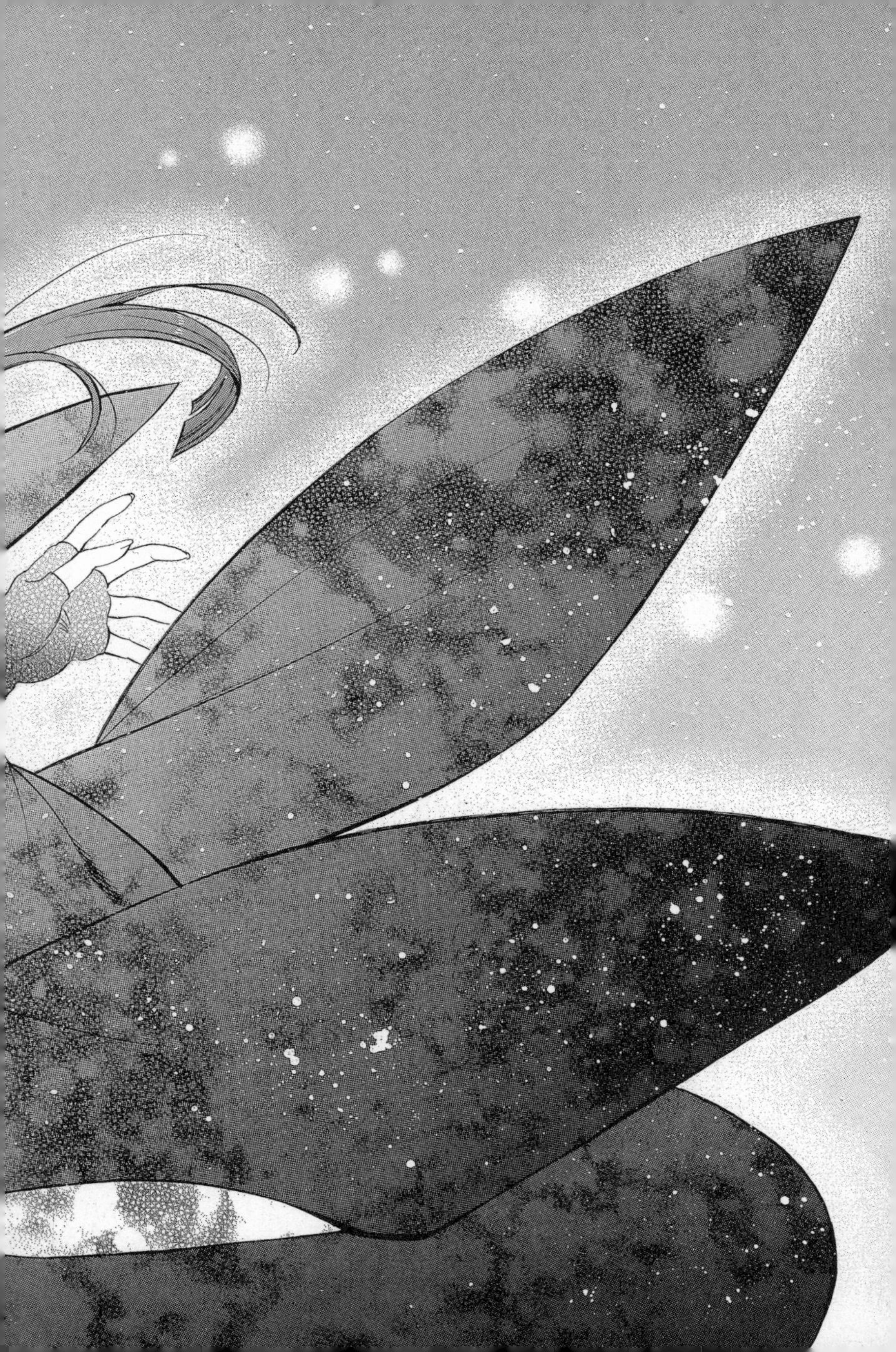

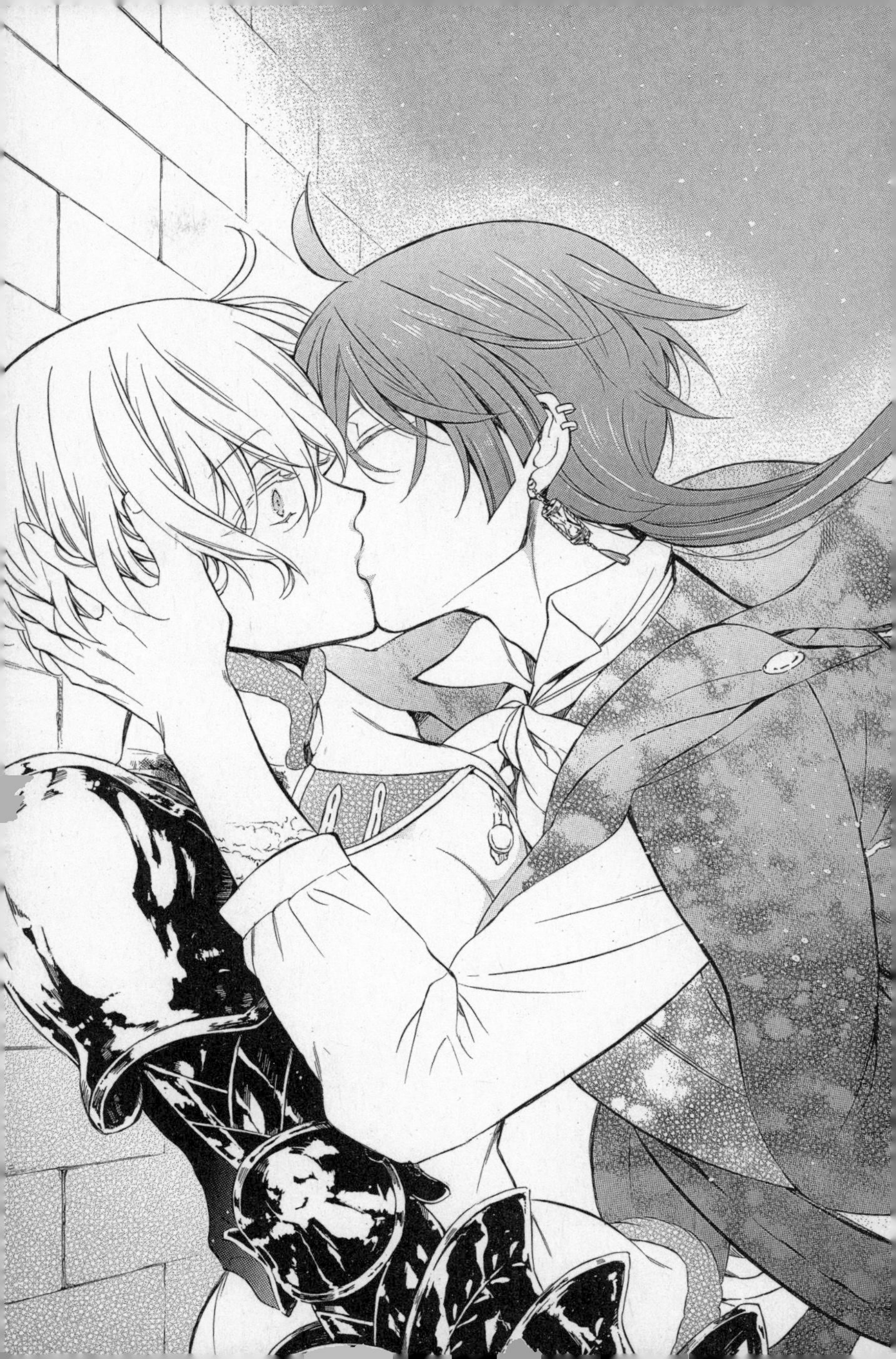

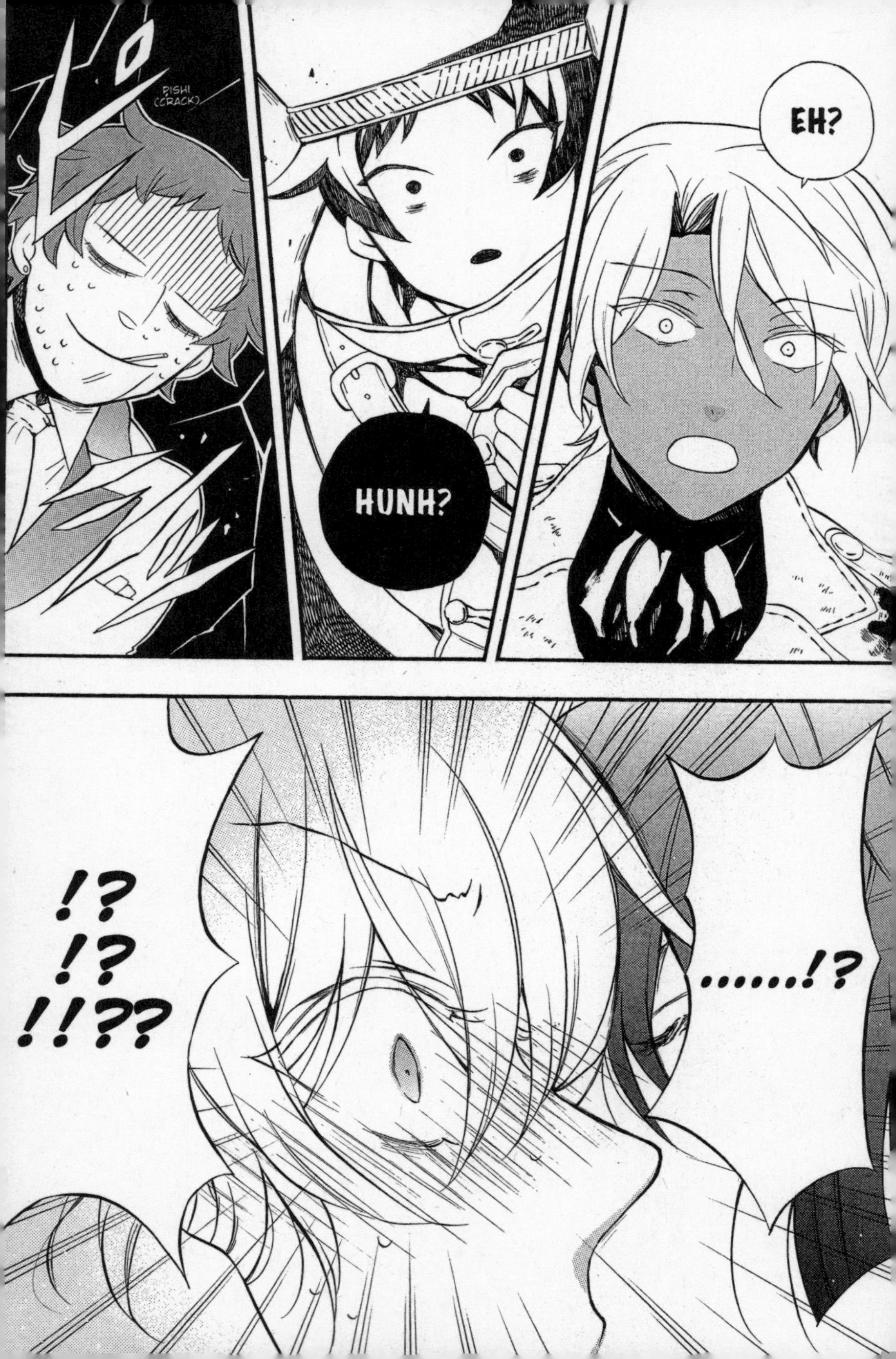
EH?
HUNH?
PISHI (CRACK)
......!?
!? !? !!??

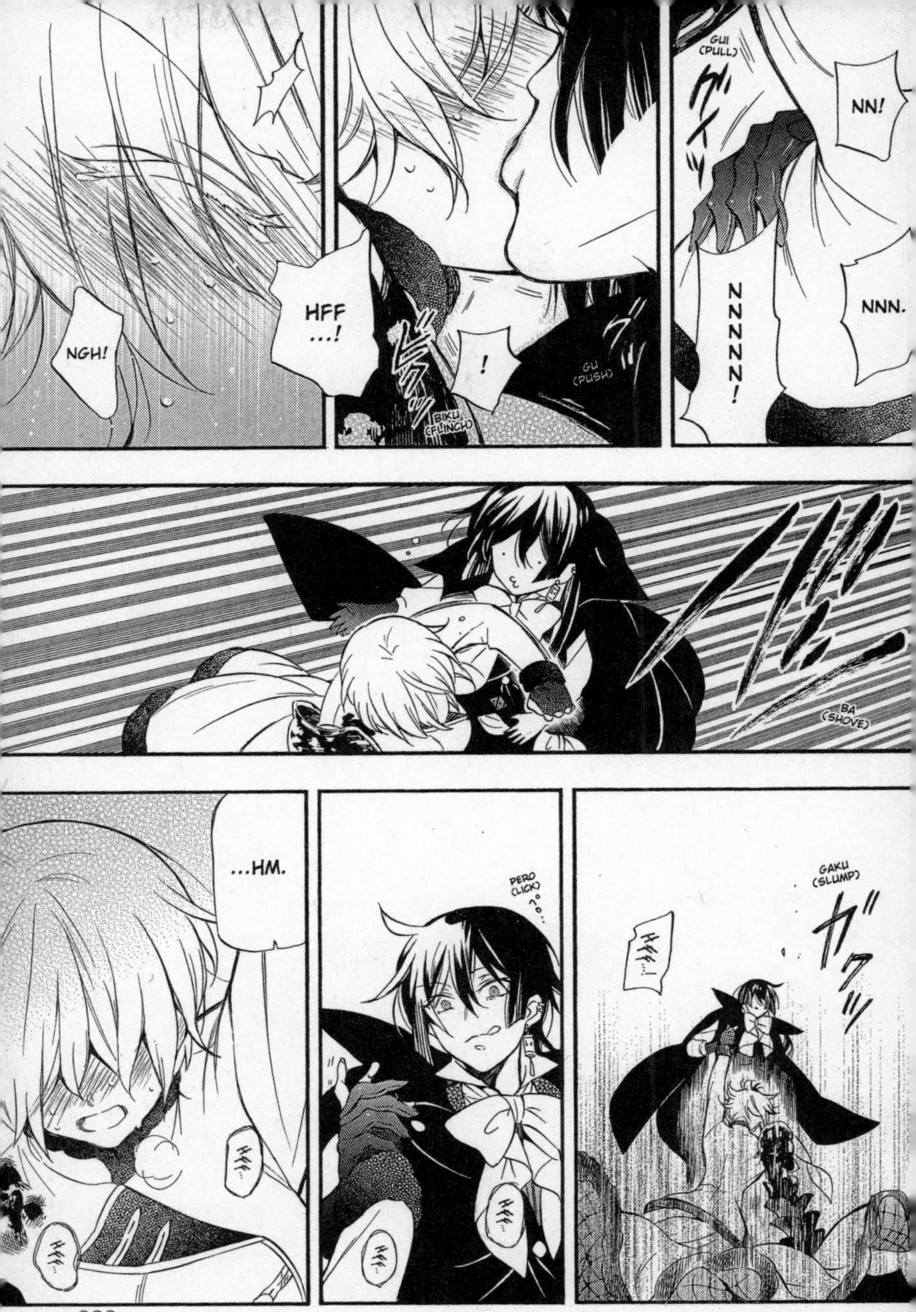
GUI (PULL)
NN!
NNN.
NNNNN!
HFF ...!
!
GU (PUSH)
BIKU (FLINCH)
NGH!
BA (SHOVE)
GAKU (SLUMP)
HFF...!
PERO (LICK)
HFF...
HFF...
...HM.
HFF...
HFF...

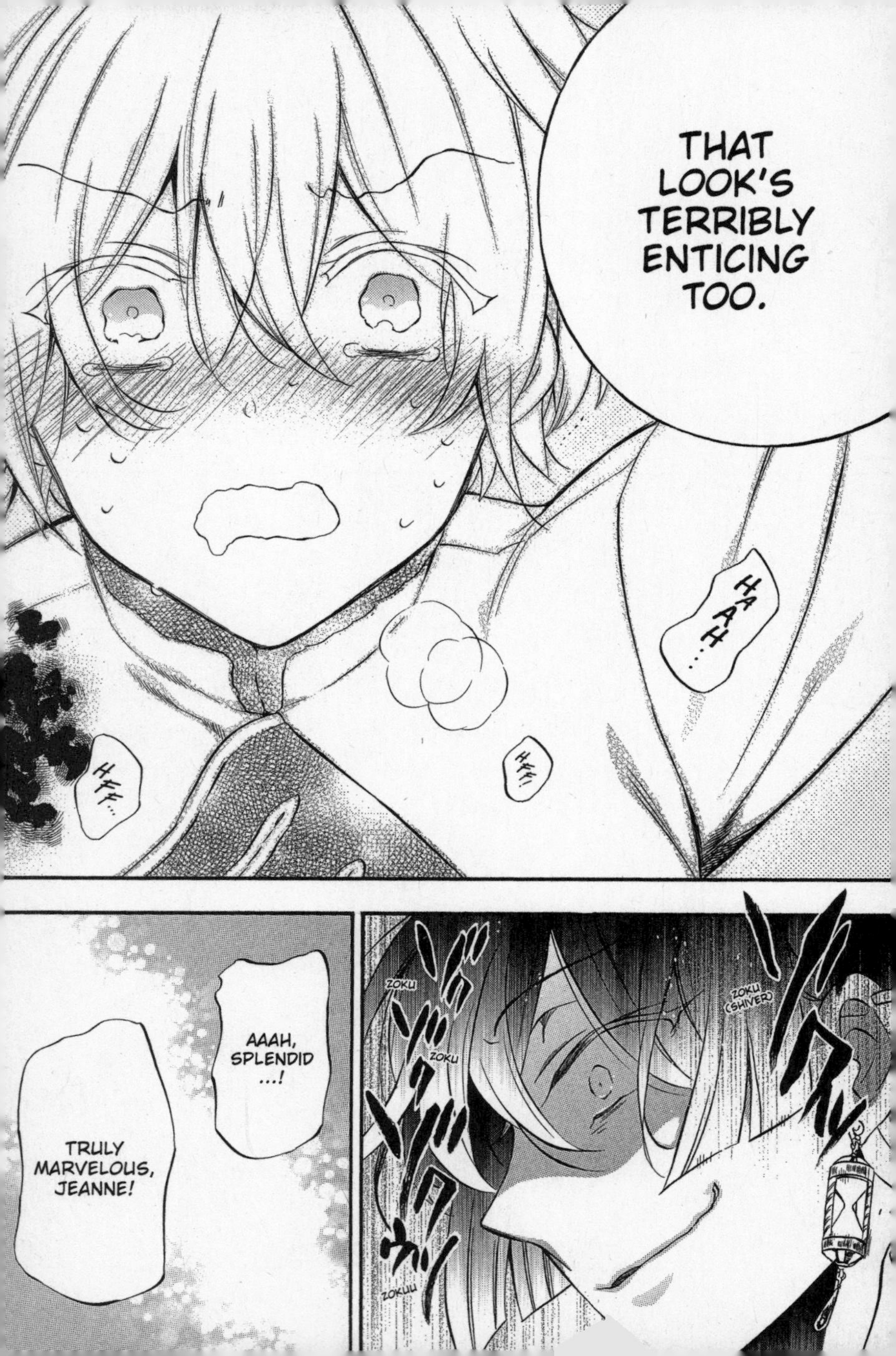
THAT LOOK'S TERRIBLY ENTICING TOO.
HAAH...
HFF!
HFF...
ZOKU (SHIVER)
ZOKU
ZOKU
ZOKUU
AAAH, SPLENDID ...!
TRULY MARVELOUS, JEANNE!

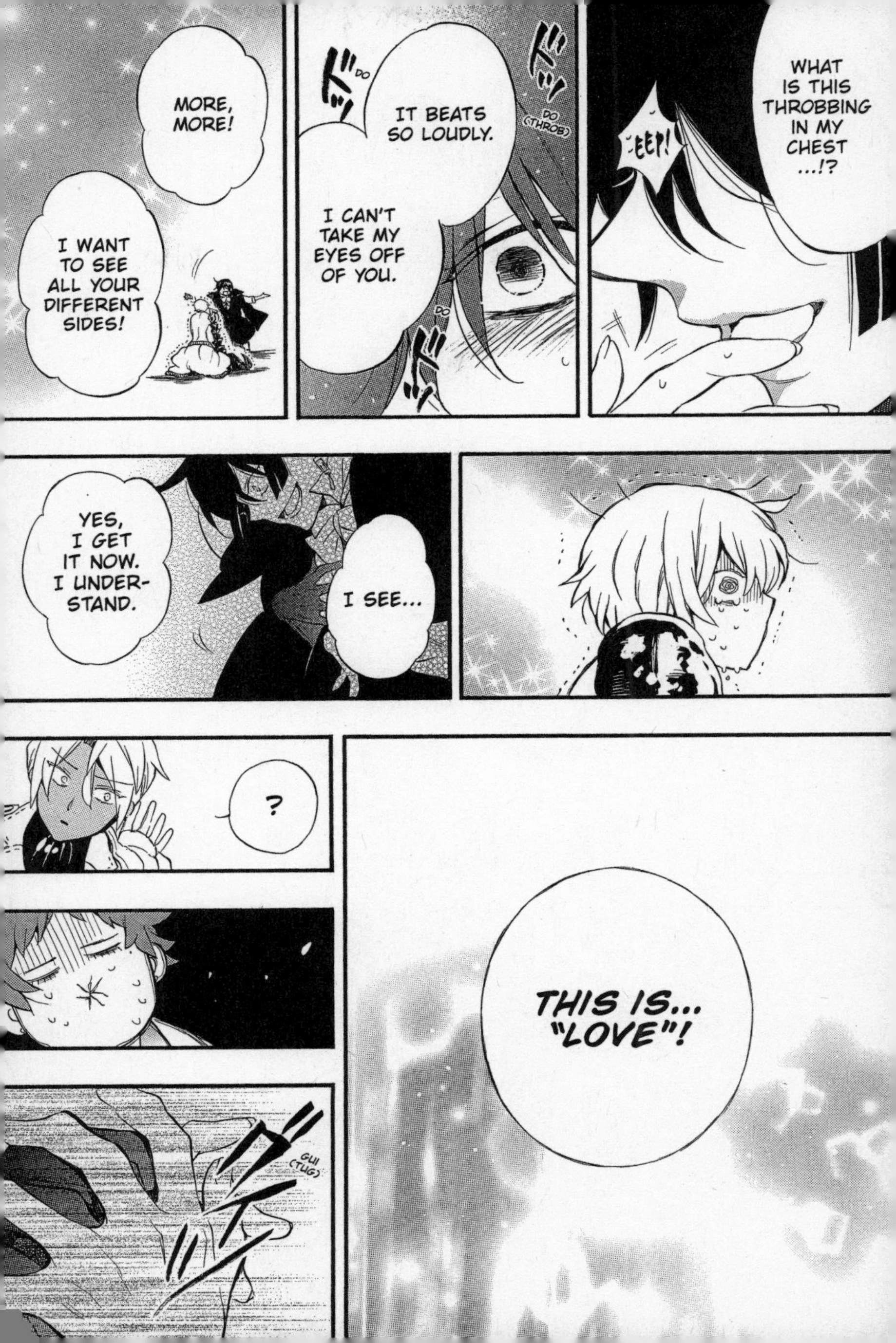
WHAT IS THIS THROBBING IN MY CHEST ...!?
EEP!
DO (THROB)
IT BEATS SO LOUDLY.
DO
I CAN'T TAKE MY EYES OFF OF YOU.
DO
MORE, MORE!
I WANT TO SEE ALL YOUR DIFFERENT SIDES!
I SEE...
YES, I GET IT NOW. I UNDER-STAND.
THIS IS... "LOVE"!
?
GUI (TUG)

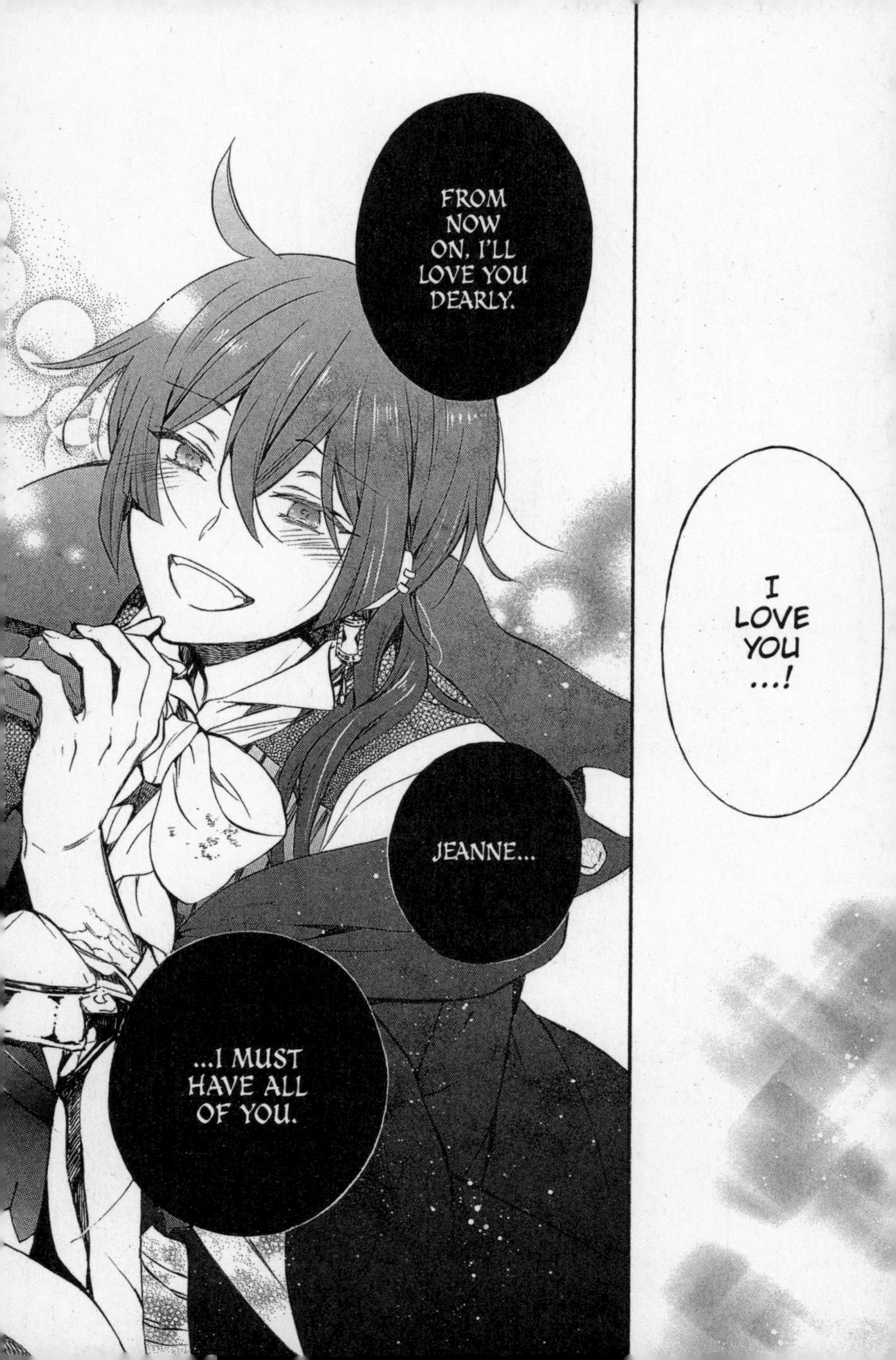
I LOVE YOU ...!
FROM NOW ON, I'LL LOVE YOU DEARLY.
JEANNE...
...I MUST HAVE ALL OF YOU.

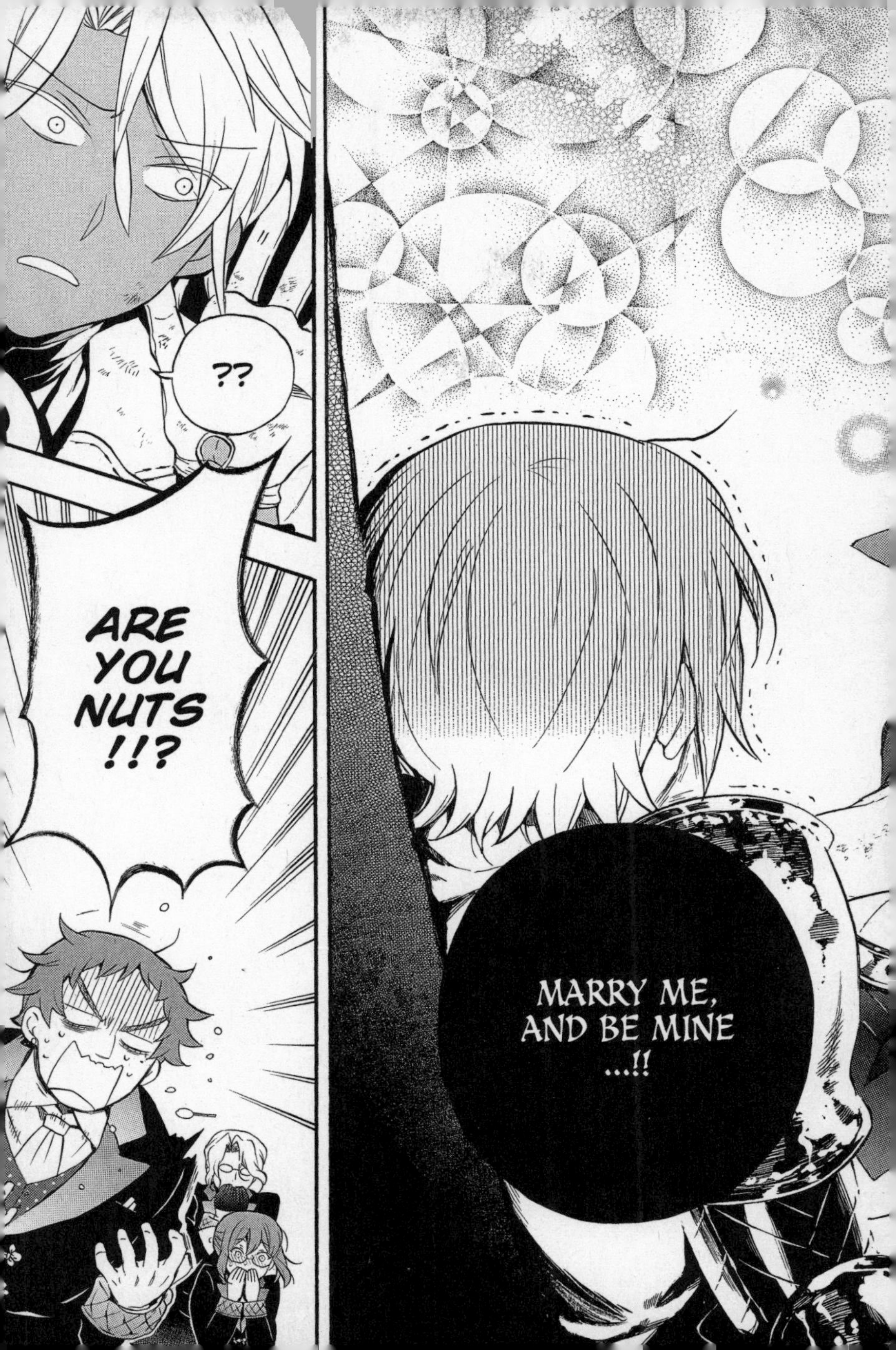
MARRY ME, AND BE MINE ...!!
??
ARE YOU NUTS !!?

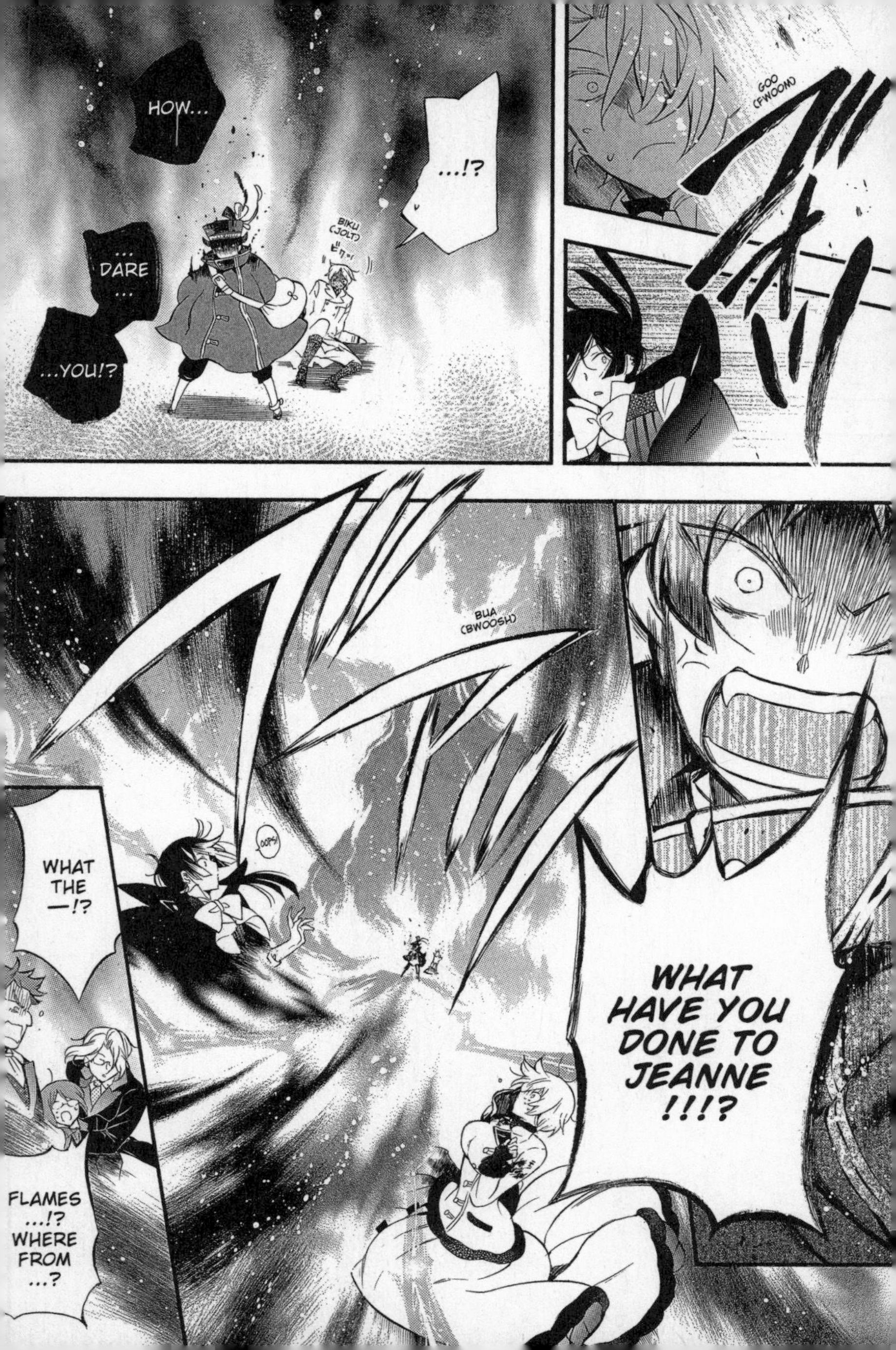
GOO (FWOOM)
...!?
BIKU (JOLT)
HOW...
...DARE...
...YOU!?
WHAT HAVE YOU DONE TO JEANNE!!!?
BUA (BWOOSH)
OOPS!
WHAT THE—!?
FLAMES...!? WHERE FROM...?

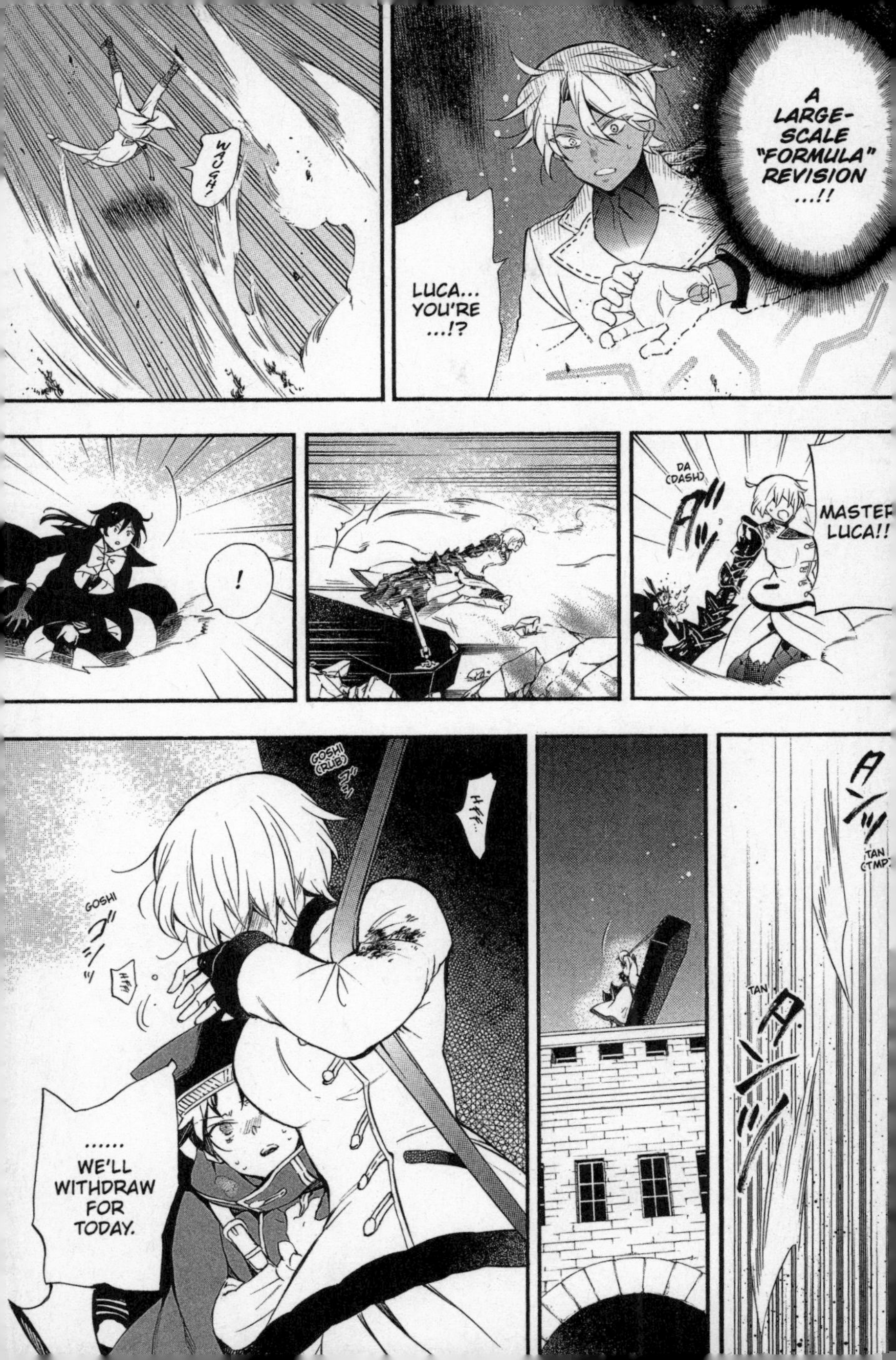

A LARGE-SCALE "FORMULA" REVISION ...!!
LUCA... YOU'RE ...!?
WAUGH!
DA (DASH)
MASTER LUCA!!
!
TAN (TMP)
TAN
GOSHI (RUB)
HFF...
GOSHI
HFF
...... WE'LL WITHDRAW FOR TODAY.

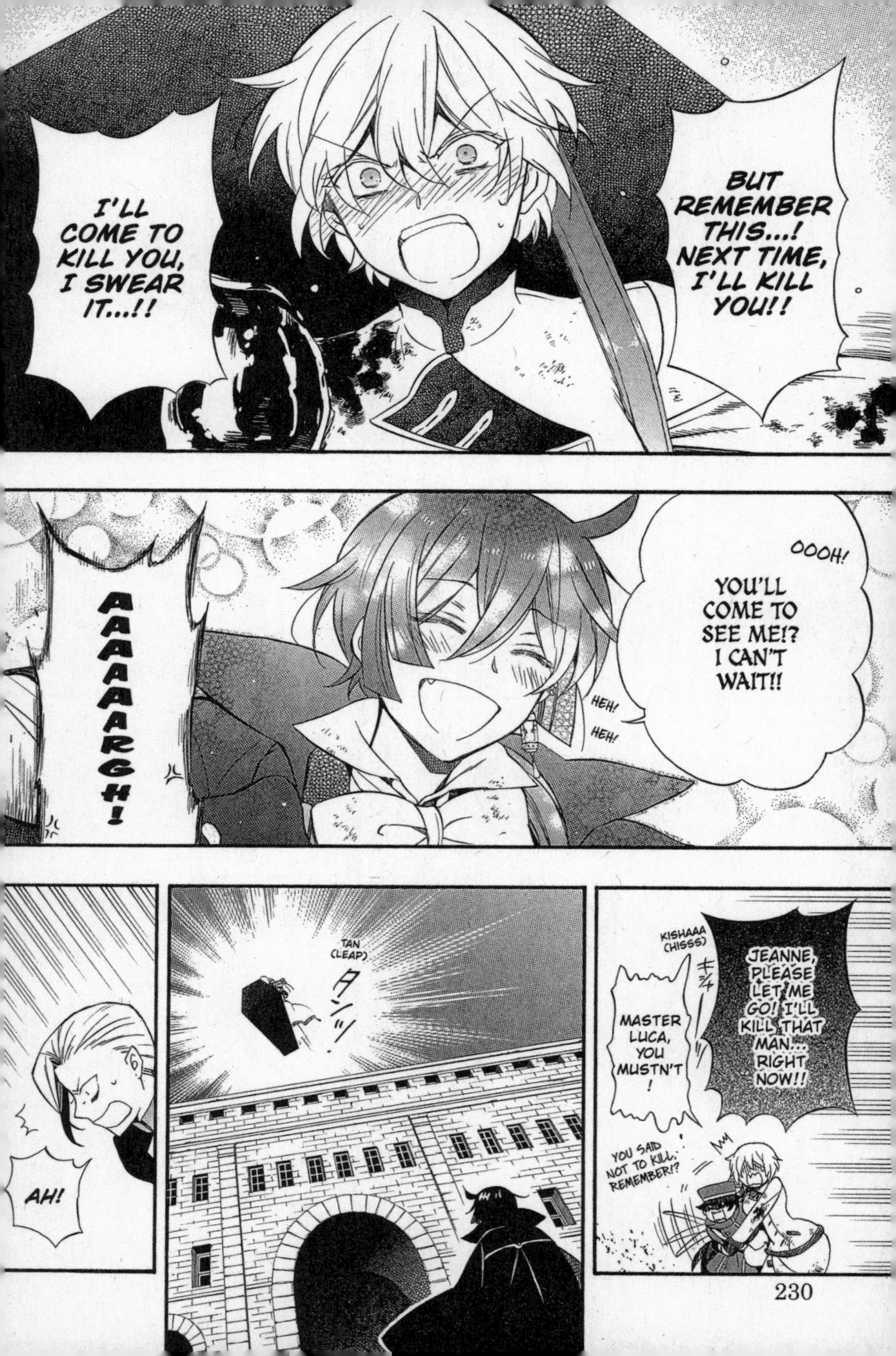
BUT REMEMBER THIS...! NEXT TIME, I'LL KILL YOU!!
I'LL COME TO KILL YOU, I SWEAR IT...!!
OOOH!
YOU'LL COME TO SEE ME!? I CAN'T WAIT!!
HEH! HEH!
AAAAAAARGH!
KISHAA (HISSS)
JEANNE, PLEASE LET ME GO! I'LL KILL THAT MAN... RIGHT NOW!!
MASTER LUCA, YOU MUSTN'T!
YOU SAID NOT TO KILL, REMEMBER!?
TAN (LEAP)
AH!

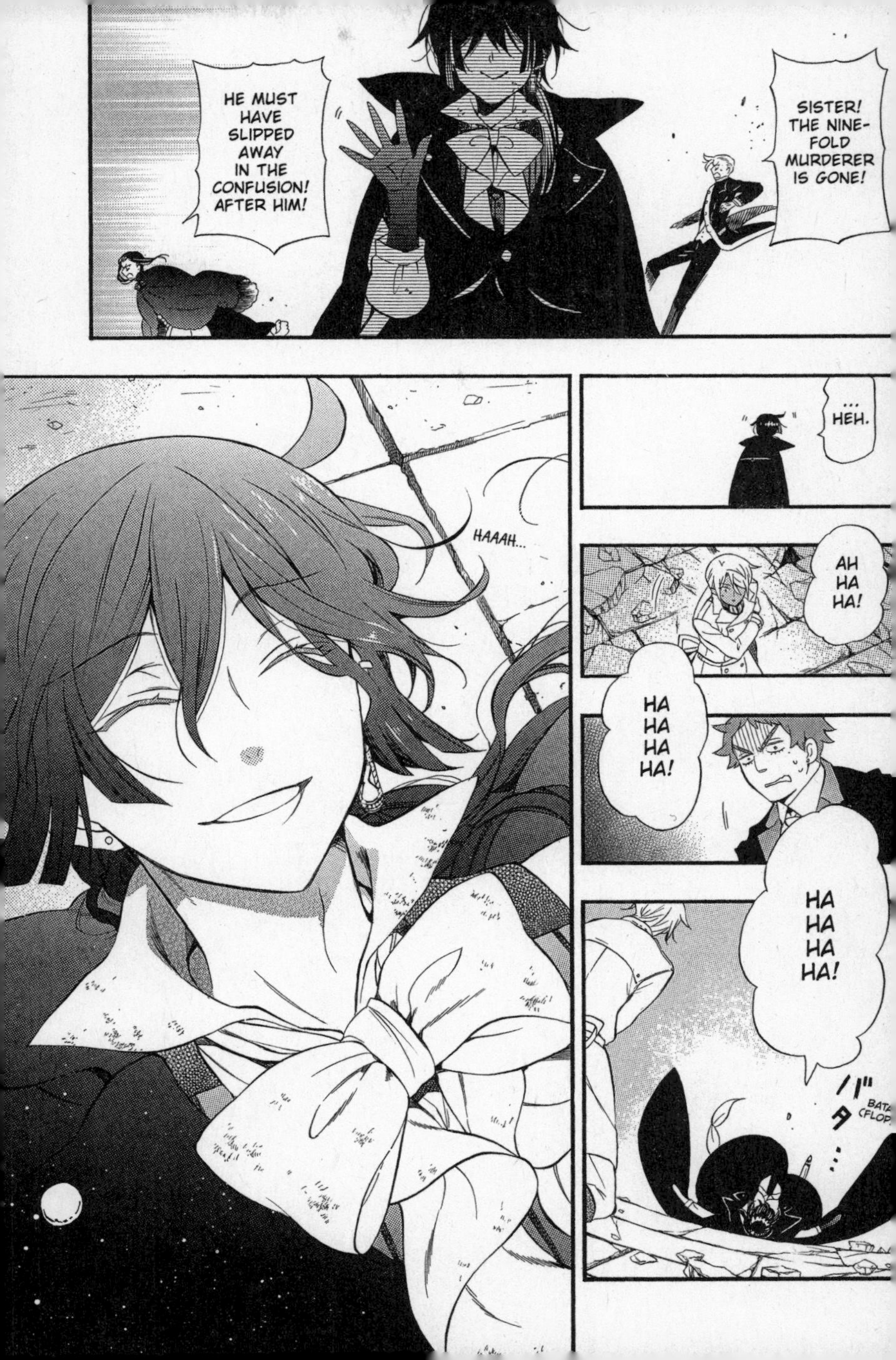
SISTER! THE NINE-FOLD MURDERER IS GONE!
HE MUST HAVE SLIPPED AWAY IN THE CONFUSION! AFTER HIM!
... HEH.
AH HA HA!
HA HA HA HA!
HA HA HA HA!
BATA (FLOP
HAAAH...

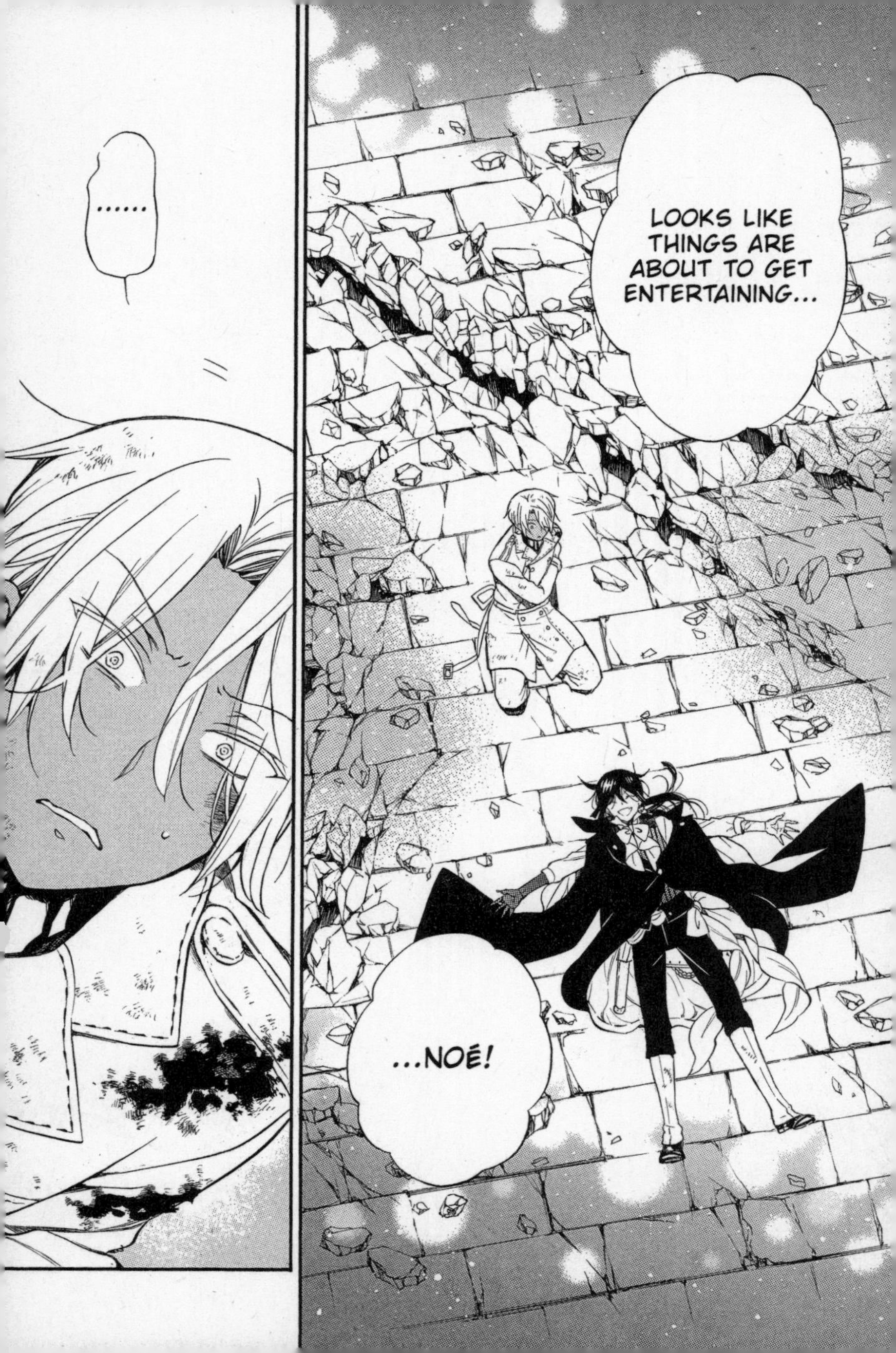
LOOKS LIKE THINGS ARE ABOUT TO GET ENTERTAINING...
...NOÉ!
......

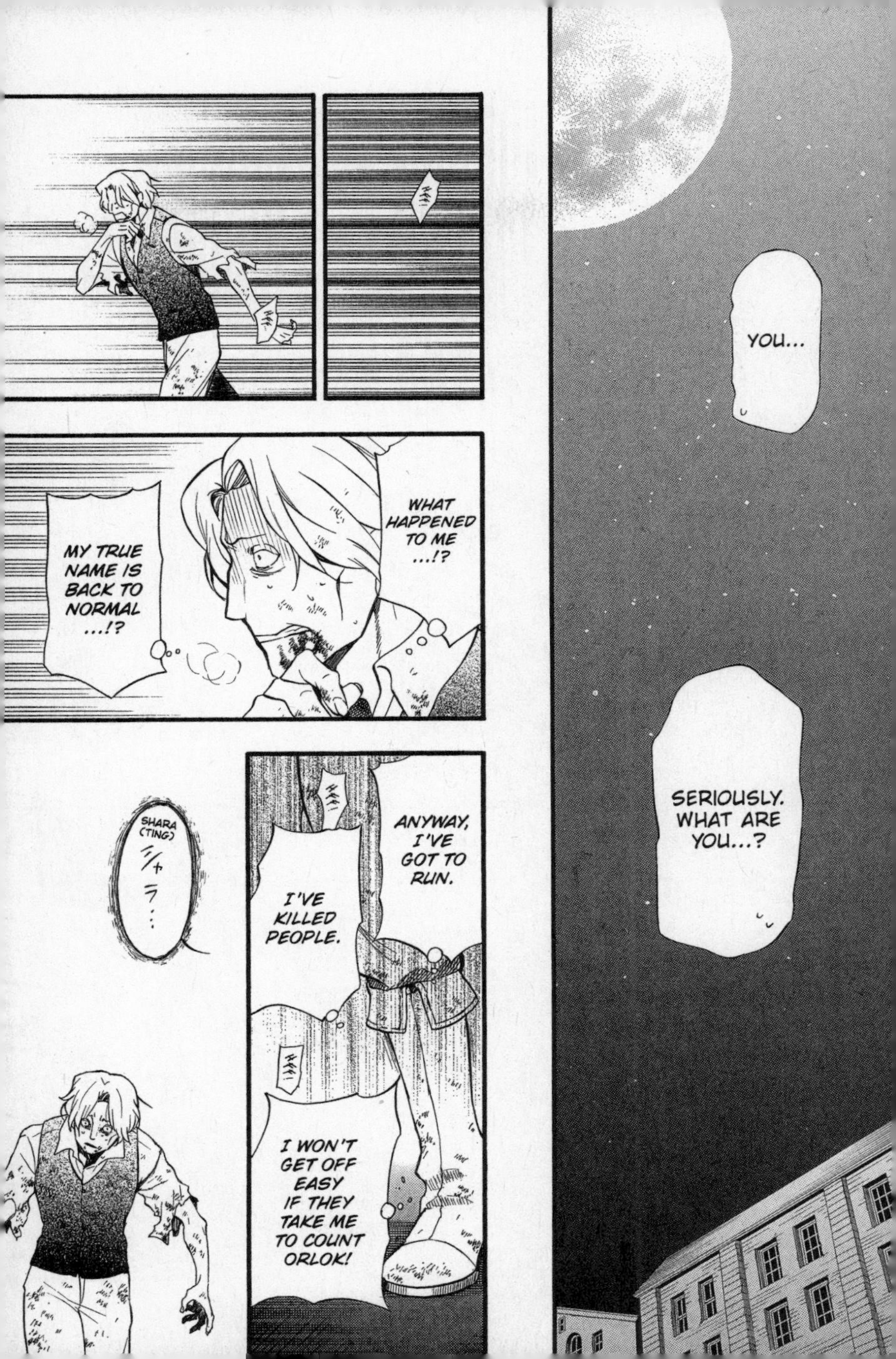
YOU...
SERIOUSLY. WHAT ARE YOU...?
WHAT HAPPENED TO ME ...!?
MY TRUE NAME IS BACK TO NORMAL ...!?
ANYWAY, I'VE GOT TO RUN.
I'VE KILLED PEOPLE.
I WON'T GET OFF EASY IF THEY TAKE ME TO COUNT ORLOK!
SHARA (TING)
シャラ…

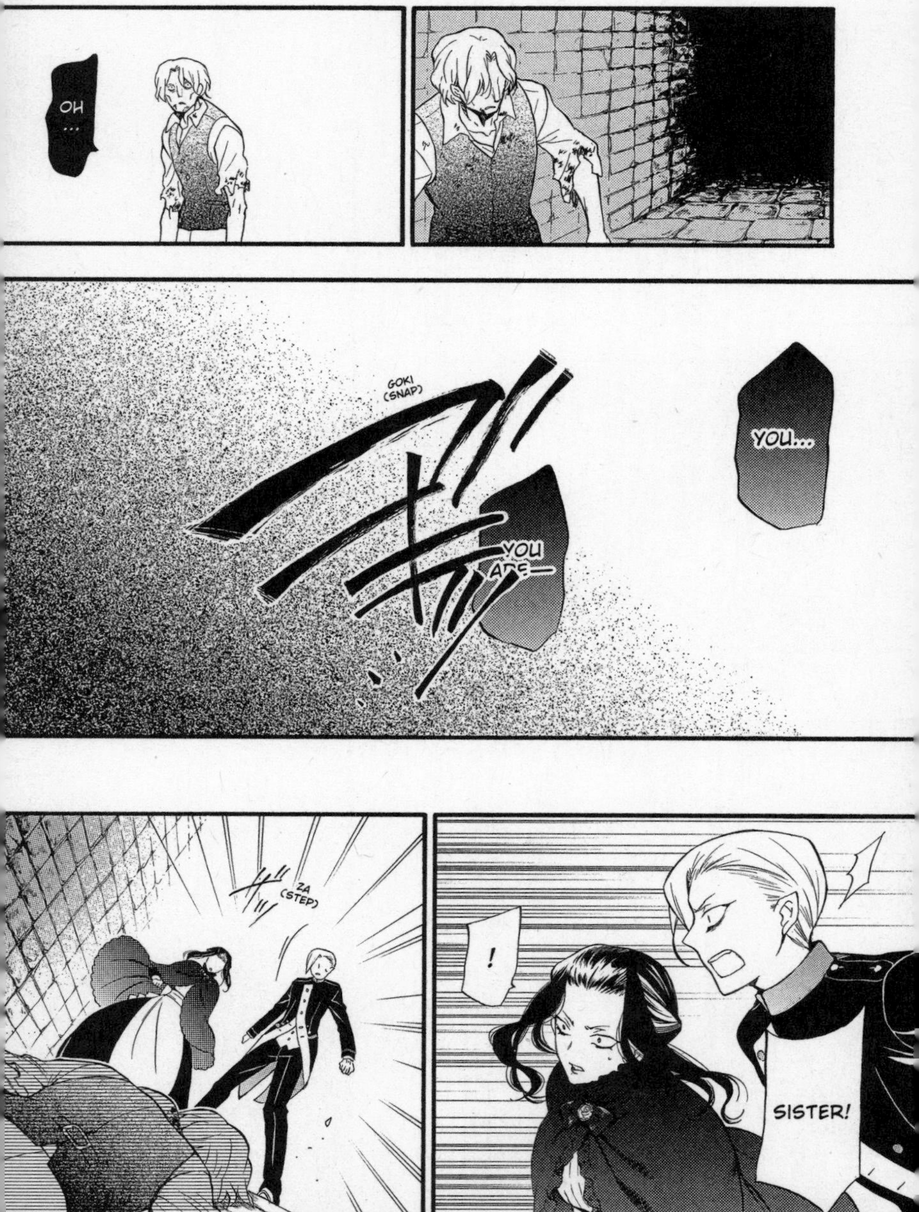
OH ...
YOU...
GOKI (SNAP)
YOU ARE—
!
SISTER!
ZA (STEP)

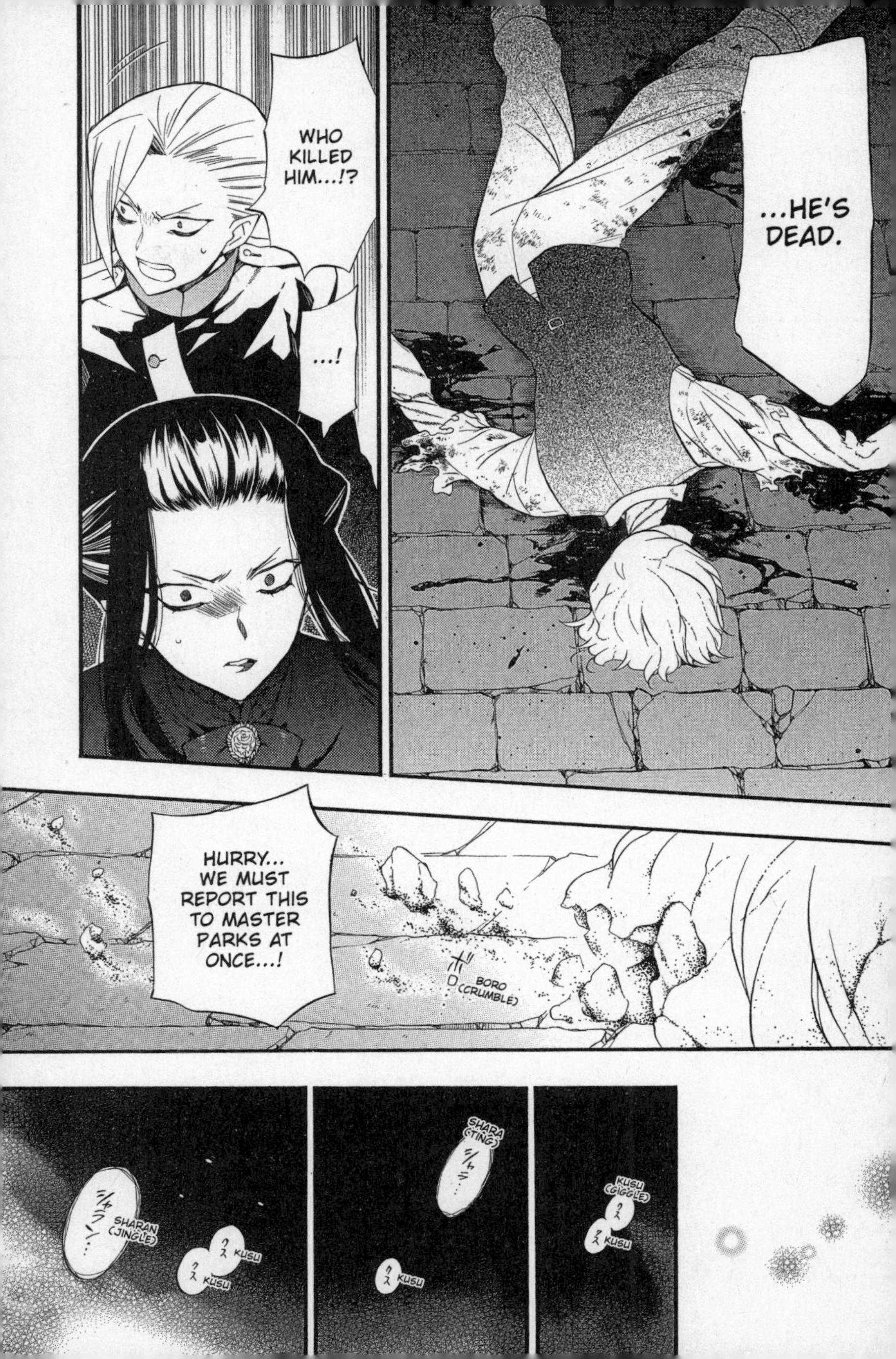
...HE'S DEAD.
WHO KILLED HIM...!?
...!
HURRY... WE MUST REPORT THIS TO MASTER PARKS AT ONCE...!
ボロ BORO (CRUMBLE)
クス KUSU (GIGGLE)
クス KUSU
SHARA (TING) シャラ
クス KUSU
シャラン… SHARAN (JINGLE)
クス KUSU
クス KUSU

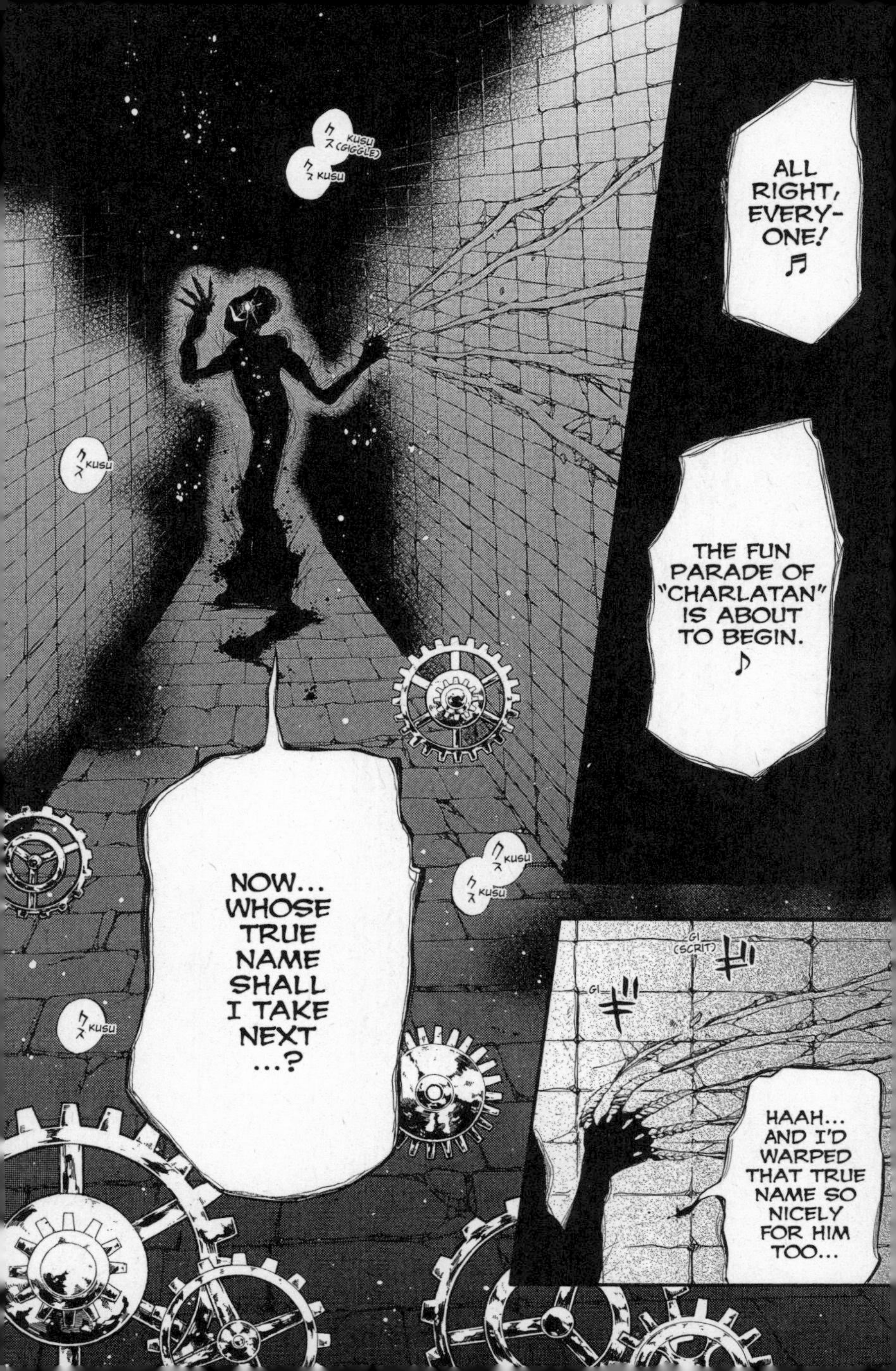

ALL RIGHT, EVERY-ONE! ♬
THE FUN PARADE OF "CHARLATAN" IS ABOUT TO BEGIN. ♪
クス KUSU (GIGGLE)
クス KUSU
クス KUSU
NOW... WHOSE TRUE NAME SHALL I TAKE NEXT...?
クス KUSU
クス KUSU
クス KUSU
ギ GI (SCRIT)
ギ GI
HAAH... AND I'D WARPED THAT TRUE NAME SO NICELY FOR HIM TOO...

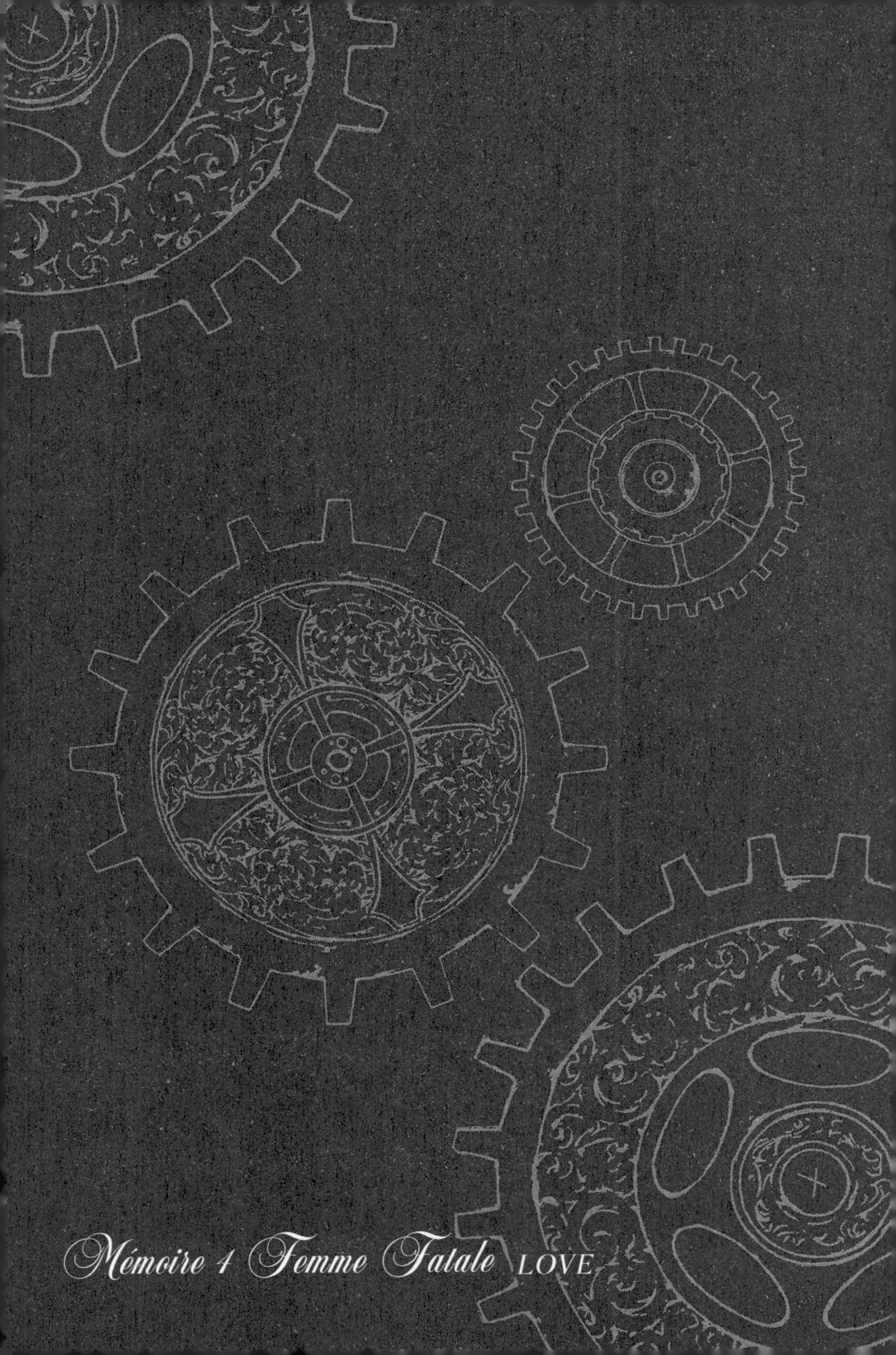

Mémoire 4 Femme Fatale LOVE

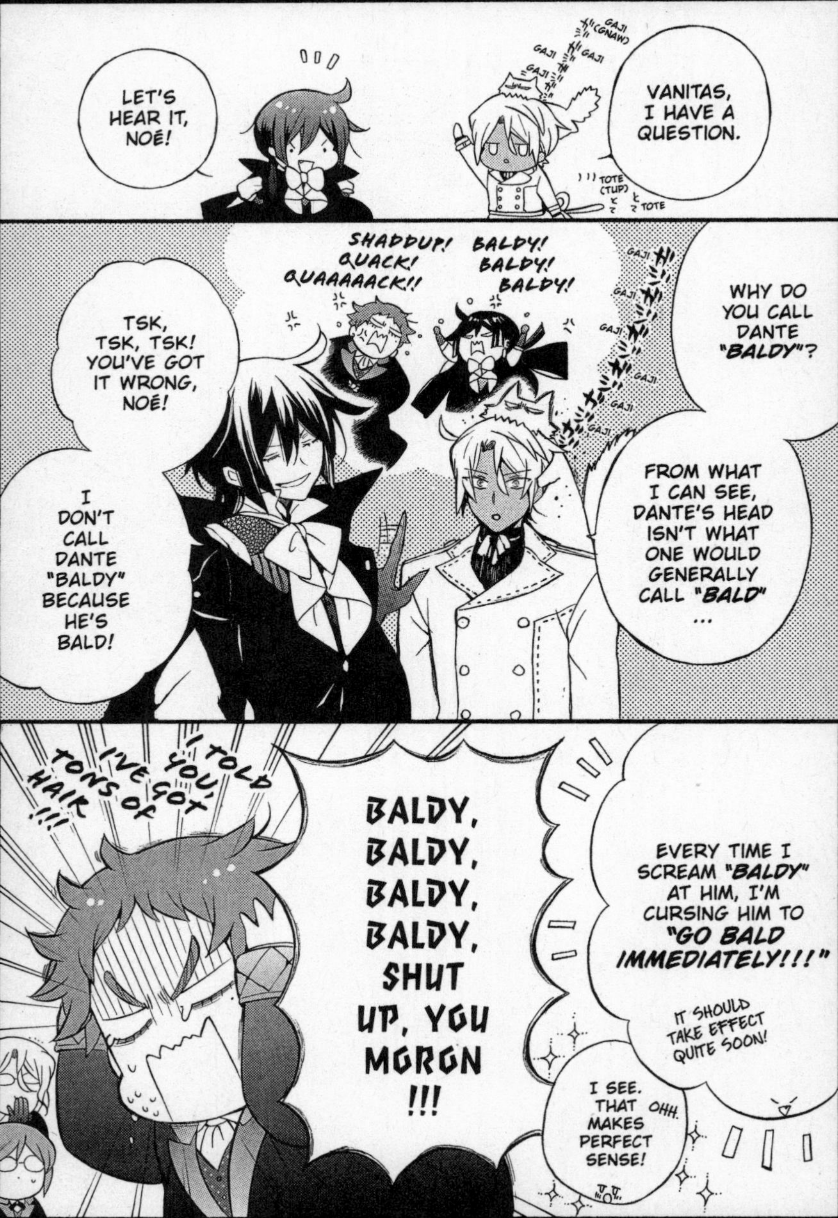

THE CASE STUDY OF VANITAS 1 THE END

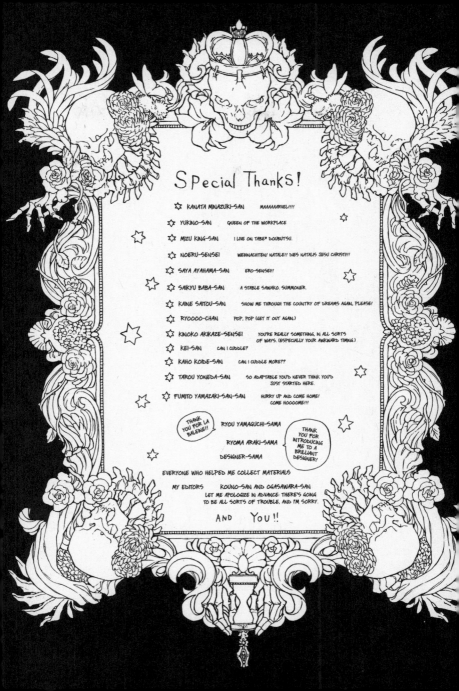

Special Thanks!

☆ KANATA MINAZUKI-SAN MAAAAAARVEL!!!!

☆ YUKINO-SAN QUEEN OF THE WORKPLACE

☆ MIZU KING-SAN I LIVE ON TABE* DOUBUTSU.

☆ NOERU-SENSEI WEIHNACHTEN! NATALE!! DIES NATALIS JESU CHRISTI!!!

☆ SAYA AYAHAMA-SAN ERO-SENSEI!!

☆ SAIKYU BABA-SAN A STABLE SAWAKO. SUMMONER.

☆ KAINE SAITOU-SAN SHOW ME THROUGH THE COUNTRY OF DREAMS AGAIN, PLEASE!

☆ RYOOOO-CHAN POP, POP (GET IT OUT AGAIN.)

☆ KINOKO AKIKAZE-SENSEI YOU'RE REALLY SOMETHING, IN ALL SORTS OF WAYS. (ESPECIALLY YOUR AWKWARD TIMING.)

☆ KEI-SAN CAN I CUDDLE?

☆ KAHO KOIDE-SAN CAN I CUDDLE MORE??

☆ TAROU YONEDA-SAN SO ADAPTABLE YOU'D NEVER THINK YOU'D JUST STARTED HERE.

☆ FUMITO YAMAZAKI-SAN-SAN HURRY UP AND COME HOME! COME HOOOOME!!!

THANK YOU FOR LA BALEINE!! RYOU YAMAGUCHI-SAMA

RYOMA ARAKI-SAMA

DESIGNER-SAMA

THANK YOU FOR INTRODUCING ME TO A BRILLIANT DESIGNER!

EVERYONE WHO HELPED ME COLLECT MATERIALS

MY EDITORS KOUNO-SAN AND OGASAWARA-SAN

LET ME APOLOGIZE IN ADVANCE: THERE'S GOING TO BE ALL SORTS OF TROUBLE, AND I'M SORRY.

AND YOU!!

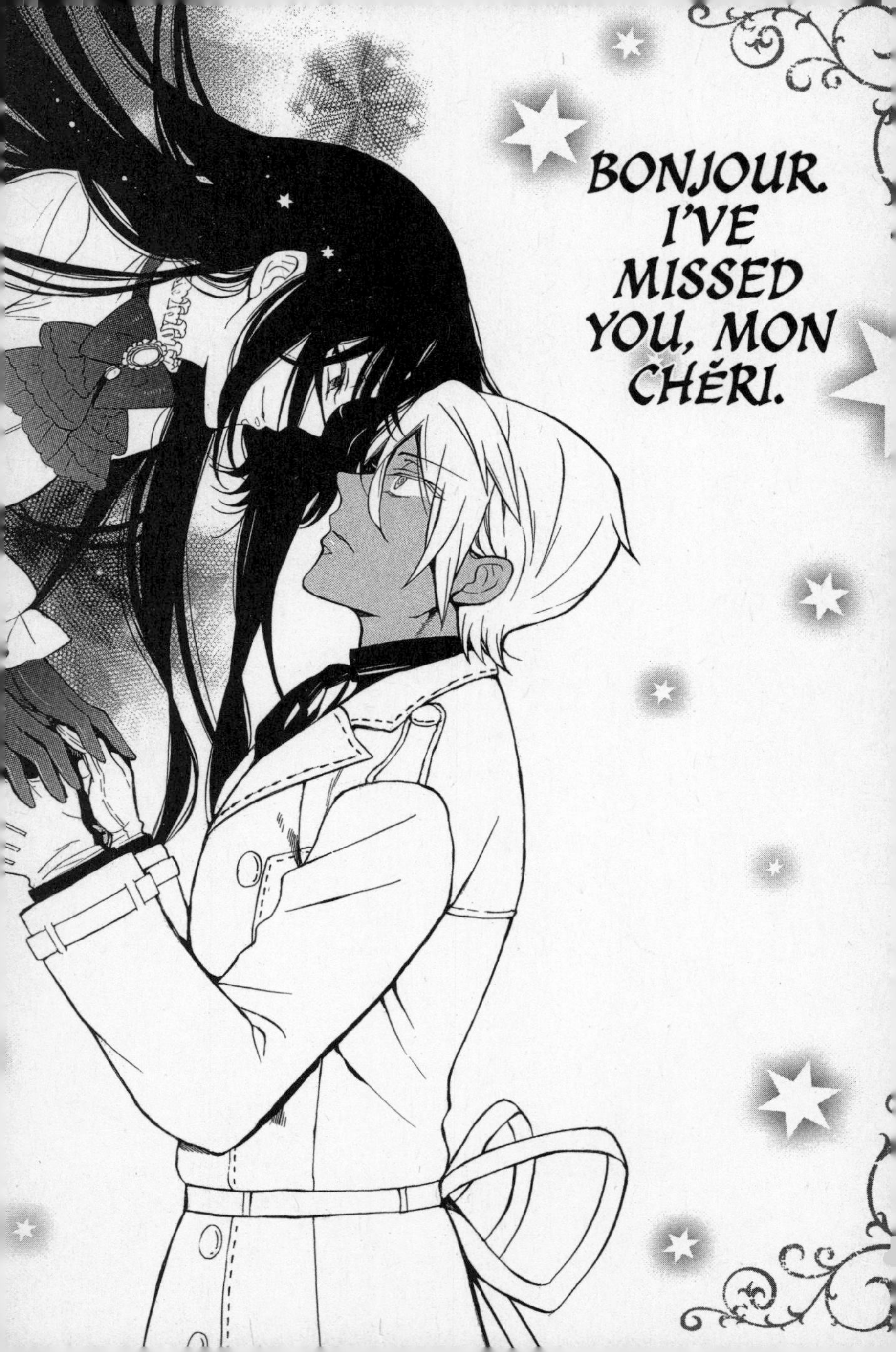
BONJOUR. I'VE MISSED YOU, MON CHÉRI.

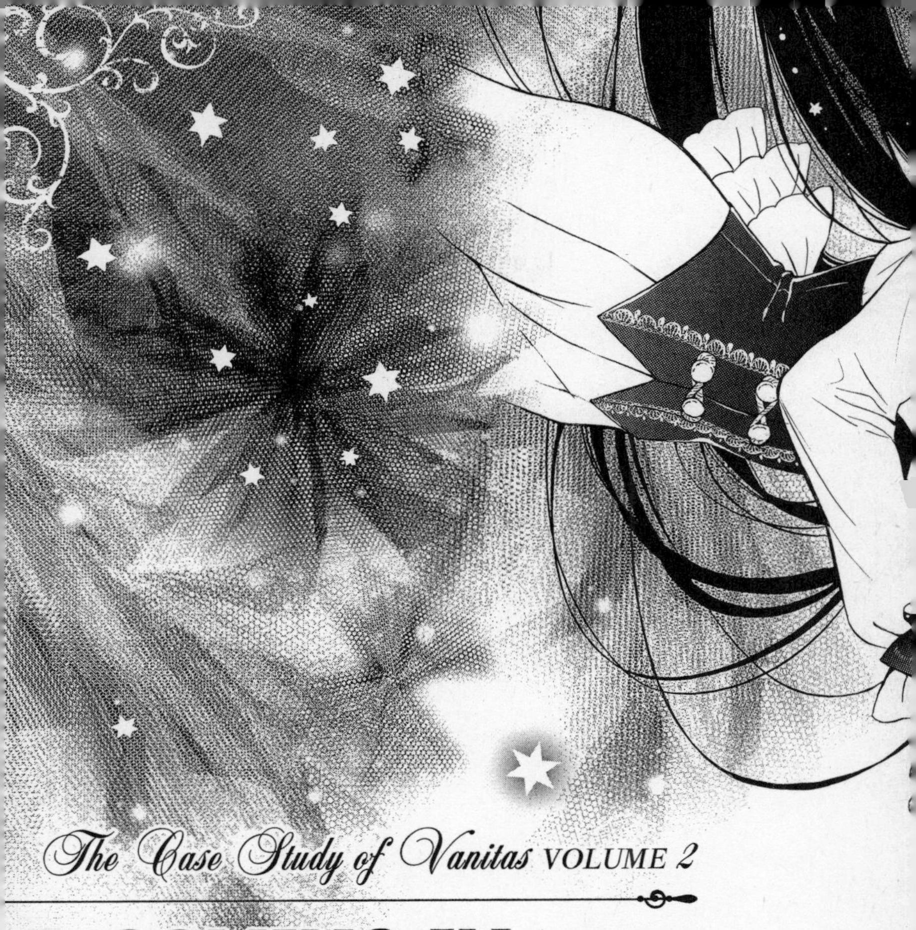

The Case Study of Vanitas VOLUME 2

COMING IN 2017

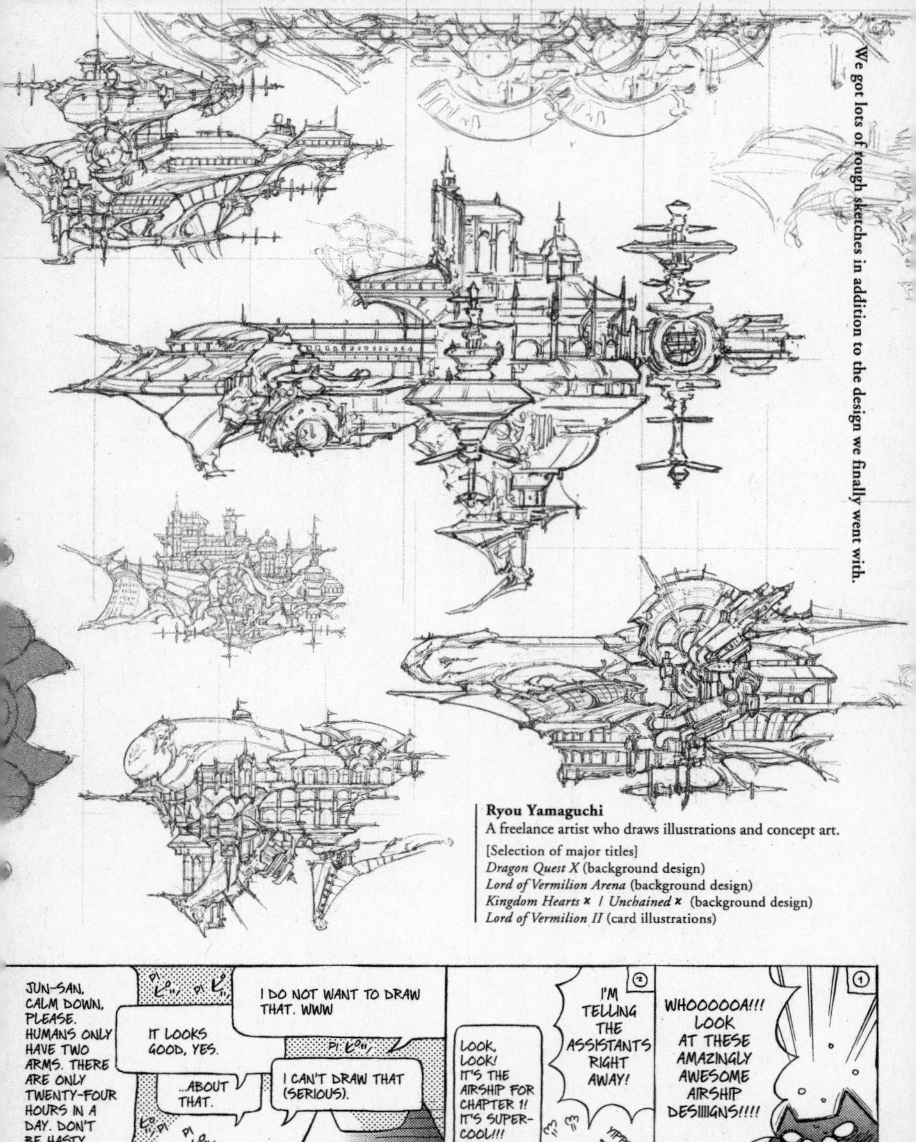

We got lots of rough sketches in addition to the design we finally went with.

Ryou Yamaguchi
A freelance artist who draws illustrations and concept art.

[Selection of major titles]
Dragon Quest X (background design)
Lord of Vermilion Arena (background design)
Kingdom Hearts × / *Unchained* × (background design)
Lord of Vermilion II (card illustrations)

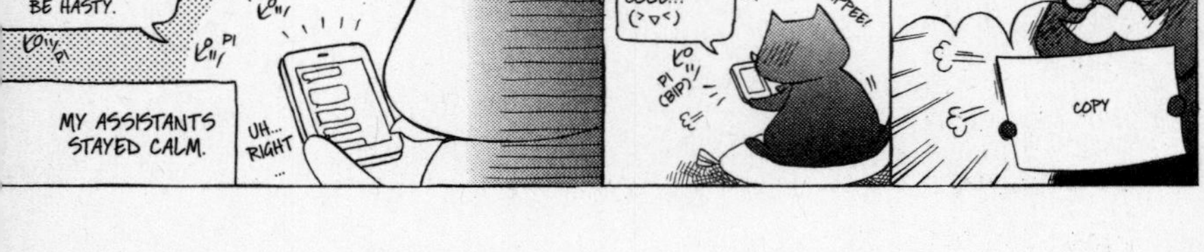
1
WHOOOOOOA!!! LOOK AT THESE AMAZINGLY AWESOME AIRSHIP DESIIIIGNS!!!!
COPY
2
I'M TELLING THE ASSISTANTS RIGHT AWAY!
LOOK, LOOK! IT'S THE AIRSHIP FOR CHAPTER 1! IT'S SUPER-COOL!!! (>▽<)
YIPPEE!
PI (BIP)
I DO NOT WANT TO DRAW THAT. WWW
PI
IT LOOKS GOOD, YES.
I CAN'T DRAW THAT (SERIOUS).
...ABOUT THAT.
PI
PI
JUN-SAN, CALM DOWN, PLEASE. HUMANS ONLY HAVE TWO ARMS. THERE ARE ONLY TWENTY-FOUR HOURS IN A DAY. DON'T BE HASTY.
PI
UH... RIGHT ...
MY ASSISTANTS STAYED CALM.

LUXURY PASSENGER LINER

"LA BALEINE"

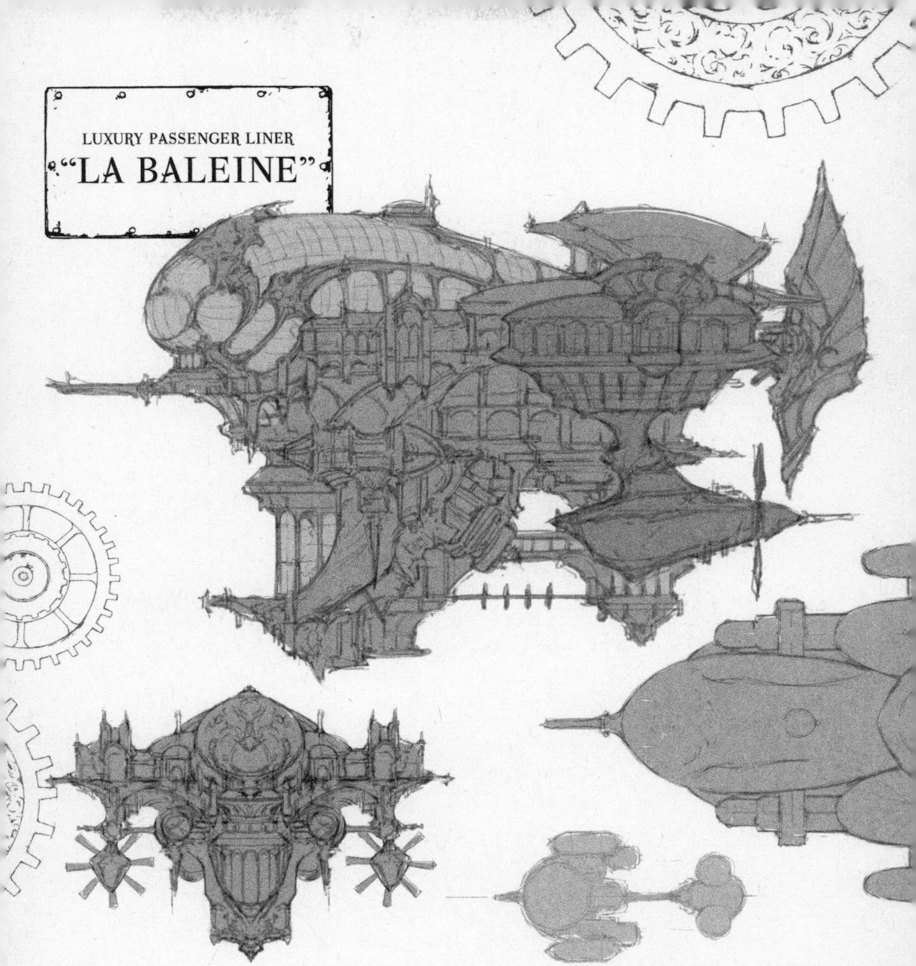

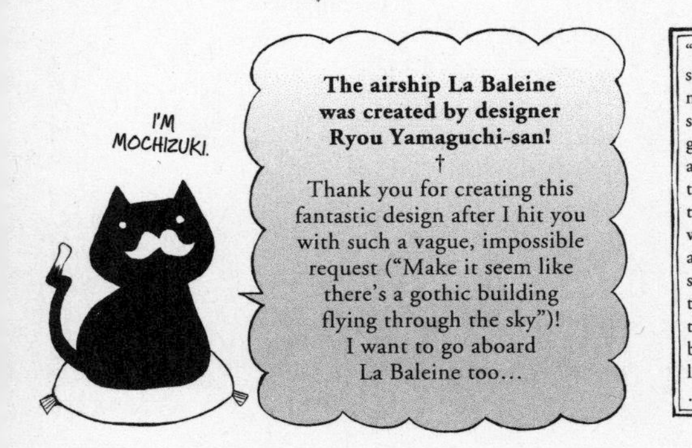
I'M MOCHIZUKI.

The airship La Baleine was created by designer Ryou Yamaguchi-san!

†

Thank you for creating this fantastic design after I hit you with such a vague, impossible request ("Make it seem like there's a gothic building flying through the sky")! I want to go aboard La Baleine too...

"A big airship that glides through the night sky over steampunk Paris, elegant and elaborately ornate, but not too much like a ship or a mecha; make it feel like something that really shouldn't be able to fly, like a gothic building, only it is flying..." Etc., etc. Even as all these words flew back and forth during the meeting, and I thought, "Wow, that sounds pretty hard," as if it were somebody else's problem, I have a very clear memory of itching to start drawing it right away. I packed the design with a concentration of the excitement I felt at the time. I'll be really happy if it conveys even a little bit of anything to you.

......by **Ryou Yamaguchi**

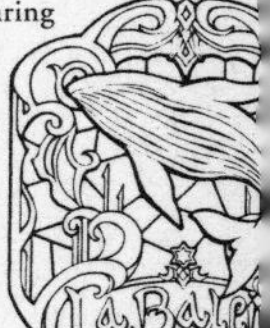
La Bale

I WANT TO GO TO PARIS ...

Jun Mochizuki
AUTHOR'S NOTE

Paris was the first overseas
destination I ever visited. This
story is made with a base of the
emotion and elation I felt back
then, packed with all sorts of
things I like, then simmered well.
I hope it suits your palate.

THE CASE STUDY OF VANITAS

VOLUME 1

JUN MOCHIZUKI

TRANSLATION: TAYLOR ENGEL
LETTERING: MORGAN HART, BIANCA PISTILLO

Vanitas no Carte Volume 1 ©2016 Jun Mochizuki/SQUARE ENIX CO., LTD.
First published in Japan in 2016 by SQUARE ENIX CO., LTD. English translation rights arranged with SQUARE ENIX CO., LTD. and Yen Press, LLC through Tuttle-Mori Agency, Inc., Tokyo.

English translation ©2015, 2016 by SQUARE ENIX CO., LTD.

Yen Press
1290 Avenue of the Americas
New York, NY 10104

Visit us at yenpress.com
facebook.com/yenpress
twitter.com/yenpress
yenpress.tumblr.com
instagram.com/yenpress

First Yen Press Edition: December 2016

The chapters in this volume were originally published as ebooks by Yen Press.

Yen Press is an imprint of Yen Press, LLC.
The Yen Press name and logo are trademarks of Yen Press, LLC.

Library of Congress Control Number: 2016946115

ISBNs: 978-0-316-55281-3 (paperback)
978-0-316-43735-6 (ebook)

10 9 8 7 6 5 4 3 2 1

BVG

Printed in the United States of America